Period Property
Manual

Published in June 2012
Reprinted April 2015, January and August 2018,
April and May 2019, June 2020 and 2021 (four times)

British Library Cataloguing in Publication Data:
A catalogue record for this book is available
from the British Library

ISBN 978 0 85733 845 7

Published by J H Haynes & Co. Ltd.,
Sparkford, Yeovil, Somerset BA22 7JJ, UK
Tel: 01963 440635
Int. tel: +44 1963 440635
Website: www.haynes.com

Haynes North America Inc.
859 Lawrence Drive, Newbury Park, California 91320, USA

Printed in Malaysia.

Acknowledgements

SPECIAL THANKS TO:
Chris Bowler of Thame, Oxfordshire and
Paul of Mike Wye & Associates Limited, Devon and
Stewart Menelaws of Studio Scotland Limited

Thanks also to everyone who helped out with photos and advice including:-
Kelly at Listed Property Owners Club,
Matthew Clements
Mike Parret of Dampbuster.com
Pete Ward
Zachary Trump
Barry Mulford
John Partridge
Sean Wheatley
David Moore
John Guest
Rob Workman
Roger Angold & Marjorie Sanders
Andrew Osmond thatchers
Chris Gare
Sean O'Reilly of IHBC
And for inspiration - The Society for Protection of Ancient Buildings
Old House Handbook

Period
Property
Manual

Ian Alistair Rock MRICS

CONTENTS

1 IS AN OLD HOUSE RIGHT FOR YOU?

Old buildings have a certain magical quality about them, something that's broadly defined as 'character'. Whether it's a thatched cottage, a Georgian townhouse or a humble back-to-back terrace, period properties ooze charm and history, making them quite different from anything being built today.

But living in old houses isn't everyone's cup of tea. Not everyone can cope with sloping floors, uneven plasterwork and potentially draughty windows and doors.

Above and right: Could you cope with sloping floors and low beams?

Below: Period house quirks – carved face revealed in cellar stonework (left) – handy integral boot scraper (right).

Are you a 'period property person'?

Estate agents often point out that purchasers of period houses are buying more than just a roof over their heads – they're embarking on a whole new lifestyle that involves living *with* the property rather than just *in* it. Period living is for those who find pleasure in genuine antiques rather than reproductions, and can be relaxed about the occasional minor shortcoming.

To discover whether you're an 'old house kind of person', try this simple test. Imagine walking into a quaint old house that's brimming with curiosities and quirky imperfections; which of the following thoughts comes to mind first – '*That's interesting*,' or '*Let's renovate*'?

Enjoying living in old houses is about appreciating their history; for example, perceiving a worn step as testament to the generations of people who have stepped over the threshold, rather than as something that needs modernising. It's all too easy to unwittingly erase history with unsympathetic redecoration and the urge to straighten and smooth out old surfaces.

If you can appreciate the patina of age without being too bothered by the odd imperfection and minor inconveniences that are part of the character of old houses, such as a door that occasionally sticks, then old-house living is for you. However, that doesn't mean you have to live in a dank and festering time capsule that's totally devoid of modern conveniences.

Adding value

When it comes to 'doing up' an old building there's a right way and a wrong way to approach it. This is a challenge that's explored in some detail in the chapters ahead. A house that's been carefully repaired in sympathy with its age is more likely to appeal to future purchasers than one that's been modernised, with all the history that made it special ripped out. So the best advice is to start by looking at what can be saved rather than what needs to be replaced. This approach should prevent character and charm being sacrificed in pursuit of 'perfection'. An old building that's too perfect can look like a Botox-injected fake.

What exactly is a 'period house'?

Everyone can visualise what a 'period house' looks like, but defining exactly what it is can be a little more difficult. The simplest definition is 'a property with solid walls', made with natural materials like brick, stone, timber or mud. This includes just about every house built up until well after the First World War, when modern cavity wall construction began to become mainstream. It's a testament to the quality and longevity of such antique properties that in the 21st century they still account for around one in five of the UK's housing stock – an incredible five million plus houses.

But old buildings are special in several other ways. Unlike today's bland developer-built boxes, they were a product of their immediate environment. Designed to withstand local weather conditions, they were constructed using materials sourced from nearby woodlands, fields or quarries, or sometimes dug from the ground beneath the builders' feet.

Distinctive regional designs were not determined by architects intent on 'challenging assumptions' but by the practical challenges of nature. A roof pitch would depend on the ability of the coverings to shed water and resist wind. The width, depth and height of houses was a function of the strength of the wall materials and the structural spans possible in timber floor joists and roof rafters.

There's something innately pleasing about an environment brimming with the weird and wonderful quirks of local building traditions that slowly evolved over many centuries. The combination of traditional materials and distinctive shapes makes a major contribution to the character and diversity of the different regions of Britain. The sheer variety of old houses crafted from local materials adds interest to an otherwise bland mass-produced world of identical buildings. Most people would agree that the towns and cities which we find most harmonious and agreeable are those that have retained their heritage and resisted intrusive modern development.

But it's not just the quirky old lumps and bumps that define old houses. The most important practical difference compared to modern buildings is the way they work. As we'll see in the next chapter, traditional solid walls were porous, relying on their ability to allow moisture to evaporate, a key quality that is only now being fully understood.

House history

Part of the joy of owning a period property is making intriguing discoveries about your home's history. Old newspapers may be lurking in lofts and cupboards, or you may unearth the odd historic coin or piece of long mislaid jewellery around the house, or dig up intriguing fragments of stone or glass buried in the garden. You may notice that ancient roof timbers show signs of being smoke-blackened, suggesting possible origins as a medieval hall. Or perhaps it started life less grandly as a 'shippon', where the original occupants shared part of their home with farm animals.

Every old house has a story to tell – its architectural history will have evolved over different eras, and changing tastes and fashions will often have left their mark on the decorations and fittings. To shed some light on the past, neighbours and previous owners are a good starting point for research. Parish councils and local history groups can all be valuable sources of information, as can old legal documents, censuses and electoral registers. Comparing maps of the local area over different times can highlight fascinating changes.

Changes over time – historical development

Many old buildings have been subject to so many alterations and changes over the centuries that in some cases the original core is largely obscured.

A single building can easily incorporate several forms of

Old house history

There were two less well-known driving forces that strongly influenced the way old houses were built, even dictating architectural styles: compliance with legislation, and avoidance of tax.

Building control

Following the disastrous Great Fire in 1666 (which destroyed 80% of the City of London), the London Building Act of 1667 stipulated that all new houses were to be built in brick or stone, rather than timber, and that streets should be wide enough to act as a fire break. For the first time restrictions were imposed on such things as storey heights, the thickness of walls (including party walls), the dimensions of timbers for floors and roofs, and the proximity of joists and rafters to chimneys and flues.

Over a century later the 1774 London Building Acts stipulated that doors and windows should be recessed at least 4in (100mm) from the front of the building. Heights and sizes were prescribed for a variety of house types, and it laid down a further prohibition on overhanging timber eaves or cornices, requiring that brick parapets rise 2½ft (0.76m) 'above the garret floor'. This gave rise to the classic Georgian townhouse with its roof hidden behind parapet walls, and windows set back 4in deep, that become ubiquitous in towns throughout much of Britain.

Tax avoidance

As we shall see in later chapters, the imposition of taxes and duties on construction materials also had a strong influence on house construction. Depending on when your property was built, its final configuration is likely to have been affected by the following taxes: the Hearth Tax, or 'Chimney Tax' (1662–89); the Window Tax (1696–1851); the Wallpaper Tax (1720–1830), the Glass Tax (1746–1845); and the Brick Tax (1784–1850), the last introduced to pay for the war in North American. Today, of course, governments know better, with VAT applied across the board to all building materials *and* labour!

Below (left and right): Clues to a building's evolution evident in varying window styles and changes in materials

construction and a range of different materials depending on what was available, affordable and fashionable at the time. For example, a house of medieval timber-frame origin may have a 17th-century extension built in stone, a Georgian rendered facade, a Victorian addition in solid brick and a modern extension of cavity wall construction. Different phases of construction can usually be spotted by looking for clues such as different sizes of bricks, breaks in the bond and building lines or variations in the type of windows, which may even indicate a former incarnation as two or more separate dwellings.

A good way to spot clues to a building's hidden past is to take a walk around the house and carefully sketch out floor plans. This can help reveal any concealed voids or identify where internal walls or chimney breasts have been removed. Evidence of past alterations can sometimes be gleaned from old photos in local history books, particularly where original Tudor timber-frame houses were re-fronted in Georgian times with fashionable masonry facades.

Which period?

Pinpointing the date of your house is made all the more challenging because styles and methods of construction didn't suddenly change with the death of a monarch. Georgian architecture, for example, didn't immediately become Victorian overnight in 1837. Nonetheless, it's useful to put a name to the period in which your house was built.

Stuart 1603–1714 (except for 1649–60, 'Cromwellian period')
Includes Jacobean period (James I) (1603–25)
William and Mary (1689–1702)
and Queen Anne (1702–14).
Architecturally the 1660s–1730s period was known as English Baroque

Medieval
1066–1485

Tudor
1485–1603
Includes Elizabethan (1558–1603)

Georgian
18th and early 19th centuries
Early – 1714–60 (George I and George II)
Mid – 1760–1820 (George III)
Late – 1820–37 (George IV and William IV)

Victorian
1837–1901

Edwardian
1901–14 (although Edward VII died in 1910)

Buying an old house

Buyers of period properties need to be prepared for a few 'imperfections', such as bowing beams and gently undulating walls and ceilings. In fact there's normally very little that's perfectly vertical or horizontal. If quirks such as these don't give you the collywobbles, then you're off to a good start.

But there's sometimes a price to pay for the pleasure of living in a unique piece of history. You may have to accept limits on the extent to which walls and windows can be insulated. So to keep fuel bills down you may need to modify your lifestyle in the cold winter months by installing thick curtains or wearing warmer clothes indoors to permit lower room temperatures.

In other words, it helps if you're willing to adapt to the house, rather than altering it to suit you. So don't, for example, buy a small cottage when you really want a far larger house, and then try to turn it into something it isn't.

Here are a few questions worth pondering before embarking on house hunting:

- Is the space right for you and your family without making too many changes to the historic layout?
- Will you be bothered by draughts, the odd spider and the occasional damp spot that won't go away?
- Are you prepared for low door-heights and beams on which unwary visitors might bang their heads?
- Can you accept that building works may cost more than you're likely to get back in added value?
- Can you accept the need for periodic maintenance inherent in vintage buildings?

Before you buy

First of all, get a building survey done by a local chartered surveyor who specialises in old buildings of the type you're buying. Mindful of their legal liability, surveyors often describe the tiniest blemish in words that sound extraordinarily alarming. It's a good idea to talk the survey through with the surveyor afterwards so that any defects can be put into perspective in terms of what is normal in old houses, rather than comparing them with the rigorous standards of new properties.

Be prepared for the survey to recommend follow-up specialist reports. Any worrying cracking is best diagnosed by a structural engineer, and services, such as drains, tested by specialists. But be wary of salesmen who offer free surveys (especially timber and damp contractors), who have a vested interest in finding 'problems'. Use impartial professional consultants instead.

Mortgage lenders can sometimes be reluctant to lend against unusual properties. Most tend to have a tick-box mentality and may, for example, decide not to lend against a perfectly sound timber-frame house because some of the walls are comparatively thin. Banks appoint panel valuers who are not usually trained in conservation, and may not be fully competent to advise on historic buildings.

Repair or restore?

Before carrying out any work on an old house it's a good idea to start by asking yourself three questions:

- Is it really necessary?
- How much original fabric would be destroyed in making this repair?
- What's the minimum amount of work required to keep the house dry and safe?

In the wrong hands an old building can easily be stripped of all the history that makes it special. Hundreds of years of irreplaceable original fabric can be destroyed in literally minutes. Often the best bits of a building wind up dumped in the skip. Of course, no one deliberately sets out to damage their own property or to carry out works that are a complete waste of money – such heavy-handed mistakes are generally well-intentioned and normally down to a lack of knowledge. So, should you 'restore', 'renovate' or 'refurbish' an old property? Most of us use these words pretty much interchangeably, but to conservationists there's only one 'R' word that's normally acceptable, and that's 'repair'.

Repair

Mending a building with the minimum loss of fabric, taking care to preserve its authentic character, is always the best approach. But in practice decisions often have to be made as to whether something can be repaired or genuinely needs to be replaced. For example, with a rotten old sash window, should you replace the whole thing, or just the decayed bottom rail? The answer is, it's always best to try and retain as much of the original historic fabric as possible, with all its embedded clues from the past that tell the building's story. Remember, the building is only authentic if original parts remain. Repair is also by far the best option from an environmental perspective, because it retains all the existing 'embodied energy', saving all the new energy and resources that would otherwise have to be used to manufacture replacements. See Chapter 16.

Restoration

People often talk about restoring a house 'to its former glory', but the fact is many properties – such as artisans' cottages or cheaply-built workers' terraces – wouldn't have had a great deal of glory in the first place. The definition of 'restoration' is 'returning to a former condition', but in practice this tends to mean putting things back to how we *think* they were when new, or taking a building back to some other selected point in time. Restoration usually involves stripping off modern layers to reveal past appearances. Such work can be acceptable if carried out with care, but if done insensitively there's a risk that a lot of its character and history can be destroyed in the process. At its worst restoration tends to be destructive, creating a forgery or facsimile of the original. On the other hand it may involve replacing ghastly, poor-quality modern additions (such as clumsy concrete roof tiles) with authentic natural materials appropriate to the original construction.

Conservationists are not generally keen on the word 'restoration', preferring the option to preserve all the marvellous history, including the small marks and scars that have accumulated over time. But in reality, preserving grotty peeling 1970s wallpaper, Artex ceilings and avocado bathroom suites is not most people's

The 1641 engraving shows a medieval timber frame house before being rendered in the 19th century and restored to original in 2004 (below).

idea of period living. So a measure of careful restoration may sometimes be desirable.

Renovation

Defined as 'to restore to a good state' – literally to 'make new again' – in practice this usually involves destroying some original fabric in the process of modernising, perhaps with the occasional nod to history in the form of a modern 'period-style' fireplace (often the wrong period) or a bit of stick-on polystyrene coving.

Refurbishment

Defined as 'to renovate and decorate', this usually involves gutting and modernising an old building using off-the-shelf materials from DIY stores. A typical 'refurb' will leave little if any original fabric, and involves installing fittings and finishes of the same type used in newbuild construction. Such work can be potentially damaging to old buildings, so this is the least desirable of the 'four Rs'.

The fact is, any work done insensitively risks destroying much of a building's history. In practice some things in old buildings may be beyond saving, although in skilled hands miracles can be performed. So the best advice is to repair wherever possible, otherwise restore as sensitively as possible. The aim should be to respect historic 'imperfections' such as bulges, bows, sags and leans rather than hide them. Happily, this is a very eco-friendly, approach. Today we are starting to realise that 'make do and mend' is the best course of action with most old buildings. For example, if a beam in a timber-frame house is broken it usually makes sense to mend it with a metal bracket or timber splint rather than to rip it out and replace it. Old houses react rather like the human body – often the less disruptive the surgery the less risk of 'collateral damage' and the stronger the recovery. So from a conservation perspective the golden rule is to do as little as possible – minimum intervention and maximum preservation. If it doesn't need fixing, leave well alone; if it does need attention, stick as closely as possible to the original.

However, few people want to live in a 'museum', without modern creature comforts such as WCs, bathrooms and effective heating. So inevitably old houses need to be adapted. Where new alterations are made, they should be capable of being reversed in future, for example timber stud dividing walls or suspended ceilings can be installed with a view to removal at a later date with minimum damage, taking care to leave the original skirting and coving etc intact. When you put your mind to it, it's usually possible to design anything from light switches to new extensions so that when they eventually become unfashionable or redundant they can be removed with minimum scarring.

When carrying out works to old properties it's important to take your time. This way you'll be rewarded by noticing subtle indications as to how the building was constructed and has evolved throughout its history. Cupboards, lofts and cellars are often rich in hidden clues. However, swift action is sometimes essential – a 'stitch in time' can prevent serious damage from damp and decay, particularly when it comes to fixing leaks from roofs and gutters. Making your home secure and watertight is obviously the first priority, even if only on an emergency basis, for example erecting a temporary roof covering that will allow work to continue in bad weather.

Doing nothing

This is sometimes the best option. One of the joys of living in an old house is that you're surrounded by 'living' history. So rather than trying to make everything artificially new, why not just relax and enjoy the old imperfections? If a number of bricks or stones in the walls have eroded, as long as the cause of the damage has been halted it's often appropriate to do nothing and leave the decayed masonry as it is. The next best option is to make an 'unnoticeable' repair.

Remedying past mistakes

Many repairs carried out in the past have turned out to be damaging, and later need to be 'unpicked'. But the cost involved in making-good previous inappropriate work can be high. So if

woodlouseconservation.co.uk

you're considering buying an old house that's been insensitively modernised, be aware that you might be taking on considerable expense and hassle to put things right. Sometimes the work necessary to rectify past 'wrongs' can be highly destructive to the remaining original fabric – for example, it's sometimes not possible to remove modern hard cement mortar pointing from old brickwork without wrenching away much of the surface of the old bricks as well.

However, sometimes you come across evidence of much older traditional repairs that actually add to the building's character. For example, badly weathered stonework walls sometimes had 'tile repairs' carried out. This involved cutting out small areas of eroded stone and filling the resulting void with several horizontal courses of plain clay roof tiles bedded in lime mortar, looking like a multi-layer sandwich replacing the missing stone. This is still a respected method of repair for small patches of badly eroded stonework.

Older traditional repairs add to a building's character

Salvage

Something else you might expect conservationists to approve of is reusing old salvaged historic bits and pieces rather than fitting something new straight out of B&Q. But the worry with many items gleaned from salvage yards is that you risk introducing inappropriate components, confusing a building's history with non-local items. A better alternative is to commission new handcrafted replacements, which has the added benefit of stimulating local craft skills.

Messing up appearances

Some works carried out on old buildings are damaging primarily because they have the unfortunate effect of trashing a property's kerb appeal – and hence its value. The fact that people sometimes lavish large sums of money on 'improvements' that actually reduce the value of the property concerned would be vaguely amusing if it wasn't so tragic. Popular 'negative value' improvements include gluing artificial stone cladding to the walls, installing ugly plastic or aluminium double-glazed windows, and re-cladding roofs with clumsy interlocking concrete tiles. Other botches that sometimes ruin the appearance of old houses include painting over lovely contrasting materials like brick quoins and flint, and adorning historic walls with clunking great meter boxes.

Sustainable design: back to the future

Old houses can teach modern developers a thing or two about eco-friendly construction. We hear a lot from architects and government about 'sustainability', yet no one seems to be able to clearly define what it actually means. The fact is, 'sustainable design' is all around us if we simply take the trouble to analyse how period buildings were constructed. Fortunately there are plenty of them still around to remind us how it's done.

For a start, old houses were built with locally sourced materials. In contrast modern materials are mostly transported vast distances, often imported, and are applied with no sense of local or cultural appropriateness. This makes today's construction industry one of the biggest consumers of energy. It has also resulted in the loss of traditional local skills, compounded by the demise of apprenticeships in many building firms. So the link with the past is being severed – something old buildings can help us rediscover.

Worse, we now know from bitter experience that modern materials (designed for new house construction) can actually cause serious damage when applied to old houses – see Chapter 2.

Modern materials aren't designed to be easily repaired and maintained. For example, hard bricks bedded in rigid cement mortar can't be replaced or reused, whereas in old walls any eroded bricks can be cut out and readily replaced, thanks to the softness of traditional lime mortar. Traditional timber windows and doors can be planed and adjusted over time so they last for centuries. In contrast, modern plastic units can't be repaired, only replaced with energy-intensive new ones. Old buildings were designed to be easily maintained over

the years with simple repairs, and hence consume massively less energy and resources over their lifespans, which are often measured in centuries.

In old buildings even materials that require higher levels of maintenance, such as thatch, can usually be replaced with minimal environmental impact as they use renewable, natural materials with a low carbon footprint. But the icing on the eco-cake is that traditional lime-based mortars, plasters and paints actually absorb vast quantities of CO2 during the setting process. You can't get much more sustainable that that – something Energy Assessors should take note of.

Planning and legislation

When you buy an old house, there's a fairly good chance that it could be a Listed building or located within a Conservation Area. This is a key consideration because in both cases there are benefits as well as certain restrictions and legal responsibilities. Your solicitor's local search should flag this up, but there's a lot you can find out yourself simply by trawling around the Local Authority planning website.

For questions about such 'protected properties' the usual point of contact at your local Council is the Conservation Officer. For Listed buildings they may be able to provide some useful background history with a copy of the original listing description that explains why it was considered worthy of conserving in the first place. Another category of protection known as a 'Scheduled Ancient Monument' only applies to unusual structures such as ruined castles or prehistoric mounds.

Listed buildings

Listed buildings are those recognised to be of 'special architectural or historic interest'. For most owners the fact that their home is afforded special recognition is very much a positive attribute, not least because it can enhance the property's value. There is also an added privilege of in effect belonging to a very select club, a benefit not accorded to owners of the average bog standard home. Listing, however, also imposes significant restrictions. If you want to carry out alterations that affect the building's character you must apply for Listed Building Consent. Should you fail to do so, it is a criminal offence to carry out unauthorised work or to instruct someone else to do it for you. So it's obviously pretty important to know where you stand before wielding the mallet.

Most buildings dating from around 1840 or earlier are likely to be listed. After this date, a greater numbers of historic buildings survive, hence more exacting listing criteria apply in terms of quality and character. There are about half a million Listed buildings and structures in the UK (covering everything from cathedrals to telephone boxes). Listed buildings can be checked via the website Britishlistedbuildings.co.uk and photos can be viewed at the respective websites Imagesofengland.org.uk, Historic-scotland.gov.uk, Archivewales.org.uk and Doeni.gov.uk.

In England and Wales, Listed buildings are categorised as either:

Grade I	Buildings of exceptional interest or rarity
Grade II*	Buildings of particular importance and of more than special interest
Grade II	Buildings of special interest which warrant every effort being made to preserve them

In Scotland the equivalent gradings are A, B and C, and in Northern Ireland A, B+, B1 and B2.

Grades I and II* actually only comprise around 6% of all Listed buildings, the vast majority being Grade II. Strictly speaking, the legal level of protection is officially the same for all Listed buildings regardless of grade, although in practice it's likely that factors such as relative scarcity and national importance may have some bearing on decision-making.

The fact that you need to go through the process of applying for Listed Building Consent is not intended to prevent alterations and improvements, just to allow a breathing space for careful consideration, to prevent any inappropriate or damaging works. It doesn't automatically mean that all change is forbidden – the system simply sets out to preserve the character of the buildings, favouring preservation. This is obviously a good thing when you consider how much less your house would now be worth if previous owners had installed plastic windows, Artexed ceilings and cheap MDF doors.

Apart from knowing when to apply for Listed Building Consent, there are two other big issues that keep owners of Listed buildings awake at night – buildings insurance and VAT, both discussed in Chapter 3.

WHEN IS LISTED BUILDING CONSENT NEEDED?

The general rule is that everything is listed, the interior as well as the exterior. Even some fixtures and fittings are included. However, it's not just 'old bits' that are protected. Consent is needed even for reversals of existing, relatively modern alterations, no matter how glaringly inappropriate. Even where you want to carry out good work, such as demolishing a hideous modern extension, or reinstating lovely period windows and getting rid of UPVC horrors, you will still need to apply for consent first. Infuriating though this can be, it's not unknown for some relatively recent additions to be deemed to have 'become an essential part of the building's character'. However, in most cases consent will be granted for 'common sense' reversions.

Providing the work doesn't affect the character of the building, improvements such as replacing recent kitchen and bathroom fittings may not require consent. However, if the proposed work involves alterations such as tearing down partition walls or removing a chimney breast to install a range cooker, or even knocking through openings for extractor fan ducts, then consent is required.

A fundamental distinction is whether the work constitutes a repair or an alteration. Consent is not normally required for repairs carried out on a like-for-like basis, providing they don't cause a loss of fabric or alter the character of the building. But there are grey areas when it comes to deciding at what point a repair actually becomes an alteration, and therefore requires consent. For example, a repair to a brick wall might just involve piecing-in a few bricks to match, or it may go further and affect the appearance. A key test is whether it 'alters the character' of the wall.

Unauthorised work

Common examples of unauthorised work (where consent should have been obtained) include:

- The use of modern materials, including plastic paints, gypsum plasters and cement mortars or renders.
- Replacement windows, especially UPVC double-glazed units.
- Replacement roof coverings with new materials that are non-matching, *eg* concrete tiles in place of original clay tiles or natural slates.
- Removal of internal partition walls or ceilings.
- Hacking off of lime renders and plasters to expose brick or stonework.
- Replacement of historic solid floors (such as brick pavers or flagstones) with concrete slabs.

The bottom line is it's best to assume that permission is required for all but the most straightforward changes, both inside and out, and that the whole building is protected, and to first consult the local Conservation Officer. Some apparently innocuous changes such as installing satellite dishes, alarms, meter boxes or even lining flues may need consent where they affect the character of the property. For re-thatching with a different type of thatch, it's best to assume an application will need to be made, unless the Conservation Officer confirms otherwise. Even changing the colour of the external paintwork or cleaning brickwork, stonework or timber beams, will normally need consent, as it can change the character of the building. Above all, the use of modern materials to repair or alter a Listed property will not usually be acceptable. This includes using cement mortars and renders, and plasterboard or expanded metal lath in place of original lath and plaster or wattle and daub.

Outbuildings

Listing doesn't stop when you walk out of the house. Structures such as garden walls and outbuildings may be included, along with assorted curiosities such as statues, fountains, tennis courts and sundials.

Usually any buildings or objects located within the 'curtilage' of a Listed property are also listed where they date from before 1 July 1948. So, for example, any old stables, storerooms and garages etc are likely to be legally protected. The 'curtilage' usually refers to the boundary of the existing property, but it can also sometimes refer to land within former boundaries where part of the land has been sold off, *ie* the 'natural' boundaries rather than current legal ownership ones. In such cases listing can impact on neighbouring properties. The precise definition is 'land that has had a close and contiguous relationship with the Listed building over many years', which leaves a fair amount of room for interpretation.

Enforcement

Where work has been done illegally (*ie* without consent), Local Planning Authorities have draconian enforcement powers. Potential penalties include unlimited fines or a prison sentence of up to 12 months.

The authorities may also require that a building is put back to its former state. Alternatively, where consent would have been granted in some form (had the owner bothered to apply) they may adopt a pragmatic approach and require that the works are revised to comply with a 'retrospective consent'.

One thing that can be particularly chilling for the unwary buyer is that there is no time limit for enforcement notices to be served to remedy illegal works – which means you have to be extremely careful when buying a Listed building, because as the new owner

Inappropriate aluminium units being replaced with new replica period timber sashes

A listed cottage with illegally installed UPVC windows

you're suddenly liable for any past misdemeanours. In some extreme cases the cost of rectifying someone else's unlawful alterations and reinstating the property to a condition acceptable to the Conservation Officer can be so enormous that it effectively slashes the property's market value – for example, where a previous owner has illegally replaced all the windows, extended the roof with new dormers and cement-rendered all the walls.

So it may be worth taking out an indemnity policy as a purchaser to protect yourself against any pre-existing unauthorised works made by previous owners.

REPAIR NOTICES

The planners also have extreme powers to force owners to make repairs where a Listed building has fallen into poor condition and has seriously deteriorated. Where an owner consistently fails to keep a property in reasonable repair to the extent that the building is now at risk, they can issue a repair notice, with the materials and details of works strictly specified and controlled. A schedule of urgent works is drafted and served on the owner who legally has no option but to comply.

Alternatively, the planners have the power to appoint their own contractors to carry out the works and subsequently recoup the cost from the owner. Local Planning Authorities (or English Heritage in Greater London) are also legally entitled to carry out any urgent works necessary for the preservation of the building. Councils may, as a last resort, compulsorily purchase buildings at risk.

Similar powers apply to properties in Conservation Areas if preservation is important for maintaining the character or appearance of the area.

Further information

See Chapter 3 for information on buildings insurance for Listed buildings and VAT.

Further advice and support for owners of Listed buildings can be found on our website, www.Period-house.com, and via the Listed Property Owners Club.

Conservation Areas

Conservation Areas are locations of 'special architectural or historic interest' where it is considered desirable to 'preserve or enhance the character or appearance' of an area. If you own a property located within one of the UK's 10,000 or so Conservation Areas you need to be aware that there is additional protection in place to prevent any unsympathetic development that could spoil its character. However, the restrictions are far less draconian than for Listed buildings, not least because interiors are unaffected. The focus largely relates to any proposed alterations visible from the street.

Whereas Listed buildings might be regarded as individual 'star players', the rationale behind Conservation Areas is that groups of less spectacular buildings within their overall setting and local environment are also worth preserving. All it takes is for one property within such a group to suffer inappropriate alterations and it will immediately devalue all the adjoining properties. No matter how beautifully maintained your house is, if the neighbours decide to cover their house with artificial stone cladding and plastic windows it will inevitably spoil the 'tone' of the area.

In practice, the main restriction is that some Permitted Development Rights (PDRs) are less generous. This means that you have to apply for planning consent for certain works that normally wouldn't need it. For example, you're normally allowed to build single-storey side extensions (up to half the width of your house) as 'Permitted Development' without the need for planning consent. But in Conservation Areas side extensions are not allowed without a planning application, although single-storey rear extensions are.

The objective is to ensure that alterations won't detract from the area's appearance – things that can be seen from the street, like changes to cladding, adding big box dormers,

Why we have Conservation Areas

Above and right: Garden walls, railings and trees are all protected in Conservation Areas

and replacement windows and doors. So properties on corner sites will be more restricted. Front boundary walls and fences are also likely to be covered. Applications are required to demolish any building in a Conservation Area, and there's a general planning presumption in favour of retaining buildings.

You can download plans showing the extent of Conservation Areas from your Local Planning Authority website. There is normally no charge for Conservation Area applications (though this may change).

It's not always appreciated that trees in Conservation Areas are also automatically protected. If you want to fell, top or lop such a tree, six weeks' notice has to be given to the Local Authority so that they can consider the contribution the tree makes to the character of the area. There are some exceptions, such as trees with a trunk diameter less than 75mm at a height of 1.5m above ground level, and ones that are dead or dangerous. See Chapter 17.

ARTICLE 4 DIRECTIONS

On rare occasions, Planning Authorities may wish to further protect certain characteristics of an area where they're in danger of being damaged by works for which a planning application is not normally required – such as re-cladding roofs and frontages, or even painting elevations, doors and windows. They can implement this by issuing an 'Article 4 Direction' which, at a stroke, removes Permitted Development Rights.

Website

Useful links and further advice can be found at the website for this book, www.Period-house.com

Period Property Manual

2 HOW OLD BUILDINGS WORK

The importance of breathability

A happy house - freshly limewashed breathable render, with stonework pointed in lime mortar

The way old buildings work is very simple. Before the days of modern cavity walls, houses had solid walls built of naturally porous materials, such as brick and stone, bonded together with relatively weak mortars. When it rained, moisture was absorbed into the external surface but was free to evaporate away once the rain stopped, helped by the drying effects of the wind and sun. This natural cycle is known as 'breathing'. In exposed locations the outer face might be given a protective coating of render and limewash as a further buffer against the elements, preventing excessive water absorption into the wall.

On the inside there was a similar process in operation. The walls were coated with lime plaster and decorated with compatible natural paints. Any excess humidity from activities such as cooking and washing was swiftly dispersed thanks to effective air circulation helped by draughts and fireplace flues, or else temporarily absorbed into porous wall surfaces. Kitchen ranges or open fires kept burning through the colder months helped interior surfaces retain a steady temperature and would also draw air through the home, all of which helped the structure to remain dry.

Lime mortar allows moisture to harmlessly evaporate away, temporarily darkening in the process

Conflict

Things began to change from the 1930s with the widespread adoption of modern cavity wall construction in mainstream house-building, combined with the advent of cement mortars and renders that were starting to eclipse traditional lime-based materials. This marked the beginning of a major transformation in the way buildings functioned. Modern houses are designed to work in a totally different way to traditional solid-wall properties. Cavity walls provide a rigid barrier against moisture, relying on impervious outer layers that simply block it out. The building

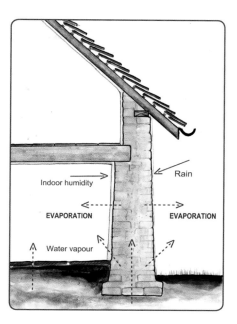

is effectively sealed in a skin of hard masonry, tough cement and impervious plastic paints and renders. Impervious materials are designed to prevent moisture entering the building in the first place, rather than relying on a natural 'breathing' cycle of absorption and evaporation.

Problems began to occur in traditional buildings when modern materials and techniques started to be applied. Materials such as rigid cement mortars, renders and 'plastic' paints were generally easier to use and were stronger than old lime-based products. Scientific progress was unquestioningly accepted as a 'good thing', and it became standard practice to use these new-generation materials for properties of all types. It was simply assumed that old houses behaved like modern buildings, with no understanding of their need to breathe.

The need to breathe

Attempts to change the way a traditional breathing building performs are doomed to failure. Modern impervious materials sometimes appear to work, at least for a while, by concealing the symptoms, but problems eventually reappear or are simply displaced to another part of the property.

For example, once a solid brick or stone wall has been cement-rendered or coated with plastic masonry paint, it's only a matter of time before hairline cracks develop in the rigid surface. And once water gets into a crack the only way it can escape is back through the same tiny crack; but it's unlikely to find the same route out again, so there it stays.

Problems have also been caused in recent years where waterproof sealants have been applied. These effectively act as barriers that interfere with a wall's natural ability to breathe.

This well-meaning but deeply flawed approach, using modern materials to protect old buildings, only makes problems worse, leading to accelerated rates of decay, sometimes to the extent of threatening the very existence of the property.

Old buildings and movement

There is another crucial difference between older and more modern houses. Modern buildings are rigid structures built on far deeper foundations. As a result old buildings tend to move in tune with seasonal ground movement, and therefore the structures need to be much more flexible. Fortunately, traditional lime mortars have a marvellous innate quality known as 'plasticity'. This allows old buildings on shallow foundations to react to movement by subtly distorting, rather than cracking and failing.

If you could observe this process under a microscope, you'd notice that fine cracks develop in wall surfaces when old buildings are subjected to small movements. As rainwater penetrates these cracks an amazing thing happens – it dissolves free particles of lime, which are drawn to the surface as the water evaporates out, effectively sealing the cracks with tiny deposits of lime. In this way lime mortar allows movement to be 'shared' between all the bricks or stones, resulting in slight localised deformation rather than cracks. No matter how alarmingly distorted an old building may appear, as long as it remains stable it's in equilibrium. And all will be fine until the day when someone decides to make an ill-advised structural alteration, or introduces heavy new loadings such as a loft conversion. See Chapter 8.

Damp

Damp finds its way into buildings from a variety of sources, not just from rain. Surprisingly large amounts of water vapour are created indoors as a result of everyday activities, such as cooking, washing, breathing and perspiring. Plumbing leaks are another potential source of damp, often remaining hidden and going unnoticed for long periods. In addition moisture from the ground can be absorbed by walls or floors in contact with it. But although most houses before the mid-Victorian period were built without effective damp-proof courses (DPCs) this wasn't normally a problem, as long as ground levels weren't too high, because any moisture that rose up the walls was able to evaporate harmlessly away.

How old houses coped with damp

A GOOD 'HAT AND BOOTS'

Builders of traditional dwellings knew the importance of a good 'hat and boots'. Roofs were designed with a wide overhang to shelter the walls, minimising the amount of rain running down them, something that's especially important with thatched roofs without gutters. But a building's 'boots' were also critical to provide protection at ground level, particularly for houses with walls constructed of timber or earth; hence these were normally erected on a substantial base of stone or brick designed to keep at bay any damp rising up from the ground.

BREATHABLE WALLS

Most traditional building materials are relatively porous. Brick, stone, timber, mud, clay and lime-based mortars and renders will temporarily absorb a certain amount of moisture when it rains, naturally drying out later when exposed to air and sunlight. Masonry walls were generally quite thick, preventing them becoming waterlogged before the next drying cycle, so the insides of solid walls stayed dry.

However, some traditional materials, such as some softer bricks and chalk, can readily absorb moisture but can't release it quite as rapidly, and therefore take a little longer to dry out. Hence in very exposed locations, such as some coastal areas, walls would often be clad or rendered for additional protection. For example, traditional roughcast render or 'harling' has a textured finish that maximises the surface area through which moisture can evaporate from the wall.

PERMEABLE MORTAR

The conduit for most of the moisture absorbed into or evaporating out of solid masonry walls is via the mortar joints, rather than through the brick or stone. Over a long period of time the mortar that has been doing most of this 'breathing' can eventually become a little worn and eroded, perhaps every 100 years or so. This is why soft mortars (and lime-based paints) are sometimes described as 'sacrificial' – because they protect the masonry, gradually wearing themselves away in the process.

NATURAL FLOORS

Earth was the original floor finish for many old houses. Trodden to a firm base and dressed with renewable straw or reeds, any ground moisture would have been dried out by natural draughts. Later, floor finishes such as brick or stone slabs laid directly upon the earth, or on a sand or lime mortar bed, were naturally porous and permeable, allowing any damp to be naturally 'wicked' out. Georgian and Victorian suspended timber floors relied upon air currents blowing through the underfloor void to disperse damp from the ground.

GOOD VENTILATION

Effective indoor air circulation aided by active fireplaces would help whisk away any internal moisture before it had a chance to do any harm. But ventilation was also important in roof spaces, to preserve roof timbers. Old roofs may not have been perfectly watertight in all conditions, but because there were tiny air gaps between tiles, slates or stems of thatch, any small amounts of rain that got into the loft could dry out thanks to effective ventilation.

Great mistakes

Much harm has been done to old buildings over recent decades as a result of inappropriate repairs and modernisation work. The great irony, of course, is that such improvements were undertaken with the best intentions. The resulting problems were largely due to a lack of knowledge as to how old buildings worked – and regrettably some homeowners and builders are still making similar mistakes today.

Problems can be traced to a combination of lifestyle changes affecting the indoor environment, and the use of modern materials that have the unfortunate effect of 'suffocating' old houses that need to breathe.

Traditional building performance

- Moisture is absorbed into the naturally porous surfaces of the building's fabric, mainly from rain and moist ground. This primarily affects the base of the walls and the ground floor.

Naturally porous traditional brick

- In dry weather, especially when sunny or windy, these same porous materials allow moisture to evaporate. This controls damp.
- Internally, fires provide background warmth and also draw ventilation through the building, assisting evaporation.
- Good ventilation via roof coverings, windows, and chimneys also assists evaporation.
- Traditional lifestyles produced smaller amounts of water vapour.

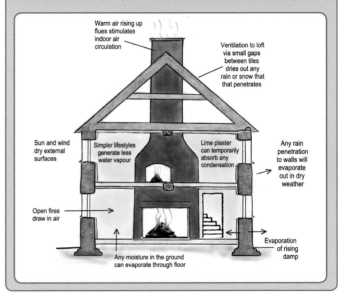

Non-breathable 'wallshield' type coatings (right) seal in damp, whilst trashing property's kerb appeal and value.

LIFESTYLE CHANGES

Back in the 1960s and '70s, as central heating systems introduced new levels of warmth and comfort to old houses, open fires effectively became obsolete, as well as deeply unfashionable. Hence fireplaces and chimney breasts were often removed or simply abandoned and blocked up. This revolutionary change in home heating was closely followed by the introduction of double glazing, which sealed up ventilation paths from windows, totally eliminating draughts. As a consequence water vapour in the indoor atmosphere no longer had the combined forces of heated chimneys and effective air circulation to help draw it away. Meanwhile, up in the loft, roofing felt was laid under the tiles, also reducing ventilation. To compound the problem, far greater amounts of water vapour were now being produced, as bathrooms were installed without sufficient

Left: Thick underlay blocks ventilation

Left: Cement plinth stops damp escaping so it is forced up through the brickwork; winter freezing causes crumbling.

ventilation (e.g. extractor fans). Together with cooking and washing activities in kitchens, this generated a lot of steam and moist air that had nowhere to escape. In some houses, cooking and bathing (especially showers) resulted in an epidemic of condensation, causing extreme damp, decay and black mould.

MODERN MATERIALS

Few older buildings have escaped the application of modern materials. The number one problem is the widespread use of modern impervious finishes such as cement mortars, renders and masonry paints. These have the undesirable effect of trying to change the way an old building works. Rather than allowing it to breathe, they force it to try and act like a modern house and exclude moisture from entering in the first place. The trouble is, they also seal in any residual moisture in old walls by blocking natural evaporation; and because these new impervious materials are hard and inflexible, they're prone to cracking as old buildings move. Moisture will then penetrate small cracks but can no longer escape. This causes damp to be displaced further up the walls, subjecting them to prolonged dampness and thereby increasing the risk to any timbers in contact with them. Where damp has become trapped it can ultimately lead to serious timber decay and encourage beetle attack.

There are five key 'disaster zones' where modern methods have been unsuccessfully applied:

1 Re-pointing

Probably the single most damaging application is where traditional lime mortar has been raked out and walls have been re-pointed using impervious modern cement mortar. This exacerbates damp problems, sometimes leading to serious erosion in masonry walls. See Chapter 5.

2 Cement render

To successfully keep out rain, cement render coatings rely on not becoming cracked – which is fine in rigid modern buildings that are designed not to move, but is virtually impossible to avoid in old buildings with shallow foundations. Sooner or later rain will enter cracks and become trapped.

3 Plastic paints

Because modern 'plastic' masonry paints don't breathe they have the perverse effect of locking damp into old walls, in a similar way to cement render. Once applied, any residual damp in the wall is blocked from escaping, as is any new moisture absorbed into the wall, for example from condensation indoors.

4 Internal plasters

The application of hard, modern, gypsum plasters or internal cement renders has the effect of sealing up the inside of the walls, thereby blocking the internal escape route for trapped damp.

5 Injected DPCs

Ironically, the above four 'improvements' are a major cause of damp in old buildings; but rather than dealing with the true cause of the problem, the standard 'solution' insisted on by mortgage lenders is to label all damp as 'rising damp' and inject chemicals into the walls. In most cases this simply makes matters worse, adding additional barriers to breathability!

Another modern 'improvement' that can sometimes contribute to damp problems in walls is where old ground floors have been dug up and a concrete slab laid over a plastic sheet damp-proof membrane and a hardcore base. The potential risk is that any moisture from the ground that used to be free to evaporate can no longer do so, and is instead displaced towards the base of the walls, exacerbating any low-level 'rising damp'. This is more

New concrete floor forces moisture towards the walls. Injecting a DPC fails to solve the problem – the wall is still damp.

likely to be a problem where the surrounding ground is a bit on the marshy side, often where gardens slope down towards the property, in which case installing a simple drainage channel may be advisable (see 'French drains' on page 25).

The alternative remedy of excavating and replacing a modern solid concrete floor is a highly disruptive job that would only really be worth the upheaval and cost where major works are already scheduled. The ideal replacement would be with a new insulated limecrete floor or a traditional suspended timber floor (see Chapter 10).

Types of damp

Most people living in an old house will at some stage experience a damp problem. There's a lot of hysteria about damp, mainly because if it's left unchecked for long periods in the vicinity

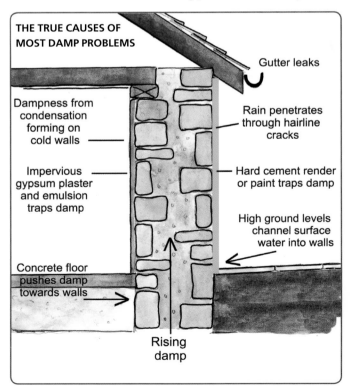

THE TRUE CAUSES OF MOST DAMP PROBLEMS

Gutter leaks

Dampness from condensation forming on cold walls

Rain penetrates through hairline cracks

Impervious gypsum plaster and emulsion traps damp

Hard cement render or paint traps damp

High ground levels channel surface water into walls

Concrete floor pushes damp towards walls

Rising damp

of timber it can cause decay. However, this only tends to be a potentially serious concern in houses where the timber structure is exposed to dampness, such as where the ground floor is of suspended timber construction. In most cases the odd spot of damp isn't a problem, and may simply need to be accepted and managed. Considerably more damage has been caused to old houses by inappropriate 'remedies'.

The important thing is to identify the true cause and treat the source of the problem, not just the symptoms. Most damp at low level can be cured by common-sense improvements like reducing ground levels. Conservationists reckon that around nine out of every ten cases of alleged 'rising damp' are actually misdiagnosed.

There are five basic types of damp: condensation, penetrating damp, rising damp, salt contamination and plumbing leaks.

Condensation

When warm, moist air or steam hits a cold surface such as a wall or window it condenses back into water. Over time any excess humidity or water vapour in the indoor atmosphere can form ugly black spots of mould, especially in nooks and crannies where air circulation is poor or the atmosphere is stagnant,

such as behind wardrobes. A big part of the solution is better ventilation, which can be improved with extractor fans or simply by adopting good lifestyle habits like opening windows regularly, particularly after steamy baths or showers. It's also important to limit the sources of moisture, such as poorly vented tumble dryers and boiled food. Insulating cold surfaces can also be helpful – but it's important to do this correctly in old houses (see Chapter 16).

Penetrating damp

Water soaking through walls from the outside is usually due to defects like broken or blocked gutters, cracked downpipes or defective sills, often combined with defective pointing. Such defects often go unnoticed for months or years, causing continual wetting of an area of wall.

Small gaps in windows and at roof junctions are also common weak-points where water can gain entry.

Right: Streaking provides clue to the source of problem

Below: Damp patch – easily mistaken for rising damp

Where damp penetrates near the base of a wall, perhaps because of high ground levels and rain splashing, it's frequently misdiagnosed as rising damp. Where ground levels are high, damp earth causes water to diffuse through lower walls, a process known as 'lateral water penetration'. It's very common for outdoor ground levels to have slowly built up over the years, sometimes reaching parity with internal floor levels, particularly where assisted by a spot of DIY patio laying. The resulting water penetration can cause mould and decay to any timbers in contact with the walls. The most appropriate remedy is simply to remove the source of moisture by reducing the ground level.

Rainwater can, of course, penetrate from other points of entry. Damp is sometimes encountered around old fireplaces. Usually the cause is nothing more than rain running down the flue and soaking into the soot and debris in the recess behind the fireplace. Simply clearing out the debris can do wonders in resolving such problems.

Right: Looks like rising damp – but is it?

scarring to old buildings over the last three decades.

'Rising damp' refers to moisture that can be absorbed from wet ground through the microscopic pores within soft brick or stonework in lower walls. The technical term for this 'sucking' process is 'capillary action'. In order to prevent any such risk, damp-proof courses became mandatory in new houses from 1875. A DPC is simply a horizontal barrier built into the lower walls. In

Nice shrubs, shame about the damp

Clumsy cement pointing looks naff and traps damp

Sometimes, however, it's not possible to remove the cause of penetrating damp, such as where buildings by main roads are subjected to persistent spray from large lorries. The optimum solution in such a case may be to physically clad the exterior walls to provide a natural barrier. However, this will inevitably mean a fairly drastic change of appearance, so it's important to choose a type of cladding that suits the age and style of house. Fortunately, for many Victorian and Edwardian houses tile hanging is historically appropriate. Another option might be to use traditional 'mathematical tiles' (see Chapter 7), which give the appearance of natural brick. As well as being visually acceptable, these solutions are more resilient to continued splashing than simply rendering the wall, which would discolour and break down due to the high level of salts present. Crucially, tile hanging also has the advantage of allowing ventilation to the newly concealed wall surface, aiding the drying out process.

Rising damp

True rising damp is extremely rare. The fact that the very words are enough to strike terror into the hearts of nervous homebuyers is thanks largely to misguided mortgage lenders insisting on the injection of chemical DPCs at the first whiff of damp. This has resulted in an enormous amount of unnecessary damage and

older houses this might comprise a course or two of slate, or a double course of super-hard engineering bricks, later superseded by a layer of hot bitumen or bituminised felt, and today by thin strips of black plastic. But the fact is, there are millions of old houses dating from before the mid-Victorian period that continue to manage quite happily without any form of DPC.

In a recent case,

No DPC, no problem

an old house with very little in the way of damp-course provision was found to be suffering from damp in a ground floor room where cement render had been applied up to a metre above floor level. By removing this impervious coating and re-plastering in lime, the walls were able to dry out and the problem was solved.

The main reason that mortgage lenders routinely insist on chemical DPCs being retrospectively pressure-injected into old walls, as a condition of the loan, is the lure of a 'guarantee'. The idea behind such works is to form a new horizontal barrier within the wall that stops any moisture getting through, but in reality it has proved virtually impossible to solve damp problems in this way.

Externally, there are two main sources of moisture to lower walls:

■ Excessively wet ground
The ground at the base of a wall may have become marshy over a period of time, because of leaking drains, defective guttering or downpipes, or the water table being very high. Excessively wet ground is sometimes the cause of subsidence, as it can no longer adequately support the walls. The solution is to fix the leaks or to drain the soil.

■ High external ground levels
Where damp earth is banked up against a wall, or there's a hard surface such as a concrete path abutting the wall, it can force moisture into and up the wall via the easiest (most porous) route. Reducing ground levels and installing a shallow gravel-

filled ditch (a French drain) allows water to escape from the base of the wall. It also provides an 'evaporation zone' for the lower wall, minimising or eliminating the effects of rising damp.

High ground levels are a common cause of damp penetration

French drains
A 'French drain' is simply a shallow gravel-filled ditch excavated near the base of a wall. By allowing the moisture to evaporate this helps disperse damp that would otherwise collect and soak into (and up) a wall. In cases where the ground is seriously damp or waterlogged, a perforated pipe should be laid along the bottom of the trench before backfilling with pea shingle. The groundwater then percolates down through the gravel and is carried away by the pipe to a soakaway, watercourse or surface water drainage system, like a mini land-drain. Ideally a rodding eye should also be incorporated so that if necessary the pipe can be periodically cleared by jetting with water or inserting drain rods.

French drain with neat protective grille to pavement

A great deal of care is needed when excavating trenches near the base of old walls that may have very shallow foundations. A trial hole should first be dug to discover how deep the property's footings (foundations) actually are, and to check the soil conditions. Where the footings are very shallow you may need to dig the trench about half a metre away from the house. This should still be sufficient to intercept and safely disperse rainwater dripping off overhanging thatched roofs, for example.

Where the garden slopes down towards the house, wet ground adjacent to the walls is almost inevitable. In storm conditions there's potential for deluges of surface water swamping the lower walls and surging through airbricks. Fitting a simple drainage channel a metre or two away from the house can usefully intercept any mini tsunamis and divert them safely away.

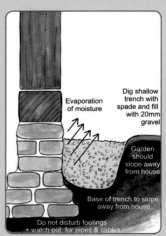

Evaporation of moisture

Dig shallow trench with spade and fill with 20mm gravel

Garden should slope away from house

Base of trench to slope away from house

Do not disturb footings + watch out for pipes & cables

Damp causes lime plaster to lose its key – but hair binds plaster together acting as a sheet

Salts leeching through. The walls should have been left to dry out before re-plastering in lime (not in gypsum plaster as here).

can set up slight stresses and tensions, enough to cause hairline cracks in grouting to wall tiles etc. When you add modern power showers to the equation you have a recipe for trouble, with water pumped under pressure into even the tiniest cracks. Damp from hidden pipework behind kitchen units, or from loose connections to dishwashers etc, is often only discovered when the units or appliances are replaced, by which time quite serious decay may have set in to timber floors.

Salt contamination

Where plasterwork has become damp it will often retain a residue of natural salts, such as chlorides, nitrates and sulphates, which were carried within the moisture. This is most common where the source of the damp was from the ground itself. But salts can also originate from salty unwashed sand used in the original mortar or plaster, or even from urine where animals were once kept in former 'longhouses' or 'shippons'. Mysterious salt patches sometimes appear in chimney breasts due to salts derived from flue gases.

Some of these salts are hygroscopic, and have the curious ability to make a wall surface temporarily appear damp. Where the air in a room is fairly humid they can absorb moisture from the atmosphere (sodium sulphate salts produce white crystalline deposits but aren't strictly hygroscopic). Although usually only superficial, this can prove quite difficult to rectify. There's not much that can be done other than replacing the affected patch of plaster with new lime plaster, but even this may not completely cure the problem. So before re-plastering it's essential the source of damp is rectified, and the masonry allowed sufficient time to fully dry out. Otherwise, salts can normally be brushed or vacuumed off, but surfaces should not be washed as they will promptly dissolve in the water and become reabsorbed back into the wall.

Plumbing leaks

One of the most common sources of damp is defective plumbing and drainage. But it's not always as obvious as you might think. Old baths, showers and toilets can quietly go on leaking for many a long year, remaining completely undetected. Tiny leaks can develop unnoticed at the back of toilet pans, which over time cause rot to floorboards (exacerbated by steamy air condensing and dripping from cold ceramic cisterns etc). Copper pipes can sometimes develop almost invisible pinhole corrosion leaks over time, and are particularly prone to erosion where buried unprotected in concrete floor screeds or if connected to pipes made from non-compatible metals, such as steel.

Another common source of damp in properties of all ages is from mastic seals around baths and acrylic shower trays. Because old houses tend to move slightly in tune with the seasons, this

The obvious precaution to prevent bursting is to lag all water pipes which run through cold areas, such as lofts, floor voids, larders, garages and cellars. Otherwise in sub-zero temperatures the water in pipes can freeze, the resulting expansion of nearly 10% causing pipes to fail at the weakest point, normally the joints.

Some original plumbing fittings are of historic value, particularly old external lead or cast iron hoppers and soil stacks, which sometimes feature decorative mouldings, or even coats of arms. These can be real works of art and very much part of a house's history, and shouldn't just be chucked in a skip and replaced with a cheap modern plastic equivalent. It's important to find a plumber who understands old buildings, as it's only too easy to damage historic ceramic fittings. The oldest bathrooms are only likely to date from around the 1860s, but even so you may possess 'first edition fittings' that should be treated as valuable antiques. So rather than replacing defective old taps, they can normally be taken apart and cleared of limescale deposits and given a new lease of life with fresh washers.

Looks like rising damp but isn't (leaking water supply pipe)

Obsolete damp treatments

Banks and building societies often make damp and timber treatment a condition of the mortgage in the belief they're protecting their investments. Unfortunately, the standard knee-jerk response to the slightest suspicion of damp has for many years been to install a new DPC, usually by chemical injection. Guarantees for such works are contingent upon the internal plaster being stripped to a metre above floor level and replaced with a waterproof cement render coat. This way, if the newly injected DPC doesn't work the rendered surface will hide the damp from view so that it *appears* to work, even though the hidden floor joists may be silently rotting away.

There are several types of damp treatment that have been tried without much success over the years:

Chemical DPCs

So bad they did it twice – injected far too high and into masonry

Daft DPC – injected up the wall in failed bid to block damp from garden wall.

In theory, pumping a silicone-based fluid or cream into a wall made from porous materials should form an impervious horizontal barrier to block any damp rising up from the ground. The chemicals used can be solvent- or water-based, and injected by pressure or gravity. But in practice this approach is rarely successful, and many historic houses have been pointlessly scarred by having rows of holes drilled in their lower walls.

There are several reasons why injected DPCs are ineffective. Poor workmanship has resulted in many being injected at the wrong height, usually at far too high a level to protect vulnerable floor timbers.

To have any chance of success injection should be into the mortar joints rather than the brickwork, otherwise any damp can simply work its way past the injected bricks via the mortar. Despite this, the masonry in old walls is commonly injected, sometimes even into hard impermeable stonework such as flint. Even where the job is done properly, problems occur when the chemical fluids don't entirely fill up the pores, or completely push out the water in the damp wall in front of the advancing injection fluid. The fluid will take the line of least resistance, via the largest pores and cracks.

As if this wasn't bad enough, injecting the walls is only part of the process. As noted above, to qualify for a guarantee the old plaster is hacked off the lower internal walls, which are then 'tanked' in cement render, which prevents the damp inside the wall from drying out. This normally succeeds in masking the problem – at least until the trapped damp builds up behind the render and is displaced to previously unaffected parts of the wall. Worst of all, in most cases damp will still be in contact with hidden floor timbers. Despite this, mortgage lenders are usually happy as long as they get their guarantee (which in the event of a subsequent claim is often worthless). In the vast majority of cases, injecting a DPC is highly unlikely to solve the problem and will be a total waste of time and money. The only thing that can be said in favour of this method is that it's less damaging than some other works that have been tried in the past!

DPC cut into the wall

Retrospectively inserting a physical DPC involves cutting out a short section of wall and inserting a length of waterproof material, then repeating the process to the full length of the wall. Mechanical cutters such as chainsaws were routinely used to cut open mortar joints. Such aggressive techniques can be highly damaging to traditional buildings with their irregular walls and uneven courses. Unsurprisingly, some properties suffered consequential structural problems.

Electro-osmosis

By applying a weak electric current to a copper wire fixed horizontally at low level around a wall it is claimed that water molecules are repelled as they try to rise up the wall (due to altered polarity). The copper wire is connected to metal electrodes inserted into holes drilled into the walls. In reality, such electro-osmotic systems have achieved inconsistent results and suffered from corrosion.

Ceramic vents (atmospheric siphons)

Porous ceramic tubes are inserted into holes drilled into the base of a wall. These are designed to draw moisture towards their surfaces by capillary action, where it can then evaporate. This is the same principle as breathable lime mortar. But because evaporation is concentrated around one point (the tube) the pores on the surface eventually become blocked as mineral salts accumulate during evaporation. Worse, they are sometimes bedded in cement mortar which actually blocks the path of water! Inserting ceramic vents into walls inevitably causes damage, although at least the tubes are flush with the surface. An aggressively advertised current version known as the 'Shrijver' method involves fitting several large projecting vents to a wall surface, which are both visually and physically intrusive, and therefore considered inappropriate for period buildings.

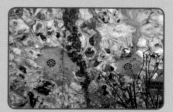

Vents set in hard flint embedded in impervious cement – pointless and damaging

Damp sealants

It would be nice to believe that damp problems could simply be brushed away, or banished forever with a quick spray. Some 'miracle solution' products found on the shelves of DIY stores rely on containing damp behind a physical barrier, such as special thick paint. The trouble is, by definition they seal damp in, rather than deal with the cause of the problem. Damp sealants are also sold on their ability to stop water getting into walls. But this is like guarding the front door only to find that you're attacked through the back door. Old walls are rarely perfectly dry when damp sealants are applied, and moisture can enter by other means, not just from rain. A surprising amount of damp is due to indoor condensation, or soaking down from faulty gutters and sills etc, and 'damp-sealing' the surface will stop it escaping by evaporation, thereby storing up future problems.

A more sensible variation on this theme, sometimes used in basements, is to apply a physical lining to a wall while leaving a well-ventilated air gap behind, thus isolating the damp from the new internal finish but crucially allowing the wall to breathe.

Mike Parrett / Dampbuster.com

Solutions

Damp problems can only be fully solved by addressing the actual causes. This can require a certain amount of detective work, because old houses often comprise a mix of traditional and modern construction that's evolved over centuries. In some cases there may be more than one cause of damp, so care is needed when devising solutions. Doing the job properly isn't a quick fix, especially where damp has been lurking for a number of years. So once the prime causes of the problem have been eliminated, a certain amount of time is then required to assess whether each measure has been successful.

Fix external leaks

The easy way to expel moist, humid air before it can cause dampness

de-humidifiers. Check also for leaks from pipes, baths and shower trays etc.

Prevent death by suffocation

To allow damp to escape by naturally evaporating away, any harmful modern materials such as cement renders, mortars and gypsum plasters need to be carefully removed and replaced with traditional breathable materials. But these can be quite aggressively attached, and in some cases it may not be possible to remove them without damaging the building's historic underlying fabric. Modern plastic masonry paint can equally trap damp, but can normally be removed from masonry or lime render without

Often the source of the problem is down to something fairly simple, like a leaking gutter that just requires clearing out or a minor repair. Other common suspects include eroded window sills, defective roof flashings and leaking drains. Run through the maintenance checklist at the end of this book to make sure all potential sources of water ingress are isolated.

Confront the enemy within

Fix any obvious internal sources of water. Condensation generated by people living in the house may be combated by improved ventilation, insulation and heating, and in the short term even

After hacking off hard cement render this wall was pointed up in natural lime so it could breathe

causing damage by using a pressurised steam system. But where you've got a cement render coating under the paint the whole lot will need to be removed and re-rendered in lime – a fairly major undertaking. However, where modern cement render is quite thin, it may be possible to carefully scrape it off over the mortar joints, to allow damp to evaporate from the wall as originally intended. See Chapter 14.

Reduce ground levels

One of the most common causes of damp in old buildings is high external ground levels. Ideally the ground outside should be around 200mm below the internal floor, but sometimes it's even higher than the floor, especially where paths or pavements have been re-laid. Ensure that earth isn't banked up against the walls. Where flowerbeds and soil have built up over time it should be a fairly straightforward job to level them.

Where you have an adjoining hard-surfaced path, rain can splash up the wall. Replacing paths immediately adjoining a house with gravel instead of concrete or asphalt can significantly reduce damp problems.

As discussed earlier, a French drain is a simple but highly effective remedy. Swapping wet soil for gravel allows damp to evaporate into the air circulating below ground level within the gravel, so it's less able to migrate up the walls. However, in order for moisture trapped in the lower wall to escape it helps to replace any cement pointing or render with breathable lime-based equivalents.

Allow time for drying out

To get rid of dampness plenty of time needs to be allowed for the building to dry out once the problem has been resolved. This famously takes about a month for each 25mm of masonry – which could mean as much as nine months for a typical 9in (230mm) thick solid brick wall, or well over a year for a thick rubble stone wall. In some cases you may need to allow a summer or two to get the full benefit. To help the drying process any external vegetation adorning the walls should be cleared. Indoors, it helps to open windows in the dryer months to encourage ventilation.

During winter months the best advice is to simply keep the house heated. De-humidifiers can help speed up the process, but beware of over-drying damp joinery, as it can be vulnerable to shrinkage and cracking. One thing to bear in mind is that, as we saw earlier, any hygroscopic salts absorbed in the plaster can do a pretty good impersonation of a continuing damp problem during the drying-out process, even though the wall itself is actually dry.

Mike Parrett / Dampbuster.com

An obvious case of rising damp (above)? – until you take a look outside (below)

Mike Parrett / Dampbuster.com

After hacking off cement render plinth, the wall should be allowed to dry out, then repointed or rendered in lime (with a bellmouth drip)

3 HOME IMPROVEMENTS

Owning a charming period property is a bit like running a classic car – you need to be prepared to dispense generous amounts of TLC on a fairly frequent basis. At the very least most old houses will require regular maintenance to keep them sweet. Many others will have suffered from inappropriate 'improvement' works using modern materials that, as we saw in the last chapter, can be very damaging and now need to be rectified. You may even be considering doing up an old wreck requiring extensive work, or perhaps extending or converting an historic house.

But as regular viewers of TV property shows will know, it's all too easy at this stage to be overcome with enthusiasm and charge ahead, only for things to later turn sour. So before getting the builders in, it's worth taking a few minutes to consider how best to go about it. This should pre-empt any risk of the best bits of the property somehow ending up in a skip, whilst ensuring you get exactly what you're paying for.

Before you start

Getting work done on old houses tends to be more of a challenge than with modern buildings, because to do the job properly requires the application of 'heritage skills'. But that doesn't mean you shouldn't tackle some of the work yourself. The step-by-step features in this book show the kind of projects that are well within the capabilities of competent DIYers. If time permits it's worth enrolling on practical courses in traditional building skills. There's something deeply satisfying about mastering the use of natural materials in the time-honoured fashion.

If you do plan to take on any of the work yourself it's important to consider how much time you can realistically devote to it. Most people are happy to undertake some decoration or landscaping work and leave the more complex stuff to local specialists. Alternatively you may have an aptitude for drawing plans, or perhaps project management is more your thing. When it comes to employing builders, the decision needs to be made whether to employ individual trades or to appoint a main contractor. Either way the key to a successful outcome is to ensure that the works you want carried out are clearly communicated to the people doing the job.

The professionals

For all but the smallest jobs you're likely to require the services of a building surveyor or architect, and quite possibly a structural engineer. But it's essential to only employ those with good experience of historic buildings as well as a genuine feel for conservation.

A building surveyor or architect can be appointed to draw up plans, write a specification and tender the job. They should be able to tactfully steer clients away from any potentially damaging ideas or unsympathetic modernisation work. Where necessary they can advise on complying with relevant legislation (never assume your builder 'knows the law'). For larger projects they should be able to perform the role of project manager and administer the contract fairly between the employer and building contractor on site, up to completion.

A good building professional will be familiar with the Conservation Officers at the local authority. They'll know what information to submit for planning and Building Regulations applications, and should be able to guide clients through more complex planning issues, such as repairs to Listed buildings.

To find the right people, start by checking out the websites of the professional bodies for architects and surveyors and of specialist conservation groups such as LPOC (Listed Property Owners Club), IHBC (Institute of Historic Building Conservation) and SPAB (Society for Protection of Ancient Buildings) should also be able to point you in the right direction – see the 'Further advice' box. Above all, pick someone you feel comfortable working with. And before confirming the appointment, don't forget to check that they have the necessary professional indemnity insurance.

Architects
Qualified architects are members of RIBA (Royal Institution of British Architects), but relatively few specialise in the conservation of historic buildings. Those that do are mostly registered with the AABC (Architects Accredited in Building Conservation) register, which lists individuals by region. See www.aabc-register.co.uk.

Building surveyors
As with architects, only a minority of chartered surveyors specialise in historic buildings. However, the RICS (Royal Institution of Chartered Surveyors) has a dedicated building conservation faculty, who should be able to provide a list of suitably experienced local surveyors.

Structural engineers
When buying a property, mortgage valuations sometimes require that a follow-up inspection is carried out by a structural engineer, to advise on significant cracking or other movement. Or you may want to appoint an engineer to design structural alterations. Clearly a good understanding of local traditional buildings of the same type as yours is essential, to avoid any unsympathetic or unnecessarily heavy-handed 'belt and braces' repairs.

A good starting point is the Conservation Accreditation Register for Engineers, which lists structural engineers skilled in the conservation of historic structures – and also scores top marks for the best acronym (CARE).

Planning and Building Control

Planning and Listed Building Consent

As we saw earlier, like-for-like repairs to Listed buildings don't usually require consent. But this is something of a grey area, so to be on the safe side it's best to consult your local authority Conservation Officer. To help explain the changes you have in mind, a few photos of the property and simple drawings or sketches of the proposed improvements can work wonders. Having to submit a Listed building application for quite minor changes may seem a bit daunting, but the majority of applications are approved. It's now quite common for a small fee to be charged for listed building applications.

In some cases you'll need to apply for planning permission as well as Listed Building Consent, for example where you want to build an extension. The good news is this can now be done on a single combined form, although it may be treated as two concurrent applications. For minor changes it should be fairly straightforward to do your own application, although you'll normally need some basic scale drawings showing the extent of the proposed works. You will also need to complete a 'Design and Access Statement' to accompany your plans. This provides an additional opportunity to set out your case and demonstrate that the changes you want to make have been carefully thought through, including any impact on the building's historic significance. Bear in mind also that the desirability of preserving the setting of a Listed building is a factor that planners must give special regard to.

Soon after your application has been submitted, the neighbours will become aware of the proposed changes, which the Council have a duty to publicise. So it's worth bearing in mind that by keeping them informed of your plans from the outset they'll be less likely to assume the worst and raise objections.

The application process usually takes around eight weeks. If it's ultimately refused you have a right to appeal within six months. But the best advice is to carefully run through your plans in advance with the local planning team to pre-empt any possible problems. Although they should offer guidance, remember that it's not their job to design an applicant's project for them. Once permission has been granted it normally remains valid for a period of three years, so if work has not been 'substantially commenced' during that time a fresh application will need to be made.

Building Regulations

A Building Regulations application is required for more types of work than you might imagine. In addition to regulating matters such as structural alterations, fire safety, drainage and major new building work, the Building Regulations are today increasingly focussed on thermal insulation and energy efficiency. Approval of additional works such as electrical wiring and replacement windows is normally delegated via approved installers, where a 'competent person' certifies that work has been carried out in compliance with the Building Regs.

For any structural alterations or new building work the application will normally require detailed drawings accompanied by engineers' calculations. Unlike simpler planning drawings, these need to include detailed information confirming compliance, such as specifying precise details of openings and the strengths and thermal performance of materials.

However, when it comes to submitting your application there are two options: a 'proper' Full Plans application, or the short-cut method known as a Building Notice. The fee is the same in both cases, but with a Building Notice you can normally commence work 48 hours after giving the minimum two days' written notice. With this method you're basically making a promise up front that you'll comply with the Building Regs on site, rather than submitting detailed drawings to prove it in advance. But the risk is that a site inspection could later uncover something that doesn't comply. And if a problem isn't picked up until late in the day, it's likely to involve considerable extra work for it to be taken down and rebuilt – which would prove highly disruptive, not to say expensive.

So for all but the smallest works it's normally best to make a Full Plans application, not least because it encourages you to think through the details in advance, thereby reducing the risk of problems arising later on site. It also means your builders will have an approved set of plans to work to. The application itself should take no more than five weeks. As with planning consent, once approval has been granted you need to use it or lose it, and start work within a three-year period. You need to notify Building Control at least two days prior to starting on site, and then at key stages so that their surveyor can inspect the works as they progress.

Culture clash

Where an old house is undergoing repair or alteration there's a potential conflict between the Planners' desire for conservation and Building Control imposing stringent thermal efficiency targets. Part L of the Building Regulations seeks to impose increasingly demanding standards of 'modern house' energy performance, which can sometimes clash with Planning requirements to retain the original fabric, particularly when it comes to works on Listed buildings. Fortunately, Building Control Officers are permitted considerable discretion in cases where carrying out such works would threaten the character or fabric of an old house. So some relaxation of the rules should be possible, perhaps with a little help from the Conservation Officer, in order to reach a sensible compromise.

The Party Wall Act

If you need to carry out building work to a wall shared with neighbours, the Party Wall Act comes into play as a legal requirement. As you'd imagine, this primarily applies to works to party walls in terraced and semi-detached houses; but it also applies where you want to excavate foundations within 3m of an adjoining property (in some cases within 6m), and can equally relate to works affecting walls on boundary lines between gardens. You have to serve a formal notice on the owners of the adjoining property at least two months before the work commences, which normally means having to appoint a Party Wall Surveyor.

Specialist work – rebuilding wall with cob blocks

woodlouseconservation.co.uk

Selecting the right builders

The success of any building project is largely down to your choice of builders. But anyone with a van can offer building services, so it's essential to do your homework. It's always worth following up recommendations from friends or neighbours, but the people who know which local builders and trades have the specialist skills necessary for the demands of period properties are Conservation Officers, although they may not be allowed to make specific recommendations. Architects and surveyors can also be a useful source of advice, as they may have worked with contractors and key trades on previous jobs.

Inevitably, the best people tend to be booked up weeks or even months in advance, but it's better to wait than take a risk employing someone less experienced.

Heritage skills

As well as appointing a builder you get on reasonably well with and feel you can trust, it goes without saying that it's essential they know what they're doing. To judge whether they have the necessary understanding of the way period properties work, try asking the following questions:

- Do you use pure lime mixes for mortars and renders (as opposed to adding cement)?
- Are you happy to repair an old window rather than chuck it out and replace it?
- Do you get on well with Conservation Officers?

In each case you're looking for a 'yes'. You might also want to check their views on the subject of damp in old walls. If their

Pointing in lime mortar

Studio Scotland Ltd

immediate response is to suggest injection of a chemical DPC then they are not the right people for the job.

Work to old houses tends to be relatively labour-intensive because it often involves careful and time-consuming piecing-in of repairs, with a higher level of skill required. So you may find there are only a small number of suitable craftspeople to choose from in your area. Trades usually work as individual one-man bands, or sometimes as small firms. Also, remember that there are legal restrictions as to who can carry out electrical work and gas installation – see Chapter 15.

Sometimes unexpected issues are encountered as work progresses, such as some unanticipated rot revealed when a concealed beam is exposed. This means that decisions need to be made about how best to solve the problem. After a certain amount of sucking in air, embellished with the odd expletive, most builders will be more than happy to dispense advice. However, the task of analysing defects and designing repairs is normally the responsibility of your architect, surveyor or engineer, particularly where there are any structural implications. On the other hand, some of the best trades will have extensive experience and practical knowledge of materials and structures, and might have encountered similar issues in the past. So they may well be able to suggest some valuable solutions, which should be discussed with your designer.

Further advice

There are a surprising number of groups dedicated to conservation of old buildings. Best known are perhaps the Institute of Historic Building Conservation (IHBC) and the Society for the Protection of Ancient Buildings (SPAB), who should be able to supply advice on locating skilled craftspeople and specialist trades, as well as suitable surveyors and architects. The Listed Property Owners Club (LPOC) is an excellent resource for owners of all old houses. Depending on the age of your house, it may also be worth approaching dedicated conservation groups like the Victorian Society and the Georgian Society. See www.period-house.com.

Preparation

Whether you're embarking on minor repair work or building a major extension (see Chapter 16), the key to a smoothly run job is to specify clearly at the outset precisely what you want done. This may sound blindingly obvious, but too often bitter disputes grow from simple misunderstandings about exactly what was included in the price and what wasn't. So taking a few minutes to clarify this in advance could save a great deal of unnecessary stress and expense later in the process.

At this point it's worth mentioning the difference between a quote and an estimate. A *quote* is a firm price that is legally binding – a fixed sum for a fixed amount of work. Even if you're presented with a larger final bill, you're only obliged to pay the agreed quoted price, unless you've requested extras or agreed to any changes. An *estimate*, on the other hand, is nothing more than the builder's best guess as to what the cost might eventually be. Because estimates aren't legally binding and are subject to change, they're generally considered too risky to rely on, even for fairly minor works.

Specifications and pricing

For smaller, more straightforward projects a brief, clearly worded description, accompanied by a scale drawing, may be all that's required for a builder to quote against. To obtain quotes for larger, more complex projects a detailed specification is advisable. Known as the 'spess', this is basically a long 'shopping list' stating each separate piece of work required, against which the contractor has to price. Specifying work to old buildings is more of a challenge than for a newbuild property (see below), so these are normally drawn up by a surveyor or architect. Together with a copy of the Building Control approved drawings, this can be used as the basis for a competitive tender to select a contractor. It can also come in very useful later on, when it comes to making payment; having individual prices quoted against each specified job means it should be clear how much money is due for each completed piece of work.

When it comes to comparing quotations, it's naturally tempting to accept the lowest price. But if one is suspiciously low, check whether it includes VAT. High standards tend not to go with low prices, and you'd normally expect to pay a premium for specialist heritage skills. However, unless you have implicit trust in an individual craftsman, or they come highly recommended, it's generally best to avoid quotes based on time taken (a price per day) because of the obvious temptation to sit around and string the job out indefinitely. Day work may be acceptable for smaller parts of the job, at agreed rates, but rarely for a whole project.

Conservation

It's particularly important with old buildings to make it very clear that you want to retain as much of the original fabric as possible, with a focus on repair. This should prevent the unfortunate scenario where historic bits of the house are unnecessarily ripped out and replaced. Expert conservation advice may be needed in advance to decide precisely which parts of the building are capable of being salvaged (and if so, what is the optimum method of repair to apply) and to identify any that are definitely beyond repair. Otherwise you'll forever be plagued by the nagging doubt that those irreplaceable items of antique joinery that the builders chucked out could have been saved.

It's only too easy to accidentally erase charming quirks and valuable clues to an old property's history.

With work to old houses you need to be constantly on the case. Whereas with a modern property you can simply write 'paint windows', here you need to define the type and make of paint, as well as the preparation and the number of coats, not forgetting the colour and sheen. This obviously involves a lot of work, but the more specific you are the less room there is for mistakes and disputes later on site.

Cost control

Having accepted a firm quote or a tendered price you should have a reasonably clear idea about how much you'll end up paying for the completed job – providing, of course, that nothing unexpected happens. And there's the rub. Work to old buildings is rarely fully predictable, and can sometimes throw up unforeseen problems. With the best will in the world it can be hard to know exactly what will be encountered until work has started and parts of the building have been opened up and explored.

Unforeseen circumstances such as concealed decay, or problems lurking underground, can result in substantially higher costs. To some extent builders will factor in a certain amount of risk in their quotes, but to guard against being overcharged for unexpected additional work you need to agree hourly or daily rates so that a fair price can be agreed at a later date (and also agree on how materials will be charged).

To ensure the job doesn't grind to a halt should something nasty pop out of the woodwork, it's recommended that your budget includes a contingency fund of at least 20%. If you do find yourself going over budget it helps to have an idea as to which parts of the job are non-essential, so that if push comes to shove some works could be postponed or sacrificed.

But if there's one major cause of hugely inflated costs it's this: clients requesting extras and changes. So the golden rule is, don't keep changing your mind after you've accepted a price.

Programming the works

Works to old buildings are best carried out between May and September, because traditional lime-based materials and finishes will be at risk from frost in the months nearer winter. This requires careful programming, with works usually needing to start in spring or summer in order to finish by the autumn. You need to calculate the time back from the completion date, allowing for any planning applications and party wall awards. Allow time for preparation of drawings, eight weeks or more for planning applications, and around five weeks for Building Regs 'full plans' applications. Contractors are usually allocated three or four weeks to price a tender. Your programme also needs to allow for lead-in times for any specialist components such as bespoke windows, which can sometimes add several months, although this may run concurrently whilst documentation is prepared, submitted and processed. Above all you need to factor in the availability of skilled trades to actually do the job.

Contracts

When employing firms of building contractors, it's standard practice – as the term contractor implies – to draw up a written contract. A building contract is simply an agreement between you and your builders for them to undertake a list of specified tasks to a certain standard for an agreed sum of money. Ready-made contracts such as the JCT (Joint Contracts Tribunal) Minor Works are widely available, or you can download a free one from the Federation of Master Builders – see links on the www.period-house.com website.

All you need to do is to fill in the key details, such as the agreed price, the duration (start and completion dates), and payment terms. Then both parties sign and keep a copy of the contract.

However, where you're employing individual trades a written contract of this type is not appropriate. Many will run a mile at the mere thought. Although, strictly speaking, accepting a verbal offer could form a contract in law, without something written down it's your word against theirs. So the best arrangement is to get written quotes and confirm acceptance in writing, making reference to the relevant drawings (by plan number and date). For smaller jobs a simple exchange of letters and copies of approved plans is often sufficient. The letter should include all the key points such as the agreed price, payment terms, and the agreed timescales, *ie* the start and finish dates.

The build

Managing the build

There seems to be an unwritten rule that building work invariably takes longer than anticipated. But correctly planned and managed there's no reason this should be the case. Nonetheless it pays to build some slack into your programme, whilst keeping the builders focussed on completion by the agreed date.

For major works it's often better for all concerned if you physically move out of the house rather than trying to survive marooned in the corner of a solitary room with a chemical toilet. If this isn't possible, create some breathing space for yourself by agreeing working hours with the contractor, and carefully programme the works so that the job can proceed safely away from your belongings, children and pets.

It's a good idea to give your tradesmen a guided tour of the house at the outset, mentioning some of its history and the important features. To assist with project management as the works progress, it's worth keeping a diary recording who was on site each day, what work was done, materials delivered, and any adverse weather that stopped work. This can come in very helpful at the final totting up process, when memories have faded. It's also worth taking photos before, during and after each stage (but do it discreetly – it doesn't pay to irritate your workforce!). By the end of the project, 'who said what to whom' will be shrouded in mystery, with inevitable scope for disputes, so all instructions to your builders should be confirmed in writing, along with any agreed changes resulting in additions or reductions in costs.

It's easy to forget that you also need to manage the neighbours. As we saw earlier with planning applications, living in harmony with the good folk next door is greatly assisted by taking the trouble to keep them informed. If they know what's going on and how long the work is scheduled to last they're likely to be more tolerant of periodic disruption and noise. Neighbours can also be a useful security device, keeping an eye on things when you're not there.

Payment

No one does their best work if they're not paid on time, so you need to agree payment arrangements well in advance and pay promptly. On larger projects and newbuilds it's common to pay for completion of key stages, but not all projects can be neatly broken down into easily priced chunks of work. This is where a detailed specification with a breakdown of costs for different parts of the job can come in useful. The simplest approach is to ask the builder to submit their invoice on a monthly or fortnightly basis; but never pay for work in advance – in case the builder goes bust or vanishes without trace!

It should be agreed with the contractor at the outset that you'll keep a retention from each payment due of at least 5% of the contract sum, payable upon completion. Towards the end of the job a snagging list should be drawn up and gone through in detail with the builder, at which point the retention should come in useful as a motivational tool. When the work is finished it's important to obtain the completion certificate from Building Control (where this applies) before making final payments to your builders.

Materials

Sourcing matching traditional materials, such as hand-made bricks or roof tiles, is crucial to the end result, but can be enormously time-consuming. Where you're employing trades direct you may decide to organise the supply of materials yourself. If so, take the precaution of agreeing with your builder in advance that the items you're ordering are technically suitable for the job at hand. This way no one can later blame the materials should any problems arise. Also, be sure to place orders well in advance and check delivery times, to avoid the nightmare scenario of paying trades to sit around doing nothing because of a 'no show' delivery – delays on site are expensive. Where you're employing a main contractor, they'll normally take responsibility for organising and paying for the materials. You should not be expected to pay for these until they've been delivered on site.

Traditional building materials tend to be more sensitive to wet and cold than their modern counterparts, something specialist suppliers will be conscious of. So suitable storage on site needs to be arranged in advance.

One final word of advice: beware of 'Sunday supplement' miracle products such as spray roof foam and 'never paint again' wall coatings – they can be extremely damaging to old buildings.

Safety checklist

It's not worth sacrificing your health even for the most fabulously restored period house. The nightmare scenario of a serious accident occurring, or being sued for negligence, can be avoided by taking a few common-sense precautions at the outset. This may not be the sexiest part of the project but the following suggestions could save you having to endure a future existence hideously scarred, blinded or brain damaged:

- Be sure to wear protective clothing, goggles, masks, gloves and steel-capped boots, plus a hard hat.
- Always carry a charged mobile phone.
- Try to avoid working alone, or else tell someone and call them at prearranged times.
- Keep a first aid kit handy.
- Keep bonfires well away from buildings (particularly thatched roofs) and don't leave them unattended.
- Take extra care when working at height, and ensure scaffolding is correctly erected.
- Comply with Work At Height Regulations, which restrict the use of ladders.

Security and protection

When it comes to major works, particularly if you've vacated the property, temporary fencing may need to be erected to protect the site from vandalism and theft. The risk of accidental damage from building works is also a major consideration. Fortunately this can be largely pre-empted by a little careful upfront planning. Vulnerable windows and doors can be temporarily protected by being boarded over. Historic architectural details such as fireplaces and staircases should be shielded from damage (and from the eyes of thieves). Old floor surfaces can be protected with sheets of hardboard or plywood. To preserve fragile items like historic ceilings from vibration, remind the builder to use screws wherever possible rather than hammering in nails. Externally, be alert to the risk of scaffolding damage, particularly to glazing and roof tiles.

Scaffolding

A high proportion of accidents arise from poor erection of scaffolding or temporary work platforms. This is definitely not a DIY job. Scaffolding must always be erected (and

dismantled) by a licensed specialist firm carrying full insurance. Normally this should be the responsibility of the main contractor, or arranged by your builder. Any platform over 2m high must have metal edge-guarding fixed to the sides, and if people are likely to be passing beneath there should be protective netting to catch falling debris.

As this is one of the major expenses of any work at height, it's worth making the best use of it while it's in place, for example by painting external joinery or overhauling windows. But tell your builder well in advance so as not to clash with other scheduled works.

CDM regulations

CDM stands for Construction, Design and Management. If the extent of building works exceeds 30 days or involves more than 500 man-hours on site, then the contractor must notify the Health and Safety Executive in advance. If you're the client, this shouldn't be your responsibility, and less extensive works are, in any case, currently exempt. However, if you directly employ more than five people on your site at any one time, the Management of Health and Safety at Work Regulations come into play. This means you must be able to demonstrate that you've taken reasonable precautions to prevent injury.

Old house hazards

Whilst not wishing to spoil anyone's period-living enjoyment, it's important to be aware that there are some additional hazards that are sometimes encountered when working on old houses.

One of the greatest potential risks is where major structural alterations are carried out, because if undertaken without due care they can easily cause instability. One recent example saw an entire flank gable wall of a Victorian terrace collapse because cowboy builders had excavated along the full length of the wall, undermining the shallow foundations. The insurance company duly wriggled out of paying (as they hadn't been notified about the works), leaving the unlucky owners on the verge of bankruptcy as well as effectively homeless. A more common scenario is where substantial new loadings are added, such as loft conversions. This can set up enormous new stresses that must be calculated by a structural engineer and factored into the design in advance. Such works are also subject to obtaining Building Regulations consent.

Probably the most obvious danger in old buildings, to people and property alike, is from fire. Fortunately, by taking a few simple precautions the most serious dangers can normally be averted.

Fire

Fire has zero respect for status. In 1986 the Queen awoke to the news that a disastrous blaze had caused extensive damage to Hampton Court Palace. It is thought the fire was started by a candle in one of the 'grace and favour' apartments. The repairs eventually cost £5 million and took six years to complete. Of course, such horrors can equally occur in humbler abodes. So with a view to pre-empting tragedies of this kind let's take a look at some common causes of fires in old buildings.

HOT WORK

A significant number of major fires in period buildings have been traced back to renovation work. But it's not just thatched roofs that

---

Top tips for employing builders

- ■ Only select builders who have suitable 'heritage skills', with good experience of traditional buildings.
- ■ Get at least three written quotes (*not* estimates). For larger jobs the quotes should be priced against an itemised specification that you've provided. Get the cost broken down into as much detail as possible, so that you can see what you're getting and use it as a guide for any additional works.
- ■ Check if VAT is included in the quote. Individual trades my have a turnover that's below the VAT threshold and quite legitimately not need to charge VAT.
- ■ Ask for references from previous jobs, and go and see them.
- ■ When comparing quotes, check for hidden extras, and don't be tempted to automatically choose the lowest price.
- ■ Agree payment stages in advance and only pay for completed work. Never pay up front.
- ■ Check that the builder is suitably insured for risks to persons and property. Ask for copies of certificates for full public liability insurance and (for main contractors) employers' liability cover.
- ■ Ask who will actually be doing the work. Will any subcontractors be able to produce work of a high standard?
- ■ Be very clear about precisely what work you want done, and don't keep changing your mind later on site or you'll be charged lots of expensive extras.
- ■ Use a written contract with firms or detailed letters with trades.
- ■ Confirm the start and finish dates in writing, along with the agreed price and arrangements for payment.
- ■ Confirm exactly what's included in the price – does it, for example, include lifting and re-laying carpets, moving furniture, scaffolding, clearing all rubbish from the site, skip hire and cleaning up?

A few simple precautions could have prevented such disasters

are at risk. Old dry timbers and wood-shavings nestling in hidden nooks and crannies can potentially be combustible, as can concealed birds' nests and accumulations of old tinder-dry straw. Consequently conservation bodies now rigorously enforce bans on 'hot work' of any kind. Flame guns and blowtorches are conventionally used for plumbing and paint stripping but the use of naked flames shouldn't really be necessary. Compression fittings can be used to connect pipes, and joints can sometimes be welded off-site.

Hot work on joinery should be avoided, not just because of the potential fire risk but because fumes from burning lead paint are hazardous and the heat risks cracking old glass. If there's absolutely no other option to using heat-producing appliances, work should take place early in the day so that it's finished at least a couple of hours before the site is vacated. The same rule should apply to any work with spark-inducing tools, like angle grinders. One useful additional precaution is to install temporary (battery-powered) smoke alarms during the work.

FAULTY ELECTRIC CIRCUITS

It's well known that old electrical wiring can potentially be unsafe with a risk of consequent house fires or electrocution, but even new electrical wiring has the potential to become hazardous, for example where mice have chewed cables or where cable runs are enclosed within thick layers of loft insulation and in danger of overheating. The simplest precaution to reduce the risk of fire and fatal electric shocks is to install a modern consumer unit incorporating both types of safety trip switches – MCBs and RCDs.

Miniature circuit breakers (MCBs) are the modern equivalent of old rewirable fuses, only much more efficient, switching off an overloaded circuit usually within 100 milliseconds. Residual current devices (RCDs) are highly sensitive earth leakage detectors

that monitor the current (amps) flowing between live and neutral. If it detects even a tiny difference it will instantly disconnect the circuit, thus saving lives.

OVERHEATING DOWNLIGHTERS
As we shall see in Chapter 15, there are

two main concerns about recessed lighting: cutting holes in ceilings significantly reduces their fire resistance (as well as weakening them), and concealed lighting can cause the build-up of heat in confined spaces within ceiling voids – which is of particular concern where you have a thatched roof in proximity. Downlighters are therefore best avoided, or else should be fitted only to new suspended ceilings.

DEFECTIVE FLUES, OPEN FIRES AND THATCH
Many old houses have hidden cavities within flues, and a build-up of soot in flues over time can fuel a chimney fire. The solution is to have chimneys swept regularly. This is particularly important with

Chimneys well clear of thatch

thatched properties, as witnessed by buildings insurance premiums that reflect the potential fire risk.

Happily a few simple precautions can go a long way towards negating these risks, such as installing a smoke alarm in the loft, lining active flues with the correct type of flue liner, (essential where there is a log-burning stove) and fitting a mesh spark-arrestor to chimney pots (but remember that these need periodic cleaning) – see next chapter.

Wise precautions
Legendary 1960s rock star Steve Marriott died in April 1991 when a fire, thought to have been caused by a smouldering cigarette, swept through his 16th-century Essex farmhouse. A functioning

Wildlife in your home

You're never entirely alone in an old house. To a certain extent it should be possible to live in harmony with the occasional uninvited guest, but it may sometimes be necessary to take action to repel rodents or insects. These are the most common cohabitants:

Birds

With most species of nesting wild birds it can be an offence to remove or destroy their nest while it's in use or being built. If you plan to remove redundant nests from a roof space after the birds have flown, make sure that the access route to the nest is sealed off with wire netting, to prevent bird ingress but maintain loft ventilation. To scare off nuisance birds, one ingenious and often effective solution is to fix an artificial bird of prey 'scarecrow' to your roof!

Mice and rats

Apart from possible health issues, rodents can cause trouble by gnawing through plastic cable insulation, so it's essential to have a modern RCD-equipped consumer unit. To deter rodents, block up holes where they're entering the house and eliminate vegetation near the house where mice can live. Traditionally cats would earn their keep by deterring vermin! Alternatively traps or glueboards can be effective.

Plug-in ultrasonic pest repellent devices claim to repel rodents. They operate by emitting short-wavelength, high frequency sound waves at too high a pitch to be heard by the human ear. Opinions vary as to their effectiveness but they're non-lethal and probably worth a try.

Bees and wasps

'Mortar bees' sometimes burrow into eroded soft mortar joints in walls. They're only seen for a few weeks in the spring and are relatively harmless. Wasp nests are surprisingly common in lofts, in varying sizes from a few centimetres in width to a half a metre or more.

Squirrels

Grey squirrels, unlike their native red cousins, are widely regarded as vermin. Red squirrels are protected as an endangered species. Like mice, squirrels might chew electric wiring in lofts. Mothballs can be an effective deterrent. Also, seal up small openings to block ingress.

Bats

It's an offence to harm a bat, or to obstruct or destroy access to its chosen habitat. Bats tend to roost in lofts or outbuildings and are usually seen flying at dusk. Droppings are a clue to their presence – these look similar to but larger than those of mice. For further information visit the Bat Conservation Trust website (www.bats.org.uk).

smoke alarm could have made all the difference. Fitting smoke alarms to provide early warning is probably the single most effective survival measure, as well as one of the cheapest. A handy fire extinguisher and fire blanket in the kitchen can also be lifesavers. You also need to consider what means of escape you could use, particularly from second-floor or higher rooms.

But there are some other fairly obvious precautions that could save your historic bacon, such as not allowing smoking in or near the building, and not hosting wild candlelit parties. While you're at it, make sure there's a suitably powerful and lengthy hose with access to an outside tap. Also try to get into the habit of shutting doors to all the main rooms at night, especially to living rooms and kitchens, where fires are more likely to start.

Toxins

Two toxic materials in particular are common in older buildings – asbestos and lead. However, these needn't be a serious concern as long as you're forewarned.

ASBESTOS

Asbestos was widely used throughout most of the 20th century (particularly from the 1920s to the 1970s) as a strong but lightweight fire-resistant material, before its harmful effects were fully understood. The most common type found in old houses – asbestos cement sheeting – utilised the much less harmful white asbestos (as opposed to the more potentially carcinogenic blue and brown varieties). This is most commonly encountered in the form of soffits to box eaves on many post-war houses (and extensions), and is especially common as corrugated sheeting on the roofs of outbuildings, garages and old lean-tos. Its use in ceilings or as wallboard was comparatively rare, but it did make an appearance in guttering and drainage pipes between the 1940s and 1960s.

Asbestos in various other forms was additionally used for insulation to heaters and boilers and for pipe lagging in the form of bandages or compounds. It was even used in fireplace caulking, in some artificial slates and tiles, and in some wall plugs. One of the most common sources of fibres in properties of all ages is in some textured ceiling paints (for safe stripping see Chapter 14).

Asbestos is potentially dangerous to health where tiny airborne particles are inhaled, so any form of sanding, cutting or drilling must be avoided. However, surveyors routinely point out that as long as the fibres are not breathed in there shouldn't be any great concern. Hence often the simplest solution is to leave well alone or conceal it safely out of sight. Only in rare cases will expensive specialist removal works be required (*eg* for pipe lagging).

But there is another potential danger. As noted above, many old outbuildings have corrugated asbestos cement roofs. These tend to be weak and brittle and can easily fracture and collapse if walked on, forming jagged shards sharp enough to slash arteries, which in some tragic cases has resulted in people bleeding to death.

LEAD

Paint containing lead-based pigments was commonly applied to joinery and metalwork, and remained in widespread use until the 1960s. Lead-rich dust particles are harmful if inhaled so the use of power sanders should be avoided, as should burning off such paint, because of the toxic fumes. So where old paintwork needs to be rubbed down it should be prepared by hand with wet sanding. When rubbing down it's important to wear mask, goggles and gloves.

Water supply pipes were traditionally either of lead or cast iron, and until recently lead was used in the solder for copper water pipes. Fortunately in hard water areas the long-term build-up of limescale should provide an effective protective coating. If it's a concern you can have drinking water quality-tested for lead content. But for most of us the main potential point of contact with lead is with old paint – see Chapter 14.

OTHER TOXINS

It's sometimes claimed that ancient anthrax spores may be contained in the old horse or goat hair in plasterwork pre-dating 1895 (when controls were introduced), but this is probably a bit of an urban myth, and there are no recorded cases of infection. Nonetheless, wearing a mask is advisable when plasterwork is disturbed, to avoid breathing in dust particles. Also, as we shall see later, some early wallpapers contained toxic cocktails, including compounds of cadmium, cyanide and arsenic.

Finances

Unless your property happens to be Listed there's precious little official encouragement for the conservation of old buildings.

In exceptional cases grants may be available from English Heritage for urgent repairs (to Grade I or Grade II* Listed buildings), with similar arrangements existing in Scotland, Wales and Northern Ireland.

However, there is one area where incentives are increasingly available – to improve the energy efficiency of existing homes. This in itself is good news, but owners of old houses need to be mindful that the advice dispensed by unqualified sales people for schemes like the 'Green Deal' may not be appropriate for historic buildings, and in some cases may be positively harmful. In Chapter 16 we shall look at how this can be done properly, to achieve good thermal efficiency standards without sacrificing any of the building's character and valuable history.

VAT

There are a number of situations where reduced VAT can apply to residential properties. Firstly, renovations and alterations to houses that have been left empty for at least two years will be eligible for a reduced VAT rate of 5%. Better still, for properties empty for more than ten years there's no VAT at all – *ie* the full amount should be recoverable.

Perhaps the most obvious exemption is where individuals or small firms with a low annual turnover below the VAT threshold (£77,000 at the time of writing) are quite legitimately not required to charge VAT. But remember, the builder will still have to pay VAT on materials purchased in connection with the project, as well as for any plant hired, and this cost will be passed on to you. Where you are charged VAT, always check the necessary VAT number is shown on the invoice.

Until October 2012 alteration works to Listed buildings were zero-rated – a substantial saving. However like-for-like repairs, usually the best method of conserving old buildings, have always attracted VAT, so conservationists lobbied hard for parity. Now all works are charged at the full whack!

Insurance

Another subject that can be quite taxing for Listed property owners is buildings insurance. Because old buildings cost more to repair than modern houses it's vital to have adequate cover in place. If in the event of even a fairly small claim you're found to be under-insured, insurance companies can reduce the amount paid out by imposing an 'averaging' clause, leaving you out of pocket. But establishing an accurate rebuild cost of a Listed building can be surprisingly difficult.

It's a common misconception that the value for buildings insurance is the same as the market value of the house. With most properties the plot typically accounts for something around a third of the market value, so rebuild costs tend to be significantly lower than the price paid when it was purchased. However, it's not inconceivable that the price of rebuilding a Listed oak-framed medieval thatched cottage could actually total more than it cost to buy. So if your house is Listed, it's essential the insurers are informed.

The cost of repair work can be particularly expensive, because you may be legally obliged to rebuild or replace damaged fabric with high-quality materials matching the original. The cost of employing specialists skilled in traditional construction techniques, or recreating ornate features and superb decorative detailing, can be very substantial. For example, the planners may insist you reinstate a finely carved oak staircase with an exact replica, and unless your insurer is aware of such risks in advance they may only be prepared to pay out for a standard plain wooden staircase. Fortunately, most Conservation Officers draw the line at insisting workmen don medieval outfits for complete period authenticity! But it's not just the cost of building works that needs to be considered. There are implications with slower rebuild processes that can mean hefty bills for alternative accommodation.

To cover yourself in the event of a claim, be sure to notify your insurer in advance of having building work done, and tell them if the property is going to be unoccupied. Where a building has to be left vacant whilst undergoing long-term refurbishment it may only be possible to insure it on a restricted perils basis, which excludes risks such as theft, malicious damage and impact by builders' plant etc. So ensure that the contractor carries adequate liability insurance. For major improvements, advise your insurer of the increasing value of the house as work progresses. You may also need additional insurance cover for tools, materials and equipment on site.

If disaster does strike, keeping a good photographic record (somewhere safely off-site) of period features such as historic fireplaces, doors and beams can be an enormous help. Finally, you need to check in advance that your insurer will allow you to choose your own contractors – loss adjusters sometimes insist you use their 'panel' firms, who may have no knowledge of the craftsmanship or materials needed for Listed buildings.

Period Property Manual

4 ROOFS AND RAINWATER FITTINGS

No matter how picturesque an old roof, it's not much use unless it does its job properly. Maintaining a good 'hat' should be at the top of the list when it comes to preventing an old building falling prey to disrepair. Prompt replacement of broken or missing tiles can be the vital 'stitch in time' that halts water penetration, thereby preventing damp and rot.

Roofs can last for hundreds of years, but when a failure does occur it's important not to panic and inadvertently damage the building's historic character with inappropriate works, such as replacing quaint original coverings with clumsy modern concrete interlocking tiles.

Much of the charm of old houses stems from the combination of local craftsmanship and traditional materials that have weathered gracefully over many years. The original choice of roof coverings would have been largely determined by their suitability

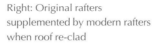

Top and above: Rough hewn roof timbers

Right: Original rafters supplemented by modern rafters when roof re-clad

for coping with local weather conditions, but factors such as cost, availability and fashion would have also influenced the types of material that ended up on your roof.

The roof structure

The shape and strength of roofs is largely a function of the choice of coverings, as the structure would be designed to support the specific type of tile, slate or thatch. Roofs were traditionally built with steeper pitches than on modern houses in order to hasten the dispersal of rain, since there was rarely any form of underlay beneath the tiles.

From medieval times it was common practice to assemble roof structures in a 'dry-run' on the ground and mark the components with Roman numerals as a guide to reassembly *in situ*. Sometimes gouged symbols called 'shipping marks' were also applied, believed to denote the quality and grading of timber.

Some of the simplest early roofs were constructed using trunks of 'rough hewn' timber with the bark left on, such as 'ash pole rafters'. Such ancient roof structures, particularly those of oak, can last hundreds of years if kept dry and well ventilated. Although the outer sapwood frequently becomes host to wood beetle, such attacks are normally superficial, with the timbers retaining their natural durability and strength. By the Georgian and Victorian eras most roofs were constructed from softwoods, but the quality of the naturally seasoned timber used at the time was far superior to that found in modern roofs.

Carpenters marks – the same mark was applied to 2 pieces of timber to be joined

Baz Mogridge / E2BN

Firebreak walls

In the roof spaces of terraced and semi-detached houses, masonry party walls normally separate individual properties from those next door. Chimney breasts were commonly built up these party walls, leading to the stack(s) above. However, jerry-building in the Georgian and Victorian periods sometimes resulted in firebreak walls being omitted entirely in a bid to save money. Consequently open loft spaces would sometimes extend all the way from one end of a terrace to the other. Today the main worry with this arrangement is that fire could rapidly spread through the entire terrace, unchecked by 'firebreak' walls.

Recent blockwork party wall in loft where originally omitted

Where you find party walls in the loft made of modern blockwork or plasterboarded studwork, it's likely that recent upgrading works have been carried out as a survey recommendation. Reinstatement of missing firebreak walls can also be beneficial from a structural perspective, providing additional support to the timber purlins that in turn strengthen the rafters that form the main roof slopes.

Some rows of terraces feature short external parapet walls built up above the roof line, effectively dividing the main roof slopes of each house from its neighbour. This requirement was originally introduced by London Building Acts to prevent builders skimping on firebreak walls by forcing them to extend the walls upwards, where they were visible to all. Such parapet walls are normally capped with coping stones or alternatively have a course or two of 'creasing tiles' projecting either side to disperse rainwater.

Movement

Some ancient roofs undulate quite dramatically, sporting a distinctly wavy profile. This may appear somewhat alarming but a certain amount of historic sagging and settlement to an old roof is usually acceptable. As long as the movement isn't progressive – *ie* 'live' – it shouldn't be a problem. Structural problems to roofs are comparatively rare. The most likely causes are:

ROOF SPREAD

Given half a chance, rafters have a natural tendency to push downwards and outwards. They're normally restrained lower

down by ceiling joists acting as collars. But where there's insufficient lateral restraint (often because joints have failed due to rot or rusted nails) the rafters will be free to do their

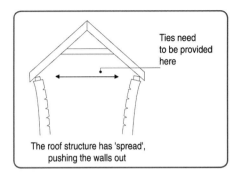
The roof structure has 'spread', pushing the walls out

Ties need to be provided here

Collars tie together roof opposing slopes

Discreet tubular metal ties strengthen roof structure.

worst, pushing out the walls so that they lean or bulge at the top. This in turn can cause the rafters to sink, so the roof sags in the middle. This is a relatively common occurrence on cheaply built lean-to roofs. To prevent further movement, the usual remedy is to improve restraint with new collars (or metal ties) or by refixing each rafter to the adjoining ceiling joist below with coach bolts.

Timber can also come loose due to the failure of iron nails (common at tie beams) – these can be replaced with stainless steel bolts.

PHYSICAL ALTERATIONS

Old structures don't much like change. Serious problems sometimes develop as a result of stupid alterations, such as cutting away an inconveniently positioned timber brace to create more headroom. Problems sometimes also arise from the addition of substantial additional loadings, such as carelessly inserted dormer windows, loft conversions, or where an original lightweight slate roof has been replaced with heavier new concrete tiles.

ROT AND BEETLE

It's comparatively rare to find significant beetle or timber decay in roof structures. As noted above, wood beetle doesn't tend to burrow far below the surface, so the affected timber often retains its strength. So a spot of woodworm in the rafters shouldn't normally be a problem. Rot is only likely where prolonged leakage has occurred. Likely areas of decay from continuous saturation include timberwork adjacent to valleys and faulty flashings, and less commonly wall plates and rafter feet. A localised repair may be all that's required, combined with improved loft ventilation to help moisture evaporate, thereby reducing the risk of such problems recurring.

Badly decayed rafter with new rafter alongside.

New roof timbers alongside of existing

Roofing work

Surveyors sometimes have a tendency to be over-cautious and to pass premature death sentences, condemning old roofs that may still have a good 10 or 20 years' life left in them. It's also not unknown for less ethical roofers to succumb to the temptation to drum up business by scaring homeowners into unnecessary major works. So how can you tell if a roof is in need of major surgery or just a quick fix?

Refixing

The lifespan of many traditional clay or stone tiles can be measured in hundred of years, far longer than their fixings. Slate is also one of the most durable roofing materials, with a lifespan often substantially exceeding a century. Of course, the longevity of a roof very much depends on its exposure to the environment, as well as the quality of the original materials; but whereas ancient oak pegs can still be found holding clay peg-tiles in place, original iron nails (or later galvanised ones) commonly used in 18th- and 19th-century slate roofs have often rusted away, resulting in extensive slippage.

There's an old rule of thumb that if the number of slipped slates or tiles exceeds about a quarter of the total then completely stripping and re-cladding a roof is more economical than spot repairs. But today's Work At Height Regulations mean that scaffolding or platform towers are required even for minor roof repairs, significantly adding to the cost. Although hydraulic platform 'cherry pickers' can often make access easier for minor repairs, they're still expensive. Nonetheless, refixing or renewing the odd slipped or missing tile should be a fairly straightforward job for a competent roofing contractor – who should also appreciate the need to avoid causing further damage to old slates or tiles whilst carrying out repairs!

Tiled roofs are typically easier to repair than those clad with slate because most tiles are just hung over the battens (as opposed to being nailed in place), making them easier to lift. It's sometimes even possible to carry out emergency repairs to tiled roofs from inside the loft – assuming there's no underlay in the way. For example, temporarily inserting a small sheet of lead from underneath in place of a missing tile might stem a roof leak before it can do any serious damage.

Slate roofs are more difficult to repair because each overlapping course is nailed in place. However, there's a time-honoured method of refixing slipped slates using 'tingles'. These are small strips of metal (lead, zinc or copper) that are nailed to the batten underneath the (temporarily removed) loose slate, and then folded up at the lower edge of the slate, clipping it in place. However, on roofs where you see a rash of tingles it's likely to indicate widespread problems with corroded nails. This is a sign that re-cladding is overdue, although it's often possible to salvage and reuse the majority of the old slates.

Several slipped slates show roof is beyond repair using tingles.

Tracing leaks

It's surprising how much rain a tiny hairline crack or a small hole can admit. Sometimes the source of a leak isn't hard to locate, such as where water's streaming down the side of a chimney in the loft, but more often than not it can be surprisingly tricky to pin down the exact cause of the problem. This is because the water can travel some distance along ceilings and down roof slopes, well away from the source. Try using a hose to methodically test small sections of roof at a time.

In older roofs (without underlay beneath the tiles) you'll normally see thin strips of daylight between the tiles but any large gaps – especially at junctions with walls and stacks – are likely to indicate defective flashings.

Satellite damage

Leaks due to broken slates and tiles are fairly rare – except in one scenario. Installers of TV aerials, satellite dishes and solar panels clambering around in heavy boots on fragile roof coverings are a common cause of damage. Despite being one of the most hardwearing of all roof coverings, individual slates are quite fragile and can crack like crockery when trodden on. Of course, by the time you spot the problem the chances are the perpetrators will be long gone, so it's worth asking the installer to take a photo of the roof to verify its condition before finalising payment.

Contractors tend to site aerials or dishes at the point where access is easiest for installation, but this may not be the best place visually for the kerb appeal of your home. So it's a good idea to consider in advance which locations are most appropriate, and ensure that cables aren't just lazily run dangling across the main walls, with carelessly drilled holes damaging the property's fabric or appearance. If reception allows it's best to position TV aerials inside lofts, and satellite dishes can often work just as well hidden in roof valleys or in gardens.

Inspecting your roof

Once every 12 months or so it's advisable to give roofs a quick visual once-over to spot any looming potential problems before disaster strikes. These are some of the common warning signs to look for:

- Check for any slipped or missing slates or tiles. This could be a one-off defect, or part of a more extensive problem such as 'nail sickness'.
- Check whether metal flashings are loose or cracked.
- Where you have mortar fillets at joints they're likely to develop cracks, and are often best replaced with lead flashings.
- Check mortar pointing at ridge tiles (and, where relevant, hip tiles and verges). If it's badly eroded it will need re-pointing.
- In terraces and semi-detached houses, check the area above the party wall. Where next door's slates or tiles are relatively new, are they neatly integrated with those on your roof? Where there's a parapet above the party wall, check the condition of flashings and coping stones.
- In the loft, try switching off the light and look for any large chunks of daylight, *ie* gaps in the roof.
- Also in the loft, check for any damp staining that's still wet under weak points such as valley gutters, flashings and back gutters to chimneys.

Leak at back gutter to stack

Above: Here the original tie beam (at purlin height) had been cut out causing roof spread. Now temporarily replaced with scaffold plank

Right: Inappropriate 1980s concrete interlocking tiles

Re-cladding

There comes a point when so many tiles or slates have slipped that it's more cost effective to have the roof completely stripped and relaid. Where roofs are stripped with care it's often found that the majority of the old slates or tiles are still sound and can be sorted and graded for reuse. Don't get exploited by builders who tell you otherwise and then proceed to sell them behind your back.

It's comparatively rare for roof structures to require repair, and failure is most commonly due to rusted fixing nails. Replacing the existing timber battens isn't always necessary. Old battens can survive remarkably well if suitably ventilated and not subject to prolonged damp. Modern softwood battens are normally treated with preservative, whereas older ones relied on the quality of timber. However, you may decide to take the opportunity to fit a modern breathable underlay that will necessitate their removal and the fitting of new battens on top – see 'Underlays and ventilation' on page 46.

It's normally possible to strip an average sized roof and cover it with sheets of breather underlay in a day (which should be sufficient to temporarily keep out the worst

Recladding with existing tiles over new battens and membrane

of the weather). For any major work scaffolding will need to be erected over the whole house, temporarily enclosing the roof in plastic sheeting to facilitate all-weather working and protect the interior. Before the job starts it's always a good idea to take photos to record the condition of the old roof, and to help reinstate the detailing correctly.

Righting old wrongs

A change in the type of covering might sometimes be worth considering for aesthetic reasons, for example where an old roof has been inappropriately re-clad with ugly, modern, concrete interlocking tiles. These were often heavier than the original slates or tiles, in which case the roof timbers should have been beefed up to support the greater weight; but the need for strengthening was commonly overlooked, causing some old roofs to sag and bow inwards quite dramatically. Where such movement is pronounced, reinstating the original roof-line is likely to significantly add to the cost, with provision of additional new rafters etc. However, replacing clumsy artificial coverings with tiles or slates authentic to the originals can work wonders for the kerb appeal, and hence the value, of an old property.

When replacing something glaringly inappropriate on a Listed building it's sometimes easy to forget that Listed Building Consent is still required. And in Conservation Areas consent would normally be needed for a change in materials where visible from the street.

Re-cladding roofs can be dauntingly expensive, so the temptation may be to reduce costs by specifying cheaper replica roof tiles and slates. These are manufactured from artificial

Above: Damaged lath ceiling cut away to reveal wattle framework under thatch – later repaired using reed mat

Below: Surviving roof truss with sarking timber 'underlay' needs to be sensitively overhauled

Above: Plain clay tiles weather naturally and will soon blend in

Right: New concrete tiles on single storey extension clash with clay tiles on main roofs, and will lose their colour over time

materials such as concrete, fibre cement or fibreglass resin mixed with slate dust, and moulded to imitate the colour, form and texture of the original. At a glance these can appear similar to traditional materials when first laid, but after a few years they'll weather differently, often developing ugly blotching or streaks, and simply don't have the enduring beauty of natural materials. Which is why Conservation Officers have a tendency to turn distinctly pale at the mere suggestion! Another reason why such economies aren't normally advisable is because much of the cost of re-roofing is actually down to labour and scaffolding. So it's worth paying a little more to acquire traditional, natural materials that not only look good but also last a lifetime, or often far longer.

Sourcing the tiles

Old roofs should be re-clad with like-for-like materials, ideally reusing some of the existing coverings where they can be salvaged. But in most cases you'll need to source at least some new matching ones.

However, this can be something of a challenge. Although handmade clay tiles are still produced they probably won't be identical to your existing ones because of variations in the local clay that was originally used. Nonetheless, these should have the subtle imperfections of a handmade product, making them distinct from machine-made equivalents that are too precise and flat with sharp edges that can appear a little bland. Small local manufacturers can often produce 'specials' to match tiles of unusual sizes or shapes.

Even if you can source modern handmade replacements the existing tiles will have weathered darker over time. Hence the new

ones won't immediately blend in when patching an old roof and a certain amount of contrast is to be expected, at least for the first few years.

So that new tiles don't stand out too obviously, they can be randomly mixed with the existing ones or located in areas where they're not so visible from ground level. Or you could try the well-known trick of swapping weathered tiles from a rear roof slope. When first built new roofs would have stood out in fresh yellows, oranges or reds, so there's no reason you couldn't do this today if you decide to completely re-clad a roof slope, rather than experimenting with 'instant ageing' methods such as painting with yoghurt or manure, or buying tiles in 'ready-weathered' colours.

Sourcing slates or stone tiles can be a little more challenging, because the quarries where they originated will very rarely still be in operation. When re-roofing it used to be common to recycle existing slates simply by flipping them over. This made sense where the outer surfaces were eroded by city pollution and starting to 'delaminate', with paper-thin layers flaking off the surface. But this needs to be done carefully, as the undersides also sometimes show signs of delamination as a result of condensation, and may have become soft and spongy.

Ridge tiles

The crowning glory of many an old roof is found at the ridge or 'apex'. This covers the point where the two slopes meet at the top, and is commonly clad with purpose-made ridge tiles bedded in lime mortar. Sometimes a different material is used from that covering the roof slopes, such as lead rolls or clay ridge tiles for

slate roofs, or sedge for reed thatch. Old ridge tiles can normally be reused (unless they've recently been re-bedded in modern cement which grips so hard it can't easily be cleaned off). Crested Victorian terracotta ridge tiles are particularly appealing and can be repaired or replicas specially made using broken old pieces as a template.

Underlays and ventilation

Old roofs were originally built without any underlay. Installing a layer of roofing felt beneath the battens only became commonplace from the 1950s as a secondary barrier to intercept any leaks from wind-driven rain blown between gaps or the odd missing tile. However, in harsher climates and exposed locations mats of rush or straw were sometimes applied under the tiles to improve insulation, and for added protection against wind and rain. In Scotland rafters were traditionally clad with loosely-butted 'sarking boards'; slates could be fixed directly on to the timber boarding, whereas clay tiles would be fixed to battens nailed over the top.

Normally, however, where the undersides of the slates or tiles are visible when standing in the loft of an old property the chances are the roof is original. Conversely, where you find a layer of thick black 'sarking felt' the building has probably been re-clad in recent years. The main worry with this is that old roofs need a through-flow of air to help moisture evaporate and keep the timbers sound and dry. But because ventilation traditionally entered roof spaces via small gaps between tiles, the addition of thick impermeable underlays could restrict air circulation.

Ventilation may also enter roofs from vents at the eaves, or sometimes via airbricks in gable walls. But it's not unusual to find that these air paths have been blocked with insulation stuffed into the eaves.

The obvious solution is to clear blocked air paths to improve ventilation from the eaves. If additional air vents are installed, perhaps to gable walls, this must be done with sensitivity, so as not to damage the building's historic fabric. As noted earlier, removing old underfelt isn't normally cost-effective unless you're

re-cladding a roof anyway, as the whole roof needs to be stripped and re-battened.

Today's new generation of vapour-permeable breathable underlays is a major improvement over old sarking felt. Such modern 'breather membranes' prevent the ingress of rain but allow air from outside to pass through, ventilating the roof space. Rather like high-tech mountaineering clothing they simultaneously allow any internal moisture to escape, thereby reducing the risk of condensation forming on cold undersides, and are therefore worth incorporating when re-roofing old buildings.

Insulating attics

Of all the possible energy-saving home improvements there's one that stands out as being especially cost-effective. Upgrading loft insulation is relatively inexpensive and can significantly reduce heat loss and condensation problems. We'll explore in detail how best to upgrade thermal insulation in Chapter 15.

Where houses were originally built with rooms in the attic the ceilings normally follow the undersides of the rafters, with eaves cupboards to the lower sides. Although lath and plaster is thicker than modern plasterboard, the degree of thermal insulation will still be pretty minimal. However, upgrading such surfaces to current standards can be difficult without sacrificing historic plasterwork.

In properties where the old ceiling to the rafters has already been replaced with plasterboard, or where a loft has been converted some years ago, upgrading should be possible; but even then it's unlikely that the rafters would be deep enough to accommodate the necessary amount of insulation whilst maintaining sufficient ventilation. Insulation boards may be wedged between rafters provided an air space of 50mm is left between the rafters on the outer side. So, for example, 100mm-deep rafters could only accommodate another 50mm of insulation board wedged between them, which means an additional layer of insulation would need to be applied to the underside, potentially reducing headroom.

With historic ceilings at rafter level a better option is to leave the existing structure in place and line the surface of the old ceiling with sheep's wool or hemp boards fixed in place with new battens and plasterboard. This can work from a conservation perspective because if necessary it could be reversed in future with minimal damage to the building's historic fabric.

New breather membrane

Traditional tmber sarking board 'underlay'

Avoiding quick-fix botches

Some old roofs have suffered from modern quick-fix treatments that actually damaged them further. For example, polyurethane spray foam is widely advertised as a miracle cure that can rejuvenate decrepit old roofs. In effect the foam glues the undersides of tiles or slates to the battens and rafters to stop them slipping. This is a classic false economy because any moisture in the roof timbers will then be sealed in, hastening decay. The foam also has the unfortunate effect of blocking essential ventilation to lofts, and in any case is often misapplied, leaving gaps in areas where access is restricted. It's sometimes even applied to underfelt, which defeats the whole point of doing it anyway! Despite bogus claims in press advertisements, spray foam offers virtually zero insulation qualities. And, to add insult to injury, spraying old slates or tiles prevents them from being salvaged and reused.

Another well-known quick-fix botch is 'turnerising'. Here old roofs are painted with a thick layer of bituminous paint, sometimes applied

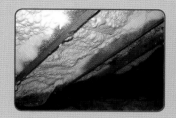

over a layer of mesh. Alternatively an unholy combination of roofing felt and tar is sometimes used. In time the coating becomes rock hard, making it impossible to recycle the slates or tiles. Because of the cost of scaffolding and labour turnerising can cost as much as half the price of a proper roof overhaul. A classic false economy that only lasts a few years.

Surveyors will immediately down-value properties subjected to such disastrous botches.

Plain concrete tiles – left.   Plain clay tiles – right

Tiles and slates

One of the first tasks for a new owner of a period property is to identify the precise type of roof covering. What you discover will depend on the property's age and local traditions, and whether it has been re-clad or altered over the years, so a spot of detective work may well be necessary. One clue to an earlier incarnation is where relatively steep roofs are clad with pantiles or slates. Because these can accommodate much lower pitches than plain tiles this may suggest that the property was once thatched.

Plain clay tiles

Early 'peg tiles' were made with small holes to accommodate wooden pegs (traditionally of oak) that hooked on to laths of oak or chestnut running across the rafters. In rural areas thick reeds were sometimes used as laths. Tile pegs were later superseded by iron nails. Traditional handmade clay tiles were made in many different shapes and sizes, although attempts had been made to standardise tile sizes by Royal decree as early as the 15th century.

In some regions it was customary for the undersides of tiled roof slopes to be 'torched' – plastered with lime or clay – to prevent driving rain penetrating between tiles, a precursor to modern roofing felt. Where this was used as a substitute for pegs it can be hard to repair, as it's easy to dislodge large numbers of tiles in the process.

By the Georgian era modern tile designs had appeared, incorporating small projecting nibs that hooked over the battens but still incorporating holes for occasional nailing, perhaps every fourth or fifth course. Sawn softwood battens were gradually introduced as a cheaper alternative to traditional laths. Slate superseded tiles for much of the 19th century, but by the late Victorian and Edwardian periods cheaper manufactured tiles had become popular, and were widely available in standard sizes. Machine-made tiles were smoother and flatter than the traditional handmade variety, which produced roofs with a subtly different character. Modern concrete substitutes became popular from the 1930s.

Handmade clay tiles exude warmth and charm

Original tiled roofs can last hundreds of years

Weatherproofing - traditional stone slate roof 'torched' underneath in lime mortar

Pantiles with distinctively wavy profile

Pantiles and Roman tiles

Traded between Britain and the Low Countries from medieval times, pantiles are still very common, and are particularly associated with East Anglian towns with ports. As their popularity spread many thatched roofs were re-clad with pantiles. Made from the same fired clay as plain tiles, pantiles were larger, with a distinctive flattened 'S' cross-section designed to interlock with the tiles on either side. This interlocking design has the advantage that less overlap is required to the course below than for plain tiles, so fewer are needed, hence the weight of the roof is less. This makes them easy to replace without disturbing the rest of the roof covering. It also means they can be laid to a much lower pitch (30° or less), which is particularly useful for shallow lean-to extensions and traditional 'Norfolk dormer' roofs.

Clay pantiles have a long lifespan, similar to plain tiles, and are hung in a similar way with projecting nibs that hook over the battens, or in more exposed locations nailed in place. They were sometimes laid over a roughly woven straw mat – an early type of 'breather membrane'.

By the mid-19th century double 'Roman tiles' had been introduced. These are similar

Above: Plain tiles shown here can't cope with very shallow pitched roofs found on some dormers

Below: Triple Roman tiles

to pantiles but are slightly larger, and typically have two or three 'rolls' rising from a flat surface. Roman tiles provide good weather resistance but are considered less visually appealing than pantiles.

Because of the severity of the winds in some coastal areas it was traditional to build the side gable walls above the level of the roof, to prevent the tiles being lifted by the wind. 'Tumbled-in' gable ends were built without copings on top of the wall.

Slates

Slate is a type of rock that splits along the grain to produce a highly durable roofing material. Vast quantities of roofing slate were once produced in many parts of Britain, the best known and probably most widely used being Welsh slate, recognisable by its subtle grey-purple hue (but appearing uniformly black when wet). Welsh slate can be split into extremely thin, smooth sheets to produce a lightweight roof covering which required less robust roof structures, with consequent cost savings. But slate was also sourced from quarries in Scotland (eg Easdale and Ballachulish), Cornwall (eg Delabole), Lincolnshire (eg Collyweston) and Cumbria (eg Westmorland), and its quality and thickness varied. The heyday of slate was in

Above and below: Slates are individually nailed to battens, rather than hung like tiles

the Victorian era, when it dominated – thanks largely to railway distribution – until cheaper manufactured tiles began to appear in the late 19th century.

Natural slates aren't perfectly flat, and have slightly rough edges. They are fixed to battens by being nailed through holes near their tops, although larger sizes are often centre-nailed to prevent wind lift. A wide variety of slate sizes were used, depending on the roof pitch. For example, larger

Slates produced in a fish-scale pattern

sizes such as 610mm x 350mm might have been laid on shallow pitches (some as low as 22.5°) or smaller 305mm x 205mm slates on steeper roofs up to 45°. Traditionally slates were laid in diminishing courses with the largest at the bottom, getting smaller towards the top, but later mass-produced slates from larger quarries were commonly laid in uniform sizes.

As mentioned earlier, it's often possible to recycle as much as 75% of the original slates from a roof and re-lay them with new fixings. You may be able to make up the difference with matching slates from local reclamation yards or 'borrowed' from outbuildings or less visible roof slopes. New natural Welsh slate can still be obtained, as can Cornish and distinctive bluish-green 'Lake District' varieties, but quality of this type costs money, so it may be tempting to use cheaper foreign imports such as Brazilian, Chinese, Canadian or Spanish varieties. However, these are generally far less durable, with a shorter lifespan, making them a poor choice for period properties. Equally, modern manufactured artificial fibre resin 'slates' are relatively cheap, but they weather differently from the real thing as well as having a considerably shorter lifespan.

Stone slates

Stone roofing slates were made from certain types of limestone and sandstone that could be split along the grain. Depending on what part of the country you hail from, these are referred to as stone tiles, tilestones, flagstones, flags, thackstones, or scantles. Large, rough and very heavy, these are probably the hardest wearing and longest lasting roof covering of all.

As with clay tiles, stone slates were fixed in place with oak pegs hooked over the battens. The pegs were inserted through a hole

made near the top of each slate, but were later superseded by iron nails. For extra stability the undersides were sometimes 'torched' with a coating of lime mortar.

Stone roofs are still laid in the traditional way with courses that diminish in size as they go up the roof. Because more rainwater flows over the lower roof surface, the bigger slates with the greatest lap are placed towards the bottom, thereby reducing the number of joints.

Due to the substantial weight of stone slates the roof timbers need to be relatively large and more closely spaced, which makes for characteristically strong roof structures. Also, the uneven texture of stone slates means that relatively large gaps are formed where they overlap; so to prevent water seeping through, roofs need to be laid to a relatively steep pitch, sometimes with the joints grouted in mortar. Because of these idiosyncrasies it's important to only employ specialist roofers with the necessary experience and expertise.

There are regional variations depending on the type of stone. For example, limestone slates tend to be relatively small, facilitating details like swept or laced valleys and small dormer roofs, such as in those in Cotswold cottages. Sandstone roofs tend to use larger slates and are therefore less detailed, but their smoother texture permits less steep pitches.

Sourcing new matching stone slates can be a challenge as the original quarries are probably long closed, but reclamation yards can be worth trawling or outbuildings can be raided to supply small numbers.

Wooden shingles

It may seem counter-intuitive to clad roofs with tiles made from wood, but shingles made from highly durable oak or sweet chestnut are a long-established, although comparatively rare, traditional roof covering. Today sawn cedar is more common, although its use tends to be restricted to outbuildings. As with slate roofs, the lower courses are usually thicker.

Flashings and valleys

Any form of watertight joint on a roof is always going to be a potential maintenance weak point, so it's no surprise that the most common areas where roof leaks occur is at junctions – typically where roofs abut walls and chimney stacks, or where they join other roof slopes at valleys. Evidence of this can commonly be seen in lofts in the form of old leakage staining down party walls and chimney breasts.

Leadwork provides robust waterproofing to stepped junction

Mortar fillets

One area where traditional building techniques didn't always excel (whisper it) was in sealing gaps at junctions between roofs and walls, using mortar fillets. Although this detail looks appropriate on thatched cottages it's not the most effective way of keeping water out, because over time cracks tend to develop as old buildings move, or as a result of thermal expansion (eg to chimneys).

On the plus side, lime mortar could accommodate a certain amount of movement; but where old mortar fillets have been replaced by brittle modern cement, premature cracking and hence ingress of damp is inevitable.

The method of choice for sealing roof joints is lead flashing, which was widely used from Georgian times onwards, especially

Left: Hairline cracks can let a lot of water in!

Below left: A traditional tiled mortar fillet

Below: Lead soaker interlaced with slates

Flashings

It's obviously important that leadwork for new or replacement flashings is of sufficient strength for the demanding job it has to undertake. Normally a thickness of either Code 4 or 5 should be specified (respectively 1.8mm and 2.24mm thick). Sometimes all that's needed is a minor repair, such as where a flashing has wriggled free from a mortar joint over time and needs to be re-fixed into the joint, secured in place with lead wedges and pointed up. But where an old metal flashing (sometimes of cheaper zinc) has split or eroded it will need to be replaced.

Builders will naturally take a practical stance on such matters, but with period properties it's important to also consider the effect on the property's appearance before making a decision.

STEPPED OR CONTINUOUS?

As well as specifying the correct thickness of lead, you also need to be clear about whether you want the new flashing fixed in a 'stepped' configuration or, alternatively, in continuous form. For example, where a roof slope abuts a brick wall a stepped lead flashing is normally the most effective solution. This is ideal for a typical Georgian or Victorian house, but would probably be inappropriate on an old cottage. But where a roof slope abuts an irregular rubble stone wall, or where brickwork is very uneven or has a roughcast render finish, a continuous lead flashing may be technically more suitable. This requires a long groove or 'chase' to be cut into the wall, into which the top of the flashing is tucked. The problem is, this effectively creates a permanent scar if applied where a stepped flashing would have been appropriate. An alternative option can sometimes be to use lead soakers concealed under a mortar fillet.

for better quality buildings, although cheaper shorter-life zinc was sometimes substituted.

Cracked mortar fillets can normally be replaced quite satisfactorily in new leadwork. But where conservation issues dictate that traditional detailing is retained, without wanting to compromise watertightness, there is another possible solution. The trick is to insert lead soakers under the tiles and then cover them with a strip of stainless steel expanded metal lath. This provides a key for a traditional lime mortar fillet, made from a reasonably strong hydraulic lime such as NHL 5. The lead soaker concealed under the mortar should keep the joint nice and watertight.

Right: Lead flashing provides superior watertight joint compared to mortar fillets

Below: New lime mortar fillet has suffered frost damage

Valleys

Valleys are found where two adjoining roof slopes meet, like a gorge running between steep hills. Traditionally, tiles would be skilfully 'swept' around or 'laced' up valleys, but slates couldn't accommodate such intricacies due to their larger size, so Georgian and Victorian slate roofs were commonly built with 'open valleys' lined with lead. Alternatively a 'secret valley' might be formed with the slates or tiles either side neatly mitred so they almost abut, with a hidden lead lining or soaker under the joint. Later, purpose-made valley tiles were manufactured to provide a simpler and more robust solution.

As always with historic roofs where repair work is required, the trick is to reinstate the original as far as possible. Today only specialist craftsmen are likely to have the right skills to execute a traditional swept or laced valley. Whilst it might be technically

Above left: Laced valley

Above: Valley tiles

Left: Open valley

OK to replace it with an open or mitred valley, the charm of the original roofscape would be compromised.

Where an open or mitred valley has leaked, the tiles or slates on either side should be stripped and any blockages cleared. If the lead has failed it's important to replace it with a matching strip of the correct thickness, typically Code 5 or 6 (*ie* minimum 2.24mm thick). Avoid using cheaper shorter-life materials such as GRP. See 'Valley gutters' on page 57.

Metal sheet

As well as being used to form watertight junctions at flashings, valleys and soakers, metal was commonly used for cladding small shallow-pitched roofs such as those to bays, porches and dormers. It was also well suited to more exotic roof designs involving curved shapes, such as domes or spires.

Flat roofs

Large flat roofs are a comparatively recent architectural feature, more likely to be encountered on modern extensions, rarely blending harmoniously with the original architecture. Problems

with leakage are common where cheaper, short-life roofing felt has been used, in which case reinstating with new lead should be considered. Alternatively asphalt can provide a longer life expectancy than felt, and is often specified for balconies or where flat roofs need to be walked on. It might instead be worth constructing a new pitched roof to blend in with the original building, where this can be done without obstructing windows or dominating the rest of the house.

Lead

Lead sheet would traditionally have been the favoured cladding material for flat or very shallow roofs because of its legendary durability. The Roman baths in the city of Bath famously employed lead linings which

Below: Lead roof with rolls

are still performing perfectly after an incredible 2,000 years. One of the qualities of lead is that it can easily be shaped by beating, hence its popularity since medieval times for a whole host of uses including gutters, downpipes, cisterns, plumbing, and glazing strips in church windows. But because of the expense its use in residential properties was limited to grander buildings, only gaining more widespread popularity from the Georgian era for use as flashings, soakers and rolls, as well as lining hidden box gutters – see page 55.

It's important to use the right thickness of lead sheet for the job, and Code 6 or 7 is usually specified for flat roofs. The higher the code, the thicker the lead and hence the larger the size of sheets that can be laid. But lead can be a deceptively complicated material to get right. As we saw earlier, it's very prone to thermal movement. Expansion and contraction can result in splits and leaks unless the detailing is done correctly. Lead sheet needs to be periodically lapped, for example, with 'steps' (drips) running across the fall, and rolls running parallel with the direction of fall. Problems due to oversized sheets or poor detailing at junctions are not uncommon.

Although good quality leadwork should comfortably last for a century, and often significantly longer, repairs are sometimes needed at potential weak points, such as upstands at joints to walls. Where lead sheet has split, welding can achieve long-lasting seams and is sometimes used to effect repairs *in situ*. However, such 'hot work' is discouraged on old buildings due to the risk of scorching the timber base – a practice that has resulted in serious fires. In some cases discreet professional gluing of lead strips or patches can be an effective and far safer alternative.

Sheet leadwork is a specialist skill and not something most roofers are familiar with, other than for flashings. Fortunately the Lead Sheet Association has made diagrams of leadwork available, which can be downloaded via the Period-house. com website. To help check the quality of workmanship, the best advice is to compare these 'right way' drawings with the details on site – and be sure to inspect the work in good time, before the scaffolding is taken down!

Where an old roof is being overhauled it's quite likely that there will be no insulation. To reduce the risk of condensation forming on the undersides and attacking the metal, new insulation should be installed.

Zinc and copper

Lead was always a relatively expensive material, and remains so today – a fact well known to illicit strippers of church roofs. To save money the Victorians occasionally substituted cheaper zinc for both flat and pitched roofs, but zinc is much lighter than lead and not nearly as durable.

On some grander buildings an even more expensive metal was the material of choice. Copper is, of course, recognisable by its trademark bluish-green verdigris patina that develops over time. Despite being lighter than slate, tile or lead, sheet copper is extremely long-lasting and can be folded readily into waterproof seams, or shaped over curved frameworks for cupolas and domes. But it needs careful detailing or water run-off can cause stains and streaks, and fixings must be of the same material (or a copper alloy) to prevent chemical deterioration.

Thatch

If you close your eyes and picture an archetypal 'dream cottage' there's a good chance it'll have roses round the door and a thatched roof. Yet to modern eyes what could be more bizarre than a roof that's knitted together from crops that are grown and harvested? The enduring appeal of thatch was traditionally down to the fact that the materials were cheap and readily available, combined with a ready supply of farm labour to build roofs. Thatch continued to be widely used in rural areas until the mid-Victorian era, when rail transport made slate and manufactured tiles available throughout the country.

A typical thatched roof has a fairly steep pitch (at least 45°) so that it can shed rainwater faster than it can soak through the stems. The thickness of the thatch keeps out the water and, thanks to a generous overhang at the eaves, rainwater is dispersed well clear of the walls without the need for gutters. Plus there's the added benefit of having a thick, insulated quilt sitting on top of your home to keep it warm and cosy.

Thatched cottages may be highly desirable, but there are two key practical concerns that buyers typically have: the likely cost of periodic re-thatching, and the potential risk of fire.

Catslide roof

A 'catslide' is a roof that sweeps down from the ridge nearly to the ground to embrace a small side room or lean-to. Catslides are usually found on the sides of houses and are particularly common on thatched roofs to timber-frame buildings. This is because the frame could be extended fairly easily at ground floor level, with extra thatch simply woven on to the bottom of the existing roof, in a sort of 'mullet' style. The pitch of these roofs at relatively low level often needs to be a little shallower to successfully accommodate the extension.

Large gaps under netting at the ridge suggest need for some re-thatching

Lower layers of thatch may date back hundreds of years

Longevity and fire risk

Thatch requires periodic work to the ridges, on average every 10 to 15 years. You would normally expect to have to replace the ridge several times during the roof's lifetime, to prolong the life of the roof as a whole. On straw thatch a matching straw ridge might be used, but for water-reed roofs ridges tend to be made from sedge, as reed is too brittle to fold.

The lifespan of the main body of the roof is harder to predict because so much depends on the specific type of thatch, the quality of workmanship and the degree of exposure to the elements. Roof slopes can last as long as 50 years or as little as 15. Straw and reed thatches are reckoned to be 'sound for a generation'. But eventually thatch loses volume. Visually this is most evident where protective wire netting was placed over the thatch when last re-laid, because over time it will slowly sink back and a gap will develop under the netting, signalling that it's time for repairs.

The longevity of thatch depends on a number of factors:

- Pitch – the shallower the roof, the more surface moisture it will retain, hastening deterioration
- Orientation – south-facing slopes age much quicker.
- Air circulation – nearby trees can restrict air, so that damp takes longer to evaporate.
- Quality of materials – rather like wine, the quality of both reed and straw varies from year to year.
- Skill of the thatchers – some firms' workmanship is better than others.

Unlike conventional roofs you don't normally strip away and replace all the old coverings. It's customary to leave the lower layers of existing thatch in place. Hence some may date back hundreds

A localised repair may be all that's necessary (here to combed wheat reed)

of years, so it's important to avoid the loss of such historic fabric by never completely stripping a roof when re-thatching.

A woven wattle frame supporting the underside of the thatch may show signs of being smoke-blackened, perhaps dating it to the 15th or 16th century when the house originally comprised one large open hall, without upper floors and with just a simple hole in the roof serving as a chimney.

Where you see a build-up of moss on the roof slopes it can sometimes look a little alarming, but moss is usually pretty harmless and can even protect the surface, as some mosses produce anti-fungal chemicals that help preserve thatch. So unless the growth is extreme to the extent that it's blocking rainwater run-off and causing a build-up of water it shouldn't be raked off, as this is likely to also remove some of the weathering thatch.

The fact that thatch is potentially flammable should be regarded simply as a risk that needs to be intelligently managed. This boils down to three key points: maintenance of chimney stacks and flues, your choice of heating appliances, and the need to take sensible precautions to prevent any harm if a problem should develop. This subject is discussed in detail in Chapter 10.

The top of the pot should be at least 1.8m above the thatch surface – a spark guard alone isn't sufficient

Assessing the condition of thatch

Thatch is a specialist area, so when buying a thatched property it's best to seek the advice of an experienced local surveyor. However, there are a number of key points that you can check visually:

- Are there any climbing plants growing over the roof? If so these will probably need to be removed.
- If there's protective wire netting over the thatch, check if it's rusted.
- Check the ridge to see if there's a gap under the netting at the apex, or if the rodwork is damaged.
- Are there any gaps or cracks to mortar joints/flashings around chimneys?
- Does the ridge appear to be a slightly lighter colour, suggesting it has recently been replaced?
- Check the highest point of chimney flues (ie the top of the pots) – they should be at least 1.8m above the thatch, and at least 2.3m horizontally from any thatched roof surface.

Left and below: Thatching in water reed

Timberline-Ireland.com

Timberline-Ireland.com

Local traditions

To the casual observer one thatched cottage may look pretty much like another, but there are rich local thatching traditions and styles, something of which Conservation Officers will be very conscious.

Although thatching skills have passed down through generations, and the tools of the trade have changed very little, there's a trend towards standardisation today. So it's important to pick a thatcher who understands the local vernacular.

Types of thatch

WATER REED

Traditionally grown in Norfolk and extensively used in East Anglia, hence the name 'Norfolk reed'. However, water reed has a long history in other parts of the country with access to reed beds, especially in Dorset. Because of its durability and strength water reed was used extensively.

New water reed thatch

Andrew Osmond Thatching

National Society of Master Thatchers

Andrew Osmond Thatching

Above: Tool of the thatching trade – a 'biddle' or 'legget'

Left: Thatching with water reed

The reeds are laid with their 'butts' down and fixed laterally by 'sways' (hazel rods) hidden beneath each subsequent layer. Only the bottom of the reed is left exposed, with the stems dressed into place to form a tight finish using a tool known as a 'legget' or 'biddle'. Modern water reed is relatively easy to lay and is imported in quantity. Although it is longer-lasting than some other types of thatch, longevity depends on a number of factors, not least the skill of the thatcher.

COMBED WHEAT REED
Sometimes known as 'Devon reed', this is mostly used in south-west England, west of Dorset. It's laid is a similar way to water reed. The raw material is actually wheat straw ('reed' being the traditional term for straw). Whereas water reed has a sharp-edge profile, combed wheat reed has a distinctive, bristly, 'ends only' look.

LONG STRAW
Once the most common as well as the cheapest method of thatching, long straw traditionally dominated in southern counties eastward from Dorset. Although the raw material is wheat straw (the same as for combed wheat reed) it uses completely different fixing techniques, being laid in shaggy layers that are then trimmed and the edges sewn into place with 'liggers' (hazel rods). The loose straw is drawn into units of thatch called 'yealms', which are fixed in courses to a base coat of thatch using hazel spars. The surface contains a mix of ears and butts. Uniquely, at the eaves and gables you'll see 'liggers' on the surface.

Tips for a successful thatching job

- Ask the contractor for a detailed description of the work in advance. Before confirming acceptance, run through it with the Conservation Officer.
- Allow for any associated repairs that may become apparent during the works, such as to roof timbers and chimneys, in terms of timescale and funding.
- A good thatch should not need an underlay.
- On the underside of some old roofs there is a thin layer of plastered woven reed that forms a ceiling, known as 'flecking'. This is easily damaged during works and needs special care.
- Any foot traffic on a thatched roof can cause damage, so make sure TV aerials etc are fixed before thatching, or site them internally.
- If you're thatching a new extension, the Building Regulations require provision of a fire barrier.
- Where a protective covering of netting is applied to straw roofs it should be close-fitting.
- Thatchers are often keen to leave their mark, with fancy ridges and decoration. However, smaller dwellings are unlikely to have been originally finished this way, so be sure to agree ridge details in advance.

New wheat straw thatch (long straw)

Andrew Osmond Thatching

Thatching in combed wheat reed

Right: Long straw thatch

National Society of Master Thatchers

Below: Wheat straw

Andrew Osmond Thatching

With long straw thatch the traditional verge detail is a 'roll barge' and, crucially, the ridge is left flush without any ornamentation. Straw roofs are normally covered by wire netting to prevent bird and vermin damage. One attraction of long straw thatch is that it can be patch-repaired because it's laid in layers – something that's more difficult to do with reed roofs.

In recent decades water reed has made inroads into traditional straw strongholds as wheat straw became harder to obtain because new short-stemmed cereal crops no longer left such an abundance of long stems. The good news is that thatching straw is now widely available once again, being grown especially in Britain or imported. One concern about using water reed in 'straw regions' is that in order to secure a fixing, all the old thatch is sometimes stripped back to the roof timbers. Straw, on the other hand, being lighter, was traditionally allowed to build up over time, often reaching a thickness of well over a metre. Conservationists are conscious that reaching down to the bottom layers of ancient thatch is like delving back through time, and these very first layers that may be blackened with medieval soot are part of the history of the house that can easily be erased.

HEATHER, GRASSES AND TURF
The current fashion for 'green roofs' on new eco-friendly buildings is essentially a modern take on traditional heather, grass and turf roofs. These were common in the mountainous northern and western parts of the UK, often in poorer areas with limited access to mainstream materials. Regional variations included seaweed and bracken, with heather more common in parts of Scotland and Ireland. In exposed coastal areas additional precautions were needed to keep thatch of all types in place. Netting or ropes over the roof would be weighed down with large stones hanging down the face of the wall, or ropes sometimes pegged to the wall tops.

Rainwater systems

In wet and windy Britain, defective rainwater systems are often the first step on the road to ruin for old buildings. It's a sad fact that maintenance is often ignored, yet overflowing gutters and damaged downpipes can cause extensive damp and rot, and sometimes even subsidence. Fortunately, despite their huge potential to wreak havoc on a building's historic fabric it's normally a relatively straightforward task to repair such defects.

A short history
Gutters and downpipes were once a luxury reserved for the rich. Whilst stately homes might proudly boast charming decorative

Right: Charming lead hopper (shame about the plastic gutters)

Below: Art in action – pristine cast iron hopper and downpipes

leadwork to hoppers and splendidly crafted guttering, complete with the occasional spouted gargoyle, nearby cottages often had to get by with little more than a generous roof overhang to throw rainwater clear of the building.

But as well as being expensive, lead was not particularly well suited for use in conventionally located eaves gutters, except as a lining to cumbersome timber box guttering or 'spouting'. Hence Georgian townhouses commonly concealed their guttering and valleys behind elegant facades, with rainwater collected behind parapets and discreetly discharged down lead pipes.

It was only the availability of mass produced cast-iron rainwater goods as an alternative to lead from the late 18th century that allowed mainstream housing to benefit from effective collection of rainwater, conducting it efficiently down to ground level for dispersal safely away from the house. Cast iron remained unchallenged until the advent of cheaper plastic in the mid-20th century.

Thatch

Thatched roofs are the exception to the rule since they don't normally have guttering. Instead they employ very wide eaves to shed water clear of the walls. Because the water drips over a wide area at the bottom of the roof slopes, it would be very difficult to retrospectively install guttering.

The clever thing about thatch is the way it naturally regulates the amount of water run-off. Much of the rainwater seeps into the

Above: Concealed parapet gutter behind balustrade

Right: Valley gutter to 'butterfly' roof hidden from view from street

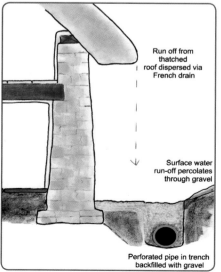

Run off from thatched roof dispersed via French drain

Surface water run-off percolates through gravel

Perforated pipe in trench backfilled with gravel

thickness of the thatch, temporarily absorbing it until it can evaporate away later. In prolonged heavy downpours, however, if there are concerns about soil becoming waterlogged where rainwater drips off overhanging eaves a good solution can be to excavate a shallow French drain in line with the run-off.

Valley gutters

Perhaps the most vulnerable type of gutters are those that are hidden from view. Concealed behind front parapet walls, 'butterfly roofs' are a feature of many Georgian and early Victorian houses. These 'M' shaped structures typically comprise two smaller lean-to roofs propped up against the party walls either side in a terrace, with a lead-lined valley gutter in between like a narrow flat roof, usually running front to rear. Unfortunately, being tucked away out of sight from street level these tend to be routinely ignored until a serious leak develops, often simply the result of blockages due to a total lack of maintenance.

More seriously the lead linings themselves also sometimes fail. As mentioned earlier, lead sheet is very prone to thermal expansion and needs to be laid in lengths that are short enough to accommodate movement without splitting. The provision of an occasional shallow step where sheets overlap (known as a 'drip') is the conventional solution. Unfortunately, this is a key detail that

Right: Downpipes serve concealed gutters behind parapet walls

Below: Double pile roof with valley

the original builders didn't always get right. So at worst the timber 'flat roof' substructure may need to be taken up and reconstructed with new steps formed approximately every 2.5m (for Code 7 lead). Needless to say, such works will considerably add to the expense.

Similar problems apply to properties with 'parapet gutters' tucked away behind the front or rear parapet walls or balustrades at the top of the main walls. In order to discharge rainwater from boxed wooden lead-lined guttering running along the front of the building (or less commonly within the roof space) it was sometimes channelled at a 90° angle to 'secret' internal gutters run within floor voids, leading to a rear hopper and downpipe arrangement or, more worryingly, diverted to an internal downpipe in the centre of the building. Inevitably such designs have led to problems with undetected blockages and leaks in floors, and consequential damp and rot.

The Georgians had a particular fondness for designing roofs with hidden gutters. The 'double-pile' design, popular in 18th century farmhouses, in effect comprised two houses built back-to-back, each with its own separate gabled roof, forming a valley with a gutter running along the middle.

In an emergency a temporary repair with modern fibreglass reinforcement may protect the property from leaks until a permanent repair or re-roofing can be undertaken, but temporary patching has a nasty tendency to be left for years. So if you come across old bitumen paint or roofing felt applied over old cracked lead, it should ring alarm bells. Factoring in the expense of scaffolding makes it more cost-effective to get the job done right first time. Although new lead sheet is expensive, some of the existing lengths will usually be perfectly sound and can be left in place, or the cost can sometimes be offset by selling redundant scrap lead.

Down to the ground

The humble downpipe plays a crucial role in conducting rainwater safely away from the property. But when things go wrong the symptoms often go unnoticed until major problems with damp or rot develop.

Over time downpipes can become blocked with debris and moss, causing overflowing. Because it can be difficult to clear

such obstructions without complete removal of the pipe, one preventative measure is to fit a leaf-guard (a wire cage) in the gutter 'hole' on top of the downpipe outlet. Although it's sometimes pointed out that guards can themselves become blocked, causing the gutter to overflow, a blocked gutter is relatively easy to clear.

At their base downpipes should ideally discharge above a gulley. A 'shoe' fitted to the bottom of the pipe helps slow and direct the flow. This 'open access' arrangement allows for easy inspection and maintenance. To avoid blockages a grille covering to the gulley is a simple way to guard against leaves and rubbish.

Surface water is normally dispersed via underground pipes to a soakaway (a rubble-filled pit) in the garden, or to a handy nearby watercourse. Alternatively it may be piped into a public drain. However, it's not normally permissible to discharge surface water via foul drains, because in storm conditions this can cause a tsunami at the sewage works, leading to unfortunate consequences – a deluge of sewage-rich storm water overflowing into rivers.

Where downpipes simply disappear straight into the ground without any sort of visible gulley, it might be worth gently excavating around them to see whether they're actually connected to an underground pipe, and if so in which direction it's heading.

Left to their own devices, gulleys can eventually become obstructed. Gulleys incorporate a simple 'U' bend trap that can become silted up or clogged with leaves, rubble, and even small creatures such as dead frogs. If no one bothers to keep things flowing, and surface water is allowed to collect near the walls, the ground will become marshy. In time this can rob the foundations of their support, leading to localised subsidence. Older underground drainage pipes commonly develop hidden leaks at joints, another potential cause of marshy ground. So if there are any suspicions of movement to the walls in the immediate vicinity it's worth excavating around shallow underground pipes to check for leaks. Another problem can arise further down the line where old soakaways become silted up, or are sited too close to buildings – they should be at least 5m from the house. The solution in both cases is to have them replaced. Thankfully this is one area where you don't need to worry about conserving original features!

Checking condition

If a wall is covered in slimy green stains or has dark, brooding damp patches it's pretty obvious that all is not well. Common danger signs are plants sprouting in gutters and around downpipes, or localised moss growing on damp walls. But sometimes tracing leaks requires a spot of detective work.

To judge whether your system as a whole is running smoothly it's worth taking a couple of minutes to stand back and see how it all fits together. Starting at the top, visually follow the route the rainwater takes, down from the main roof via assorted gutters, hoppers, pipes and subsidiary roofs until it ultimately arrives at ground level. It's not unusual for a single leaking downpipe or an overflowing water butt to bear ultimate responsibility for discharging most of the surface water from the main roof. It's important to check whether there's a sufficient number of downpipes to cope with a heavy downpour – for example, on the front elevation of a typical terrace you need at least one downpipe per three houses, or roughly one every 10m.

To spot any less obvious problems it's worth investing in an umbrella and observing the system in full flow during a storm. Check for leaks at gutter joints or from missing stop ends and monitor the flow of discharging water. Gutters should be set at a gentle fall – normally around 20mm to 25mm per 3.5m run, or a shallower 10mm fall for deeper 'ogee' or moulded profile gutters. Alternatively use of a watering can or garden hose can help pinpoint smaller leaks. But there's one thing above all that's essential to check – whether it's all securely fixed and not about to come crashing down.

Brackets and fixings

Rainwater fittings have a tough life, exposed for centuries on end to the ravages of storms, wind and driving rain, and then periodically tested to breaking point with back-shattering loadings of snow and ice. As if that wasn't taxing enough, brackets designed to support only the weight of a gutter have had to withstand ladders leant against guttering by generations of decorators, window cleaners, and aerial installers. So keeping your gutter brackets in good shape is key to pre-empting serious problems from leakage-related damp and decay, as well as preventing the nightmare scenario of heavy gutters toppling off and plunging earthwards.

Most original cast-iron guttering is the familiar 'half-round' shape supported on brackets, but 'ogee' or moulded styles with a distinctive wavy front were also popular, and were screwed directly to timber fascias. Brackets were most commonly screwed or nailed directly into protruding rafter feet, or sometimes driven directly into mortar joints in the walls. In more recent properties they are generally fixed to fascia boards.

To judge whether fixings feel soundly attached start by getting up close and taking a good look – but be careful not to tug at them so vigorously that it risks dislodging heavy lengths of cast iron. Check whether there are sufficient numbers of brackets to support the additional weight not just of rainwater but also of heavy snow loads piled up in mini drifts with thick icicles, bearing in mind that a litre of water weighs 1kg. Normally one bracket per metre run of guttering is necessary, with more closely-spaced support where there are corners or junctions, such as to bays.

Old brackets are part of the history of the house, so even where

they've become redundant it's worth leaving them in place, supplementing them with matching new ones that take care of most of the heavy lifting. Modern replacement brackets are available in traditional styles, but need to be made from galvanised or stainless steel for durability. Special 'rise and fall' brackets can be adjusted to the correct fall *in situ* using a threaded bar.

The traditional method of fixing cast iron downpipes and hoppers to walls was by means of iron spikes driven into the wall through integral cast iron 'ears', but these can be tricky to remove. One common problem is where downpipes have been positioned too close to the wall for ease of painting, so when it comes to replacement it's worth adding a spacer around the fixing bolt so that they're positioned out from the wall by at least 25mm. This should allow for future redecoration and help prevent water from soaking into the walls in the event that a pipe becomes cracked or blocked. New fixings into masonry can be made using stainless steel screws or expansion bolts.

Maintaining cast iron

To conservationists, cast iron is king. The original is still the best, largely because it looks right on old buildings. Cast iron has the potential to last a very long time indeed, but it needs to be periodically painted or it will eventually rust.

Restoring old cast iron systems tends to be a specialist job because of the need to work at height and manhandle cumbersome lengths of heavy guttering. Ideally every component should be removed and dismantled before stripping and painting, but it's not always possible to take down complete runs of heavy guttering without damaging it. That said, you might be lucky, as some types of bracket hold heavy cast iron guttering like a cupped hand rather than clipping it into place, which should allow it to be lifted free unless it's rusted in place.

Early cast iron gutters were joined with caulking and putty that, over time, can become brittle and crack (as do modern neoprene gaskets). Where old joints are still sound they can just be painted over, but where rust has set in the joints need to be dismantled, stripped and painted before being rejoined using a suitable silicone mastic.

Any rusted areas need to be exposed by stripping back to bare metal. The presence of old lead paint means that chemical strippers are a safer option than power-sanding. Any sound paint is best left and lightly sanded by hand (taking safety precautions) to provide a key. Traditionally it was common to coat the insides of gutters with bituminous paint and any remaining bitumen will need to be removed, otherwise it can trap damp. Rust can be chemically neutralised with special anti-corrosive gels or liquids. Bare metal can

be primed with two coats of zinc-based protective metal primer, which also provides chemical protection against future rust. This is followed by two further coats of MIO (micaceous iron oxide) paint, which can also be used as a protective finish to the insides of gutters. Finally visible areas can be given a top decorative coat, either before or after refixing. Because metal doesn't need to breathe this is one of few parts of an old house where modern paints can be used with a clear conscience.

The connections between lengths of downpipe are less troublesome than for gutters because they simply interlock, relying on gravity to make an effective joint – one reason why they generally last much longer than gutters. However, weak spots at risk of corrosion can be found in any areas that avoided regular painting – notably the back of downpipes and around gutter brackets. To check, feel behind downpipes for any roughness indicating rust. Hoppers should be checked inside for rust and small holes. If possible hoppers should be taken down so that their backs can be protected by repainting.

One problem is where downpipes are partially built into walls or embedded in render. Because the surfaces in contact with walls are impossible to paint, eventually they will rust. Despite this, conservationists tend to favour leaving such pipes intact until failure finally occurs, as attempted removal is likely to cause damage. Or you could leave it in place but fit a new matching downpipe nearby as a substitute for rainwater dispersal.

Replacement parts

When restoring an old cast iron system it should be possible to replace any severely rusted components with matching replica parts. Because period cast iron rainwater fittings were manufactured in reasonably standard sizes it's normally possible to source new or recycled parts without too much trouble. Where a particular historic fitting is damaged beyond repair and impossible to replace, one solution can be to have a copy made from moulded fibreglass and reinforced epoxy filler. However, for

components that carry water it's normally necessary to take them down so that a specialist bolt, braise or weld repair can be carried out. Wooden stop ends were sometimes fitted, so suitable replicas may need to be made up specially.

Alternative materials

If your house boasts original cast iron or lead rainwater fittings, the best option is to overhaul the existing system before considering replacement. But where complete replacement is essential, or you want to replace inappropriate modern fittings or to extend the

house, new cast iron systems are readily available. The main drawback with cast iron is its weight, plus the fact that it requires periodic decoration to prevent rust taking hold. It's also quite a bit dearer to buy than off-the-shelf plastic fittings from DIY stores, although if you factor in its

Downpipes embedded in walls are prone to rust

Well maintained cast iron

long lifespan (subject to maintenance) it costs about a third of the price of the plastic variety in the long run.

There are a number of possible alternatives, each with their pros and cons (see boxout). It's generally reckoned that the next best option to cast iron is cast aluminium, which looks pretty similar and is highly durable and long-lasting. Crucially aluminium is also considerably lighter, doesn't suffer from corrosion and can be customised on site. But as with cast iron, it's not the cheapest option. Bear in mind that for Listed buildings you need to apply for consent to replace rainwater fittings with anything other than like-for-like, no matter how authentic a substitute material looks.

Cast aluminium looks like original cast

New installations

Traditionally, new metal gutters and downpipes needed to be fully painted prior to installation. Fortunately new cast iron rainwater systems now come ready primed, and even fully pre-painted with ten-year protective coatings. Heritage aluminium rainwater fittings can similarly be ordered with a powder-coated finish.

When installing new gutters it's important to ensure there are sufficient numbers of brackets, as described earlier. You also need to allow a degree of flexibility to accommodate thermal movement, particularly with aluminium or PVC guttering, otherwise it can cause twisting and fractures at joints.

Gutters must be set to a sufficient fall, and if you're fixing gutter brackets to old timber fascia boards check they haven't rotted, otherwise the whole lot could collapse. But avoid fitting ugly new fascias to an old building where none existed previously, as they'll look sorely out of place.

Materials

Lead
Pros
Long-lasting.
Maintenance-free and does not require painting.
Often features historic decorative detailing on downpipes and hopper heads.
Cons
Expensive.
Can split and sag.
Repairs are a specialist job.
Because downpipes are fixed tight to walls to prevent movement, any leaks will soak into walls.

Cast iron
Pros
Traditional material that looks right.
Long-lasting and strong.
Resistant to damage from ladders or snow loadings.
Fairly consistent interchangeable sizes and bolted into place, so parts easily replaced.
New components come ready-painted.
Cons
Expensive.
Fairly brittle, and if hit hard can crack, or bits can snap off.
Prone to rust and needs periodic painting.
Heavy, and needs sound fixing.

Copper
Pros
Does not require painting, as it develops a pleasant natural green patina.
Suitable for modern extensions to old buildings.
Long-lasting and strong.
Light weight makes installation easier.
Cons
Expensive.
Non-traditional.

Cast aluminium
Pros
Looks very similar to original cast iron, so good substitute.
Long-lasting and strong.
Resistant to damage.
Light weight makes installation easier.
Does not corrode, so is easy to maintain – no need for frequent decoration, or can be left in its natural state.
New components come ready powder-coated.
Cons
Expensive.
Not traditional and lacks surface texture of cast iron (but with thick coat of paint can mimic it).
Cheaper extruded aluminium formed in seamless lengths is relatively thin.

Plastic
Pros
Cheap.
Light weight makes installation easier.
Useful as a temporary solution.
Cons
Non-traditional.
Looks cheap and is rarely acceptable on old buildings.
Prone to warping and creaking.
Becomes brittle over time due to the effects of UV light.

Period Property Manual

5 WALLS

Beats going to Wickes: freshly dug earth for use in mud construction

One of the joys of owning a period property is the charm of old walls built from natural materials that have mellowed harmoniously over many years. Old houses were constructed from a wide variety of different materials, depending on local tradition and the age and status of the building, but one thing all old walls have in common is that they tend to improve with age, developing an attractive patina and texture over time.

Unlike their modern equivalents, built to an identical specification from one end of the country to the other, the use of locally sourced, natural materials conferred a distinctive character on different towns and regions. Of course, this came about for purely practical reasons. It was generally cheaper, easier and more sustainable to use readily available materials. So in heavily wooded areas it made sense to build in timber frame; other regions had a ready supply of stone that could be hewn from quarries or simply collected from the fields, and in places where subsoils were clay-rich it made sense to dig it out and build from unfired clay or to bake it into bricks. Similarly, early mortars were nothing more than clay-rich earth dug from the ground, used to pack the spaces between rubble-stones in walls.

Brick

Bricks were traditionally made from clay dug out of the ground close to the building site and baked in temporary kilns erected on site. Today many adjacent ponds or pits are still visible where clay was originally excavated.

Part of the beauty of traditional bricks was their subtle lack of uniformity. Old bricks were hand-made, thinner than their modern counterparts, and of uneven size and finish. Because it was impossible to make perfectly identical ones, bricks displayed a lovely range of hues, from pinkish red to deepest plum.

Manufactured bricks only became widely available from the later Victorian period, with most towns having their own brickworks. There were remarkable variations in colours between different towns and regions, from reds, yellows and silvers through to purples, blacks and chalky white 'Gaults'. This was a result of differences in minerals and impurities in the local clay (such as chalk, sand, flint or iron), as well as added ingredients such as salt and ashes. The predominance of iron in most soil types accounts for the disproportionate weighting towards red.

Brick wars

For nearly a thousand years after the collapse of the Roman Empire, wood was the predominant house-building material across much of Britain. Only the most important structures – cathedrals, palaces, castles, churches – were afforded the luxury of fine quarried stone. The reason stone was so rarely used for houses until as late as the 18th century was because it was hugely expensive to extract, cut and transport on account of its enormous weight.

Bricks have been around in Britain from Roman times. However, the Romans lacked the technology to fire them to a consistent hardness, so they made thinner bricks that were more like tiles. Bricks had enjoyed a resurgence as a home-produced building material by the time of the Tudors, and their popularity was boosted following the catastrophic Great Fire of London, when draconian new restrictions signalled the death knell for traditional timber-frame and thatch construction in urban areas. Subsequent Building Acts introduced standardisation of bricks and further restricted the use of timber on house fronts.

Bricks had the great advantage that they could be made on site from clay dug from the ground. The main drawback was that if any of the manufacturing stages was flawed – if the clay mix was wrong, or the moisture content high, or the heat of the kiln not exactly right – it would result in less than perfect bricks. And imperfect bricks were common.

By the 1770s brick had become the primary material for house building, except in a few traditional stone regions and for some smaller cottages. But increased demand and the imposition of the 1784 Brick Tax resulted in hefty price rises and hence a switch to alternatives such as tile hanging or weatherboarding.

The appeal of brick for homebuilding waned further as fashions changed in favour of stone. Red brick became especially distasteful. Many houses of brick or timber were re-clad behind fashionable stone facades, or given a permanent 'facial' of simulated stone by the application of a creamy layer of stucco.

Brick might have been permanently marginalised as a domestic building material but for one unexpected consideration – pollution. Coal burning was carried out in prodigious volume  by the early Victorian period and coal smoke was particularly hard on stone buildings. Structures that looked radiant when new could rapidly deteriorate to a shabby, stained shadow of their former selves. Whereas some sandstones adopted a dramatically blackened tone, Portland stone assumed a brilliant whiteness on faces exposed to the wind and rain whilst sheltered corners became filthy black.

Pollution was the making of modern brick, though several other factors helped. Canals and later railways made it possible to ship bricks greater distances, and the removal of the Brick Tax in 1850 reduced prices further still. But it was the invention of the Hoffmann kiln in the mid-Victorian period that allowed bricks to be produced continuously along a primitive production line, to a relatively uniform size, colour and appearance. Since then brick has remained largely unchallenged as the material of choice for mass house construction.

Brick bonding

By far the most common pattern of brick bonding in standard 230mm thick solid walls was Flemish bond, where bricks laid lengthways ('stretchers') were alternately punctuated with bricks laid crossways, showing their heads ('headers'). Modern cavity walls, in contrast, are built in 'stretcher bond' with all the bricks laid end to end.

Other variations were also used, such as English bond (courses of stretchers interspersed with courses of headers above or below).

Above: Header bond – with all the bricks laid crossways. Here the style replicates dearer.

Above right: English bond – alternating courses of headers and stretchers.

Right: Flemish bond

Bricks and mortar

Old bricks were fired at much lower kiln temperatures compared to those used in modern brick making and as a result they're relatively soft and porous. This wasn't a problem traditionally because the lime mortar used to build walls at that time tended to be slightly weaker than the masonry around it. This allowed the mortar joints to act as an escape channel, so that any rain absorbed by the porous brickwork in wet weather could easily evaporate out later. However, after a century or more of acting as a conduit for escaping moisture, old mortar joints tend to gradually wear away and eventually require re-pointing. Hence mortar pointing is sometimes described as performing a 'sacrificial' role. (Compare this to today's houses with a projected lifespan of a mere 60 years, where the whole building is in effect 'sacrificial'!) Moisture always takes the easiest route out of a wall, so if the mortar is too strong it will be forced to escape via the brick or stonework instead, which then adopts the sacrificial role. As we saw in Chapter 2, as moisture evaporates from the pores of the masonry it is vulnerable to expansion from frost, and from the crystallisation of salts (dissolved in the moisture), which can blow off the face of the brick or stone.

Eroded original mortar needs a little 'topping up' after more than a century's service

Lime mortar can accommodate movement in old buildings

This is a common problem, because so many old walls have been damaged by being re-pointed with the wrong stuff. Compared to lime mortar, hard modern cement is simply too tough and too waterproof, and blocks moisture from escaping via mortar joints.

But lime mortar is also kind to masonry in another way. Over the years many old walls have gradually twisted and distorted as old buildings shuffled about on their shallow foundations. Yet the bricks haven't cracked or snapped, thanks to the amazing flexibility of lime mortar, which can accommodate and even heal small cracks.

Jerry building

Periodic shortages of experienced bricklayers throughout the 18th century led to a general lowering of standards, and financial pressures meant malpractice was not unusual. One well-known shortcut involved hastily constructing the carcass of an entire terrace using cheap single thickness brickwork, often comprising poor quality underburned bricks. The facing elevations were later clad in brick or ashlar stonework by skilled bricklayers or masons to give the appearance of quality construction. Externally

this might give the impression of a traditionally strongly bonded wall with intermittent bricks (headers) running across both rows, tying them together, but this could be an illusion where 'snapped headers' (bricks split in half) were used. Sometimes the inner carcass would incorporate projecting 'bonding timbers' inserted at various heights in the walls in order to tie-in the outer face, but being susceptible to rot this eventually resulted in bulging walls on many house fronts. Another example of 'jerry building' was the occasional use of wooden beams in the footings, resulting in subsequent settlement of some load-bearing walls. But serious cracks were often avoided thanks to lime mortar allowing bricks to adjust rather than crack.

To save money, unscrupulous builders devised ingenious ways to economise on the numbers of bricks, and you can sometimes spot clues to such deficiencies. If what appears to be a standard 230mm (9in) thick wall has unusually tall bricks, it may actually be built in 'rat trap' bond – a money-saving method used in some cheaper houses. Here although the bricks are laid in a Flemish bond pattern, they're actually placed on their sides, forming very thin leaves with

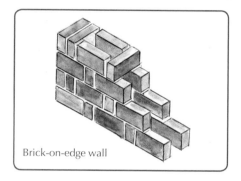
Brick-on-edge wall

a series of small flue-like cavities within the wall (in an 'H' pattern when viewed from the above). Worse, some walls were only built of single-thickness brickwork, half the width of a normal 9in solid wall, and potentially unstable over more than one storey. This is not uncommon on rear additions and cheaper back-to-back housing. There should be a clue apparent in the bonding, since all the bricks are laid lengthways in stretcher bond like a modern cavity wall (but only comprising a single leaf). However, cunning builders commonly rendered such walls externally to disguise such shortcomings.

Even the wealthiest clients could be hoodwinked by fashionable rendered walls concealing a multitude of sins. External stucco plasterwork was widely used to simulate expensive stone dressings on elegant creamy white Georgian and Victorian 'wedding cake' houses built in expensive areas such as London's Regent's Park. But hidden behind the smooth stucco surface there could be poorly constructed walls of soft, under-fired bricks.

Cavity walls

Although it had long been known that walls built as two relatively thin leaves with a space left in the middle were more effective against penetrating damp than walls of traditional solid masonry, this modern method of construction didn't become mainstream until the 1930s. However, a few Victorian and Edwardian homes pioneered cavity construction – often those sited in exposed locations – and are identifiable by their telltale stretcher bond brickwork (ie with all the bricks laid lengthways).

The two leaves of a cavity wall are held together with wall ties at periodic intervals. Some early walls were simply tied with an occasional brick laid across very thin 'finger cavities', but most used metal ties fabricated from wrought or cast iron (in some

areas recycled iron hoops from cotton mills were used). These have generally performed satisfactorily. However, wall tie failure is not unknown, particularly in coastal areas due to the corrosive effects of salty air. Failure is due to rust causing the ties to expand, resulting in horizontal cracking at regular points in mortar joints corresponding to the position of the ties. Such defects are usually most prominent at more exposed higher levels. Specialist wall tie repairs can be carried out, but it's important that lime mortar is used when reinstating mortar joints.

Ivy and climbers

Climbing shrubs adorning old walls can look quaint and picturesque, but any uncontrolled plant left growing up the side of a wall can potentially cause problems. Excessive foliage hinders the

drying out of damp walls, particularly on northern elevations, and left unkempt can block gutters. Ivy is by far the worst offender, taking root in any handy crevice such as a soft mortar joint and working its way into the wall. As it grows it slowly expands, eventually blowing apart the masonry and even destabilising the structure. However, ripping live ivy off a wall once it's gained a firm foothold can cause damage. The best approach is to cut it off at its roots and snip through stems so that it gradually withers away, losing its grip.

Repairing brickwork

The telltale sign of frost damage is 'spalling', where the face of the brick has been blown off so it looks like it's been in a war

zone. The exposed, soft insides then become very vulnerable to penetrating damp. However, if the damage is fairly localised it's normally possible to repair individual brick faces *in situ*. The test of a skilled brick repair should be how discreet and unnoticeable it is. There are three ways this can be done:

■ Individual decayed or cracked bricks can be cut out and turned round to expose the undamaged face. Because lime mortar is relatively soft, it's sometimes possible to rake it out using a hacksaw blade. The problem with hammering with a bolster and mallet is that it can weaken old bricks – no matter how carefully you chip around a brick, it can be disheartening to find when it's nearly out that it suddenly shatters in your hand. Although the use of power tools tends to be frowned upon by conservationists, a series of carefully drilled small holes can help loosen the mortar around the brick, followed by a handsaw to cut around it. Alternatively the 'Allsaw' is a power tool designed to individually extract old handmade bricks, and claims to be able to discreetly cut into joints as thin as 3mm. It goes deeper than a grinder, and causes less vibration to delicate structures.

Once safely extracted, if the reverse face of the brick looks OK it can simply be turned round, dusted off and fixed back in place. This is a very green and sustainable method, getting extra mileage out of the existing materials.

■ Where an old brick has become eroded to the extent that it's beyond reuse, the next best option is to replace it with a good matching one (old bricks are in imperial sizes). But replacements need to match not just in terms of colour and size, but also

in porosity and texture. Modern bricks are harder and more uniform in appearance than older bricks that were made from less compacted clay dug from layers closer to the surface, and fired in small batches. But be cautious with second-hand bricks – as some may be under-fired and unsuitable for external work. If you need to replace a fair number it's worth ordering a batch made specially from a local brickworks. But whatever the source, replacements are best left to blend in naturally over time rather than trying to tone them down artificially. Once the new bricks are carefully bedded in with matching lime mortar they should be indistinguishable from the old wall once they're fully weathered.

■ Cosmetic surgery is an alternative way of repairing eroded bricks by building up the damaged face using tinted lime mortar. Whilst this won't last as long as a replacement – perhaps 10 to 15 years – it can be almost invisible to the eye if skilfully done. Blending coloured pigments with lime mortar can, with care, provide an excellent match.

The first step in the process is to brush away any loose surface material. Then mix a small amount of lime mortar to a stiff consistency with a matching tint. Just before it goes off the mix is applied to the surface of the eroded brick. Finally, the carefully made-up face is finished with a special wooden tool (which gives a better finish than a metal trowel). Once set the mortar joints can be re-pointed around the brick.

However, there's a potential risk with this method that the repair may weather differently to the surrounding brick and change colour over time. An alternative is to build up decayed faces using thin brick slips, but this isn't recommended as such repaired bricks suffer from inherent structural weakness that can sometimes cause them to crack or drop off.

For cleaning old brickwork, see Chapter 12.

Pointing

The pointing is the visible edge of the mortar joints between the masonry. The walls of Georgian, Victorian and Edwardian houses are commonly finished with discreet flush or very slightly recessed joints. Thin joints were equated with top-quality construction and some extraordinarily fine workmanship can often be seen, far thinner than today's typical 10mm wide joints. The key thing about original pointing is that the mortar doesn't dominate the wall. Even on cheaply built homes the pointing wouldn't stand out.

With care, an oscillating tool can be used to cut through and loosen mortar joints allowing individual bricks to be safely removed

Above: Discreet traditional pointing (left) contrasts with inappropriate new projecting 'weatherstruck' cement pointing (right)

Below: Original super-fine joints (left) need specialist repointing – not a botched DIY job (right)

RUBBED AND GAUGED BRICKWORK

Precision-engineered joints became fashionable in the Georgian era. Some parts of the wall would have super-fine joints, notably to the arches above window and doors openings. Known as 'rubbed and gauged', this was achieved by rubbing relatively soft 'red rubber' bricks to create a perfectly smooth surface, allowing extremely fine joints, with each brick forming a close contact with its neighbour. Arches were formed by each brick being rubbed into a slightly tapered shape, known as a 'voussoir'. So thin were these that the term 'penny joints' was coined, being about the width of a chunky old penny. The repair of such fine craftsmanship is inevitably a specialist job, not something the average brickie should attempt. The original joint thicknesses should be respected, as clumsy larger modern joints can ruin the appearance of historic properties.

TUCK POINTING

As fine quality rubbed and gauged brickwork became popular, a cheaper alternative method was developed that could give the appearance of fine quality work applied to an entire elevation. Known

Fine tuck pointing applied to front elevation only (not to side and rear walls). Ten Downing Street has distinctive black tuck pointed brickwork

as 'tuck pointing', this employed an ingenious deception. The brickwork would first be pointed perfectly flush using specially coloured mortar that matched the face of the bricks, making the mortar joints virtually invisible. Then a fine line just 2mm or 3mm wide was cut along the hidden joint and filled with a mix of extremely white lime putty and marble dust or silver sand to give the appearance of a superfine joint. Whether by design or error tuck pointing sometimes ignored the real underlying mortar joints altogether, with the fine line cut into the brickwork instead.

Re-pointing

There are few subjects that cause as much gnashing of teeth amongst conservationists as re-pointing. It would seem that people either do nothing for years on end, completely ignoring severely eroded mortar joints, or they go completely bonkers and cover the whole house in virtuoso re-pointing that stands out like virulent spaghetti.

Given the choice, a little benign neglect is probably the safer option because lime mortar joints are often condemned prematurely. The fact is, old masonry only needs re-pointing where the joints are so badly eroded that rainwater can settle in the grooves. Being a little soft or 'powdery' compared to hard modern cement pointing doesn't mean it's failed, it's just doing its job as the sacrificial element. A fingernail can make an impression on lime mortar in sound old brickwork, but over the years many perfectly healthy old walls with apparently soft lime mortar have been damaged by needless re-pointing with much harder modern cement.

Eventually, however, there comes a time when a certain amount of re-pointing is necessary. Often only small patches of walls require re-pointing, because exposure to the elements varies even within the same wall. South-facing walls at higher levels or in exposed locations will typically receive more of a battering from wind and rain. It's therefore highly unlikely that all the mortar will fail at the same time. So this is a job that's best done piecemeal in small areas where needed, rather than blitzing entire elevations at a time. Watch out for unscrupulous builders who tell you otherwise.

Sadly, the character of many old walls has been drastically damaged as a consequence of bad re-pointing. There's a definite art to getting it right. The aim should be to match the original with new lime mortar. The new pointing should blend in as

Nicely repointed in lime to match the original

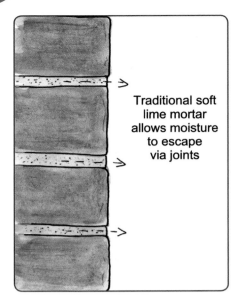

Traditional soft lime mortar allows moisture to escape via joints

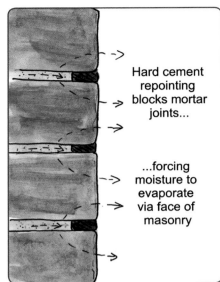

Hard cement repointing blocks mortar joints...

...forcing moisture to evaporate via face of masonry

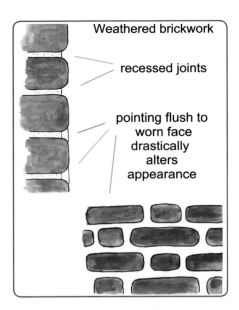

Weathered brickwork

recessed joints

pointing flush to worn face drastically alters appearance

Weathered brickwork with rounded 'shoulders'

New pointing should weather-in over time – but must be kept moist to prevent extreme whiteness

unnoticeably as possible and shouldn't be at all obvious. As well as selecting the right mix of sand and lime, it's important that the style of pointing should replicate the original. The two most common traditional styles were 'flush' and 'bucket handle'. Flush, as the name suggests, is level with the face of the brick or stonework, whereas bucket handle is curved slightly inward (like a handle has been run along the joint). Avoid modern styles that stand proud, such as angled 'weatherstruck', because it simply looks wrong on old houses.

The success with which the new work weathers-in will particularly depend on the width of visible joints. Ham-fisted, uneven, badly done joints can make the bricks appear much smaller, drastically altering the look of a house. However, one thing that can sometimes make re-pointing old masonry walls a bit more challenging is where the exposed edges of the bricks have eroded away over time where they abut mortar joints. Such brickwork will have a 'rounded shoulder' appearance that isn't immediately obvious because the old mortar has receded; but as soon as new pointing is applied flush with the face of the wall it will fill these eroded areas, resulting in absurdly wide joints that make the bricks appear tiny. So rather than traditional flush pointing in such cases, you may need to set the face of the joint slightly back in order to keep it looking reasonably thin. The golden rule is to only appoint trades experienced with old buildings. It's only too easy to end up paying good money to get re-pointing that screams 'I'm new – look at me!' for years on end.

Mortar mix and colour

Re-pointing using lime is an exacting skill, as any mortar that gets on to the face of the bricks or stone by mistake will usually leave a whitish mark. Lime also has more limitations in use than modern cement. As well as being highly caustic, it is weather-sensitive and mustn't be used in winter. Understanding how to work with lime

is at the heart of maintaining old buildings, so this is a subject that will be explored in some detail later in the next chapter.

Mixing mortar of the right colour is key to a good job, and this is largely determined by the choice of sand. A basic repair mix would be one part lime putty to three parts sand. Achieving the right consistency may require a mix of both sharp sand and soft sand of a suitable colour. There are also some time-honoured tricks of the trade. To help new mortar blend in builders would sometimes add a little soot or strong tea to the mix. In skilled hands it's also possible to add colour using small amounts of natural earth pigment (but remember that too much additive can affect performance).

However, don't get too hung up on instant ageing techniques, because as long as the basic mix is right lime mortar will naturally darken over time. Any wall that's freshly re-pointed in new lime mortar is likely to stand out slightly for the first year or so while it weathers in to match, no matter how sensitively done. In fact it should ultimately match better by itself than if treated with colourants, as these sometimes weather unpredictably over time.

It's also best to avoid the temptation to use white cement. This is a product that builders sometimes throw into cement mixes to fake a lime appearance, as a substitute for lime. The problem is it looks *too* white, and although not as strong as ordinary Portland cement it still has cement's negative qualities.

Preparation

Preparation of the wall is key to any successful re-pointing job. That means carefully raking out loose, soft mortar to form a square edge for the new lime mortar to sit on. Joints should be raked out to at least twice the height of the joint, using a screwdriver or other hand tools. The joints are then dusted before being wetted prior to receiving the mortar, to allow for the 'suction' of the bricks.

Cement pointing

In the 1990s conservationists began to realise how much damage cement was doing to old buildings, even when it was only added to a mix in small quantities. It was belatedly realised that hard cement pointing had the effect of trapping moisture in walls, causing old soft brick or stone to become saturated and prone to shattering at the first frost. But by then many old houses had already suffered from inappropriate re-pointing and traditional lime skills were largely forgotten. Fortunately in the intervening years a lot of good work has been done to help revive and encourage such heritage skills.

There are some key differences between cement and lime pointing that can help you tell them apart. Cement mortar very often has a drab grey (or dark greenish grey) colour, whereas lime tends to be sandy or off-white. However, in both cases the colour will depend to a large extent on the choice of sand and strength of the mix. The real test is hardness. Try pushing the tip of a blade or screwdriver against a mortar joint – it usually sinks into lime mortar but not into cement. Or take a small lump of mortar out of the wall and try to crumble it between your fingers – lime will break up fairly easily but cement is far harder and remains in a rigid lump.

Urghh! - cement damage is obvious

1 and 2 Cement mortar pointing. 3, 4 and 5 Loosening cement with hammer and chisel. 6 Risk of damage to masonry

RE-POINTING BRICKWORK

Materials

Tub or bucket of lime mortar, hessian sheeting

Tools

Raking out tool and hammer, fine water spray, pointing tool (or cutlery knife), small mortar hawk, stiff bristle brush

1 Rake out at least 10mm or as required to get back to sound mortar.

2 Clear away the dust with a dry paintbrush or bristle brush working from the top down.

3 Wet the joint thoroughly before the work begins. If you apply new mortar to a dry joint it will not carbonate properly and will crumble and fall out.

4 Place some mortar onto the hawk. Mortar should be of a smooth yet fairly stiff consistency.

5 Before starting practise lifting a sliver of mortar off your hawk.

6 Working from the top down, apply the mortar to a clean, damp joint. Mortar should be pressed in and left slightly proud of the brick face without spilling over. Avoid fiddling with it too much at this stage.

7 Wait for the mortar to go 'green hard' – between a few hours and a couple of days, depending on the volume of mortar and the temperature. Prod it gently with a finger to see if it makes an impression – if not, the joint is ready to be finished. Any excess mortar can be scraped off.

8 To finish off, once the mortar has begun to set, hit the joint with a bristle brush. This helps compact it slightly, forcing the mortar to the back of the joint, and closing any hairline shrinkage cracks. Finally, give the joint a fine mist spray and cover it with hessian. This slows the drying process and encourages optimum carbonation – particularly important on warm or windy days.

HOW TO UNDO OLD DAMAGE

Cement by its nature is incredibly grippy stuff that, once set, clings like a limpet. So where an old wall has previously been re-pointed in harmful modern cement it can sometimes prove difficult to remove it without bits of the adjoining brickwork also coming away, damaging the

Moisture trying to evaporate from the wall is blocked by masonry paint - until frost blows face off damp brick

historic fabric. Thankfully slack workmanship often comes to the rescue. Where the cement mortar was poorly applied, or has simply been smeared over the surface of the joint, it won't be adhering so firmly. Or if you're lucky, much of the hard cement pointing will have already come loose, cracked or dropped off, and it may be possible to pick off small strips from the underlying lime. In contrast, soft lime mortar can't be picked out intact in pieces.

Problems tend to arise where the cement re-pointers did a really thorough job and first raked each joint out by 25mm or more. In such cases it may only be possible to remove the pointing by causing damage to the surrounding soft masonry, which could actually be worse than leaving it in place. The only way to know

is to have a go on a hidden area and judge whether it can be removed without causing collateral damage.

In some circumstances a little careful preliminary drilling using a thin bit may help to loosen hard cement, but as mentioned earlier, avoid the temptation to use angle grinders. These have a habit of skidding and permanently disfiguring bricks. Where previous re-pointers have made this mistake it may be possible to conceal existing scars with skilled cosmetic surgery using a mix of brick dust and lime.

Checking new lime pointing

Until you've mastered the art and done the job a few times you need to keep a close eye on new pointing. Don't worry if it's not right first time – the trick is to assess the cause of any defects and adjust your technique accordingly. There are three key problems to watch out for:

Problem	Possible causes
It's gone all crumbly	Wall not sufficiently wetted or properly prepared. New pointing wasn't kept moist. Frost damage – *eg* when done too late in the year.
There are shrinkage cracks	Mortar applied too wet. Mortar not 'pressed back' during curing process. Wrong sand – soft building sand used instead of sharp sand.
It's extremely white	Mortar not fully finished curing. New pointing wasn't kept moist.

Stone

Stone was traditionally one of the most widely used building materials across much of Britain, with enormous variations in durability, texture and colour. Even stonework of the same material can have differences in quality that only become apparent over time, as some varieties weather better than others. So before undertaking repair work, it helps to know what you're dealing with, and to understand its strengths and weaknesses.

Ordinary houses were often built using rough 'unquarried' rocks and stones found lying around in fields, or from rubble left over from local quarries. But it wasn't unknown for raw materials in the form of quarried stone to be 'liberated' from derelict monasteries and ruined houses and usefully recycled. At the other end of the scale smooth, labour-intensive dressed stone was generally reserved for use in more expensive homes and mansions.

Rough stone walls were commonly built to a thickness of 2ft (0.6m) or more. But thick stone walls are not always as solid as they look. Internal cavities were often left between the inner and outer leaves and filled with rubble. Stonework was commonly bedded in earth or lime mortar, although in some parts of the country rubble stone was traditionally left dry on the outer face.

Above: Damage limitation: removing paint from joints allows wall to breathe

Left: Cement render can be hard to remove

The three principal forms of stone construction, from dearest to cheapest are:

ASHLAR

Fine-grained prepared stone such as Bath and Portland stone. Precisely cut, squared blocks laid in parallel courses and finished to a smooth dressed surface. Defined by joints often just a couple of millimetres thick.

COURSED RUBBLE

Roughly dressed quarried stone laid in courses of similar thicknesses.

RANDOM RUBBLE

Stone taken directly from the ground and laid in random arrangements. Often rendered.

Much cheap random rubble stonework was never intended to be seen, being concealed from view and protected from the elements by a decorative render or at the very least a coating of limewash.

Where walls were left exposed, mortar often contained small 'pinning stones' or 'gallets' pushed into the surface of the joints. As well as having a pleasing decorative effect, these reduced the amount of mortar required to fill the joints, and hence minimised shrinkage. They were also a useful way to balance larger uneven stones, thereby adding structural strength to a wall. In some parts of the country small stones embedded in mortar joints were believed to function as lucky charms, warding off evil. Either way, the best advice is to leave them in place!

Types of stone

There are several well-known types of stone used for building, hailing from different regions where they were quarried.

SANDSTONE

Sandstone is composed largely of silica or quartz, being similar in its make-up to loose sand. But the stone's strength and colour are determined by the extent of local impurities, such as clays, iron and chalks. Once quarried extensively in many parts of Scotland, sandstone quarrying was also a major industry in central and southern Wales and much of northern, western and south-eastern England, including central Devon and the North and South Downs. Colours range from yellow or grey through to browns and reds. Glasgow is built of an especially distinctive reddish stone. 'York stone' is a popular name for Yorkshire sandstone.

LIMESTONE

Although limestone is closely related to chalk (both being formed from calcium carbonate) it is a much stronger building material, because of the presence of impurities. Colours range from white through to honey yellows and browns. Widely used varieties include whitish-grey Portland stone and warm, mellow Bath or

Cotswold stone. One variant commonly used in rubble form in southern England was known as 'pudding stone'. Some types of hard limestone can look very similar to marble when polished, the best known being Purbeck marble (true marble hardly occurs in the UK). In England the 'limestone belt' sweeps across the country in a broad arc from Dorset on the south coast to the Cleveland Hills of Yorkshire in the north.

CHALK AND FLINT
Chalk is a softer, purer version of limestone, largely constituted from the crushed remains of tiny, shelled sea creatures. Where it was of sufficient strength it was sometimes used as a relatively soft and porous building material. For example, 'clunch' is chalk cut into building blocks, although it can alternatively comprise a softer chalk mixed with clay. Quarried principally in southern and eastern England, chalk was chiefly used as the raw material for lime

mortars and renders.

Flint is the tough, impervious cousin of chalk, often found in seams running through chalk quarries. Composed of very hard silica it is totally different from the chalk that

bears it, yet these two contrasting building materials are often found together in the same walls. Flint was also used to provide a decorative banding in stone or brick walls. (See also page 76.)

GRANITE
Granite was widely used as a building material. Predominantly composed of silica and minerals originally derived from molten magma, granite has long been prized for its strength and extreme durability, as well as its attractive appearance. Its hard-wearing qualities made it ideal for buildings in very exposed locations (famously being used to clad Tower Bridge), as well as for kerbs and paving. Aberdeen is well known as the 'Granite City', but it was also quarried in the Highlands and south-west Scotland, as well as in Leicestershire and Cumbria. Houses built of both quarried and unhewn granite (ie stones collected from the land) are characteristic of Devon and Cornwall.

ARTIFICIAL STONE
Manufactured building components became immensely popular from the 1760s to the Victorian period. Artificial 'Coade stone' was moulded into decorative forms that would have normally been carved from real stone, such as lintels and columns sporting elaborate flower patterns and classical figureheads, as well as ornate friezes, statues and prancing lions etc. It is actually a type of stoneware made from baked clay that looks and feels exactly like worked stone. Over the years Coade stone proved incredibly resilient to the assault of corrosive acids that have seriously eroded natural stone, surviving remarkably intact. Perhaps the best-known example is the large lion on the south side of London's Westminster Bridge.

mikewye.co.uk

Repair or replace?

Despite its hard image, a lot of stone used for building is actually relatively soft. The hardest rocks – granite, slate and some sandstones – are the most resistant to erosion but, inevitably, at the time of construction factors such as cost and local availability often trumped long-term durability. Also, using a less hard stone obviously made life a lot easier when it came to carving or cutting it into blocks.

Different types of stone weather in different ways. Some softer stones such as chalk, some varieties of limestone and many sandstones can erode relatively quickly. Problems tend to occur where walls are particularly exposed to the weather, or where there's persistent dampness due to faulty sills and gutters etc. Once stonework becomes waterlogged over the course of many years freezing will cause expansion, and the natural layers that make up the stone will start to fracture. Where stone is exposed to pollution or extreme weather the surfaces can eventually turn powdery as the natural glues that bind all the granules together start to fail. But it's important not to overreact to signs of mild erosion. Naturally weathered stone needn't be a problem, and is simply a subtle sign of age that adds character.

Repair

There are several options where you have a small number of individual stones that have eroded. In order of severity these are:

■ Do nothing

The first question should be 'is repair really necessary?' Worn stone is often part of the charm of historic buildings. Even where some of the face has been lost, it's sometimes better to leave well alone unless it can no longer perform its function. However where

Above: Is repair really necessary? Here some minor repointing may be all that's required

Right: Original fine pointing

Right: Messy repointing is worse that doing nothing

possible the cause of the problem should be repaired. For example, it's important that window sills throw rainwater clear of the wall below, which depends on the thin drip groove running along the sill's underside; so where this has worn away it must be remedied or damp will soak into the wall.

Check for 'water traps'
Ledges, sills and decorative string courses were originally built with a slight outward fall so that they could 'throw off' water away from the house. But over time slight settlement or erosion can cause subtle but potentially damaging changes, allowing water to pond and penetrate through the walls. A discreet layer of lime mortar can provide the necessary slope away from the building.

Enhanced protection
Limestone walls can be protected from erosion with a 'shelter coat' of limewash. Adding some powdered stone can help achieve a better match. More sophisticated mixes can be used with natural additives such as casein, which helps bind and strengthen the mix. Limewash dries to a composition that is essentially the same as limestone, and can last up to five years, but isn't suitable for some other types of stone.

Cosmetic repairs
The stone face can be repaired using lime mortar that's specially tinted to blend in with the wall. Cosmetic repairs are often a better option than highly invasive cutting out and replacement. Localised surface decay can be filled using a carefully blended mix of lime mortar and stone dust or coloured sands or earth. Skilfully done repairs are indistinguishable from the surrounding stonework.

Tile repairs
Where only a small area of stone has eroded badly, a traditional 'tile repair' may be appropriate. The worst affected area is cut out to form a deeper hole, which is filled by pushing in layers of clay tiles bedded in lime mortar. This way the minimum amount of eroded stone is lost.

Fit a new face
The eroded area is chiselled back and a new matching stone face carefully pieced in.

Replace the whole stone
The damaged stone is completely removed so that it can be replaced with a matching new piece, *eg* badly cracked stones can be cut out and replaced, if structurally necessary.

The decision whether to repair or replace often depends on the location of the stonework. At low level it may be better to simply leave an eroded stone face alone. But where stonework to parapet walls at roof level is damaged, it's probably best to replace it because it's at the mercy of the weather. Given the cost of scaffolding it can makes sense to combine this with any necessary roofing work.

Above all, before embarking on any major repair or replacement work it's important to address the cause of the problem, for example:

Rusted iron cramps
Where a wall has cracked, if you go ahead and replace the stone without first addressing the cause the cracking will more than likely recur. Smooth-faced stone ashlar blocks are often held in position by iron cramps bedded into small pockets in the stone

and caulked with molten lead. Where the protective lead coating has cracked and allowed water to penetrate, the iron will rust and expand, blowing apart and cracking the stone it was meant to restrain. Cracked stone may have been repaired in the more recent past using a similar method employing iron cramps, with unfortunate results, which is why today stainless steel cramps are used instead.

Dodgy past repair work
Where soft stone has been re-pointed with hard cement mortar it will accelerate decay (see 'Re-pointing'). The rules for brickwork also apply to stone – *ie* not sealing up walls with modern paints or cement mortars and renders. Even super-hard granite is porous to an extent, and flint prefers being bedded in flexible lime mortar rather than being gripped by cement. But cement isn't the only culprit. Synthetic chemical repairs have been widely applied to stonework in recent decades. Unfortunately these have since proved to be quite damaging and are no longer recommended. One unpredicted side-effect has been a noticeable deterioration in the colour of the stone over time. Another modern cure that

Old eroded stonework replaced to lower floor wall only. Projecting new stonework could have formed a 'rainwater trap' on top of new upper course, so this is reasonably flush.

turned out to be damaging was the painting of wall surfaces with damp sealants. The problem with such impermeable coatings is that they trap water inside the stone, which has the effect of accelerating the process of decay from within.

■ Traffic spray and defective sills

Erosion at lower levels to walls adjoining roads is often due to spray from traffic. A relatively simple solution may be to lime-render and limewash the lower wall in the form of a traditional plinth. This should protect the surface from further erosion. Similarly, where defective window sills can't be fully repaired rendering the wall below should help protect it.

For cleaning old stonework, see Chapter 12.

Replacement

Where stonework is so damaged that it needs to be cut out and replaced, either partially or fully, it raises the question of where to source matching new materials. Where possible it's best to reuse existing stones. With luck you might have a redundant outbuilding built in compatible stone. Finding suitable new stone can be a tall order because it's unlikely the original quarry will still be in operation. Even stone of the same geological type can vary from quarry to quarry.

The replacement stone should match the original as closely as possible, not just for aesthetic reasons but because different types of stone placed together can react chemically. For example, limestone and sandstone shouldn't be used together because

the interaction between them can set up a damaging process of erosion.

Even with perfectly matching stone there may still be aesthetic issues to consider. This tends to be more of an issue with expensive dressed, squared ashlar, where erosion is a lot more obvious than in rough stone walls. Also, where a smooth-faced stone wall has eroded, its surface, having been eaten away, will now be set back from the original face as it was built. This presents a bit of a dilemma when it comes to replacing whole stones in smooth-faced walls. Should the new stone be positioned to match the original face as it was when new, thereby projecting slightly from the adjoining worn surface, or should it be inset a little so that it aligns with its weathered neighbours? The general view is that it's better to reinstate level with the original face.

RE-POINTING STONEWORK

Putting right previous generations' misguided attempts at re-pointing has become a major part of the conservation job on many properties. Mortar should always be weaker than the surrounding masonry, otherwise it can't do its job properly, allowing moisture out and absorbing movement.

So the first task is to remove all the harmful old cement pointing.

Great care is needed, as cement is incredibly grippy, so removing it can also pull away chunks of the adjoining masonry, potentially damaging the face of some softer types of stone.

Finishing new lime putty mortar pointing

To make matters worse, in recent years the fashion for projecting 'ribbon pointing' in hard cement has proved visually disastrous, standing out like varicose veins. Traditionally, pointing was usually flush, so that on rubble walls, for example, only the peaks of the stones project out. Avoid anything that shouts 'look at me', drawing the eye to itself and upstaging the stonework, such as dark pointing on light-coloured stone.

Re-pointing fine-jointed ashlar stonework is very skilful and best left to the professionals. However, rubble stonework should be reasonably straightforward to re-point. But the relatively large joints in exposed rubble walls can be prone to shrinkage.

Above: New 'look at me' cement ribbon pointing trashes old wall

Below: Stonework freshly pointed in natural lime mortar. Looks good and feels right.

Raking Out Stonework

A lot of damage can be caused to old stonework trying to remove hard cement mortar by hammering joints with conventional bolsters or chisels. The problem with this method is that it relies on brute force

in an attempt to break the surface of the joint and shatter the cement mortar. This can also disrupt the bond between original building mortar and the stonework, weakening the wall.

Although the use of mechanical tools is often prohibited in specifications, in experienced hands they can be a far better option for removal of dense hard cement mortars. Cutting with an oscillating tool is the best option (rather than spinning discs).

Once the centre of the joint has been cut out it should then be relatively easy to break off the remaining cement mortar into the 'open space' created. The ideal tool to use is a mason's chisel – a thin, sharp, narrow throat chisel – which is far less damaging to masonry than thicker chisels and bolsters. Unlike bashing with hammers and bolsters, this shouldn't cause stress to adjacent masonry.

Simply tapping around the edge of the cement pointing should cause it to break away from the masonry cleanly and harmlessly, exposing the face of the stone.

It is essential to remove all the cement mortar, right the way back until the old lime mortar is exposed.

The vertical 'perps' are usually less well filled than horizontal bed joints where the weight of stone has compressed the mortar.

Where hard cement mortars need to be removed, first carefully mark along the middle of the joint in chalk.

Use an appropriate mechanical oscillating tool to cut along the centre line.

Then use a narrow-throated chisel to chip off the remaining cement, and to clean up the joint.

Brush the exposed joint to remove any remaining particles prior to re-pointing.

RE-POINTING STONEWORK

Materials

Lime mortar, hessian sheeting, mortar board / hawk

Tools

- Fine water spray
- Brush
- Hammer
- Pointing tool (a double-ended trowel with a smaller square end at the handle for use where joints in stonework are narrow)

In rubble wall construction you often find a variety of types of masonry – the wall shown here for example contains sandstone and granite. The traditional style of pointing demonstrated below is known as 'pointing to the weathered edge' or 'recessed'. Alternatively 'fully flush' pointing was sometimes used prior to rendering or harling, or on less stable walls where the original lime has become loose such as on ruins.

1 Clean the joint with a brush to remove dust etc. Joints should be spotlessly clean before re-pointing.

2 Thoroughly dampen down the wall, allowing excess surface water to soak in. This is essential for control of suction in old joints – to avoid rapid water loss from new mortar.

3 Conventionally, mortar is applied from a hawk. The pointing tool used should as closely as possible match the width of the joint.

4 Placing mortar into a rubber palmed gloved hand allows you to shape the mortar on the trowel more accurately than taking it off a hawk.

5 Apply the mortar to a clean, damp joint, starting at the top and working down. The main thing is to get the mortar well compacted by pressing it in to the back of the joint, bringing it slightly proud of the face.

6 For larger voids (about 2cm or more square) pack the joint with small 'pinning stones' (aka 'gallet stones'). This reduces the amount of mortar required and hence the risk of consequent shrinkage. It's best to use similar types of stone to that in the wall. Some may need to be shaped so they fit the space – and don't protrude from the face of the wall.

All images courtesy **Studio Scotland Ltd** from **The Master Stroke** DVD Tutorial series.
To view DVD trailers go to **www.themasterstroke.com**

7 First fill the void with mortar. Then push in the pinning stones. Gently tap them into the mortar with a hammer – this forces the mortar back in so that it fully fills the void.

8 More mortar is then pressed around the pinning stone to hold it in place. Here a narrow strip of pinning stone placed in between sandstone adjacent to granite.

9 After the initial set (up to 24hrs later) any excess mortar on the surface can be scraped off and the mortar tamped back with a brush. This helps compact the joint, forming a flush joint that's free from cracks, and should leave the edges of the stone clean and free from staining. Setting is weather-dependent, taking from 2hrs to the next day.

10 Finish with a stiff brush to give the joint a roughened open texture, which helps breathability.

11 Cover the finished wall with damp hessian so the new mortar doesn't dry out too quickly for at least the first 72hrs or so. In hot weather it can help to give the joint a fine mist spray. Finally, any old bits of mortar that have accumulated on the ground can be collected and recycled for later use in a new fresh mix.

Above: 2 schools of pointing on one wall: Criminally incompetent in hard cement (top) and the correct traditional approach in lime mortar (lower)

Below: Types of flintwork: Random with whole nodules (top left), interspersed with chalk blocks (top right), squared (lower left) and knapped (lower right)

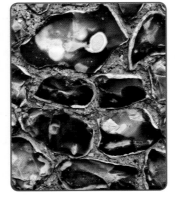

The mortar for pointing should be mixed using coarser sand than for brickwork because the larger sand particles help minimise shrinkage. There's a simple rule of thumb for calculating the maximum particle size: note the average joint width and divide by three. So for 15mm average width pointing you would choose a well-graded sharp sand with maximum particle size of 5mm. The other traditional technique for minimising shrinkage in rough stone walls was to insert small stone gallets to pack out wide joints. Otherwise rubblework would commonly have been rendered or given a protective limewash finish.

Flint

Flint is virtually indestructible. It was commonly used for house building across England's 'flint belt', from the southern counties through to East Anglia. Flintwork is one of the most skilled and labour intensive forms of stone construction, and there are various different styles.

At their simplest flint walls are built using whole stones (known as nodules) bedded in lime mortar. Better quality work used knapped flint, with individual stones split to expose their shiny inner face. The art of knapping involves chipping the flint into shape using a special blunt instrument, a process that requires great skill (and fireproof trousers). Flintwork was generally built to a substantial thickness in the form of panel infills contained between bricks or stone quoins. The finest flint walling is called 'flushwork', where pieces of flint have been knapped on five sides to create squarish blocks. Laid like bricks with thin joints, these are often interspersed in the wall with larger blocks of stone or chalk.

Although flint isn't prone to erosion like other types of stone, it isn't entirely immune to problems. Most flint nodules used for building are of a smooth, rounded shape, so there are no flat sides on which to bed the mortar. This can make it a difficult material to build with, so small shards of flint, or gallets, were sometimes used to help wedge individual nodules in place.

This relative lack of grip can also contribute to quite dramatic failures in old flint walls, with whole sheets of facework becoming detached. The problem is made considerably worse where walls have been re-pointed with cement, which traps moisture, causing a build-up of pressure that can eventually blow off the entire outer face – and rebuilding a whole section of loose facework is a painstaking and expensive job.

Old flint walls with their shallow foundations also depend on the inherent flexibility of lime mortar to accommodate seasonal movement without cracking. Where walls have been repaired or re-pointed with rigid cement mortar, sooner or later it will crack around the edges of individual flints, and cement patch repairs will eventually drop off altogether.

As with other types of masonry, clumsy re-pointing that dominates the wall can be visually disastrous, swamping the flint pattern. So for repair work it's important to select the right mortar mix for the job. Note that the mix for surface pointing is normally different from that used in the deeper inner wall construction.

There is one other potential drawback with flint that is sometimes overlooked – it's impossible to drill into it, which can make installing things like internal fixings and kitchen wall units a bit of a challenge. One traditional solution was to embed small wooden plugs in walls at key points during construction – preferably of oak to resist any subsequent dampness. But even this requires considerable forethought, as the mortar joints are at relatively inconsistent levels.

Earth and clay buildings

Being cheap and widely available, earth construction was extensively used for homebuilding. Techniques varied across the country, but there are three basic types: clay blocks, mass earth walls and 'mud and stud'.

CLAY BLOCKS

Buildings constructed using traditional unfired clay blocks known as 'clay lump', which resembled modern concrete blocks, were a traditional form of construction in Norfolk and the eastern counties where suitable stone was hard to come by. The blocks were made by mixing clean, weathered clay soil with straw by trampling with horses or cattle (hence that well known extra ingredient – dung). The straw or grass used to reinforce the mix was formed into moulds and air dried in the summer until firm. Walls were built up in courses onto a protective brick or flint plinth and the completed walls coated with lime or earth render, or sometimes with sanded tar.

MASS EARTH WALLS

Cob is perhaps the best known form of mass earth wall building, and is native to Devon and south-west England. However, similar building techniques are found in many other parts of the country. In some chalky clay areas of Buckinghamshire there are entire villages of Wychert (meaning 'white earth'). In west Wales there are houses made of 'clom', in the Midlands 'mud' and in Cumbria 'clay dabbins'. The precise mix of materials varied with locality, sometimes incorporating soft chalk, fine gravel or heather.

In the Scottish lowlands 'cat and clay' walls were constructed from bunches of straw mixed with soft clay and packed into a wooden framework. Mud walling extended right up to the harsher climate of the Highlands and Islands, where it was even used for townhouses and manses. Here clay was mixed with straw and the walls built up like Devon cob cottages, but hewn stone was incorporated in more vulnerable areas such as the corners of the house and reveals to the sides of doors and windows.

Cob is made from a similar recipe to clay lump, but once the clay-based subsoil has been mixed with straw to bind it together, and water to a gooey consistency, instead of being cast into blocks it was used to form thick walls built up about a foot (300mm) at a time. The mix was trampled direct into the wall by means of human foot-power, sometimes laid between formwork of wooden boards that moved up the building as work progressed.

Unshuttered construction needed very thick walls (600mm or thicker) which would be finished with a protective weathering coat and whitewashed or colour-washed. Such buildings tend to have distinctive rounded-off corners to avoid cracking, the most common weakness of cob walling. Finally, a generous overhang at the eaves would provide further protection to the walls beneath. This was especially important with thatch (without gutters), which was the normal roofing material.

MUD AND STUD

Mud used in combination with a timber framework was common in Lincolnshire ('mud and stud'), with close relatives in Cumbria ('clam and staff') and, of course, wattle and daub, originally from the Midlands. Timber-frame buildings and wattle and daub are explored in detail in Chapter 7.

The existence of a studwork load-bearing frame allowed greater economy with materials, so mud walls might only need to be around 250mm thick, a mere third of the width of cob wall construction.

The timber-frame walls were erected on top of a low plinth of stone or brick to protect the base of the wall, and typically consisted of a series of posts with horizontal rails, braces and a wall plate running along the top. A layer of timber laths (commonly of ash) was applied right across the frame. This would be coated with a daub of earth mixed with chopped straw and water, applied in a stiff consistency in gradual stages ('lifts'). Unlike wattle and daub infill panels, here the mud covers the entire framework on the outside. A plain limewash with an animal fat or linseed oil additive provided a waterproof exterior coating.

MAKING COB BLOCKS

Mixing subsoil, straw and water – a job traditionally done by livestock

Placing the mix into a mould

Firming and smoothing off the cob mix

Carefully lift off the mould...

...to reveal the finished block

A cob block that's ready to lay, having been left to dry

Laying cob blocks with a lime putty mortar (4:1 parts sand to lime)

All images courtesy
Mike Wye & Associates Limited
www.mikewye.co.uk

Buildings at risk

Many earth and clay buildings have survived perfectly well for centuries. However, with this method of construction good maintenance is essential. Unlike brick and stone, which retain their strength when damp, earth will soften and eventually disintegrate if subjected to persistent wetness. So to help keep earth walling dry, a 'good hat and boots' was an essential part of the design. Wide overhanging eaves helped protect the walls from rain running down them and a robust stone or brick plinth at ground level (known as a 'grumplings') kept damp at bay.

Common causes of failure are due to:

■ Persistent leaks from roofs or gutters.
■ High ground levels where soil has built up against the plinths.
■ Poor surface water drainage where water can't drain away from the building.
■ Cement render that cracks and traps damp.
■ Rodents burrowing through the walls (although an occasional redundant burrow shouldn't be a problem).

Repairing damage

Many traditional earth walls have been rendered in modern cement and can appear similar to walls of rendered rubble stonework, sometimes even fooling surveyors. Earth and clay walls naturally need to move slightly due to thermal expansion and they also need to breathe. Inevitably, covering them with coatings of rigid cement results in the render fracturing and eventually bits dropping off. Then once rain enters the wall and becomes trapped behind the hard cement it can accelerate deterioration and dissolve the earth wall behind.

Even when render has been applied over a metal or plastic

mesh, cracking still tends to develop at points corresponding to the edges of the sheets of mesh. The application of modern non-breathable paints make matters worse.

So how should you go about righting such wrongs? Normally it's possible to remove the cement render and replace it with a traditional breathable lime or earth equivalent, but this requires great care. Large sheets of render should never be levered off in one go, in case the earth behind has been washed away and the cement is literally all that's holding the building up! The best approach is to first investigate by cutting out a small square of render with an angle grinder. The walls will probably then need to be repaired using a suitable matching mud mix, but this requires skill and experience.

Unlike wattle and daub infill panels in timber-frame buildings, earth and clay block walls are load-bearing, supporting roofs and upper walls, so repairs should be made in small horizontal layers. The simplest approach is often to use cob blocks, which you can buy

or make yourself. These can be bedded in an earth mortar, which can be made from some subsoil, sieved to remove larger stones and mixed with water to form a sticky mortar. Once the repairs are complete the wall is protected with a coating of earth and lime putty render.

Wall eroded by water from defective former sill.
Fissure filled with cob mix and coated in lime putty render

6 THE WONDER OF LIME

Above and opposite: Naturally beautiful lime render

Right: Basecoat applied to traditional timber lath

Lime is a wonderfully versatile material. It was used extensively in old houses, not just for mortar mixes and renders, but for internal plasters, grouting, lime-ash floors and, of course, limewash paint finishes, both indoors and out. It's a testimony to the long-term durability of the material that enormous numbers of buildings constructed using lime still survive perfectly happily today, after hundreds of years.

Although cement was used experimentally in some late Victorian buildings, it was not the same sort that we use now – the modern variety is far denser and more impermeable. Initially cement played a fairly restricted role as an occasional additive to mixes used for underground footings and drainage pipes or in solid floors, rather than any widespread application in walls. Only in the 1930s did it really start to take over from lime in mainstream housing. But one thing lime and cement have in common is that they're both made from limestone – a hugely abundant material.

Lime making

Lime was traditionally made by heating chunks of pure limestone or chalk to over 900° in large lime-kilns. By driving off the CO2, this process converted the raw material, calcium carbonate, into calcium oxide, better known as 'quicklime'. Calcium carbonate was sometimes also sourced from cheaper, less orthodox materials such as large quantities of seashells or bird droppings. Modern cement is also formed by burning limestone, but at far higher temperatures (1,300°–1,500°) and with the addition of clay and other ingredients.

Lime making was a very widespread industry, with numerous kilns dotted across the countryside. These resembled large wells or

small stone castles set into hillsides. The process involved building up alternating layers of coal and chunks of limestone (about the size of large bricks) to the top of the kiln. Then a fire would be started at the bottom and the whole thing left to burn slowly for three or four days and nights. It must have been an eerie sight as thin wafts of smoke rose like dry ice from the ground. Stories abound of weary travellers sleeping around the edges of kilns on cold winter nights, enticed by the warmth. Unfortunately there was a very real danger of being rendered unconscious by odourless carbon monoxide fumes, and rolling into the steaming void below to be roasted alive. Human bone is, of course, largely composed of calcium carbonate.

Eventually the super-heated limestone would be transformed into small rocks of quicklime, the raw material for making the lime putty used in building. However, to produce lime putty the quicklime first needs to be added to water, or 'slaked'. This is a spectacularly violent process as the quicklime cracks up and fizzes, transforming itself into lime putty (calcium hydroxide) – a thick, creamy-looking substance. Because of its aggressively caustic nature quicklime must be treated with respect. The dust readily reacts with moisture, so if it touches your skin it will burn, or if the dust is inhaled it can cause throat irritation. The final stage in producing the building material simply involves mixing the lime putty with sand. Once the lime is exposed to air it starts to set by re-absorbing carbon dioxide from the atmosphere, reversing the production process until it ultimately reverts to its original chalky state. This makes lime very eco-friendly

Right: Be prepared for a lively reaction when slaking lime!

Below: Creamy lime putty

Below right: Mixed with sand to make mortar

Jack in the Green Conservation

Types of lime

There are two basic types of lime: non-hydraulic and hydraulic.

Lime putty ('non hydraulic' lime)

Ordinary non-hydraulic lime, or lime putty (calcium hydroxide), looks rather like thick white yoghurt, and can be purchased ready-made in airtight plastic tubs. It's produced as described on the previous page by burning pure limestone to form quicklime, which is then slaked with water. Non-hydraulic limes set on exposure to CO_2 in the air, reverting to a form of calcium carbonate similar to the original limestone – thus completing a full circle. Unlike cement, which sets by chemical reaction, lime putty needs exposure to the air to cure and won't set in water. Hence lime putty can last indefinitely if stored in an airtight container.

Sometimes called 'pure lime' or 'fat lime', lime putty is mixed with sand for added strength and bulk to make mortar and plaster. These offer excellent breathability, which makes them ideal for use with soft, porous masonry, as well as being well suited to mortar pointing, and especially for very fine work such as tuck pointing. Although non-hydraulic lime isn't as durable as the hydraulic (NHL) variety, its strength can be improved and its relatively lengthy setting time dramatically reduced by mixing in a small amount of pozzolanic additive (see opposite page).

Lime putty can be moulded, poured or painted. It's a bit like liquid stone. It can be purchased from builders' merchants in two forms:

■ Tub lime

Ready-mixed lime putty is available in plastic tubs. This is generally considered to be the best way of buying it, because the pre-mixed quality is more consistent. Some reckon that it improves with age, which is why 'mature' lime putty is sometimes specified. But containers must be kept airtight.

■ Hydrated lime powder or 'bagged lime'

Available as a dry white powder sold in paper sacks, bagged hydrated lime is used primarily as a plasticising additive for mixing cement to improve its workability.

A bag of hydrated lime can be soaked (slaked) for a few days in water and will thicken up to form lime putty. However, hydrated lime isn't recommended because if the bag is past its sell-by date, or hasn't been kept perfectly dry and airtight, the powder will have already reacted with the moisture in the air and reverted to useless chalk. The resulting putty will then be of poor quality and is likely to fail in use. If you do attempt the slaking process, it's essential to protect your eyes with goggles, and to wear a face mask and gloves.

Natural hydraulic lime ('NHL')

NHL is a tougher, more durable form of lime that offers some of the benefits of cement. It's produced from limestone containing natural impurities, such as clay and earth. Because it sets comparatively quickly and has greater strength, NHL is ideal for laying new brick or stonework. It's also suitable for relatively damp or exposed environments like chimneys and ridge tiles.

Unlike ordinary lime, NHL doesn't depend exclusively on drying by exposure to air. It sets largely by chemical reaction as soon as it comes into contact with moisture, and is therefore more able to cure in wet applications (hence its name 'hydraulic lime'). This makes it more like cement. NHL lime mortars cannot be kept for long once mixed, as they set even if kept airtight.

Available in powder form, NHL has a relatively short shelf-life and the bagged powder must be stored in dry conditions.

Until recently hydraulic limes weren't easy to obtain, although they've long been widely available at low cost in France. Fortunately home-produced NHL is now available (see website for suppliers).

NHL is sold in different strengths, which reflect the amount of clay and impurities contained in the raw limestone. But there's a downside: the higher the strength, the less flexible and breathable the material will be. Stronger NHLs are more like cement, making them easier for mainstream builders to use. However, even high strength NHL 5 still isn't cement, and the two materials shouldn't be mixed.

There are three commonly available strengths:

NHL 2   'feebly hydraulic'
NHL 3.5   'moderately hydraulic'
NHL 5   'eminently hydraulic'

The numbers relate to the compressive strengths achieved after 28 days, NHL 5 being the strongest.

For most pointing or rendering NHL 2 or 3.5 is suitable, but where high levels of breathability or flexibility are required, such as with softer base materials like cob or wattle and daub, a lime putty mix is preferable. On the other hand, where you need a quicker-setting durable mix, such as for exposed work at high level to chimneys, stronger NHL 5 may be the best bet. Hydraulic lime mortar hardens slowly over time, and doubles in strength over the first 18 months or so.

Choosing the right lime

Suitable lime mortars and renders are available for any situation without resorting to cement:

Application	Location	Lime strength
Soft brick or stone	Exposed	NHL 2 or 3.5
	Sheltered	Lime putty
Hard brick or stone	Exposed	NHL 3.5 or 5
	Sheltered	NHL 2 or 3.5
Timber frame or cob	Exposed	Lime putty (in some cases with additives)
	Sheltered	Lime putty
High level (roofs and chimneys etc)	eg ridge tiles, mortar fillets, flaunching on stacks etc	NHL 5
Below ground	eg footings, cellar pointing or rendering, retaining walls etc	NHL 3.5 or 5

Lime putty render applied to timber lath front wall and stonework side wall

A mixed background comprising mud, clay, chalk, timber frame, wattle, lath plus a few bricks for good measure!

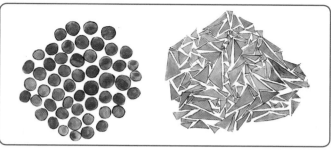

Under the microscope – soft sand left, sharp sand right

Additives

The Romans knew a thing or two about building with lime. Whether by accident or design, they discovered that adding a dash of volcanic ash, or *pozzolana*, to the mix had the effect of speeding up its setting time as well as adding strength. So weaker non-hydraulic lime can be made to set much more rapidly by the addition of a pozzolanic additive, effectively making it hydraulic. This practice is known as gauging. In the absence of a suitably active local volcano, modern substitutes can be used. Brick dust is a cheap and highly effective pozzolanic additive. Even waste materials like pulverised fuel ash (PFA) are sometimes employed. Special additives containing silica and alumina can also be mixed in. Tests of different lime mortar mixes (carried out on Cardiff castle) have shown that using a magnesium stearate additive can be very effective at reducing penetrating dampness.

A small proportion of such additives should be stirred into the mix just prior to use. The resulting mortar is usually a little darker in colour, with slightly reduced porosity. However, there is one material that should not normally be added to the mix – cement.

Pozzolanic additives are generally acceptable to conservationists. This is because when lime was historically manufactured in rural kilns there would have been natural impurities such as ash, mud and clay from the sides of lime pits, making it more like NHL. Clinically pure modern lime is relatively sterile and devoid of such natural additives that probably contributed to the longevity of old mortars and renders.

Sand

Your choice of sand not only determines the colour of the mix, but also helps achieve the right strength. When it comes to selecting the right sand there's one major difference when mixing lime mortar compared to cement: you need to use well-graded *sharp sand*, rather than the ordinary soft sand (aka building sand) that's used for mixing cement mortar. Builders who aren't used to lime sometimes use the wrong sand, but soft building sand isn't so good as a binder and is likely to lead to failure. The exception to this rule is where a certain amount of soft sand is sometimes blended with the sharp to formulate a plaster or render of just the right texture or colour (e.g. 1 bucket of soft to 2 of sharp). The performance of the end product is very much affected by the sand particle sizes, so getting the right mix of grades is important – specialist firms can provide this service.

Soft sand comprises lots of evenly sized round particles that, when looked at under a microscope, resemble thousands of tennis balls. Cement works by simply 'gluing' all these tiny particles together. In contrast, sharp sand comprises lots of tiny shards with angular edges and flat sides that interlock, leaving tiny voids between the sand particles. These pockets of air typically comprise around a third of the volume of well-graded sharp sand. When mixed, the lime fills these voids rather than rigidly gluing them. This accounts for the flexible quality of lime mortar.

Sand is normally specified as 'sharp well-graded and washed'. 'Well-graded' means it has lots of different particle sizes, ranging from microscopic dust to a few millimetres long, which helps form a stronger mix. 'Washed' means salts and impurities are absent. Salts are potentially damaging to masonry as they dissolve in damp walls and expand when they crystallise as the moisture evaporates.

Mortar biscuits

mikewye.co.uk

Getting a good colour match with mortar is particularly important if you're re-pointing the odd mortar joint here and there. To help select the right sand colour it can be useful to make up small 'mortar biscuits' in advance. Once dry, you can then snap them in half and compare them with your existing mortar.

Mixing mortar

For laying new brick or stonework, a weaker hydraulic lime such as NHL 2 or 3.5 is usually best, either mixed by hand or mechanically in a cement mixer. Alternatively you can buy ready-mixed lime mortar, which saves all the hard work of mixing. With experience you get to know the colours of different brands of ready-mixed mortar, but getting precisely the right colour for your house will depend on selecting a suitable sand – which means mixing it yourself. Hydraulic limes are generally easier to mix than lime putties, as they come in powder form and can be mechanically mixed in a similar way to cement, at about three parts sand to one part lime.

For re-pointing, non-hydraulic putty mortars are normally the best option. They're easier to apply and offer greater breathability, being slightly softer than traditional soft brick and stone. Mortars for re-pointing need to be relatively stiff and are best mixed by hand.

MIXING MORTAR

Dry pre-mixed hydraulic lime mortars can be purchased in bags, so you just need to add water. But it is much less expensive and considerably more satisfying to mix your own. For smaller quantities this can be done by hand – or alternatively you can use a mechanical mixer. The word 'mortar' is sometimes also used to describe sand/lime renders and plaster mixes.

Whichever mixing method you use, it's important to select the optimum type of sand for the intended use. Sharp sand with a good range of particle sizes makes the best mortar for pointing and should be free from salts and other impurities. For some plastering work a finer sand may be preferred containing a variety of sharp angular and soft rounded shapes.

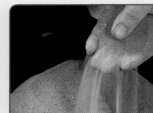

Where you need to add hair for lime plasters and renders it is best mixed in by hand just prior to use.

HAND MIXING

Lime mortar can be mixed by hand using either lime putty or powdered NHL. It can be tempting to make the job easier by adding generous amounts of water, particularly if it looks too dry. But mortar that's too sloppy won't be controllable for repointing, and can suffer from excessive shrinkage.

Before you start, be sure to protect your eyes, lungs and skin.

Non-hydraulic lime mortar
To mix non-hydraulic lime mortar you will need:-

- Mature lime putty (the binder)
- Sharp sand (the aggregate)
- A shovel or a traditional 'larry' (a wide hoe with large holes)
- Protective goggles and gloves
- A large mixing board (for smaller amounts e.g. for pointing) or a metal tub (plastering & rendering)

Lime putty mortar is generally mixed in a ratio of 3 parts sand to 1 part lime. This ratio is based on the fact that well-graded washed sand is assumed to have 33% air voids between the grains. So 1 bucket of lime putty to 3 buckets of sand should fill all the air voids in the sand matrix – hence it produces 3 buckets (rather than 4) of mortar.

2 Empty mature lime putty onto a mixing board – or for larger amounts use a metal tub.

3 Add sand and mix with a suitable shovel or hoe.

It may be necessary to add more lime binder and water where the sand turns out to contain more air voids. Together with any additives, this can be pre-mixed in a bucket and poured into the tub.

Hydraulic lime mortar (NHL)
Mortar can also be made by hand using hydraulic lime. This comes in powder form and can be mixed in a similar way to cement at a ratio of around 3 parts sand to 1 part lime.

Here you will need a bag of NHL (in this example NHL 2) plus a mortar trowel and a drill with a paddle mixing attachment. When mixing lime powder it's important to wear a mask. Although experienced practitioners sometimes pre-mix the sand and lime dry, to minimise the risk of inhaling lime dust or getting it in your eyes it is better to start by slowly adding the NHL powder to a bucket of clean water. This is mixed by hand with a trowel, then using a paddle mixer to the consistency of whipped cream before adding the sand. Note that NHL must be stored in dry conditions and bags should be covered almost immediately after use or the remaining lime powder can start to degrade.

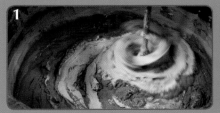
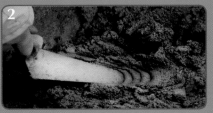

The mortar can be chopped up and kneaded like dough, using the back of the shovel. It's normally sufficiently pliable when you can mould it into a ball – if it's still crumbly it needs more mixing. Putty mortars will last indefinitely if stored in sealed airtight containers, but hair mortar should not be stored for too long as the lime will break down the hair.

POWER MIXING
HYDRAULIC LIME NHL MORTAR

Hydraulic limes are well suited for use in mixers, which makes them easier to mix than lime putty. Depending on the strength required, they are usually mixed in a lime/sand ratio of 1:3 (or sometimes a stronger ratio of 1:2) for at least 15 minutes until 'fattened up'.

Machine mixing requires a wetter consistency, which is ideal for laying new bricks or stone, and for plastering. To make a wet mix stiff enough for re-pointing, tip it on a board and cover with a plastic sheet before leaving overnight. By the next day the mix should be firmer. Then knock up the mix immediately prior to use.

Adding sand

Adding water

Adding binder (NHL)

Mixing

Cover the mixer to protect from…

…binder dust

Mixing

Adding kiln dry sand if required

All images on opposite page courtesy
Studio Scotland Ltd
from
The Master Stroke
DVD Tutorial series.
To view DVD trailers go to
www.themasterstroke.com.

Images on this page courtesy
Mike Wye & Associates Ltd,
www.mikewye.co.uk

The mix is pliable enough when it can be rolled into a ball

Sticky and ready to use

Working with lime

It's a bit of a myth that lime is difficult to use. Of course, learning a major new skill takes time, and you probably won't get it 100% right first time, but for anyone with reasonably good hand skills

(like brickies and most DIYers) it shouldn't be difficult – it's just a matter of getting used to working in a slightly different way. True, working with lime requires more patience and planning ahead, but it can actually be a more forgiving product to use than cement. Many people find working with lime highly satisfying, in a way that cement somehow isn't.

Like any material, you need to understand its qualities to get the best out of it. The most important thing to realise is that you can't use lime-based products all year round. Lime is very sensitive to frost until it's set, which can take several weeks. So pointing, rendering and limewashing should only really be undertaken between about May and October. Frost damage is identifiable by a crumbling outer surface of mortar. Even in mellow weather, lime putty-based mortars (ie non-hydraulic) can take a very long time to harden if laid too thick. This long setting period means works need to be programmed for the warmer months.

For jobs in exposed locations, such as re-pointing chimneys or ridge tiles, using NHL or a pozzolanic additive helps speed up setting times.

When working with lime it's also important to be aware that it's notoriously caustic, so skin contact is best avoided until it has set and reverted to docile calcium carbonate.

Cement or lime?

For the last 60 years or more, cement has been in pretty much universal use. Its success was down to the fact that it was easier to

mix mechanically and could be reliably used in large volumes for modern concrete strip foundations. Unlike highly frost-sensitive lime, cement was guaranteed to cure within days, and with anti-freeze additives could be worked in cold weather, making it useable for more of the year. Because of cement's ability to set without exposure to air it could even cure underwater – hence one of its earliest applications was for building lighthouses. In comparison, lime required more skill to judge the mix and could take weeks or even months to harden fully. This makes cement an unrivalled material for new construction. However, we now know that using cement mortar or render on old buildings is positively harmful.

Lime also differs from cement in the way it releases water when setting, via evaporation and background suction. Whereas faster-setting cement and gypsum plasters harden before the water comes out, lime putty (and to a lesser extent hydraulic limes) release the water before hardening. In the process, the volume of the mortar reduces, causing shrinkage and hence resultant cracking if excessive water is added to the mix.

WHAT'S SO GOOD ABOUT LIME?

Lime may be more costly to use, but in the long run it works out cheaper because it doesn't cause damage like cement, thanks to its three unique properties:-

1 Breathability

Lime products are inherently vapour-permeable. This means moisture that's absorbed by old walls made from soft brick or stonework is able to naturally escape by evaporating away.

Lime mortar allows walls to breathe, acting like the lungs of the building, a process that can eventually start to erode the mortar. Mortar pointing should always be softer than the surrounding brick or stone, but where a wall has been re-pointed in cement it clogs the evaporation path, forcing the moisture to try and escape via the masonry, which then erodes instead of the mortar. It's better to have to replace lime pointing every hundred years or so than replace damaged bricks or stones every decade or two.

2 Flexibility

Lime can accommodate seasonal shifts and minor settlement without cracking. As if by magic it can even reset itself in the new position. In contrast, modern cement render is hard and rigid. Where it's been applied to old walls there will invariably be a myriad of fine cracks that develop over time. And once water enters it becomes trapped.

3 Repairability

Small surface cracks in lime render can be 'healed' with a coating of limewash. When repairing old buildings, existing lime-based mixes can be scientifically analysed to determine their original composition (although in some cases the original composition may not have been ideal).

Protect yourself

- Lime is hazardous if it splashes into your eyes, because it's very alkaline. Wear protective goggles and keep a flask of lukewarm water handy for emergency eye washing.
- Lime burns on contact with skin. Brief contact is OK, but on a prolonged basis it can cause serious burns. Wear tight-fitting surgical gloves.
- Avoid breathing-in powdered lime, as it will 'slake' inside your throat and lungs. Wear a face mask and try to hold your breath when opening bags.

External render and roughcast

External plasterwork, known as render, traditionally used similar materials and techniques to internal plastering, described in Chapter 11. The main difference is found in the traditional styles of finish, such as pargetting, stucco, roughcast and pebbledash.

Pargetting

Decorative exterior plasterwork known as pargetting was popular in the 17th century and is most commonly found on timber-frame buildings in the eastern counties. A wide variety of designs were produced using sticks or combs, often in the form of framed coats of arms, or geometric and floral patterns.

Pargetting was suitable for backings of timber lath or wattle, so the craft declined as bricks became more freely available.

As fashions changed in the Georgian period, the 'pargework' exteriors of many timber-frame buildings were concealed behind new smooth-rendered elevations. However, the art enjoyed a revival with the late Victorian Arts and Crafts movement.

The original raw material is 'parge', a mixture of sand and slaked lime with an animal hair binder, similar to the stuff used for parging flues and sealing the undersides of roof tiles. However, various additional 'secret ingredients' were added including soot, tallow, dung, blood and salt, all geared to producing a viscous material that cured slowly to a leather-like hardness. If it cured too quickly it would be difficult to work into complex patterns, but if it cured too slowly the frost might catch it.

Moulds of wet plaster were applied in two or three layers, and the decorative surface finished with a limewash sheltercoat. Where cement was used in the mix for more modern pargetting, or for repairs, the ornamentation can often appear quite harsh. Repair work is similar to lime render repairs, although reinstating original patterns clearly requires an artistic bent and sculptural skills.

Traditional pargetting in Essex

Reviving the tradition

Freshly crafted 'rude man of Cerne Abbas'!

Chris Bowler

Chris Bowler

Applying traditional stucco to chimney stack:

Right and below: First coat for corner blocks.

Below right: corner blocks complete and Ashlar rendering finished

Seanwheatley.co.uk

Seanwheatley.co.uk

Seanwheatley.co.uk

Above and right: Roughcast with decorative motifs

Stucco

Stucco is smooth, exterior plasterwork that was a fashionable finish on Georgian and early Victorian 'wedding cake' townhouses. It was usually incised with horizontal lines to imitate fine stonework, thus giving a more expensive appearance with relatively cheap materials.

The raw materials used to create stucco ranged from simple lime render (lime putty and sand reinforced with animal hair), to quicker-setting mixes with pozzolanic additives, or stronger hydraulic lime mixes. Some more exotic stuccos known as 'mastics' were designed to repel water; these were based on linseed oil with ingredients such as limestone dust, silver sand, crushed pottery or glass, and yellow lead monoxide (known as 'litharge' – a highly toxic powder added to speed up drying times). As with conventional renders, stucco was generally applied in two or three coats of similar thickness. The topcoat was given a smooth, trowelled finish, to replicate ashlar stonework, before being limewashed.

Roughcast

As the name implies, roughcast is a rough, lumpy render that originated as 'harling' in Scotland and northern England. It was most commonly used in exposed locations on the west side of the country on account of its weather-resistant qualities, but is also found further afield, for example in Northumberland with its characteristic limewashed roughcast farmhouses.

Roughcast became fashionable as a 'rustic' finish on some more expensive late Victorian and Edwardian houses. The rough texture is derived from shingle or pebbles mixed into the final lime render coat, which is thrown on to the wall (both masonry and timber lath) and given a painted finish. Because of its increased surface area, which maximises evaporation and protects against driving rain, roughcast provides very effective protection.

Sometimes it's mistaken for pebbledash, a more recent variation that enjoyed similar popularity in Edwardian times. The main difference is that pebbledash is formed by throwing smaller chippings, or dry pea shingle, on to a wet final coat of smooth render.

Cement render

As we saw in chapter 2, hard cement render can be disastrous for old buildings. Because it's impermeable it traps moisture in the walls, and being rigid and inflexible makes it prone to cracking. The solution is normally to hack it off and re-render the walls in lime. Using a hammer and chisel, a small area should be removed first as a trial, to check that it can be removed without causing too much damage to the building's fabric. Where it's very firmly adhered some may have to be left, and only removed at the base of walls or on any hollow-sounding patches.

New coatings of cement render have often been applied in place of perfectly sound old lime renders that were misdiagnosed

as 'failed'. Like lime mortar, lime render is a relatively soft material, so to the untrained eye can appear superficially crumbly. Consequently much has been replaced or overcoated with cement in the mistaken belief that 'harder was better', or to provide a more stable background for masonry paints.

Failed cement render – can cause structural defects when applied to mud buildings

Was it once rendered?

It's not always obvious whether a property was originally rendered or not. Although oak timber-frame buildings were traditionally built with their timber structure exposed, those using cheaper timber, or with less substantial structures, were often rendered. Other formerly 'naked' houses were later concealed behind fashionable stucco coatings to satisfy the Georgian taste for stylish classical front elevations. Others may simply have been rendered for improved weather protection.

In properties where original coatings have subsequently been removed, there may at first glance be no clue that the visible timber-frame or masonry wall was ever any different. But if you know where to look, there may be telltale signs, such as where the window surrounds stand proud of the building's face. Also, traces of an original render finish may survive in tucked-away areas behind fascias and guttering etc.

However, spotting where modern cement render has been removed requires less detective work – it normally pulls off part of the underlying old soft brick or stone with it, leaving a pock-marked surface; hence the need to re-render in lime.

New work

It takes skill and experience to successfully apply lime render and achieve a stable, crack-free finish. This is specialist work, so rather than risk employing someone who'll be learning on the job it's better to wait to get the right craftsman. Conservation Officers will know who's worth approaching. (See 'Choosing your plasterer' in Chapter 11.)

Mixes and materials

There's an art to preparing the optimum mix for a specific type of surface. Walls made from relatively soft materials such as wattle and daub, cob or soft porous brick need a render that's flexible enough to accommodate movement without cracking. Such walls may also be prone to higher levels of dampness, so lime putty renders are normally ideal as they offer maximum flexibility and are highly breathable. Made with non-hydraulic lime, these are the same as lime putty plasters used internally, but should not be applied externally later than September, as they're very vulnerable to frost. Lime putty should be 'mature', *ie* at least three months old. Where larger quantities are required, non-hydraulic lime render can be purchased ready-mixed and delivered to site.

With less rigid traditional backgrounds such as timber laths or wattle, the base coats need to be reinforced with chopped animal hair to reduce shrinkage and cracking. Usually cattle or goat hair is best since it grips the render better than horse hair (human hair is far too smooth). With soft earth backgrounds such as cob, broken tiles are sometimes inserted into the wall prior to applying the first backing coat in order to provide a good key.

Where a tougher mix is needed, such as for more exposed masonry walls, hydraulic lime render may be more appropriate, but there's always a trade-off between increased strength and reduced breathability. A less strong mix such as NHL 2 can often be a good compromise as a step up from weaker non-hydraulic lime. NHL 3.5 tends to be used where exposed walls take a battering from the weather. Even stronger NHL 5 isn't widely used for render due to its limited breathability.

Goat hair is perfect for hair lime plasters and renders – but don't mix more than you need at one time as the lime will gradually break down the hair if stored too long

Lime rendering

A local specialist will know how to formulate the right mix for particular types of wall surface. Although lime renders and plasters are essentially the same mix, working outdoors is far more demanding because the material is exposed to the full force of the elements. Hence the aftercare process (known as 'tending') is crucial to stop moisture evaporating too quickly.

Lime plasters perform best with two or three coats of similar thicknesses (although each coat can be a little thinner than the last), with the surface of each layer being roughened ('scratched') to provide an adequate key for the next. To help reduce shrinkage and cracking on drying, the mix should be as dry as possible but

New timber lath background (left) with hair lime putty render scratched (right) awaiting finish coat

Top tips – the art of rendering

■ **The background must be properly prepared.**
Salts leeching from the masonry can cause loss of bond with new render (especially to chimneys and low-level walls). Brush them off with a bronze or copper wire brush (not steel as tiny bits can become embedded and rust). Any surface moss or lichen should be removed, e.g. with diluted bleach.

■ **Suction must be controlled.**
High suction backgrounds such as porous brick or stone must be dampened. On low suction backgrounds (e.g. hard modern materials) or mixed backgrounds an initial 'pricking up coat' should be applied (a.k.a. 'slurry', 'bonding', 'scudding' or 'splatterdash' coat). Here a lime/sand **s**lurry is cast onto a damp surface using a harling trowel. The surface is then 'pricked up' by brush with a stippling action.

■ **Apply each coat to a consistent thickness** and key the surface before the next:-
i.   Straightening ('base' or 'rendering') coat
ii. Intermediate coat
iii. Flatwork – then rubbing firmly with float to take out any abrasions.

■ Allow adequate curing time between coats and protect new work. NHL render must be cured for around a week between coats without drying fully before the next.

■ Use physical guides (rules and screeds) to help form corners and angles, and to achieve a flat and straight finish.

All images courtesy of Studio Scotland Ltd

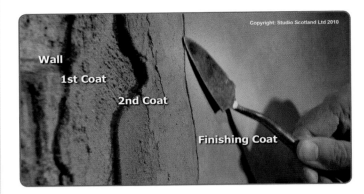

Wall
1st Coat
2nd Coat
Finishing Coat
Copyright: Studio Scotland Ltd 2010

Above: The surface of each layer must be lightly scratched with cross hatching to provide a key for the next coat

Left: Tending – vulnerable new work must be shielded with moist Hessian sacking

Below: Over the centuries a wide range of scratching tools have been devised – from simple spatulas (left) and trowels to special multi-fingered devices (right) or nails embedded in floats

Studio Scotland Ltd

still be workable. Prior to the application of each coat the surface should be sprayed down with clean water to prevent moisture from being sucked out too rapidly.

Lime render takes a relatively long time to set. It's sometimes claimed that the longer it takes to dry out the better the finished render will perform. Depending on the weather and the mix, each coat of lime putty render (ie non-hydraulic lime) may have to be left to dry for a week or more (7–21 days) before the next one can be applied, but for a stronger NHL mix the interval between coats can be as little as three or four days.

It's essential to tend it after application to prevent it drying out too quickly – or too slowly. In warm weather the finished render

A selection of wood and fibreglass floats and spatulas – in skilled hands these can work wonders

needs to be kept damp with a mist spray. To shield it against the drying effects of the sun and wind it helps if new work is covered with moist hessian sacking (also sometimes necessary for cement rendering, but for a shorter time). Lime carries on setting long after it's been applied, remaining vulnerable to frost during this period, hence its use tends to be restricted to spring and summer. Although lime render has a naturally beautiful finish it's normally limewashed to help protect it.

Lime render mix

For softer wall surfaces, such as earth, wattle and daub, or soft masonry, a weaker non-hydraulic (lime putty) mix is normally best. However for hard external masonry hydraulic lime (NHL 2 or 3.5) is generally better suited. The optimum mix of sand, lime and hair will vary according to circumstances and local tradition, but a guide to typical proportions for both lime putty and NHL plasters and renders can be seen on page 156.

Roughcast lime render mix

Roughcast is generally applied in two coats and can be similarly made with either non-hydraulic lime putty or hydraulic NHL. The ingredients are mixed to a sloppy, porridge-like consistency and thrown on to the wall using a dashing trowel, with a motion similar to serving in tennis. The mix proportions should be:

	Lime putty (non-hydraulic lime)	Hydraulic lime (NHL)
Sand	2 parts sharp sand (well-graded)	1½ parts sharp sand (well-graded)
Lime	1 part mature lime putty	1 part NHL 2 or 3.5
Shingle	1 part washed pea shingle/ pebbles	1 part washed pea shingle/ pebbles

Repairs

Hairline cracks in lime render can often be healed simply by applying a coat or two of limewash. Larger superficial cracks can be wetted and filled with a compatible mix, but bigger patches need to be filled and built up in layers. As with new work, the surface of each completed layer is roughened to provide a key for the next; each layer also needs to be wetted and requires 'tending' until set. With patch repairs it's important that the depth of the base coats must allow sufficient space for the final coat to be flush with the surrounding surface.

Other lime products

Lime is an incredibly versatile material. In addition to mortars and external renders it's used in internal plasters, floors and paints. All are explored in later chapters.

Lime plasters

A similar sand/lime mix to that used for external renders, usually with added animal hair for the base coats. Finishing coats may be richer in lime and use finer sand for a smoother finish. See Chapter 11.

Limewash

A slurry of lime putty and water used as a painted finish applied to lime-plastered and rendered surfaces or direct to masonry. For strength and colour, additives such as earth or vegetable dyes, very fine sand or powdered stone were sometimes mixed in (up to about 10% of the mix). The caustic alkaline nature of lime gives limewash natural fungicidal properties, helping to sterilise mould on walls. See Chapter 14.

Lime-ash floors

A stiff mix of lime, wood ash and sometimes also sand was used as a simple covering to earth floors, or to a wattle or reed mat background. A lime-ash floor broadly appears similar to a concrete floor. See Chapter 12.

Limecrete

Limecrete (lime concrete) is a mix of hydraulic lime, sand and insulating material that's ideal for new solid floors. See Chapter 12.

7 TIMBER FRAME BUILDINGS

Ask someone to describe a classic period house and the chances are that a 'Shakespearean' timber-frame cottage would come to mind. Charming images of such Olde Worlde gems resplendent in glorious black and white routinely leap from the covers of innumerable '*period living*' magazines.

Properties of this type are sometimes dubbed 'half-timbered', because the walls were infilled with other materials, such as wattle and daub. But with timber-frame buildings all is not always what it seems. For a start, the tradition of painting the framework black is now thought to have been a Victorian invention. Original medieval timbers were most likely limewashed along with the rest of the wall, or simply left exposed to slowly weather to a silvery shade over time. Appearances can sometimes be enormously deceptive, to the extent that it's not always evident that a building is of timber-frame construction at all. As we saw in the last chapter, many were rendered over to conceal or protect the structure. Others may have subsequently been re-clad with elegant brick or stone facades, or hung with tiles or weatherboarding. So at a glance they can sometimes appear indistinguishable from more conventional period houses.

Types of timber frame

The two main types of timber-framed building are medieval cruck frame and later post and beam 'box' construction, but there are numerous variations on both themes depending on the age of the property and its locality.

Cruck

Cruck houses are found predominantly in and around the Midlands, many parts of Wales and the north and west of England, as well as in Scotland where they were known as 'couples'. They were the earliest and simplest oak-frame homes,

being built around a series of giant A-frames rising all the way from the ground up to the roof ridge. The sides of each 'A' were formed from matching pairs of curved posts that inclined inwards to meet at the top. Each pair of these matching 'cruck blades' was made by splitting a large tree trunk down its length. The 'A' was then completed by linking the blades with a horizontal collar (tie beam).

A simple 'single bay' cruck

building could be constructed with just a single A-frame at each end, linked together lengthways by horizontal wall plates, and at roof level with big purlin beams carrying the rafters. By lining up and connecting a series of crucks, larger buildings comprising two or more bays could be constructed. The walls were often relatively thin since the roof loadings were supported by the cruck frame.

As supplies of large oak trees started to diminish, cruck frames were gradually superseded by other types of construction, although in areas where oak was more plentiful (*eg* Wales and the west of England) houses of this type were still being built into the 18th century. Cruck frames were also commonly used in stone-walled buildings, but the structure is rarely identifiable from outside and is usually most evident from inside at first-floor level.

Post and beam

The majority of surviving oak-frame homes (and most new timber-frame buildings) are of post and beam construction. Here, rather than relying on large A-frames to support the roof, the walls provide the strength of the building. At their simplest the walls are formed Stonehenge-style, with pairs of upright posts supporting

Heritage-house.org

a timber beam laid horizontally across the top. The rectangle is completed at the base by the introduction of a sole plate (aka a sill beam), into which the feet of the timber posts are tenoned. The sole plate would in turn be laid on a masonry plinth to protect it from damp emanating from the ground. By joining a series of these goalpost-like frames together with tie beams, the living space was formed as a series of bays or boxes – hence the term 'box framing'. It's also possible to stack two or more storeys on top of each other, making it a very flexible building system compared to cruck framing, which is limited by the size of the oak available to form the cruck blades.

The roof provides a 'lid' sitting on top of the boxes. Although methods of construction vary, roofs generally comprise a series of connected roof trusses, or rafters and purlins, supported by the external walls. To prevent the roofs from spreading, each pair of rafters is tied together with collars.

Aisled framing

Timber-frame houses of any form can be extended relatively easily by adding an 'aisle' down one or both sides at ground floor level – hence the name 'aisled framing'. This is quite a common feature on some oak barns and is achieved by simply building a new outer wall and extending the principal rafters down so that they're supported on the new wall posts.

How they were built

Early carpenters designed the frames with mortise and tenon joints held in place using timber pegs. The main components would be

fabricated in workshops, where huge green oak timbers were cut, planed and shaped to form a massive skeleton, ready to be transported in kit form and joined together on-site. With the structural skeleton erected the joints were secured using tightly cleft oak pegs or dowels and hammered wedges. Tudor timber-frame walls were originally left exposed, the spaces in between packed with a simple infill of wattle and daub, later superseded by panels of brick noggin.

Oak was the timber of choice due to its strength and incredible durability, although elm was also widely used. Oak is a harder timber than elm as well as being denser. The inner heartwood of oak is technically classified as being naturally very durable, and therefore doesn't need treating with chemical preservatives (it's actually extremely resistant to such treatment). English elm is classified as non-durable, and is potentially more prone to

physically snapping, hence loadings and spans would be less demanding than for an equivalent piece of oak. Trees were selected for individual parts of the frame depending on their height, girth and shape, particularly for cruck frames.

However, demand for oak from the shipbuilding and iron industries eventually led to a shortage of native hardwoods. By the 18th century, deal (pine redwood timber) was becoming more commonly used in house construction, but, being less durable than traditional oak, would usually be clad externally, for example with tiles or weatherboarding. This also led to the demise of traditional wooden-pegged joints, with most jointing of timbers instead relying on wrought iron nails, or sometimes straps and bolts.

Durability

The oak used to build house structures was usually green, ie unseasoned, making it easier to work. In contrast, timber used for joinery would be well seasoned. Oak is so dense that it can take many years to reach the state where the natural sap fluids have dried off and it's finished twisting and cracking. Once seasoned, oak becomes extremely hard. So in a building's initial years the internal moisture in the green oak would naturally dry out, shrinking widthways across the grain more than lengthways. This had the effect of tightening up the joints in the structure and making the frame even stronger, but it also created minor splits along the grain known as 'shakes'. To modern eyes these can look quite alarming, but were simply a natural part of the drying process. The propensity of green oak to shrink needs to be borne in mind when carrying out repairs. Specifying winter-felled timber, which contains less sap, should help reduce the extent of subsequent shrinkage.

The key to longevity with timber-frame buildings of all types is to ensure they're protected from prolonged dampness, especially by keeping the lower timbers well clear of the ground. So keeping an eye on maintenance, especially when it comes to fixing any leaks, and giving wattle and daub panels an occasional lick of limewash, should keep the framework healthy. Thanks to the amazing durability of oak, old posts or beams are often found to be in surprisingly sound condition even where their outer appearance is poor. So stripping out and replacing timber sections should rarely be necessary, unless a building has been severely neglected or mistreated.

Above: Daisywheel symbol

Right: Fire insurance tag

Below: Original carpenter's alignment marks

Baz Mogridge

Cladding, infill and finishes

Not all timber-frame houses display their structures openly. As we have seen, some were covered up from the word go, particularly when oak was unavailable and less durable types of timber had to be employed. A thick external coating of lime render was sometimes originally applied over a backing layer of lath, or a surface cladding of tiles or weatherboarding may have been added in a bid to protect the structure concealed behind.

Properties were sometimes also modified retrospectively as a means of improving insulation. Bare walls could be prone to draughts and heat loss, and in exposed locations wind-driven rain might penetrate junctions between frames and infill panels. This is one reason why so many timber-frame buildings had their original thin wattle and daub replaced with more robust solid brickwork.

One clue to whether a property was originally clad is where there are telltale rows of nail holes on the posts. This is likely to indicate that timber laths were previously fixed to the frame for plastering.

However, the reason why many such buildings were subsequently given a new look is simply down to changes in architectural taste. Numerous houses in both urban and rural areas were re-fronted with fashionable brick or stone during the Georgian era. Few could afford to live in a new classically-styled house, so more economic ways of transforming existing buildings became popular. Many outmoded Tudor homes were given a radical makeover, sprouting symmetrical facades of solid masonry with high parapets, and fashionable sash windows in lieu of old casements. To make these remodelling works more affordable, often only the elevation facing the street would be re-clad. Hence one clue to such alterations can sometimes be gleaned where there is an alleyway to the side or rear of the house; here you can often spot the surviving original Tudor structure in all its glory. So a large number of what appear to be classic 'Georgian' houses are in fact re-faced Tudor concealed behind new frontages.

But re-fronting sometimes comprised more than the addition of a simple facade. The Victorians were particularly fond of building large extensions along the whole front elevation. These might be one room deep or at least of sufficient depth to form a new entrance hall.

Timber frame walls are relatively thin

Historic markings

During restoration work be sure to keep an eye open for ancient symbols and historic markings. One symbol found ingrained in timber posts is the 'daisywheel'. This was a geometrical constructional reference comprising a numerical sequence to help calculate which timbers to join together and in what order to erect them. But similar ritual flower petal markings are believed to have been good luck symbols, affording protection against ill fortune.

Ships' timbers were sometimes recycled for housing and in coastal areas subject to fierce winds and storms, tales abound of wrecked sailing ships providing a welcome windfall of well-seasoned building timber. So where inexplicable marks or odd-shaped cuts are encountered it can sometimes suggest a piece of timber had a previous maritime incarnation.

Repairing wattle and daub

There's nothing quite as satisfying as repairing your house with the materials from which it was built, especially when they are available locally, and are mostly free.

- Cement render should be removed with care, to preserve as much of the historic fabric as possible.
- Gently pick out any rotten or beetle-infested withies. These can be replaced by weaving in new hazel wands wrapped around riven oak laths. Where a panel has completely disintegrated, a new one will need to be made, as shown below.
- Ready-mixed daub can be purchased or conventional hair lime putty render can be applied to the wattle base. But it can be more satisfying (and cheaper) to mix your own daub. This is made traditionally from sticky clay-based earth (originally dug from the subsoil around the house) mixed with straw and water. A typical daub mix might contain approximately 35% local subsoil, 35% sharp sand plus equal measures of chopped straw and non-hydraulic lime (lime putty) – with the option of adding a final dollop or two of dried cow or horse dung. Recycled ground-up old daub can also be added to the mix.
- To make daub, first lay the clay-rich earth on a board and remove any large stones. Then break it into lumps using a long-handled sledgehammer. Add any salvaged old daub and sprinkle on loose straw. Mix it fairly dry then add small amounts of water until the daub is sticky and pliable with the consistency of Plasticine – *ie* fairly stiff. If it's too wet it won't grip the wattlework and will slough off.

- Apply the daub by pressing it firmly into the wattle panel. Push the mix through the sticks so it wraps around each one.
- Build up the daub in horizontal layers with minimal air voids. The daub is set back about 10mm from the face of the timber frame to leave space for a later lime render finish. The inside face can either be left exposed or built up with daub so that it combines with the mix you've just squashed through the wattlework – once the outer face is complete, but before it starts to dry out. A better option is to employ a friend do this whilst you're building up the outside, so you can have fun daubing from both sides at the same time!
- While the face of the daub is still sticky, use a wooden stick to scratch a criss-cross pattern as a key for the later plaster coat. Depending on the weather and the thickness of panel, the daub may take a few weeks to dry.
- Once dry it should be finished with a thin layer of lime plaster. The optimum mix will depend on local conditions, but experts swear by a mix of one part sand to three parts lime putty incorporating finely chopped donkey hair. A slightly rougher traditional finish can be achieved with a wooden float.
- Finally paint the panels with two or three coats of limewash (and an annual coat thereafter).

Freshly cut hazel wands placed within new oak timber framework to build up new wattle background. Daub can be mixed by welly power (left) or hair lime pressed into the wattlework (right)

Unstable brickwork was exposed behind render; rotten timbers were replaced with reclaimed oak

Mix of new and recycled brick infill

Types of cladding and infill

Maintaining claddings, infill panels and finishes is fundamental to the health of timber-frame houses. However, there are a number of different types of cladding:

WATTLE AND DAUB

Wattle and daub was the most common original method used to infill panels between timber posts and beams. A thin fence-like grid of wattlework was woven from bendable sticks of hazel or riven strips of oak or chestnut. Alternatively sticks were sometimes tied together with twine. The ends of the horizontal withies and vertical staves were then wedged into small holes or grooves cut into the sides of the surrounding timber-frame members.

Above: Viewed from indoors - with instruction to builders not to damage the historic fabric

Left: Render hacked off reveals infill of clay-rich mud

Below: Cement rendered panels exacerbate decay

On to this backing grid, a sticky mix of mud or 'daub' was pressed and applied in layers. Daub comprised a mix of clay-based local earth and lime reinforced with chopped straw, and sometimes with added chalk, grass or animal hair. Traditionally cattle were used to tread the mix, hence the extra ingredient of cow dung often found in daub mixes, but this isn't essential for repair work!

Being relatively easy to apply and the materials being free, this ancient method of producing cladding continued in use in rural areas up to the 19th century.

The finished surface was either simply limewashed or, more commonly, given protective coatings of lime render and limewash and distempered internally.

Today, when modern cement render is removed from old timber-frame walls, the hard cement coating will usually pull away some of the daub, but with luck the panels may only need re-rendering with lime plaster. However, moisture trapped for many years behind hard render is a common cause of deterioration to ancient wattlework, and where fungal decay or wood beetle attack has caused it to lose some of its structural strength it will need repair or replacement. Where old daub has become friable and loose it can normally be recycled by being ground up for reuse in the new mix, as described opposite.

Where larger areas of wattle and daub need to be replaced, such as to gable end walls,

Breathable modern infill material - woodwool boards (magnesite bound) can be lime rendered; here shown hammering oakum caulking into the gaps at edges

modern hempcrete blocks can provide an excellent alternative. Made from a mix of natural hemp fibre and a lime binder, these are readily available from specialist suppliers. Hempcrete has long been used in France in traditional properties, because it has the same stiffness, breathability and flexibility as wattle and daub. It also has the important added benefit of being a very effective insulation material.

LIME RENDER

A simple coating of lime render applied to the walls was a popular way of protecting timber-frame structures. This would normally be applied over a background of timber laths, in a similarly way to ceilings and internal walls. You may also come across evidence of more recent repair attempts where render has been applied to a backing of expanded metal mesh in lieu of timber laths.

Render was sometimes given an ornamental finish known as pargetting, as described in the previous chapter. This was particularly fashionable between the 16th and 18th centuries. In the later Georgian and Victorian eras the deception was sometimes elaborated further with a coating of fashionable stucco, designed to mimic expensive cut stonework. Even roughcast finishes were sometimes applied. So it's not always obvious whether an old house with rendered elevations is of timber-frame or solid masonry

Above: Lime rendered infill panels

Above right: External nail holes indicate it was clad originally

Right: New lath nailed to frame

construction, though one obvious clue can sometimes be gleaned by thumping the wall and listening for a hollow sound.

The most common problem today is where modern cement render and plastic masonry paints have been applied. Hard cement render is extremely grippy, and if it's very firmly adhered removing it might pull away the original fabric, causing damage. This is more of a problem on softer backgrounds such as wattle and daub panels or earth buildings, where trapped damp may have caused further erosion, in some cases even making the wall unstable. However, even where a wall suffers some cosmetic damage in the removal process it shouldn't make much difference as you'll probably want to apply new lime render.

TILE HANGING

Many timber-frame buildings have had their walls weather-proofed by being clad with clay tiles (or less commonly with slates), hung from timber battens fixed across the main walls. As with mathematical tiles (see next column) it was the imposition of the 1784 Brick Tax that led to a surge in the popularity of tile hanging as a more economic alternative, ultimately changing the character

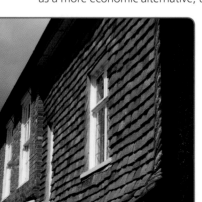

of many towns. Tile hanging was particularly popular in Surrey, Kent and Sussex where it suited the lightweight timber-frame techniques in use in the early 19th century. This is generally a long-lasting form of cladding. Where problems do develop over time, they're much the same as for roofs, *ie* the original fixing nails can be prone to rust, although it's comparatively rare for battens to suffer timber decay.

BRICK TILES

One of the most ingenious methods of tax evasion yet devised arose in response to the 1784 Brick Tax. Special tiles designed to imitate bricks, known as 'mathematical tiles', could provide what appeared to be a fashionable brick facade entirely tax-free. In fact brick tiles had originally been introduced in the mid-18th century, as a way of giving the front of timber-frame houses a more fashionable appearance, but the Brick Tax boosted their popularity until it was eventually repealed in 1850. A later version with a black-glazed face can also be seen in some seaside towns, mainly in Kent and Sussex.

Mathematical tiles are hung in the same way as conventional plain wall tiles, nailed to battens or wood lathing fixed to the timber frame. To complete the deception, the tiles were pointed in mortar, just like conventional brickwork. The amazing thing is just how convincing the tiles actually look – even to the extent of fooling professional surveyors. However, telltale signs can be seen in the detailing around windows, which only have a shallow reveal, and the comparative thinness of the walls compared to solid masonry. Sometimes the tile profile can be glimpsed at corners, where for example they might abut a rendered side elevation, although the illusion of brickwork is sometimes perpetuated with special corner tiles designed to maintain the bond.

WEATHERBOARDING

The practice of cladding timber-frame houses with overlapping horizontal weatherboards to throw off rain from the walls was customary in Essex, and became fashionable in nearby counties such as Kent, Sussex and Surrey

Lead apron protects vulnerable ledge at base of cladding from ponding of rain water

from the early 19th century. After the Brick Tax was introduced oak and elm weatherboarding was widely used as a relatively cheap form of cladding for poorer cottages and terraces, particularly in rural areas, in lieu of more expensive tiles.

The simplest type would be made from oak or elm with the bark left on, known as 'waney edge'. These rough-hewn, undulating boards with a wavy profile were traditionally used for farm buildings, but had become fashionable for homes by the late 18th century.

Early 'straight plank' weatherboarding used thick feathered boards pegged to the timber frame in broader widths. This was superseded in the 19th century by cheaper softwood nailed to studs, some later examples having a beaded edge.

But timber cladding doesn't always resemble the traditional black 'barn style' variety so familiar today. In the Victorian era smooth timber boarding was sometimes cunningly disguised to mimick stone blocks by means of highly skilled paintwork. To further resemble masonry, simulated vertical 'joints' were sometimes scored into the wood to augment the horizontal tongue-and-groove joints of the cladding. Where you find relatively narrow boarding of a perfectly uniform width and finish it's likely to be more modern machined softwood.

It's generally best to avoid disturbing old timber boarding, as it tends to be rather brittle. Where there's localised decay, try to replace the rotten areas in a way that causes minimum disturbance to surrounding boards. Being relatively thin, modern softwood boards are unlikely to match the originals, and can be prone to curling. So sourcing suitable replacements for repair work may mean ordering specially milled boards.

LIMEWASH

Although not a cladding as such, limewash was commonly applied as a finish to new timber-frame buildings to provide protection to the fabric. This was particularly important at the vulnerable crevices and joints between infill panels and the main timbers. Today limewash is recommended because it allows buildings to perform as originally intended – as breathing structures.

Above and below: This property required major structural repair work, retaining sound original timber where possible

Above and below left: A classic case of rot to timber posts revealed by removal of cement render.

Below: A bad sign - cement rendered panels

John Partridge, timberframerestoration.co.uk

What can go wrong?

Traditional timber-frame buildings work in a very simple way, with the loadings transferred entirely through the timber skeleton. The role of the panels in between is essentially to insulate the house and keep the weather at bay. Where such buildings haven't been altered over the years and still function in this way, in order to survey the structure you simply need to think of it as a load-bearing framework. Starting at the top of the house, by considering how each timber member is connected to the next you can trace the route that the loadings follow down to the ground.

However, things can become considerably more complex where buildings have been altered. For example, it's very common for old infill panels to have been replaced with brick. Sometimes parts of the frame itself have been removed and bricked up. As a result the frame may no longer be functioning as originally intended, with some walls having now evolved into what is effectively a masonry structure with a few timbers embedded in it. In fact most surviving timber-frame houses are a combination of a partially load-bearing frame and a masonry structure. This isn't necessarily a problem. What is of concern is where such alterations have inadvertently caused instability or timber decay. To make matters worse,

such defects are often concealed, so if repairs are needed they're likely to be costly and disruptive. To get an accurate assessment of condition it's important to obtain a survey from a specialist surveyor.

Why timber-frame buildings fail

There are five main reasons why timber-frame buildings fail:

1 Cement rendering

Many properties have suffered from being rendered or repaired with modern cement render, especially to wattle and daub panels. Unlike traditional lime render, cement is hard and impermeable. Because it's not sufficiently flexible this leads to cracking and ingress of water, particularly around panel edges. The damp then becomes trapped, raising the moisture content of the timber and making it more vulnerable to decay. In time the timber becomes weakened and the joints start to fail.

Removing cement render from panels of wattle and daub or soft red brick can raise a bit of a dilemma for Conservation Officers, because the works are likely to cause damage, by pulling off the face of the daub or brickwork, or as a result of vibration dislodging whole panels. But this risk needs to be balanced against the importance of saving the timber structure. Brick noggin infill is, in any case, rarely original.

2 Change to infill panels

Timber frames were commonly built with 4in (100mm) thick timbers, containing wattle and daub infill panels that were originally plastered flush with the framework. But in many properties the wattle and daub panels have long ago been replaced with a brick infill.

Sometimes bricks were laid on edge, but this made panels very thin and cold, so most were laid flat, often in a herringbone pattern. But because the bricks were slightly wider than the 4in deep frame (typically 115mm) they may no longer be entirely flush, projecting slightly and forming a ledge on which water collects. Over time this can cause the timbers to rot from the bottom up.

3 Quality of timber

Sometimes elm or less hardy softwood timber was used to build the structural frame. Being less resilient to rot and beetle attack than oak, such timbers can be more prone to decay when exposed to

Less durable softwood frame

Sole plate at very low level will be vulnerable – reducing ground levels could help

persistently damp conditions. Even so, compared to most modern timber they're generally of superior quality and are relatively durable.

4 Botched alterations

It's not unknown for careless owners to saw through inconveniently located tie beams at the base of roof trusses in a bid to create extra headroom, *eg* for a new doorway. But without lateral restraint from the tie beam the roof may be at risk of spreading.

5 Rotten sole plates

Sole plates are the big horizontal timber beams that sit on top of a building's masonry plinth, forming the bottom rail or sill of the frame, hence they're also known as 'sill beams'. The vertical posts and studs that make up the frame above are fixed at their bases into the sole plate with mortise and tenon joints. Sole plates are very effective at distributing these point loadings across the base of the building. Unfortunately, despite their size, these chunky beams can be vulnerable to rot if exposed to damp over a long period of time, usually at the point where they sit on the plinth below. This is typically due to high ground levels or because the sole plate has been sealed by a coat of cement or plastic paint. The most vulnerable area is at the bottom outer corners, where any softening of the timber from rot can cause the timber frame above to lean.

Above: Painted joints trap water, with decay accelerated by cement filler and mastic patching

Below: Rotten lower timber studs cut away awaiting splicing in of new

How tough is wattle and daub?

The spray test

There's a very simple test that demonstrates how wattle and daub panels in traditional timber-frame buildings cope with rain. If you wet the panel using a hose to simulate rain, being a porous material it naturally absorbs much of the water. As a result there's surprisingly little initial water run-off at the base of the panel where it meets the timber frame. Despite the extent of the absorption, the water doesn't actually penetrate all the way through the relatively thin (4in) wall panel. Once the weather is dry, the water temporarily absorbed into the wattle and daub evaporates away and naturally dries out.

But what happens where wattle and daub panels have been coated with modern masonry paints, or rendered in hard cement render? Substituting a concrete paving slab for the original panel for the purpose of testing simulates such impervious surfaces. When subjected to the same spray test there's a dramatic change in performance. Instead of being absorbed, all the water runs off and much of it penetrates through small cracks around the panel. Then later, when it comes to the drying-out process, the impervious material prevents the water from easily evaporating, with the result that the timber frame is subjected to prolonged damp.

This demonstrates why, when modern masonry paints or cement renders are applied, trapped water will encourage the early onset of decay to the timber frame. However, this test doesn't take into account the fact that hairline surface cracks that develop over time in modern paints and renders will exacerbate the problem by admitting and trapping moisture, a common cause of damp and decay to old wattle and daub panels.

Based on tests conducted by Richard Oxley.

Damaging thick sealant painted over timbers has started to peel

Timber decay

Oak is remarkably resistant to water, to the extent that it was sometimes even used for pile foundations in marshy ground. But original softwoods can also prove surprisingly durable, hardening with age. The durability of a particular piece of timber very much depends on what part of the tree it was originally cut from. Timber from the outer sapwood will have less resistance to attack from rot, whereas the inner heartwood is far tougher, the heartwood of oak being especially resilient.

Hidden structure revealed

Assessing timber-frame houses

Above: Not the real deal - stick on mock timber has dropped off!

Left: Movement evident to a joint

Right: Typical post and beam structure

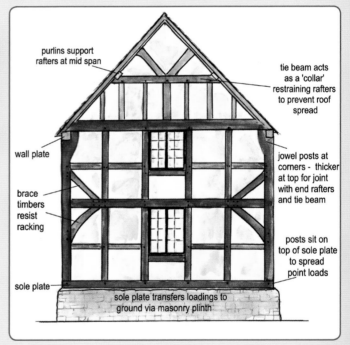

purlins support rafters at mid span

tie beam acts as a 'collar' restraining rafters to prevent roof spread

wall plate

jowel posts at corners - thicker at top for joint with end rafters and tie beam

brace timbers resist racking

posts sit on top of sole plate to spread point loads

sole plate

sole plate transfers loadings to ground via masonry plinth

Identification

- What type is it – cruck, box frame, or aisled?
- How are the joints between main timber members formed – mortise and tenon, or bolted?

Structure performance

- Is the timber frame still performing as intended? If any timbers have been altered or are missing the building may have become a 'composite' structure, where some masonry walls are inadvertently playing a supporting role.
- Are the masonry walls strong enough to provide support? A common problem is where relatively thin brick infill panels have assumed a structural role to which they're unsuited, because the timber sole plate below has rotted.
- Are the joints to the timber skeleton sound, with sufficient flexibility to accommodate minor movement? Retaining flexibility at joints is now understood to be a key part of maintaining timber-frame structures. Some past attempts at repair using epoxy resin with steel or GRP dowels have caused problems by making the once flexible joints rigid.

- Consider the timber framework as a 3D skeletal structure where internal walls and ceiling joists are as much part of the framework as the main wall timbers.
- Are any areas suffering from decay?
- Have any past repairs been carried out?

Cladding and infill panels

- Was the original timber frame exposed or was it protected, for example by cladding, lime rendering or limewash?
- Have any alterations been made, for example have original cladding or finishes been removed or concealed?
- Have any damaging modern materials been used to clad or repair the building?

Thick cement render cut away to check condition of decaying beam

Frame repaired in matching oak (left) clad in new lath ready for lime rendering (right)

Intricate repair to historic oak frame detailing uses original as template (from house below)

Heritage-house.org

sensible to 'correct' irregularities. Where repairs are needed it's important to try and retain original features, such as wattle and daub panels and historic windows, even if a certain amount of decay is evident.

On Listed buildings Conservation Officers may take the view that some old repairs or alterations have over time become part of the building's history, in which case they may need to be retained, although such decisions can be debateable.

As a rule it's best to avoid the 'nuclear option' of stripping the timber-frame structure right back to its bare skeleton. As well as saving a lot of unnecessary extra work and expense, it pre-empts the likely loss of original fabric. Stripping old structures can cause them to become unstable, particularly where decay has occurred. Cladding, infill panels and roof battens all help provide strength by bracing the overall structure. Where stripping can't be avoided, it's best carried out one section at a time.

In theory a timber-frame structure should be relatively easy to repair, but careless surgery over the years may have dramatically altered the way the building works. Inconvenient beams might have been cut or radically trimmed to make space for a new doorway, or a projecting roof brace might have been sawn off to install a dormer window. As a result, a building can morph over time into a complex matrix of interconnecting parts. Once a structural member has been cut away or has failed the building will jiggle about as the loadings find a new way to transfer to other supporting members, so things aren't always held up by the obvious route.

So as long as a piece of timber that's periodically exposed to damp is able to dry out, rot shouldn't take hold. The chance of fungal decay occurring is far greater where damp becomes trapped, usually as a result of buildings being decorated inside or out with modern waterproof renders, plasters or impermeable paints. Persistent damp softens fibres, turning wood into an attractive food source for fungi and insects.

The risk of rot and deterioration also depends on the timber's location within the building. Most vulnerable will be those exposed to persistent leaks from defective roofs, sills, gutters and downpipes, as well as those located near ground level, especially the horizontal sole plates at the base of the frame.

There are a number of simple tests you can do to assess the extent of surface decay. Some selective probing with a blunt screwdriver is a simple method of checking resistance. To see if there's any deeper hidden decay below the surface try 'sounding' the timbers by tapping them with the wooden handle of a screwdriver and listening for any hollow sounds. Gently inserting a thin blade at timber joints should reveal whether the tenons are still present.

A professional assessment is likely to employ in addition more sophisticated, non-destructive techniques such as micro-drilling, ultrasound scanning, or even heat-sensitive photography.

Timber frame repairs

Timber-frame structures naturally flex and settle, and over the course of several centuries many have evolved into pleasingly distorted shapes, something that's very much part of their character. Movement is natural in timber, so it's not usually

Localised decay to dormer timber frame sensitively replaced in new oak

Heritage-house.org

ROD AND RESIN BEAM REPAIRS

Where historic timber beams have been weakened, and replacement is not an option, a 'rod and resin' repair can provide a useful solution. This 'invisibly' strengthens the beam, increasing its overall load capacity by around 100%, allowing it to continue performing a structural role.

The beam is supported and a slot is cut along the top.

Reinforcing bars are placed into the groove as per structural engineer's calculations.

Bars are laid one above another separated by small spacers.

An epoxy grout is poured into the slot, covering the upper bar completely. If a cosmetic finish is required to the upper surface, the top can be filled with a timber fillet.

Trace Remedial Building Services

TIMBER RESIN SPLICE (TRS) METHOD

'TRS' is a method of making in situ repairs to structural timbers such as internal beams and floor joists. It has the advantage of retaining sound original fabric with minimal upheaval to adjoining ceilings etc. Decayed beam or joist ends are first removed. Suitable new lengths of replacement timber are cut to size with connector rods factory-fitted. Holes or slots are then cut into the remaining original beam to accommodate the new rods. Finally special resin is injected or poured in forming a very strong bond between the new and old materials. The completed repair is claimed to have greater structural strength than the parent timber.

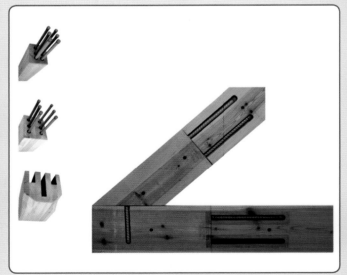

All photos courtesy   DC Moore and PropertyRepairSystems.co.uk

'To cut or not to cut'

The reason timber is an excellent structural material is because it works well both in compression (resisting crushing forces) and in tension (resisting being stretched). For example, in a typical beam or floor joist supported under each end both these forces will be acting simultaneously; as the upper half of the joist is compressed (as gravity and loadings from people walking on the floor push it down), the lower half is being pulled apart in tension. This is why cutting notches in joists must be done where it has least impact: notches for pipes should be cut from the top no deeper than one-eighth the depth of the joist, and holes for cables should be drilled in the narrow central horizontal band running halfway down between the tension and compression zones. No cuts should be made in the first quarter of the span from either end.

Structural repairs

Hacking off cement render reveals brick infill and extensive decay to frame. Structure needed substantial rebuilding with new oak posts (mainly to ground floor), new corner posts, sole plate and horizontal floor beam. As much of the original framework was retained as possible.

For anything other than minor repairs it's always advisable to consult a structural engineer with experience of period timber-frame buildings. With all repairs, the cause of any rot and decay must first be treated. And before any work commences it's important to record the condition and position of individual elements by taking photos and making drawings. Where repair work involves removal of timbers they should be numbered and labelled.

It's worth noting that removed sections of old timber are likely to have been of much better quality and durability than any modern replacement, because unlike much of today's timber it was naturally seasoned. So it may be possible to salvage some choice cuts from larger removed lengths that aren't decayed.

A lot of repair work involves strengthening individual broken or weakened timbers. There's normally more than one way this can be achieved, but the optimum solution will depend to some extent on how visible the finished repair will be.

There are three main repair options where a structural element is failing:

1 Resin repairs

Although widely specified until quite recently, the use of resins is now frowned upon by conservationists for the repair of exposed external timbers. The concern is that filling rotten pockets in timber can accelerate decay if moisture gets trapped between the timber and the resin. However, where the wooden body behind a decorative timber surface has rotted away resin can be a useful material to replace it, helping to preserve the original appearance of the timber.

Graphite reinforcement bar encased in resin

2 Metal straps

Purpose-made iron and steel straps are a traditional and widely used method of strengthening failing joints. Alternatively a pair of steel plates can sometimes be very effective for reinforcing a section of weakened timber, with one plate fitted either side and bolted through. A more subtle, indeed virtually invisible repair can sometimes be achieved using steel 'flitch plates', where a length of steel is sandwiched inside a timber beam. This option is explored in Chapter 12.

Repairing a major component such as a cracked roof plate might involve piecing in a new section of oak using stainless steel rods to stop any further movement, and the repair concealed if necessary by covering with pieces of matching timber.

Where leaning walls – particularly at gable ends – need to be restrained, steel cables can sometimes be used to provide

2 forms of steel ties

almost invisible support. Because these methods involve minimal intervention or disturbance to historic fabric and are also reversible they're generally acceptable to conservationists.

Where steel has been used, rather than traditional iron, it can be prone to corrosion from tannic acids found in oak, so it's important to specify stainless or galvanised mild steel, or paint it with protective red oxide. To ensure that straps remain secure even with future movement of the timber, stainless steel nuts and bolts are usually the best fixing option.

3 Carpentry repairs

It's often possible to cut out a section of timber, such as a rotten beam or floor joist end, and replace it with a matching new piece. 'Scarf joints' are commonly used to join two pieces of timber in the direction of their length. The simplest type of scarfing involves cutting out a matching section of wood from the ends of both the new and the old beam so that they neatly overlap when joined together. With skill, new pieces can sometimes be designed to lock in place simply by force of friction, but more often they're bolted or cramped to allow for shrinkage over time. For small patch or scarf repairs it's best to specify air-dried timber (ideally seasoned oak) for added strength, and to minimise subsequent movement from drying out and shrinkage.

New oak brace timber and brick infill

Beam repair using TRS system

Bladed scarf joint

For larger repairs, in some cases there may be no option but to completely remove a damaged component and install an entirely new timber member in its place. As with smaller repairs, the problem with using new green timber is that it will naturally season and continue to shrink, so there's a danger it can push itself out of place and add damaging stresses to the existing structure. It's therefore better to select an older, seasoned piece of oak (for example, six- to nine-year-old English oak).

DC Moore / Property Repair Systems

New oak beam being cut to size (above) to replace original rotten section under window. It is joined to the remaining original beam on either side and secured with bolts

Omec

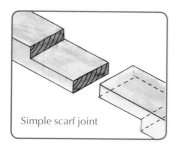

Simple scarf joint

However, where extensive areas of a building's timber framework need replacing in their entirety, green oak may be suitable, as when it was originally built. But this, of course, means you need to allow for subsequent shrinkage and movement. The fresh oak will slowly shrink across its width, so the infill panels are liable to develop cracks around their outsides. Exposed external joints can be finished with marine caulking or hemp/Stockholm tar, which will allow them to flex and move.

Where a piece of timber is of historic interest but is weak or broken, to save cutting it and losing part of the original fabric additional support could be provided by propping it with a strut, or suspending it from above with a vertical hanger. Alternatively a weakened section of timber can be reinforced by attaching a wooden splint or metal plate alongside, which will have the effect of reducing loadings, whilst retaining the original material. Cutting a deep central groove along an old beam and inserting a metal plate or rods is another possible option – see pages 108 and 164.

However, the simplest solution is probably to just run a new

temporarily supported by using suitable Acrow props. Also it's quite common for the masonry plinth to need at least partial rebuilding.

When replacing key structural timber components such as this it's a false economy to try to save money using cheaper wood – it's normally best to specify oak because of its incredible durability.

Until recently it was standard modern practice for builders to place a strip of lead directly underneath when a new sole plate was installed, with the intention of protecting it from damp from the masonry below. But in fact this can often have the opposite effect, as rainwater running down the building can accumulate and become trapped under the timber beam, setting up the conditions for deterioration and decay. It's now considered better to use traditional methods and sit the new plate on a bed of lime mortar that allows water to drain freely. Pieces of slate or tile can be used to help level any uneven surfaces.

Where rotten sill plates have been removed in the past, instead of replacing them with a matching oak beam builders have sometimes botched the job by inserting a couple of courses of brickwork. The trouble with this method is that whereas a lengthy beam will automatically accommodate and spread the very high point loads at the base of each post, individual bricks are likely to move under pressure, resulting in localised settlement. For the same reason it's best not to replace a rotten sole plate with short lengths of timber. If it's not replaced entirely, then a new beam of reasonable length will be necessary to spread the point loads.

Acrow prop supports structure above

Sole plate and lower framework replaced whilst retaining sound upper structure

Heavy lifting – repaired oak frame being re-installed

Substantial new sole plate with original posts retained

length of timber alongside the old one to relieve it by taking most of the load. In some cases it needn't even be attached to the original beam. Obviously it's important to select a suitable piece of timber, both in terms of strength and aesthetics. It may initially look a little stark against the old one, but over time it should blend in, which from a conservation perspective is preferable to staining.

Replacing a sole plate

Timbers at low level are relatively vulnerable to decay, and this is particularly the case with the sole plates that sit on top of the masonry plinth at the base to the timber structure. Where a sole plate has rotted to the extent that it's no longer able to perform its structural role, it will need to be replaced. This is clearly a major undertaking. In order to remove the defective beam and jack a new one into position, the structure above will need to be

8 STRUCTURAL MOVEMENT

There's a clue in the name. It's not unusual for old dormers to have settled over time

That should stop it! Buttress plus tie bars.

Old buildings rarely come in perfectly square packages. Over their lifetime they'll invariably have suffered a certain amount of structural movement, often due to shallow foundations or because ancient timbers have naturally seasoned and twisted. Indeed, much of their character is down to the fact that not everything is precisely true and level.

Although cracked or wonky walls can sometimes appear quite alarming, it's important not to panic; most properties have stood the test of time and are perfectly sound. But that hasn't stopped some owners from embarking on a misguided crusade to try and straighten things.

Fortunately there's a lot of truth in the saying 'old buildings don't subside, they just find a more comfortable way of standing up'. But

as with any property, structural problems can sometimes develop, often as a result of prolonged periods of neglect. Poor maintenance is often the catalyst that leads to structural failure. A drip from a broken gutter can, over time, rot a structural timber. Or a drain left leaking for years on end can ultimately be the cause of subsidence. Botched structural alterations are another common cause of movement, as the house tries to accommodate new loadings.

Footings and settlement

Many old houses were built with little in the way of foundations. A strip of topsoil would typically have been scraped away to reveal a firmer layer of subsoil onto which brick or stone footings would be laid.

Timber frame buildings are renowned for their ability to accommodate movement

Classic stepped footings below ground level

Spot the culprit – corner cracking with adjacent tree

Footings are traditional foundations, pre-dating modern concrete strips which superseded them from the 1930s. They were built in a stepped configuration, widening out at the base to spread the load, like sticking out feet.

Old footings may extend into the ground by anything from a few inches to about half a metre. As a result, in the early years after construction it was common for walls to settle down as the ground beneath compressed. Only where properties were built with basements would the foundations have been much deeper.

Temporary timber props support cob wall while movement is investigated

One of the key differences between period properties and their modern counterparts is the way they cope with movement. Modern houses are designed as rigid structures, with deep concrete foundations normally extending at least a metre underground, penetrating below the relatively unstable upper layers of the soil that are prone to frost penetration and seasonal moisture changes. In contrast, old houses were built to accommodate a certain amount of movement rather than trying to prevent it occurring.

As we saw in the previous chapter, it's the use of lime that's crucial in allowing gentle movement to occur over a wide area through mortar joints. In contrast, hard modern cement is rigid and inflexible, firmly resisting movement instead of accommodating it, resulting in cracking, often through the brick or stonework.

It's a similar story with rendered walls. Whereas hard cement coatings simply crack, allowing rain into the wall and trapping it, lime render can absorb a certain amount of deformation.

Soil types and seasonal movement

The type of ground the house is built on is a major factor in determining its potential for movement. Chalk and rock are generally the firmest types of subsoil. Sand and gravel also have good load-bearing strength when well compacted. Worst of all is peat, which has very poor load-bearing capacity.

Shrinkable clay is one of the most common subsoils in Britain and is prone to seasonal changes, drying out in summer, shrinking and cracking in times of drought. In wetter months it's prone to swelling, and heavy frosts can cause the ground to expand and heave. All of this is exacerbated by the effects of tree roots and changes to the underground water table.

Inevitably, houses with shallow foundations built on shrinkable clay will be more likely to experience seasonal movement, but with our modern-day paranoia about even the tiniest of cracks we sometimes forget that where a building has stood for hundreds of years it will have been exposed to such movement many times before. By monitoring cracks over time it can be established whether they simply open and close in tune with seasonal ground movement. As long as cracking gets no worse year on year, the chances are that no further action will be needed. The advice from the insurance industry is that there's only likely to be a long-term problem if cracks don't eventually close, or if they continue to open beyond widths of 5mm, in which case you should notify your insurance company.

Subsidence

The mere word 'subsidence' is enough to strike terror into the hearts of all but the hardiest of homeowners. It refers to the ground beneath a footing or foundation giving way as a result of external conditions that have nothing to do with the loadings placed on the ground by the building. This downward movement of the ground supporting a property is very different from a house that's settled over time as the ground is slowly compressed.

Subsidence tends to affect localised parts of a building after a change in the load-bearing capacity of the ground directly beneath it, and is usually identifiable by corresponding tapered cracking to the wall. One common cause of such 'ground collapse' is where leaking drains wash away or soften the soil, causing the structure above to drop. The effects of tree roots, droughts and heavy frosts can also contribute to destabilising the ground. Old mine workings can be another cause. As a direct result of such changes to ground conditions, the unsupported part of the wall immediately above can suddenly drop, separating itself from the rest of the structure.

But in our haste to lay the blame for cracking at the door of subsidence, the opposite problem of 'heave' is often overlooked.

Subsidence damage

Cracking in walls due to subsidence usually has the following distinctive features:

- Cracks extending through the damp-proof course down to the foundations.
- Vertical or diagonal cracks that taper in width from top to bottom (*ie* are wider at the top or V-shaped).
- Diagonal cracking is often symptomatic of localised subsidence, for example where the ground under a corner of the house has subsided due to a broken drain.
- Cracking on a wall is visible from both inside and outside the property.
- New distortion to the walls is likely to be reflected in doors and windows sticking severely.

Although much less common, heave is caused where the ground swells up and exerts an upward thrust on a building. The most likely cause is where large thirsty trees are felled (ironically, often as a precaution against the risk of subsidence!), causing the ground supporting the building to swell up as a direct result of all the moisture that's no longer being extracted.

Trees

Fast-growing trees and shrubs, especially thirsty broadleaf trees, will extract a lot of moisture from the soil and can upset ground conditions. A mature deciduous tree can remove in excess of 50,000 litres per year. Some of the worst offenders are poplars, oaks, willows, ash, plane and sycamore trees, but you need to be wary of any species of tree or shrub in close proximity to buildings. Roots can potentially extend more than one and a half times the mature height of the tree, so any structure within this 'influencing distance' may be affected, particularly where built on shrinkable clay. If the ground under part of the footings shrinks, normally as a result of dry weather and moisture extraction, it can rob the wall of support. The majority of subsidence claims involve trees, although sometimes they're an indirect cause – for example, where moisture-seeking roots enter underground drains, causing leakage, the ground can eventually become soft and marshy.

Despite these risks, there's a lot of paranoia about trees thanks largely to mortgage lenders insisting on standard tree warning phrases being inserted in valuation reports. This has sometimes panicked homeowners into a slash and burn mentality and unnecessary bouts of pre-emptive tree-felling which, as already mentioned, can actually make matters worse by causing the ground to heave. There's also a potential risk of legal issues arising where trees are subject to a Tree Preservation Order or protected within a Conservation Area. The sensible thing to do is obtain an arboricultural report from a tree specialist before firing up the chainsaw. Often the best approach is simply to manage the risk by reducing the amount of moisture being taken from the soil with some periodic pruning or pollarding.

Underpinning

Where part of a wall has cracked and sunk because the ground below has become unstable and can no longer support its weight, the standard response is to restore the lost support by underpinning it. This involves excavating down to stable ground and pumping the void full of concrete, which can be a very effective solution for modern houses with deep foundations.

But if the same remedy is applied to an old building it can prove disastrous. This is because the super-stiff new underpinned foundation will provide rock-solid support to one part of the structure, whilst the rest of the house continues its centuries-old tradition of gently flexing on its shallow footings. This simply moves the problem along a bit, with new stresses set up between the part of the building that's now rigid and those that remain flexible. This is likely to result in 'differential movement' causing fresh cracking at the junction of the repaired area.

If you suspect subsidence and notify your insurers, in the worst case they may insist on underpinning. Insurers and mortgage lenders actually have little understanding of old buildings, but this doesn't prevent them from sometimes stipulating inappropriate works. Underpinning is highly invasive and disruptive and can cause irreversible damage to old houses. It's not unknown for old buildings to actually collapse as the works are carried out, particularly properties with very shallow foundations or of earth construction. Underpinning is too heavy-handed a way of dealing with minor movement at the base of old walls. A better approach is to restore the support that's been lost using traditional materials rather than trying to bring part of the structure up to modern standards of rigidity. This can be done by 'underbuilding' the defective section of wall, laying down a few courses of brick or stone to re-establish contact with firm ground. The important point with structural repairs is that they should be in tune with the whole house and not just restricted to modernising one small part.

Assessing cracking

Cracking can sometimes be a danger sign, but more often it's simply telling you that the building is adjusting to changes in the weather and surrounding environment as the year progresses. As a rule of thumb, superficial cracks up to about 1mm wide are unlikely to be of any great concern. Localised movement can sometimes also be the result of the expansion and contraction of materials reacting to temperature changes from one season to

another, although lime can normally accommodate such forces. Cracks arising from these causes tend to be fairly narrow and uniform in width, and can be filled during routine maintenance or redecoration. This sort of cracking is more likely to occur where hard, inflexible modern plasters, renders and mortars have been applied to old walls.

It's extremely rare for cracking to be so bad that a building becomes structurally unsafe, so if you're confronted with what appears to be a gaping crevice in your wall the best advice is to keep calm. Cracks can easily be misinterpreted, which can result in unnecessary and damaging repair work. Surveyors who are unfamiliar with old buildings (and mindful of the risk of claims against them) may sometimes overreact to apparent structural problems.

The professionals best equipped to assess such concerns are structural engineers, although it's important they have experience of historic properties in the local area. Before recommending any action an engineer will normally try to establish which part of the building has moved and which has remained static. This normally involves monitoring over time and recording any further movement to determine whether or not it's continuing. Even if it turns out to be progressive, it may still not be considered serious enough to warrant carrying out any major remedial work. Monitoring should be carried out over at least a 12-month period to check whether cracks are simply opening and closing with the seasons, which shouldn't normally be a concern.

Before employing expensive experts it's often worth monitoring the cracking yourself. The simplest way to see if a crack is 'live' is to mark where it ends with a pencil and record the date. If the crack continues to grow, do the same again at regular intervals – rather like a height chart for growing children.

External cracks should be pointed up with lime mortar to prevent the ingress of water, and smaller internal cracks can be filled with a flexible plaster filler. With wider cracks it's worth recording the date they were filled in case they later open again.

Where structural repair work turns out to be necessary, a masonry wall can often be stabilised by 'stitching' the crack. This involves the insertion of stainless steel 'helibars' bedded horizontally into mortar either side of the crack. The bars are bonded in polyester resin and span across the crack, binding it together. Such repairs should be invisible once the wall has been pointed, and are completely reversible.

Historic movement

Most old buildings show signs of having moved in the past. Leaning walls and cracks in masonry are often symptoms of old foundation settlement or other longstanding structural movement that has now stabilised. All kinds of bulges and leans may have existed for many years and the building has adjusted quite happily and found a comfortable 'position of repose'. Old cracks will often have been filled with mortar, and if the crack hasn't subsequently reopened it indicates that the movement has ceased.

Long established leaning is rarely a problem

Helifix.co.uk

Left and below: Horizontal stainless steel reinforcing rods inserted to stabilise wall

Above: Old movement confers character

Right: Original timber doors can be adjusted over the years to fit distorted openings

Some very old buildings have moved so much over time that openings have distorted quite radically. Yet somehow the original timber windows and doors have been adjusted over the years to fit ever more bizarre shapes – a source of delight and character, and proof of sustainable construction.

Common areas where signs of historic movement can often be spotted are:

■ Distorted door openings where old doors have been trimmed into a tapered shape to fit.
■ Brickwork courses that rise and fall in old walls. The bricks were originally laid reasonably level but as the ground has shifted slowly over time the walls have adjusted. Crooked walls are rarely a cause for concern.
■ Old spreader plates and tie rods fitted to provide lateral restraint and tie in bulging walls. Sometimes installed at ceiling joist level to prevent 'roof spread', where the rafters push out the walls.

Right and below: Steel bars retain and strengthen walls whilst adding to period charm

■ Sloping floors where the resulting gap at the base of the skirting has been concealed by fitting beading or adjusting the skirting boards.
■ Parallel vertical cracks extending up the main walls. In houses where the window openings on each storey are positioned directly above each other – a common feature with Georgian architecture – thin vertical cracking can appear in the wall directly above or below the window reveals. This is because loadings are concentrated via tall masonry 'columns' either side of the openings.

Structural movement

Structural movement can manifest itself in different ways. Some common signs are:

■ New cracks appearing in the main walls or internal walls. New cracks can be distinguished because they're clean inside, whereas an old one reopening will contain dust or dirt. Cracking is generally tapered. Stresses in the main walls are sometimes accompanied by fresh cracking to ceilings.
■ Any openings in a wall are structural weak points, hence cracking commonly runs diagonally from the corners of windows and doors. However, cracks to plasterwork above windows may be a sign of rot in a hidden timber lintel.

Above: Dropped arch supported by Acrow prop

Helifix.co.uk

Above and below: External view of cracking and 'helibar' repair to stone building on opposite page

Helifix.co.uk

- Cracking due to foundation movement is usually more than about 3mm wide – the thickness of a one-pound coin.
- Bay windows are notorious for movement as they're often poorly tied to the main structure and have very shallow footings, but cracking between bays and the main house is sometimes seasonal, as the structure adjusts to changes in ground conditions.
- Windows and doors suddenly start to stick – but in winter this could simply be due to swelling from damp.

Recent alterations

There are plenty of old houses with inadequate foundations by today's standards that remain perfectly upright thanks to the walls being reasonably thick, with adequate restraint from floors and internal walls. It's only when such walls or floors are disturbed – such as when new openings are cut, or internal walls removed, causing new stresses – that trouble can really begin. Structural alterations are a fairly common cause of movement, but sometimes this is simply due to inadequate propping during works that caused temporary redistribution of heavy loadings on to weaker parts of the building. More worrying is where lofts have been converted, adding major new loads on the assumption that the existing structure can accommodate the weight.

Sometimes mysterious signs of movement arise because of the activities of neighbours. In a row of terraces each property is reliant on the adjoining houses for some degree of support, for example where floor joists are built into party walls. A terrace is effectively one long cellular structure where the internal walls of individual rooms all help stabilise the complete row. It's not unknown for works such as illegal basement excavations to undermine party walls, causing dangerous structural cracking in the adjoining houses.

Extensions and differential settlement

Where new extensions are added to old houses, current Building Regulations require that the extension is built with super-deep modern foundations that make it extremely rigid. But the old house will want to carry on in its old ways, shuffling about on its footings in tune with seasonal ground changes. This is a classic

Illegal basement conversion next door has caused serious structural movement

recipe for 'differential settlement', as vertical cracks appear at the abutment between the two structures. One way to accommodate this is to provide a flexible joint between the two parts of the building to accommodate these stresses, allowing them to move harmlessly against each other.

For Listed buildings there is a planning preference for new extensions to be 'reversible' – ie potentially removable without leaving a scar on the historic house. So anchoring new structures

Trench for new foundations excavated well below depth of existing Victorian footings

Bowed front wall to house in centre restrained with tie bar. House on left has rebuilt front elevation set back from neighbour

aggressively into existing old walls is inappropriate and could even result in chunks of the old wall being pulled away.

Differential settlement is, of course, nothing new. Some Georgian and Victorian houses built with cellars beneath part of their ground floor effectively have two different foundation depths – the basement area extending relatively deep into the ground, and much shallower foundations elsewhere. This has sometimes had dramatic consequences where the shallow half has settled and pulled away from the more stable part over the deeper basement, in the process splitting the side wall of the house with a giant V-shaped crack! Differential settlement can also occur where foundation depths are reasonably consistent but one part of the building is substantially heavier than the rest – for example where church towers have settled more than the rest of the building.

Bulging walls

In Chapter 5 we looked at some shocking examples of Georgian and Victorian 'jerry building'. You may recall that some solid walls were built cheaply in two separate rows with very little tying them together. Sometimes traffic vibration or decay to bonding timbers in the walls has eventually caused the two rows to separate, causing localised bulging. A similar problem due to 'out of sequence' construction can occur where the internal party walls (built by apprentice labour using

cheap materials) weren't properly tied into the main facing walls (built by experienced bricklayers) other than perhaps with a few bonding timbers. Again these may now have rotted, causing 'bellying' of front walls due to lack of restraint.

So if a solid brick wall shows signs of bulging, the first question to ask is whether the outer surface layer has parted company from the inner row. Alternatively the wall may have shifted as a whole, for example where joist ends have rotted away leaving a large expanse of wall unrestrained. Structural alterations are also a common cause of problems, such as where concentrated loadings from new beams lead to bulging of the wall below.

Other than localised rebuilding of the wall, which may not be practical or economical, the solution tends to involve the insertion of tie bars or spreader plates in order to provide lateral restraint and tie in the affected parts of the walls. But there's no law that says you have to advertise this to the world with an enormous 'S' or 'X'-shaped piece of iron stuck on the front of your house. Discreet modern 'bow ties' are frequently used to secure a bowing wall by anchoring it to newly installed floor joists. Or where a main facing wall has pulled away leaving a gap at the abutment with an internal wall, grouted 'cem ties' can be installed to reconnect them.

However, a wall bulging out can cause further problems, because floor and ceiling joists are likely to come loose so that they no longer meet the wall. One useful solution can be to install joist extenders that, as the name suggests, extend the joist so it can rejoin with the wall in its new position (see Chapter 12). Once reconnected to the masonry this should restore lateral restraint and resist further bulging.

Different types of wall construction can be prone to particular problems. For example, with thick rubble stone walls damp can sometimes swell the 'earth core' in the centre, pushing out areas of stonework. And as we saw earlier, bulges in flint walls can be caused by a loss of bond between the smooth rounded flint nodules and the surrounding mortar into which they're bedded.

Arches and lintels

Arches support the walls sitting on top of them by locking together under load and pushing out at their sides. Consequently they rely on a sideways compressive force to retain their shape. So where an old wall has moved around over the years, it can sometimes allow the arch to relax out of compression so it can drop or sag. With skill, dropped arches can sometimes be reset by inserting thin

Classic method of restraint – tie bars to part rebuilt wall (left) and newly installed (right)

New oak lintel has to be strong enough to support end bearing of ceiling beam

Above: Settlement to main walls affects lintel (with only light loadings above)

Right: Top arch limits loadings below. Brickwork can be discreetly repaired with inserted rods

Helifix.co.uk

Helifix.co.uk

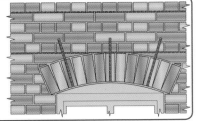

wedges, or support can be provided by purpose-made stainless steel supports inserted underneath. Such repairs are normally acceptable to Conservation Officers as they're entirely reversible. Alternatively arch lintels can be invisibly reinforced by applying self-tapping 'Dry Fix' rods from below. These are inserted up through the lintel and into the masonry above, having first stabilised the brickwork over the lintel with horizontal steel reinforcing rods bedded in mortar joints.

Lintels in older houses are commonly of highly durable oak, but in Georgian and Victorian properties they are more likely to be of good quality softwood, concealed behind lime plaster or render.

Poor original design – door frame should not support ceiling beam

Failure is unlikely unless the wall has been exposed to prolonged periods of water ingress, which can eventually result in the timbers succumbing to rot or beetle. Cracking to plaster or render above openings may be indicative of such decay.

Stone lintels are also common, and with the advent of railways in the Victorian era were increasingly incorporated into brick-built houses. Vertical hairline cracks can sometimes be seen running through the centre of a lintel, caused by an old building having shifted slightly and redistributed loadings. This is rarely cause for concern because the lintel is effectively locked in position.

Iron corrosion

Iron fixings embedded in walls were commonly used to secure stonework, or as iron 'saddlebars' in stone mullion windows. The embedded iron was protected by being caulked with molten lead to form a watertight seal around the end. As we saw in Chapter 5, caulked joints can eventually fail, allowing water ingress to rust and expand the metal, exerting sufficient force to cause cracking. The solution is to carefully remove the rusting item and either replace it with a non-corrosive metal replica or have it professionally re-tipped with bronze and reset.

Iron cramps were common in the 18th and 19th centuries when they were used for fixing ashlar stone cladding to provide a smooth, expensive-looking face to a cheaper masonry structure. Where rust has taken hold this can be a major repair job, as the cramps can be hard to access. At worst the entire front face of the building may need to be carefully taken down and refixed using new non-ferrous cramps.

Worrying lean to roof parapet restrained with high level tie bars

Timber frame

Timber-frame buildings are renowned for their ability to accommodate distortion over the centuries. As well as coping with natural changes in ground conditions each year, their structure is inherently prone to movement – originally from the seasoning of the timber, and subsequently in response to the variations in temperature and humidity throughout the year.

As we saw in the previous chapter, the jointed nature of their skeletal construction is key to allowing far greater flexibility and tolerance of movement than masonry buildings. The infill panels between the main posts and beams could similarly accommodate movement, being made of naturally flexible materials. However, past attempts at repair using such materials as epoxy resin with steel or GRP dowels may have caused more problems than they've solved, rendering the once flexible joints in the timber frame rigid and arthritic. The proper assessment and repair of such structures is a specialist job.

Rafters pushing out mud walls

Roofs

Old roofs commonly show signs of quite pronounced undulation, but a wavy roof that dips along its ridge is not necessarily in distress. Most movement of this type is long established, often reflecting old settlement in response to the changes in loadings over many years from wind and snow etc. This can lend a certain charm to an old building, to the extent that if you want to rebuild such a roof Conservation Officers may insist that the waviness is faithfully replicated!

Where repairs are needed, it's normally possible to strengthen the roof structure from inside the loft, retaining the distortion that gives it its character. For example, where a roof slope has dipped and the rafters have deflected excessively, inserting an extra purlin under the rafters may be all that's required to provide additional support. Or where individual rafters have weakened they can be strengthened by bolting steel plates across weak joints.

Of course, roofs very much depend on the walls for support,

so any settlement down below can have knock-on effects higher up. This includes internal load-bearing 'spine walls' which can be prone to settlement or ill-advised removal or alteration.

One fairly common sight in old houses is where the roof has, over time, pushed the upper walls outwards so that they lean at an angle, and the roof has consequently sagged as it has spread. As we saw in Chapter 4, roof spread is normally prevented because opposing rafters are held together by horizontal tie beams, or simply by the upstairs ceiling joists that act as collars. But if a collar or tie beam suffers from rot, or is deliberately cut (eg to improve headroom) it will free the rafters so that they can push outwards.

Fortunately it should be fairly simple to contain such forces by fitting new collars that connect the rafters on opposite roof slopes at as low a level as possible. Further movement can also be restrained by bolting metal plates to the upper walls on either side, linked by a metal tie bar running through the building at ceiling joist level. 'Racking' is another problem sometimes found in roofs of trussed construction. Here the trusses can all start to lean like a series of dominoes due to insufficient lateral bracing. This can normally be rectified by strengthening the trusses with

additional diagonal braces, or with planks of timber nailed across the undersides of the rafters.

When it comes to the roof coverings themselves, an enormous amount of movement can easily be accommodated as they're designed to be inherently flexible. As the roof timbers flex, the overlapping tiles or slates are free to adjust, sliding across each other by small amounts. As we saw earlier, the real weak point is at junctions between roof slopes and with relatively rigid chimneys and walls. Lead flashings allow for a certain amount of movement, whereas mortar fillets are prone to cracking and leakage.

Further advice

There's normally more than one solution to a structural problem. With old buildings, carrying out repairs *in situ* is always preferable, and it's usually cheaper to repair than to rebuild. As a rule, simple traditional techniques and materials are more likely to be compatible and successful. If a solution sounds draconian it may well be unsuitable. Remember, you can always get a second opinion.

9 TIMBER DECAY AND BEETLE

Beam in damp wall completely rotted away

A house may be subjected to repeated ineffective treatments

Timber is fundamental to the structure of old buildings, and not just those built with a timber skeleton. Without it holding up roofs, supporting floors and spanning openings in walls, our homes would simply collapse into ruins. But if exposed to persistent dampness it will eventually succumb to the forces of nature and start to soften and decay. This explains why there's so much fuss about damp in old buildings.

Natural decay

As part of the natural cycle, dead wood on the forest floor is cleared up by insects and fungi consuming it as food. However, timber used for construction should, in theory, be safe from such ravages. But all it takes is a persistent leak or a build-up of damp soil against the walls to replicate the conditions found in nature. Dark and damp conditions make wood attractive to fungal spores floating about in the air and also encourage wood-boring beetles. To make matters worse, modern paints and cement-based materials seal in damp that would otherwise evaporate harmlessly away. So behind neatly painted walls, old timber lintels might be crumbling, or an historic timber frame could be slowly rotting away.

Despite these risks it's important not to overreact: things are rarely as bad as they look. Considerable damage has been caused in recent years by ham-fisted 'remedies' that have actually made matters worse. Often a few simple repairs are all that's needed to kill off the fungi and beetle before they can do any serious harm.

The timber and damp scam

A whole industry has developed around the treatment of timber decay over the last few decades. Until recently the sight of a few old beetle boreholes in a property was enough to trigger a course of spraying with toxic chemicals, some of which are now known to be harmful to health and have recently been banned. It's now generally realised that most defects are simply a result of timber getting persistently damp because of maintenance issues. Repairing the fabric of the building and allowing the timber to dry out can usually halt further decay or infestation. So identifying the source of moisture is fundamental to preventing timber decay. Unfortunately, as we saw earlier in Chapter 2, damp is widely misdiagnosed as 'rising damp', triggering remedial work that may simply cause further damage. A big part of the problem lies with banks and building societies insisting that mortgage valuation reports include standard phrases that recommend further inspections by 'timber and damp contractors'. Such firms have a vested interested in finding work, with a sales-orientated approach. Some are paid by the square metre to spray and inject chemicals and re-plaster walls. Mortgage lenders want quick-fix instant solutions backed by guarantees. But a guarantee is worthless where the problem was misdiagnosed in the first place and the works carried out cover up the symptoms. Traditional buildings don't lend themselves to standard solutions, particularly when applied to timber frames, stonework, rendering and flintwork. Despite this it's not unusual for the same property to be subjected to repeated courses of ineffective spraying and injecting every time it's bought and sold!

The upshot is that homeowners have long been conned by an industry intent on selling chemical treatments that often do nothing to resolve the real problems. It's also a sad reflection on the surveying profession that rather than taking the trouble to diagnose one of the most fundamental problems faced by older buildings, they instead allow the banks (of all people) to dictate potentially damaging advice on property matters.

Why old buildings decay

There are two big reasons why buildings decay: lack of maintenance and the wrong kind of maintenance. In rainy Britain the primary task when caring for old houses is to prevent water collecting in places where it can seep into the fabric of the building and eventually cause decay. Making a few periodic checks is all that's needed to spot small problems before they get out of hand, potentially saving you a lot of wasted time and money further down the line – the classic 'stitch in time'.

So what are the key areas on which you need to keep a watchful eye? One of the most common sources of water invading our homes is from neglected rainwater fittings. An overflowing gutter or leaking joint, if ignored for long enough, can create ideal conditions for rot and beetle to wreak havoc inside the house. Similarly, small leaks from slipped or missing roof tiles or from defective joints at flashings and valleys often go unnoticed for surprisingly long periods. Chimneys are another common source of damp ingress from defective flashings, or from rain entering unprotected chimney pots. A certain amount of rain in old flues isn't normally a problem as it should evaporate away in dry weather (as long as they're well vented), but larger amounts can collect on ledges or in old rubble inside flues, soaking through chimney breasts and disused fireplaces as damp patches. Walls beneath eroded window sills are particularly vulnerable to penetrating dampness, and at ground level earth banked up against walls is notorious as a cause of damp and decay. To compound the problem, once damp has got inside a wall the application of modern masonry paints and cement renders will have the effect of sealing it in.

But whatever the cause, saturated solid walls will inevitably transmit damp to adjacent internal timbers such as skirting or floor structures. And once higher levels of damp find their way into old buildings it's an open invitation for uninvited guests in the form of wood beetle and fungal spores to take up residence. When the moisture content of wood gets above 15% it can become attractive to insects; and above about 20% (some experts say 25%) conditions start to favour rot. Hence reducing dampness is key to an effective solution.

Above: Timber floor at risk due to high outdoor ground level

Left: Overflowing hopper caused adjoining lath to rot, since renewed

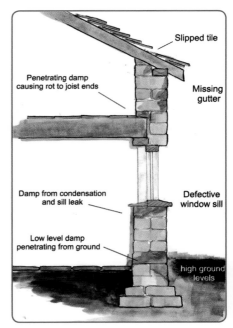

Slipped tile

Penetrating damp causing rot to joist ends

Missing gutter

Damp from condensation and sill leak

Defective window sill

Low level damp penetrating from ground

high ground levels

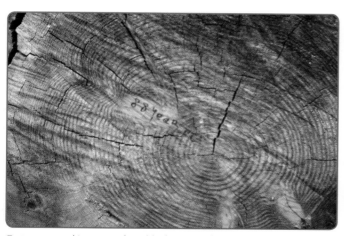

Outer sapwood is more vulnerable than inner heartwood

Cuboidal cracking – usually indicative of dry rot

How durable is wood?

To assess how resistant a piece of timber in a building is likely to be, you need to consider which part of the tree it originally came from. If you peel back the outer layer of bark on a tree the wood you've exposed is known as sapwood. This is the living part of the tree that transmits water and minerals for growth. Sapwood has little durability and is far more vulnerable to beetle and fungal attack than heartwood – the dead inner part of the tree which is particularly resilient to decay. The centre of the trunk contains the pith, which is less durable than the surrounding heartwood.

When timber is used for building it's common for a certain amount of sapwood to be left on the corners of the timbers, and these can potentially be attractive to wood beetle. Heartwood has a natural resilience to decay provided it's kept reasonably dry, but when subjected to prolonged moisture even this will eventually succumb to the natural process where old trees fall down and ultimately start to rot, providing nutrients for other plants.

Microclimates

Timbers in contact with north-facing walls are potentially most vulnerable to decay. Walls on the north side of a property get very little sunlight and are relatively sheltered from prevailing south-westerly winds. Because they don't benefit so much from the warming and drying effects of the sun and wind, any water (from leaks or condensation etc) tends to linger longer, resulting in prolonged dampness. Hence any adjoining timbers will be more at risk of decay. In contrast, south-facing walls enjoy a periodically sunny outlook with variable temperatures and are more exposed to prevailing winds.

Fungal decay

Rots are fungi, and like their close relatives, mushrooms, they thrive in moist conditions. Where rot is afflicting a property, the first task is to identify what type you're dealing with. But as with mushrooms, fungal decay comes in a variety of shapes, sizes and colours and can sometimes be a little difficult to distinguish. Most people have heard horror stories about 'dry rot', the dreaded fungus that if left unchecked can reputedly consume entire buildings – at least if urban folklore is to be believed. 'Wet rot' is

the other well-known, if slightly less exotic, type of timber decay that also occasionally pops up in surveys to scare the pants off house buyers.

However, experts have now adopted a more accurate way of categorising rot. Brown and white are the two principal types of fungal decay to timber. The key difference is in their respective methods of attack that destroy different parts of the timber. Brown rots work by removing cellulose from the wood, leaving behind a brown matrix of lignin (a chemical found in plant cell walls that makes them rigid and woody). White rots also consume the lignin, leaving behind blanched-looking decayed wood with an anaemic tinge. Despite this, brown rot is actually far more destructive than white.

Brown rots

Included in the brown camp are all types of dry rot, along with their similar-looking cousin 'cellar fungus'. However, this category also includes some types of wet rot (although most wet rots are classed as white). Timber that shows signs of distinctive cuboidal cracking is brown, usually of the dry rot variety.

DRY ROT

Spores of dry rot are present in the air around us searching for a suitable habitat, such as damp timber in unventilated conditions. Once settled they start to germinate, sending out thin grey-white

Dry rot fungus

Mike Parrett / Dampbuster.com

Above: Dry rot in floor joist

Right: Cuboidal cracking in joinery adjacent to damp wall

Above: Wet rot under suspended timber ground floor with blocked air bricks

Left: Wet rot to floor board

root-like strands known as hyphae. These quickly spread across the surface of the wood, multiplying and engulfing it in a matted web (mycelium). If suitably damp and unventilated conditions persist dry rot will develop a fluffy, grey-white, cotton-wool appearance with lilac and yellow patches. Finally it morphs into a mature pancake-shaped, rust-coloured fruiting body. This looks a bit like a dusty pizza with white edges, and proceeds to emit millions of spores that float off into the air – starting the whole process over again.

The fungus itself feeds by sucking out the moisture from the affected wood. This leaves the unfortunate piece of timber dry, shrivelled and structurally useless, cracking into brittle cubes or square blocks and eventually disintegrating.

Dry rot is often misdiagnosed because its appearance is constantly changing. It can sometimes look similar to other types of rot, depending on what life-cycle stage it's at and where it's growing. But whether correctly identified or not, because of its fearsome reputation people are sometimes panicked into taking drastic action at the slightest whiff.

CELLAR FUNGUS

King of the dry rot impersonators, 'cellar rot' thrives in the same sort of conditions. The reason it's frequently mistaken for dry rot is because it displays very similar symptoms with an almost identical fruiting body. But unlike its more famous cousin its mycelium strands are blackish brown rather than grey-white. For example, a length of skirting that's clearly suffering from timber decay with deep cracks across the grain as well as along it would appear to be a classic case of dry rot. But once removed a closer inspection of the skirting board might well reveal dark-coloured strands characteristic of cellar fungus.

White rots

White rots thrive in wetter conditions than the brown variety, eating away at any timber surface where water settles. External joinery is commonly affected where water accumulates and can't drain away freely. Rotten wood has a soft, spongy feel, caving in easily when prodded with a screwdriver. But it's not always obvious, particularly since painted timber can sometimes appear perfectly sound whilst decaying away from the inside.

The good news is that white rots only affect localised areas and aren't prone to spreading. This makes them relatively simple to defeat, for example by cutting out the decayed wood back to a sound surface and then piecing in a replacement section of timber.

Included in the white camp are most types of what used to be called 'wet rot'. But the term 'wet rot' covers a host of different fungi, ranging from those with a white and furry appearance, to mushroom-like growths and even big colourful fruiting bodies, depending on where it's growing. So a few varieties of wet rot may actually be classed as brown. With the brown variety, the affected timber grows darker in colour than the healthy wood surrounding it, ultimately breaking up with small cracks. In contrast, the white type causes timber to become lighter and the damage can be seen along the grain. Wet rot is commonly found around window and door sills and frames where flaking paint has let in rainwater, as well as internally to skirting boards, and timber floors and joist ends adjacent to damp walls.

Treatment

Just as fatal errors are sometimes made picking apparently edible mushrooms, accurate identification of fungi is a specialist task. This sometimes involves using specially trained dogs to sniff out dry rot. But all rots are fungi, and can only germinate if timber is damp with a moisture content consistently above about 20%. Fungi also like warmth, so a centrally-heated atmosphere that's tropically moist and steamy would be an ideal environment.

The best way to kill all types of rot, like any living organism, is simply to cut off their water supply. Common sources of moisture include damp walls in close proximity, water collecting on timber, leaks from defective plumbing or from baths and showers, leaking

Moist and humid indoor atmosphere is ideal for fungal decay

Got rot? What not to do

- Don't panic – even the worst outbreak of rot can be stopped by starving it of moisture.
- Don't allow the source of damp to persist – fix it.
- Don't rely on a 'free' survey from a timber and damp contractor.
- Don't hack off historic plasterwork because of rot strands behind it – they'll die off once the main outbreak's been tackled.
- Don't remove unaffected timber around the outbreak. As long as it's dry it's safe.
- Don't treat the whole area with chemicals – targeted boron-based treatments can be used sparingly.

roofs and guttering, and excessive indoor condensation. So all that may be required to deal with an outbreak is to simply isolate the timber from damp surroundings and boost ventilation to reduce moisture.

However, profit-driven timber treatment firms have an incentive to hype up the danger to justify expensive, destructive works. But the water-based chemicals they often use have the effect of introducing large amounts of moisture into the building, the very thing the rot needs to thrive! As well as blanket spraying with chemicals, for several decades the standard approach for treating suspected outbreaks of dry rot has involved aggressive cutting out of timber to a metre or more beyond the last known area of outbreak and then burning it, as well as hacking off all the plasterwork in the vicinity. Timber ground floors are the area most commonly targeted for such works, although any part of a house with a suspected outbreak may have suffered damage and unnecessary loss of historic fabric as a result of these obsolete methods.

The important point is that without damp the spores won't germinate, and the timber will be safe. Dry timber won't rot even if the spores are sitting on its surface. So to successfully treat rot the source of water must first be found and dealt with. Then the area affected must be allowed time to dry out and effective permanent ventilation installed, for example via new airbricks inserted in the walls. The timber must be well ventilated and able to breathe on all sides. A de-humidifier can help speed up the initial drying out process by extracting excess moisture from the building.

Where rot has attacked structural timbers like lintels then physical repairs may be needed. Care should be taken in historic properties to retain as much of the original fabric as possible. Before condemning an affected piece of timber, you may find that the core is still sound and it's salvageable. With the aid of specialist techniques such as scanning or micro-drills (also used for beetle – see page 128) it's surprising just how sound old pieces of timber can prove to be despite outward appearances. Where badly rotten timbers aren't salvageable they'll need to be cut out and replaced with new pre-treated timber. Where joists are in contact with damp masonry walls they can be protected by inserting strips of plastic damp-proof membrane.

Dry rot can sometimes be triggered in buildings that have been flooded, or saturated by hoses extinguishing a blaze, but more often outbreaks are simply due to a leak that's gone unnoticed for months or years. One common source of problems internally is from persistent leaks to shower trays and bath seals.

One of the things that tends to alarm people about dry rot is its mobility. In the past it was believed that fungal growths transported moisture to 'wet up' fresh dry timber, causing new outbreaks as the fungus spread relentlessly through plasterwork and solid walls. But the fact is, once the source of the outbreak has been controlled and allowed to dry out these strands should naturally die off. So there should be no need to strip away historic plaster. Even so, it's a wise precaution to check for secondary outbreaks. If in extreme cases it's considered necessary for timber treatment to be applied as a precautionary measure, targeted use of a boron-based fungicide is probably the best option. But normally all that's required to kill the beast is a dry environment and good cross-ventilation.

Inserting a plastic DPC under floor plates or joists can protect them from damp masonry

Excessive dampness to arch brickwork risks rot to timber lintel behind

Decayed lintel being removed

Mike Wye & Associates Ltd

Robust oak window timbers are perfectly salvageable despite superficial beetle activity

Beetle infestation

Virtually every old building will have a few boreholes as evidence of past beetle attacks. As with damp and rot, the mere suspicion that beetle once trod the boards in an old house can provoke hysterical overreaction and a rash of inappropriate works. It's estimated that as many as 50,000 unnecessary treatments are carried out each year in Britain. And needlessly removing old timbers is an expensive mistake, with a consequent loss of valuable historic fabric.

There are good reasons not to panic if you encounter boreholes. For a start, the infestation is likely to be of considerable age and no longer active. It may also have been repeatedly sprayed every time the house has been sold or re-mortgaged, at the insistence of the banks. But the main reason for guarded optimism stems from understanding the way beetle interacts with timber.

Wood beetles are particularly fond of surface sapwood since it's much easier to consume than the tougher heartwood. This explains why beetle infestation rarely extends much deeper than the outermost few millimetres, and hence is unlikely to affect the structural integrity of the timber.

There are other reasons why a few old boreholes are rarely an issue. Medieval carpenters frequently used oversized posts and beams of much larger dimensions than structurally necessary. This left plenty of 'sacrificial' wood in the outer layers that if necessary could be nibbled away. And oak is incredibly durable – whilst it might appear to be rotten, in the majority of cases it will be perfectly solid on the inside, and still able to fulfil its structural function. Prodding with a penknife can quickly determine the condition of the heartwood timber below the surface. If you can sense firm resistance the timber may be perfectly sound, with only the outer layers close to the surface affected.

The beetles

The two most common wood-boring insects in Britain that are attracted to timbers in old buildings are common furniture beetle and deathwatch beetle. Sometimes known as woodworm (because the larvae burrow or worm their way into the wood), furniture beetle is considered the less harmful of the two.

Deathwatch beetle is particularly attracted to hardwoods such as oak, which often compose the structural timbers in old houses, and can potentially cause serious damage. Fortunately for homeowners north of the border, properties in Scotland are less likely to succumb to deathwatch infestation, as the climate has (to date) largely deterred intrusions. However, in some more southern parts of the country with warmer microclimates, it's possible that more exotic, rarer species of beetle might be encountered. Longhorn beetle and wood-boring weevil aren't common in Britain, but, for the record, their exit holes are respectively large and oval-shaped, and small and ragged. But with future climate change we may yet see termites dining out on our skirting boards.

COMMON FURNITURE BEETLE ('WOODWORM')

Furniture beetles are matt brown and about 3mm long from head to tail. As the larvae munch their way through the nutritious cellulose in a piece of wood they form telltale exit holes about 1mm or 2mm in diameter.

Furniture beetle attacks the outer sapwood (of both softwood and hardwood) if the environment is sufficiently damp with a moisture content above about 15%. This means

Stripping floorboards exposed flight hole tunnels close to surface

Evidence of beetle and rot to removed lintel (see last photo on page 127)

Deathwatch exit holes – but are they still active?

that poorer quality timber containing a lot of sapwood is most at risk. Softwood floorboards are particularly vulnerable due to their relative thinness. On rare occasions this can result in the odd isolated board becoming weakened, with a risk of collapse when walked on. However, where boards have been stripped you can often see the remnants of little bore tunnels, looking a bit like Arabic script. But this evidence of beetle activity is normally confined to an area close to the surface. Common places where you might find boreholes include damp under-stairs cupboards and timber floors around WCs (they like the moisture and are especially partial to the proteins in urine-soaked floorboards).

DEATHWATCH BEETLE

Deathwatch beetles are more than twice the size of their junior cousins, at about 6–9mm long, with a similar matt brown body. Their exit holes are correspondingly larger at around 3mm in diameter. They're mainly attracted to hardwoods, oak being a particular favourite, but as with other forms of beetle infestation usually only the damp outer sapwood is attacked, stopping short of the heartwood. However, where timber has already been softened up by fungal attack beetle can cause havoc, undermining its structural integrity.

Famously, deathwatch beetle can sometimes be heard during the spring emergence season making a distinctive tapping noise coming from within the timber. This sound is similar to a fingernail drumming very quickly against a piece of wood about five times in succession. The slightly macabre name is believed to stem from times past, when long nights were spent tending the dying, the silent vigil accompanied only by the sound of the beetles' tapping.

If you hear the trademark deathwatch sound, before rushing to exterminate it it's important to first understand its modus operandi. These insects exist to mate, and are active and visible from around March to June, flying about well into the summer. So the beetle-monitoring season is limited to this fairly short period each year.

You sometimes find dead beetles lying about in an old building. These should not be confused with the good guys – the smaller Korynetes variety, identifiable by their blue-black colour with a distinctive metallic sheen. These are helpful predators that in spring and summer consume deathwatch larvae. Some species of spider can also help cull the deathwatch population, so it's best to leave cobwebs in place during the flying season.

Monitoring beetle activity

Each year, the larvae buried in the wood start to hatch. As the insects grow they munch their way to the surface, finally emerging as adult beetles from early spring to summer. Active infestation is revealed by piles of very fine timber dust, known as frass, left behind near the flight holes. Existing holes are often reused to deposit eggs, starting the life-cycle all over again.

However, the presence of sawdust isn't an entirely foolproof method of spotting current activity as vibration from building works can sometimes dislodge old frass.

To judge whether infestation is still active, take a close look at the exit holes. If they're clean and light it's indicative of recent activity. As you might expect, old, inactive holes tend to be dark and dirty. The simplest method of testing is to glue tissue paper over the holes using wallpaper paste or alternatively wax polish timber surfaces that are potentially at risk. Then observe whether the tissue or wax is chewed through as the insects emerge in the spring, either from new flight holes or via reused old ones. Emerging wood beetles instinctively head towards the light, which explains why you sometimes find dead beetles around windowsills or on the floor in front of windows. Based on this principle, special 'light traps' can be used in dark spaces like lofts, designed to attract beetles and trap them on sheets of sticky paper.

Fine dust or 'frass' indicates active infestation

Mike Wye & Associates Ltd

Non-destructive testing

Testing

Where a length of load-bearing timber shows signs of beetle attack, clearly the big question is whether its strength has been compromised or whether the damage is merely superficial and limited to the outer surface area. To assess the condition of the core, non-destructive testing can be carried out by carefully drilling into the timber using a micro-drill with a long, fine bit. Where the core is sound it will offer resistance, making penetration difficult, whereas a rotten core will allow the drill to pass easily through.

Other specialist techniques that can be brought to bear to determine structural integrity include ultrasound scanning – foetus-sensing technology – and advanced fibre-optic systems.

To undertake professional testing, a specialist firm will need to be employed. Although this will involve paying a fee, it's important to bear in mind that in most cases the cost will work out substantially less than a 'free survey' from a sales-driven firm that recommends a lot of unnecessary and expensive replacement work.

Overkill

Past approaches to treating suspected beetle infestation primarily involved indiscriminate attempts at mass poisoning. But the blanket application of toxic chemicals combined with radical surgery proved to be largely ineffective, not to say positively damaging. Cutting out timber for some distance beyond affected areas inevitably destroyed much historic fabric. Worse, spraying chemicals has resulted in unpleasant side-effects to human health.

In spite of such chemical warfare techniques proving ineffective, many 'Timber and Damp Contractors' persist in selling such obsolete treatments. But blanket spraying of chemicals rarely reaches the infestation, and simply results in toxins being distributed throughout the building. In any case, chemicals are difficult to apply beyond the outer surface of the timber, only penetrating a couple of millimetres, making them ineffective for more serious established infestations where insects have burrowed deeper.

Another problem with this approach is that insecticides don't discriminate, and un-targeted spraying is more likely to eliminate natural predators like spiders and other species of beetle – even harming protected species like bats (a criminal offence). Smoke treatments are similarly destructive. Deathwatch beetle larvae

can be particularly difficult to eradicate, staying deeper within the wood for a very long time, before finally emerging to a world where all the spiders and insects that wanted to eat them are dead.

Another problem is that the most serious beetle outbreaks tend to affect damp structural timbers such as joist ends that are embedded in walls, where access is almost impossible. Although organic solvents can penetrate further than water-based ones they remain very flammable for some time after application, as well as being polluting and toxic. But regardless of such concerns, such potentially damaging treatments are routinely made the subject of mortgage retentions that can only be released once the contractor has provided a paper 'guarantee'.

Treatment

Today, property professionals have adopted a more intelligent and relaxed attitude to dealing with suspected beetle infestation in old buildings. The focus is now very much on correct identification of the problem in the first place. As with fungi, wood beetle will only cause serious damage where there's damp, so the key to eradicating beetle is to cut off their fuel supply by reducing the moisture content of affected timbers. Once the dampness has

Above: A good start: exposed timbers allowed to dry out

Below: Part of the solution: ventilate to reduce humidity

Keep air grilles clear so voids to timber ground floors are well ventilated

been resolved and timber allowed to dry out, the beetle colony should diminish over time.

As wood dries out it becomes less attractive to beetle and activity decreases. Once moisture content drops below 12% they struggle to survive and their numbers decline naturally. Heated buildings are very hostile environments for them, so controlled drying out and permanently improved ventilation should prevent any need for expensive and damaging remedial treatment.

But the single most important thing is to fix the root cause of the damp first. This means prioritising the repair of leaks and removing any modern sealants, paints and renders that are preventing the damp from naturally evaporating out of walls and floors.

Applying gentle background heating to affected areas will help to reduce moisture content in the surrounding timbers – but take care not to dry out timbers too quickly, otherwise they're likely to crack.

Saturated masonry can take several years to fully dry out after the source of the problem has been removed. Although any timber in contact will remain vulnerable during this period, good ventilation should allow damp to evaporate, thereby reducing moisture levels. So where an outbreak has affected timbers under floors or within roof spaces, ventilation to these areas will also need to be improved. Where condensation is a significant source of damp, extractor fans may need to be fitted to expel moist, steamy air from cooking areas and bathrooms etc.

If you have a serious and active outbreak, then in addition to the above works a targeted application of insecticides to the affected areas can sometimes be justified. Until a permanently drier environment has been achieved, a brush treatment can be effective if applied sparingly and locally to only the worst signs of live infestation. Where chemicals are used, special gels and pastes containing permethrin are most effective. By spreading toxic pastes directly on to affected timbers, the theory is that when the beetles emerge they eat through the paste, which poisons them. But as noted earlier, this can also kill natural predators that otherwise could have done the job for you.

Defrassing

'Defrassing' is the name given to the removal of beetle-riddled surface timber, by stripping away the affected outer sapwood to get back to virgin heartwood. Although this is fine from a technical perspective, hacking off the surface wood inevitably alters its appearance and means sacrificing part of the original fabric. Such 'tidying up' works are rarely necessary.

Employing professionals

If you're buying a timber-frame property it's obviously essential to get competent advice on any suspected timber decay or beetle infestation, as the structure of the house is made of wood. So you need someone with the right expertise, not a timber treatment company with a vested interest in finding problems.

This is more of a dilemma where a mortgage lender has insisted on the purchaser obtaining a report from a 'specialist' timber and damp contractor. The best advice is to appoint instead a chartered surveyor specialising in timber-frame properties. A qualified expert will be able to identify the type of timber and advise whether it's naturally resistant to attack. Having inspected the property, they should write a report as an impartial expert identifying the cause of any decay or infestation and a recommendation of the appropriate action that needs to be taken. This approach should avoid the risk of unnecessary, expensive and damaging treatments being carried out. A letter from the Conservation Officer can also be helpful in persuading awkward mortgage lenders to release retentions.

Decay detection drilling using the Sibert microdrill

TRADA Technology Ltd

The development of the fireplace was one of the great breakthroughs in the evolution of the modern house, radically changing the way domestic buildings were designed and revolutionising internal layouts and lifestyles. Today, although the full significance of the fireplace has long been consigned to history, no period home is considered complete without a merry blaze emanating from the hearth. Yet poorly maintained fireplaces and flues remain one of the principal causes of fires in old buildings, so it's important to understand how they were built and what can go wrong.

Fireplaces

Early houses were built as large, open halls, with numerous people all sharing the same communal space. On the floor in the centre of this spacious room a fire would be crackling on the hearth. Fires were essential for warmth and light, as well as for cooking food, so were never allowed to go out, sometimes being kept burning for generations.

An open hearth had certain advantages – it generously radiated warmth in all directions and allowed people to sit around it on all sides. The smoke would gradually rise up and hang thickly in the air before dispersing via holes in the roof. These openings took the form of gaps between roof tiles that allowed smoke to escape. But they also let in rain and draughts until the development in the 14th century of roof lanterns with louvred slats that

enabled smoke to escape whilst resisting the worst of the weather.

But to our way of thinking an open hearth must have been like having a permanent bonfire in the middle of your living room. With all the windows glassless, smoke and sparks went wherever passing draughts directed them. Stinging eyes and dry throats were part of everyday life, especially on still days when smoke would thicken the indoor air, leading to much coughing and cursing. And because nearly all the space above head-height was generally filled with smoke it remained unusable.

By Shakespeare's time – the late 16th century – a new phenomenon was entering domestic architecture that would consign smoky open halls to the history books. Although fireplaces and chimneys had been a feature of mansions and castles since the 12th century, they were enormously expensive to build and hence something of a status symbol. A favourite way for owners of grand Tudor houses and palaces to project their wealth was through a profusion of elaborate chimney stacks. But early fireplaces were generally considered unsafe for use in ordinary timber-frame houses. What made the difference was the development of affordable, good quality bricks that were highly effective at containing heat.

Enclosing the fire within a substantial brick chimney breast effectively led to the subdivision of large open halls into smaller spaces or individual rooms. But not everyone was happy with the loss of open hearths and the relative inefficiency of the fireplaces that they depended on for warmth. Enclosing open hearths made homes much colder, with most of the heat being directed straight through the roof.

iron hob grates were developed for burning coal, and these were installed within decorative surrounds or 'chimney pieces'. These fashionable additions to the home were made from a variety of materials such as painted or gilded wood, stucco, slate or expensive carved marble. Smoky fires nevertheless remained a common problem, so in order to create a better draught detached fire baskets or 'dog grates' raised up on legs (or 'dogs') were introduced. Efficiency improvements continued in the Victorian era, notably in the development of the

'register grate' with an integral iron fire basket and an adjustable metal plate that regulated airflow by restricting the throat of the flue, thereby retaining more heat within the room.

A place for fire

Capacious inglenooks were designed to burn large logs, and in smaller houses the fireplace would also be used for cooking, incorporating a bread oven to one side. Hence during restoration work metal meat hooks are sometimes discovered hanging down from flues above an old fireplace. Some inglenooks were enlarged to incorporate benches so that people could sit within the fireplace enclosure, almost the only place in the house where they could be really warm. But large openings were extremely inefficient with their wide flues that lost most of the heat up the chimney.

charnwood.com

A major evolution occurred in the Georgian period, as coal started to replace wood for domestic heating. This change to a hotter-burning fuel allowed fireplaces to become smaller and more efficient. Consequently much alteration work was carried out to modernise old medieval inglenooks and chimneys. Cast

Opening up a fireplace

Today, one of the joys of doing up an old house is the exploration and opening up of long-disused fireplaces. Many have intriguing stories to tell.

Over the years old inglenooks were often reduced in size and fitted with smaller, more efficient cast iron fires or tiled surrounds. The temptation may be to remove such later additions and to restore

woodhouseconservation.co.uk

Pointing fireplace masonry prior to lining flue and re-plastering chimney breast

Flues

A flue is simply a funnel, or vertical exhaust pipe, designed to safely transport smoke from the fire to the outdoor environment. It's based on the simple principle that warm air generated by fires naturally rises, and in the process disperses the smoke and combustion gases.

At its simplest a flue comprises the space enclosed by the chimney breast masonry and the stack. But in order for smoke to rise efficiently, a smooth internal surface had to be created. This was achieved by lining the internal masonry walls with 'parging' – a coat of lime plaster, sometimes reinforced with a little cow dung added to the mix. This helped seal the masonry to prevent leaks, as well as smoothing over internal ledges where soot might have built up.

Construction became more complex with the provision of additional fireplaces in bedrooms and adjoining reception rooms, with multiple flues needing to be accommodated with a single chimney. This was achieved by building thin internal partitions of brick, slate or stone known as 'withes' or 'mid-feathers'.

Beautiful stone fireplace long concealed behind modest façade (above)

Flue failure

Flues fail for two main reasons:

- Over time, cracks or holes develop allowing combustion gases to escape into rooms or roof spaces. Internal partitions between flues within chimney breasts can deteriorate, allowing smoke to leak into adjacent flues.
- Soot and tar can build up on ledges inside a flue and may eventually ignite, causing a chimney fire. This is more common where the fuel being burnt is green unseasoned timber, as it generates excessive tar. Soot deposits can sometimes become damp from rain penetration or condensation, causing ugly tar stains that bleed through chimney breasts.

Smoke containing combustion gases from fires is potentially dangerous to human health. Leaks can sometimes go undetected for long periods, particularly within lofts or to adjoining houses, and if a flue becomes blocked a build-up of poisonous combustion

the original inglenook. But this raises a classic conservation issue – what era should you 'restore' a property to? Ripping out a later fireplace may destroy an interesting, if more recent, historical feature which was actually better at heating the room. Of course, where an original opening in a chimney breast has simply been bricked up there are no such dilemmas, and reinstating the fireplace will have the added benefit of improving ventilation.

Brick flues are common in stone buildings

Damp staining from leak at flashing

View down a flue

gases will blow back, re-entering the room. The dangers are graver still where old unlined flues are used for gas- or oil-fired appliances that produce deadly, odourless carbon monoxide, which can prove fatal. Therefore it's essential to check the condition of flues before lighting fires.

It's a fairly simple task to test the airtightness of a flue using smoke pellets. First create an upward draught (or 'draw') by burning some crumpled newspaper in the fireplace. Then light some smoke pellets placed on the hearth before taking a look in upstairs rooms and in the loft for signs of smoke leakage.

Check also that there are no nesting birds blocking the chimney. The best advice is to have the flue swept, as this should remove any loose soot deposits.

Sweeping

After many years of coal burning, the acrid chemicals released in combustion gases will eventually eat away at the parging lining in flues, and degrade mortar joints. As a result individual pieces often fall off and collect on internal ledges. Damp from condensing gases, or from rain pouring down uncapped chimney pots, can soak into any loose internal parging, which soaks up water like a sponge, causing damp patches on interior walls.

But old voids and ledges in flues can also play host to large piles of soot accumulated over the years. The worry with deposits of old soot and tar is that they can eventually ignite, causing a chimney fire. Flues serving former inglenook fireplaces tend to be particularly well endowed with odd nooks and crannies, usually as a result of past conversion works installing narrow coal grates. Hence the importance of regular sweeping.

Fortunately, Conservation Officers are unlikely to insist that traditional flue sweeping techniques are faithfully replicated. One such method involved dangling a rope down the chimney pot and attaching it at the bottom to a large clump of holly, which would duly be hauled up the full length of the flue, loosening embedded soot in the process. Alternatively, the job was sometimes done with more dramatic effect with the insertion of a live cockerel, which would eventually re-emerge in a predictably sooty state after much clucking, flapping and scratching. Most infamously of all, in the Victorian era small urchins were compelled to toil up chimneys, with disastrous consequences for their health. Despite such abuses, there remains an old superstition that seeing a chimney sweep is lucky (King George III's life was supposedly saved by one).

On a more practical basis, having your flue regularly swept should certainly ward off the dangers of chimney fires and blockages. Modern sweeps employ specialist brushes on flexible rods (like drain rods) and remove the dislodged soot with a powerful commercial vacuum cleaner. After sweeping it's generally advisable to have a final smoke test carried out, and to check the masonry to chimney breasts in the loft for any gaps where mortar might have become dislodged during sweeping.

Disused flues

In most old properties today, some of the original fireplaces will be disused and boarded up, particularly those serving bedrooms or bathrooms. But behind the scenes all may not be well. Unless chimney pots have been capped off rain can come trickling down redundant flues, causing damp in disused fireplaces, or birds may have taken up residence. Damp patches on chimney breasts can also be caused by moist air condensing on the inside of cold disused flues. This is why redundant pots should not only be capped off, but also ventilated (for example with an airbrick or purpose-made vent). And to encourage a healthy through-flow of air, a vent should also be fitted to the blocked-up former fireplace in the room below.

Such concerns pale into insignificance compared to the dangers posed by botched structural alterations. It's surprisingly common to find that chimney breasts have been removed in a bid to make more space, and yet the remaining masonry above (leading up to the main stack) has not been fully supported. To make matters worse, rain may be pouring down the chimney pot straight on to what is now a ceiling below. In older houses the removal of chimney breasts can weaken the structure of the property where they helped buttress adjoining walls. All such structural alterations should be carried out with Building Regulations consent, so unless a completion certificate was obtained it's advisable to contact Building Control and have a structural engineer verify that it's safe.

One thing to bear in mind if you propose to reinstate a long-disused flue is the possible risk that in the intervening years it might have been used as a handy shortcut for pipes or cable runs. It's also not unknown for new timber joist ends to have been inserted through the masonry, so to be on the safe side it may be worth having a video survey made of the flue.

Special brush system and vacuum used to sweep stove flues

Substantial steel gallows brackets support masonry above removed chimney breast

Blocked up fireplace opening to disused flue with vent in place

Black-horse-chimney-sweep.co.uk

Air supply

The provision of a sufficient amount of oxygen to ensure the efficient combustion of fires and appliances is a key part of compliance with current Building Regulations. The main reason for this concern is to ensure that occupants have enough air to breathe and aren't asphyxiated in competition with large open fires that can consume more than 260m³ of air per hour (in addition to burning the fuel, a large amount of air is needed to create a draught that flows over the fire and up the flue).

Traditionally ventilation wasn't a problem in old houses, as draughts emanating from small gaps in floorboards, or from window and door frames, ensured a healthy supply of oxygen to fireplaces. In the process this helped dry out any moisture in the fabric of the house. But today our modern obsession with sealing houses up means that ventilation can often be insufficient. Instead we have 'controlled' ventilation in new homes in the form of trickle vents in windows and extractor fans. A more sophisticated method is passive stack ventilation (PSV), a green alternative to mechanical ventilation and air conditioning. PSV relies on the principle of warm air rising through a vertical vent or flue – which may sound familiar! Opening up redundant fireplaces in old properties should provide similar improvements.

Wood-burning stoves

If you have an old inglenook that's inherently inefficient, installing a wood-burning or multi-fuel stove can be a useful solution. Not only are these stoves very effective at heating rooms, they also boast such impressive green credentials that with a bit of luck you may qualify for a grant towards the cost of installation. Note, however, that if you live in a smoke control area you're not allowed to burn fuels such as wood or coal that emit smoke, either in stoves or fireplaces (although smokeless fuels such as coke briquettes are permitted). Fortunately, some cleanburn stoves approved by DEFRA are exempt. These produce low emissions when wood-burning, and some are also approved for use with coal. Your local Council should be able to advise you whether you're located in a 'smokeless zone'.

It's important to be aware that stoves can generate enormous heat within the flues, far exceeding that of traditional open fires, and hence must never be used with flues that aren't lined. It's not unknown for old houses to have joist ends embedded in chimney breasts which may have coped with temperatures generated by open fires; but the intense heat generated by stoves has been known to transfer through solid brickwork in unlined stacks causing adjoining timbers or thatch to ignite. This is why it's now a condition of installing new appliances that a suitably sturdy flue liner is fitted together with a register plate. As an additional precaution in thatched properties temperature sensors linked to an alarm should be fitted. As part of the installation process it's also normally advisable to fit a 'rain hat' to the chimney pot to prevent rainwater seeping down flues and corroding the appliance.

Metal 'rain hat' cowl keeps out birds

birdstop.co.uk.

Lining flues

If a flue and chimney are in good condition, accommodating a conventional open fire burning in the hearth shouldn't be a problem. This is, after all, precisely what they were designed to do. But the reality with old flues is that small faults aren't always easy to detect, and hidden defects can develop quite quickly. So for peace of mind's sake it's advisable to have them lined. Lining is, in any case, essential if you plan to install a new gas fire, or any gas, oil or solid fuel appliance in an existing fireplace. Traditional masonry flues are simply inadequate to cope with these more aggressive exhaust gases.

charnwood.com

Hot flue gases in unlined flues can condense on cold walls and leach through, staining brickwork

Fitting a flue liner

Right: Flexible steel Lining being inserted into pot

Below: Once lined, new cowl fitted over pot. Disused flues (left) are capped and vented

Craig Hunter - Allchimneys Ltd

Craig Hunter - Allchimneys Ltd

Fitting a flexible steel flue liner should be a fairly simple operation. Liners are inserted from the top down, which means you need two people. Proceed as follows:

■ First have the chimney professionally swept to remove accumulated soot and debris.
■ Select a liner of the correct type and diameter for your appliance.
■ Arrange safe access to the stack with scaffolding.
■ Attach a long cord to the end of the liner, and from the top of the chimney feed the cord down the flue until it reaches the fireplace below.
■ At the fireplace one person gently pulls the cord down, whilst the person up top gently feeds the liner 'snake' down in small stages.
■ To close the space between the liner and the top of the chimney a 'top plate' can be fitted underneath the chimney pot, with a 'top clamp' to take the weight of the liner.
■ At the bottom, a support bracket holds the liner in place. A flex adapter can be used to join the liner to the flue pipe from a stove or appliance.
■ Once in place, the gap between the outer skin of the liner and the masonry flue should be insulated, which can be done using non-combustible loose fill (eg leca) poured down from the top. Alternatively you can fit special insulation wraps or sleeves that just clip around the liner as it goes down the chimney.
■ Finally a rain cap should be fitted to the top, because unlike 'naked' traditional masonry flues steel liners won't absorb rain.

Where a flue is already lined you may still not be home and dry. Old flexible steel liners eventually suffer from corrosion, and it's now a requirement whenever an appliance is changed to renew any existing metal liners. In addition gas and oil appliances need special chimney-top terminals to prevent blockage from birds or debris, and to help disperse gases.

When it comes to physically inserting new flue liners, the geometry of old chimneys can sometimes be surprisingly contorted, which can pose a bit of a challenge. For example, if a flue liner gets stuck during installation at a concealed bend, it may mean having to cut a hole in a chimney breast to remove it or to help channel it down.

Stainless steel chimney liners

There are three main methods of retrospectively lining a chimney, but only one is generally considered suitable for older properties – flexible stainless steel flue liners. These are comparatively easy to install and their flexible design means they can get round bends. They're also acceptable to conservationists because the installation process isn't as aggressive as other methods, and it's also a reversible option. Building Regulations recommend a minimum diameter of 150mm.

The downside is that they don't last forever, needing renewal every 10 to 15 years, depending on how regularly the fire is used. Flexible single-skinned liners are used mainly for gas fires and for oil- or gas-fired boilers, whereas hardier double-skinned liners are required for burning solid fuels and for wood-burning and multi-fuel stoves. In terms of size, a 150mm or 200mm diameter liner is generally required for a wood-burning stove, but larger inglenooks with open hearths need wide-diameter flue liners, 300mm minimum, which are relatively expensive.

Other methods
There are two other methods of lining flues, which in most cases aren't suitable for period houses:

Solid liners
Ready-made concrete or clay liners that can be pieced together like drainage pipes and built up in short interlocking sections are widely used in new buildings. In theory it should be possible to insert these retrospectively, with each component lowered down the chimney. The surrounding gaps can be backfilled with loose insulation so that the new flue is largely independent of the old structure. However, in reality it's only possible to carry this out where an old chimney is very straight and also fairly wide, making it unsuitable for the majority of period properties.

Lightweight concrete liners
Concrete is pumped down a chimney containing an inflatable elongated thin 'balloon' that runs the full length of the flue, and sets *in situ* around this temporary balloon to form the new flue. This method isn't advisable for old buildings because poured concrete can't easily be controlled and finds its way into every cavity and crack. Also, in elaborate old flues where the concrete is thinly spread, weak spots can form at corners. Conservationists also dislike the fact that the process is permanent and irreversible. The fact is, inserting a heavy mass of incompatible rigid concrete inside an old masonry 'funnel' will inevitably set up stresses as the old building continues to naturally flex over time, because the newly solid chimney can no longer move in harmony with the surrounding house.

Chimneys

The word 'chimney' refers to the masonry structure that surrounds one or more flues. But that description hardly conveys the harshness of life endured by stacks high up at roof level. Exposed sometimes for centuries to violent storms, driving rain and everything the British weather can throw at them, chimney stacks are one of the most vulnerable and yet commonly neglected parts of a building. As if that wasn't bad enough, they also have to cope with a highly aggressive internal environment. As hot

Stepped lead flashing should provide many years' service (right). Botched job – short-life taped flashing (below)

exhaust gases condense on the cold flue walls, the toxic products of combustion – such as tar acids, ammonia and sulphates – can eat away at the mortar joints and parging. As a result chimney masonry is likely to require re-pointing or re-rendering far more frequently than less exposed walls.

High-level failure
The last thing you want balancing precariously on your roof is a dangerous structure weighing several tonnes, so an annual check with a pair of binoculars is advisable to spot any potential problems before they can become seriously dangerous. There are several areas where maintenance is commonly required.

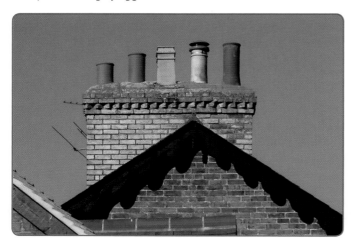

Left: Danger signs: loose, damaged pots

Below: Localised repointing required to stack brickwork (eroded bricks and flashing also of concern)

A scary sight: loose brickwork and flaunching. Partial rebuild required

RE-POINTING

The most common maintenance task with stacks is the need for at least partial re-pointing to the brick or stonework. Because of the extremes of exposure, a more durable hydraulic lime mortar mix is normally suitable, such as NHL 3.5 or NHL 5. But as is often the case with walls elsewhere on old buildings, past re-pointing in hard cement mortar has sometimes hastened the erosion of the surrounding masonry. See Chapter 5.

FLAUNCHING

The flaunching is the great mass of mortar at the base of the chimney pots that helps secure them in place. When stacks were built the pots would traditionally be placed on slivers of tile or brick laid across the corners of the stack, before being bedded in thick layers of mortar, but after many years of exposure the flaunching can eventually crack and disintegrate. And although chimney pots are reassuringly heavy, there's a potential risk they can become dislodged by a severe gust of wind or even by a sweep's brushes. Some builders find cement is more reliable than lime for use at high level, being faster setting, but because cement is brittle and potentially prone to cracking a strong NHL 5 hydraulic lime mix is generally preferable.

MASONRY REPAIRS

Modern stacks incorporate a damp-proof course to prevent any risk of water soaking down through the masonry and below roof level. But old stacks were built of relatively soft brick without the luxury of a DPC, so there's a potential risk that in severe weather conditions rainwater could saturate the stack. As a result the damp masonry

Stack repair

ALL PHOTOS COURTESY:
Baz Mogridge and E2BN / National Education Network

The 10 courses of brick need to be removed and rebuilt

Damaged chimney pot to be renewed

Victorian bricks being removed

All of the bricks removed ready for rebuild

Rebuilding the chimney with bricks to match the originals

Completed chimney – but the bricks are too bright

Bricks soot washed for instant aging effect

Scaffold removed

Job done, with lower courses re-pointed

just below the roofline can sometimes be eroded by frost (or by salts crystallising as the water evaporates). Any such damage should be visible from inside the loft, but is only likely to require repair in the rare cases where erosion is severe. This involves opening up the roof around the stack so that any badly damaged bricks can be cut out and replaced. But as always with historic buildings, the aim should be to retain as much of the original fabric as possible.

Redundant stacks

As we saw earlier, disused chimneys should be capped to restrict the ingress of rain, and also properly vented to prevent damp from forming condensation within old flues. One solution is to fit purpose-made vented hoods on the pots. Alternatively a pot can be capped completely and an airbrick inserted in the stack, as high as possible on the least visible side. If possible try to avoid taking down redundant stacks as they add architectural interest to a roofline, and their absence can spoil the appearance of a house.

Dangerous leanings

It's very common for old stacks to not be perfectly vertical. Many ancient chimneys have adopted a comfortable leaning stance that has existed quite happily for at least a century or two. The big question is, does it need fixing? Surveyors are likely to take an overly cautious approach, so the best advice is to consult a structural engineer with experience of old buildings. Where stabilisation is required, rather than expensive rebuilding, a stainless steel tie rod and strap may be all that's required. 'Stay bars' are a traditional way to secure tall or exposed chimneys and prevent the risk of rocking in high winds that could potentially lead to collapse. Any existing stay bars should be checked for rust and security of the fixings. Where severe distortion has occurred to a stack the only option may be to take down at least the upper courses of brickwork and rebuild them using like-for-like materials.

In most cases leaning will have come about as a gradual reaction over time to the aggressive forces described earlier – storm force winds and rain combined with chemical erosion inside. Fatter stacks that accommodate multiple flues tend to be warmer, and hence better protected from internal erosion. In contrast, the thin, tall, single-flue variety are more exposed to the weather, which means hot flue gases are more prone to condensing on cold masonry.

Constant wetting can cause sulphates present in the brickwork and in acrid chemicals from combustion gases to attack the mortar in chimney walls. Such sulphate attack can cause mortar joints to expand and crack horizontally, and tends to be more pronounced on the cold, windward side of the stack, which is wetter from internal condensation as well as from wind-driven rain. As a result the masonry can be 'jacked up' on one side, causing the stack to lean away from the wind. Cement mortar is especially prone to sulphate attack – another good reason to use traditional lime.

Another cause of damage to chimney masonry is from poorly fitted TV aerials (or from attached power and telecom cables). Loading such additional forces on to old chimneys does them no good, despite being convenient for the installer. Also, rust-staining from bolts and brackets can disfigure masonry – one reason why such protuberances aren't permitted on Listed buildings or in Conservation Areas.

Thankfully it's extremely rare for a leaning stack to be the result of botched removal of chimney breasts down below.

Above: Most old stacks are not perfectly vertical

Right: Steel tie rods can provide discreet support to tall thin stacks

Below: Wonky but stable

Chimney checklist

Even if you do nothing else, the following five essential checks will help you live in peace with your fireplace:

- Have the chimney swept annually.
- Check the condition of chimney stacks every 6–12 months, using binoculars.
- Check annually for smoke leakage inside the loft while the fire is lit.
- Fit a smoke alarm and CO detector in the loft.
- Never go to bed and leave an open fire unguarded.

The Victorians made chimney pots into an art form.

Chimney pots

Chimney pots weren't common until the Georgian era, although it was the Victorians who introduced them on a grand scale. This was the period when fireplace technology was taking dramatic strides in efficiency. The addition of chimney pots helped reduce the problem of smoky fires by improving the draw to the fire whilst helping to resolve problems of downdraught. Pots were a handy way of endowing chimney stacks with an instant height increase without adding to their bulk. But fashion sometimes conspired against technical efficiency. In some Georgian developments the chimneys were quite squat and shallow for purely aesthetic reasons, with pots sunk within the flue, only projecting an inch or so, to make them invisible from street level.

In earlier eras chimneys serving big inglenook fireplaces were built with large chunky stacks, with their tops simply left open. This wasn't necessarily a problem because rain falling down the flue would be temporarily absorbed into its walls until it could evaporate away. And with constantly burning fires down below, the combined action of heat and draught meant that moisture would swiftly be dispersed. Today, with less frequent use, such stacks can benefit from the addition of a 'rain cap' – a sort of mini roof built over the top of a flue. Comprising a flagstone raised up on bricks, this is a simple and visually appropriate alternative to chimney pots. The openings at the sides need to be large enough to allow sufficient air to reach the fire below, and nesting birds can be excluded with wire grilles. Above all it's essential that rain caps are anchored firmly, to resist powerful uplift forces from high winds

To protect flues with chimney pots from ingress of rain, a simple stainless steel 'rain hat' with an integral bird guard should suffice. Purpose-made pots that incorporate a cowl are also available, but must be suitable for the type of fire or appliance. Where a pot is missing or has cracked or badly spalled it will need to be replaced. Reproduction pots are readily available, but finding a precise match for some period pots can prove difficult; your best bet is to trawl through local reclamation yards.

Traditional rain cap flat roof over stack

As a rule it's best to leave the chimney termination as it was originally built, unless there are specific problems such as:

- The fireplace is suffering from a downdraught.
- Nesting birds are entering the chimney.
- The masonry of the chimney is deteriorating due to saturation from rain entering at the top.
- A stainless steel flue liner has been fitted and, being non-absorbent, could channel rainwater down to a puddle on the hearth or cause corrosion to a stove – hence the need for a rain hat.

Thatch and chimneys

Thatched houses have successfully accommodated fireplaces and chimneys for many centuries. However, where roof coverings are potentially flammable there will inevitably be a greater potential risk of fire – something that insurance premiums are likely to reflect. Conventional wisdom has it that thatch fires are brought about by rogue sparks; this may be true in some cases, but there are other, more insidious dangers.

Stack rises well above thatch surface

As we saw earlier, log-burning stoves can generate extreme temperatures within flues. A single skin of stack brickwork can, in time, allow as much as 85% of the flue gas temperature to pass to the outer surface of the chimney and into the thatch surrounding it. When you consider that modern high-efficiency stoves can generate flue gas temperatures in excess of 300° it's easy to see how the critical ignition temperature of 200° could conduct through the chimney masonry, causing the adjoining thatch to spontaneously combust.

The situation is compounded by the traditional practice of overlaying existing thatch, with new layers periodically applied. This leads to an increase in thickness over the years, and it's not uncommon for thatch next to a chimney to be well over a metre thick. This has an insulating effect on the masonry, facilitating high temperatures and hugely increasing the surface area of thatch in the critical area around the stack. Also, because thatch is steadily built up over the centuries the relative height of chimneys diminishes – in effect they become shorter, adding to the risk.

Despite such concerns, living in peace with thatch and fireplaces is perfectly possible. You can ensure complete safety in thatched properties simply by following some common-sense tips to protect yourself and your home. See the boxout.

Thatch and chimneys: wise precautions

- Install a flue gas temperature sensor linked to an alarm system – this is vital with wood-burning stoves.
- Consider inserting a physical fire barrier between the thatch and the stack masonry.
- Install a linked mains-powered smoke alarm or automatic fire detection system in the loft.
- Chimneys should extend well above the roof. The uppermost termination point of the flue should be at least 1.8m above the thatch level, and at least 2.3m horizontally from any thatched roof surface. It may be necessary to raise the stack by building it up a few courses (not just by adding a pot), or alternatively reducing the thickness of the thatch. Some insurers stipulate minimum terminal heights – check your policy or you might find you're not covered.
- 'Spark arrestors' can be fitted to the top of stacks or chimney pots. These comprise a metal mesh that's designed to trap sparks and hot embers and prevent them from floating up and settling on the thatch, but over time they can become caked with soot and transformed into a torch waiting to be lit. Unless regularly cleared, spark arrestors can actually increase the risk of fire.
- Metal flue liners should always be insulated to inhibit the conduction of heat from hot flues through stack walls.
- Flue liners must be installed by a reputable firm experienced with thatched properties.

Smoky fire solutions

Getting a fire to burn efficiently without room smoke can be difficult. Common problems include:

Cause	Solution
Blocked flue (nesting birds deposit large quantities of twigs in spring).	Get the chimney swept.
Fireplace opening is too large for size of flue.	Fit a fire hood canopy to assist in channelling smoke and reducing the effective size of the opening.
	Fit a 'register plate' to seal off the remaining flue opening (this is a horizontal plate that restricts the size of the lower flue, fitted above a large fireplace), particularly with inglenooks.
	Raise the hearth or place bricks under a fire basket to raise the height and assist the draw.
Lack of room ventilation.	Try opening the door to the room to see if it improves the draw. If it does, fit an underfloor grille in the hearth or insert air vents through the external walls.
Downdraught blows smoke back into room.	The proximity of a high building or a large tree or hill etc on the windward side will divert air currents, causing a downward draught. Raising the height of the stack, *eg* with a pot extender, can help.

For further information see guides available from the National Fireplace Association.

Smoky fires

The joy of an open fire is somewhat diminished if the smoke refuses to disappear up the chimney and instead comes billowing into the room, lending a distinctly medieval atmosphere to your indoor air quality. To diagnose the cause of such problems, it helps to go back to basics.

Fireplaces rely on the principle that hot air rises. So you're off to a head start with a regularly used flue (or a flue adjoining one that's regularly used), because this helps keep the escaping smoke warm. The next best type of flue is one that's well insulated. Some chimneys are inherently too cold to draw well, particularly those on outside walls.

Next consider any obstacles the smoke and gases are likely to encounter as they pass up the flue. Clearly the less resistance, the faster the flow. Hence the importance of smooth flue walls, or a flue liner.

Other problems that can contribute to smoky fires include flues that are damaged or blocked (hence the need for regular sweeping) and stacks that are too short or overshadowed by surrounding buildings. Problems with indoor air supply are common in houses where draughts have been totally sealed up because there's just not enough air being sucked into the fireplace.

But sometimes a smoking fire is simply down to the weather – a change in wind direction can distort the air pressure differences between the fireplace and chimney pot that normally give the smoke an extra push up.

Three examples where overshadowing could divert air currents causing downdraughts and smoky fires (left and below).

Old galvanised metal high reach pots with terminals raise flue heights (right)

11 CEILINGS, INTERNAL WALLS AND JOINERY

Old hay loft originally accessed by ladder

Above: 'Classic' beamed ceiling – but were the timbers originally painted black?

Right: Simple early ceiling construction

Open-plan living isn't something that you necessarily associate with period properties, yet many medieval houses were originally built as large halls open up to the rafters, entirely devoid of ceilings or permanent partition walls. As we saw in the previous chapter, smoke from a central fire would have filled the upper part of the house, slowly blackening the exposed roof timbers – something that can be an important clue today to the origins of old houses. It was the advent of enclosed fireplaces in the late 16th century that revolutionised internal layouts, as large open living spaces were divided into separate rooms. Freedom from smoke also made the provision of upstairs accommodation a practical proposition, with upper floors built from timber boards laid across joists.

Medieval wattle screen nicely repaired

BMulfordHistoricCarpentry.co.uk

Early partition walls would have comprised little more than curtains or fabric screens, barely sufficient to spare the blushes of well-to-do residents. Rooms were later divided with fence-like wattle hurdles woven from rushes or from sticks of willow or hazel. So in many surviving houses from this period the upper floors and internal walls are likely to be later additions.

Original features

One of the charms of old houses is that some of their features are quirky, even bizarre. A quaint corner fireplace or a curiously located partition wall may not be the ideal arrangement, but such oddities give old houses their character. So try to resist the temptation to 'tidy things up' by removing or altering them. The destruction of original fabric is a sure-fire way to devalue the special historic quality of a period property. Over the years much valuable history has been unwittingly vandalised in this way. For example medieval decorative designs were painted on internal walls and beams even in quite humble dwellings, and all it takes is a bout of over-enthusiastic decorating for such hidden treasures to be permanently obliterated. So it's important to be vigilant when work is carried out.

Medieval door to small cupboard in attic – part of this old building's story and character

Dark forces

One of the fascinating things about renovating an old house is that you sometimes stumble upon intriguing historic objects. Generations of former residents may have mislaid small items such as coins, jewellery or old toys. Even old newspapers can be a source of fascination. But there is a darker side with some houses of medieval origin.

To defend the home from the forces of the occult, objects known as 'apotropaic' (evil-averting) charms were sometimes hidden in voids, particularly beneath stairs and in fireplaces, or sometimes under floors and within walls. This might take the form of a child's shoe, bottles, dolls or written charms and marks. To propitiate evil spirits, chickens were sometimes 'walled up' – even dried cats have been unearthed.

The charm was believed to work rather like a lightning conductor, so if an evil spirit attacked the house, it would be thrown off the scent and instead drawn towards these sacrificial objects instead of coming after the people in the house. Essentially these objects were guardians that defended the property.

It was thought that at any point where air could enter the house, so too could something evil. Hence charms are most commonly found in fireplaces, because unlike doors and windows, which could be closed, flues were always open to the sky. This may explain why some houses have a void down the side of the chimney and a little opening in the loft where things could be dropped down into it. Some such voids have been found to contain collections of artefacts spanning several generations.

Some finds simply represent good luck charms. For example, when renovating you might come across a small compartment hidden in a beam, with a bag of low value old coins in it. This is the house's 'lucky money' – coins hidden by past owners over several hundred years for good fortune. The best advice is to add a few more and put it back!

Pieces of clay pipe, 2 thimbles and a pair of scissors found under oak floor boards

Baz Mogridge / E2BN

Old nail marks show joists were once concealed behind lath & plaster

Was it once plastered?

Today's obsession with hacking off old plaster has resulted in some houses losing much of their authenticity. The fashion for exposed stone or 'feature' brickwork is very much a modern concept, as traditionally the internal masonry wall surfaces would have been plastered.

However, in medieval houses the ceiling joists would originally have been left exposed, but as fashions changed in later centuries – particularly in the Georgian era – layers of lath and plaster were applied to conceal the joists and create a more sophisticated look. One clue to this is where ancient ceiling joists have chamfered lower edges, which suggests they were originally displayed. Such discoveries in Listed buildings can cause a bit of a dilemma. For example, should you tear down a comparatively youthful 18th-century ceiling to leave the original structure exposed as intended when it was built? A Conservation Officer may take the view that such additions form part of a building's history and are best retained.

Chamfered lower edges suggests joists were originally displayed

Ceilings

Ceilings originated as a simple means of enhancing privacy. Gaps between upstairs floorboards could allow light and sound to reach the prying eyes and ears of the folk downstairs who, God forbid, might hail from the serving classes. To avoid any risk of social embarrassment a thick coating of lime render was applied to a layer of timber laths nailed directly to the undersides of floorboards, literally sealing the gaps.

As we saw earlier, fashions later changed, with ceilings becoming fully enclosed to give a less rustic look. This was achieved by nailing timber laths (of split oak or chestnut, or later sawn softwood strips) to exposed joists and plastering them. This form of traditional lath and plaster construction continued until eventually superseded by modern plasterboard from the 1930s.

Decorative plasterwork

From around the 17th century, ceilings in some more expensive houses became a canvas for artistic expression. Exotic detailing sprouted from above in the shape of fabulously sculpted plaster roses and elaborate cornices made from a similar lime plaster mix to the main ceilings. Cornices would be skilfully formed by craftsmen on site, running a profiled metal sheet over a ridge of wet plaster, rather than prefabricating them as was increasingly the case from the 18th century.

Varying degrees of sophistication – from simple joist and beam (top right), vaulted (top left), and 2 examples of Victorian panelled ceilings

By the mid-Victorian period artistic ceiling ornamentation had filtered down the social scale, and a huge variety of manufactured plaster details, such as cornices, ceiling roses and corbels, became available to speculative builders. This 'fibrous plasterwork' was produced from plaster of Paris, using flexible moulds with a reinforcement of hessian scrim or a timber backing. Heavier items like ceiling roses would be nailed or screwed through the ceiling to the floor joists above, whereas lighter cornices were simply stuck in place with dabs of plaster.

Original cornice showing the oak leaf enrichments continuing on a mitre

Cutting the repeat pattern to use as a mould

Running new cornice ready to accept enrichments

Jigsaw puzzle of reclaimed original ceiling centre

Cleaning new enrichments with multi tool

Fixing individual enrichments

Nearly complete – comprises 81 individual pieces.

Repair of decorative plasterwork is a skilled job. Fortunately, even where much of it has been lost, missing sections can normally be re-cast by taking a mould from the surviving original work. New cornices can be formed in the traditional *in situ* way in stages of increasing refinement. First the basic shape is 'cored out' using a rough lime and sand mix. Then, once dry, a finer mix gauged with plaster of Paris is applied. Finally an accurate profile can be created by carefully running a fine template known as a 'running mould' along the full length of the cornice, taking care not to sneeze en route! See Chapter 14 for restoration and decoration.

Assessing your ceiling

The first thing to check with an old ceiling is whether it's original or has been replaced with sheets of modern plasterboard, usually with a skim plaster finish. Plasterboard is uniformly flat and often develops hairline cracks in straight lines at joints between sheets. Traditional lath and plaster ceilings, on the other hand, have a pleasingly undulating texture and are chunkier, often with a slight bulge evident here and there. If it's still not obvious whether a ceiling is ancient or modern, try lifting a floorboard above and taking a peak. If you can see a lot of thin timber laths with creamy blobs of plaster in between, it's an oldie.

There are good reasons for retaining original ceilings. As well as enhancing historic interiors, traditional lath and plaster has far better soundproofing qualities than modern plasterboard, being substantially thicker. Unfortunately some builders never hesitate to condemn old lath and plaster ceilings on the flimsiest evidence, such as the odd crack or bulge, or where there's a small missing piece of plaster.

Plasterers can also be quick to recommend taking down

This 300 year old ceiling could easily be replaced with angular plasterboard, erasing part of the building's character

Removal of surface plaster reveals clay and reed backing

whole ceilings and replacing them with plasterboard. But try to avoid this – plasterboard ceilings in old houses convey a flat, sterile appearance.

Such advice is sometimes aimed at drumming up extra profits, but more often is simply down to ignorance of traditional skills and materials. The fact is, traditional hair-reinforced plasters can withstand a great deal of deflection and still retain their strength. Despite appearances they may be perfectly sound, and repairable for a fraction of the cost of replacement. So never assume that an old ceiling needs replacing just because the surface is no longer flat and a few cracks have appeared.

Strengthening ceiling joists

No matter how delightful an old ceiling may look, you need to be confident that it's safe and not about to collapse. So where any

Close spacing of joists with shorter spans means ceiling is relatively strong

Right: Notches cut for pipes weaken joists and should be no deeper than 1/8th of joist depth

Below and bottom: Bowed ceiling joists can be strengthened from above in loft

Lime mortar repair to reed ceiling helps key in plaster below

underneath them. This is a non-invasive repair that prevents further deflection in old ceilings.

Clearly a different approach is required where you have rooms above a ceiling in need of strengthening. Here, once the upstairs floorboards have been lifted, new floor joists can be inserted running parallel to the old existing ones. Alternatively it may be possible to support an old ceiling from below, with the provision of a new timber beam running underneath – subject to there being sufficient spare headroom. But such 'in your face' alterations would clearly need to be undertaken with great sensitivity, and in a Listed building would require consent. Remember that structural alterations also require Building Regulations consent.

Repairing lath and plaster

Traditional ceilings were formed by nailing a web of thin timber laths across the undersides of joists. Laths are strips of wood (traditionally oak, chestnut or larch) about 25mm wide and anything from 4 – 12mm thick, spaced about 6mm apart. On to this background a base layer of thick plaster (reinforced with animal hair) was spread. This was stuck to the laths by being pushed in between them when soft, forming thick bulges on the upper side that, once dry, 'key' the plaster in place.

serious cracking or bulging is evident the first thing to investigate is its structure – the condition of the joists. To check for a weak floor, ask someone to walk around in the room whilst you calmly observe from the room below, checking for signs of excessive movement. A little light jumping up and down upstairs may reveal a certain amount of 'springiness' which is not unusual in old floors, but not to the extent that all the bedroom furniture physically gravitates towards you.

If very pronounced dipping is evident in a ceiling, lift the floorboards in the room above (or look in the attic space) to check whether the joists have deflected. Perhaps they were undersized or set too far apart when the house was originally built. Or more likely, notches or holes for pipes and cables may have subsequently been cut, further weakening old joists. A heavy load, such as a water tank in the loft, may be imposing extreme stresses. Either way, the floor structure may need strengthening. This can normally be done from above.

Where there's a loft above a weak ceiling, it's often possible to strengthen the joists by inserting a new thick timber beam or

Above: New riven chestnut lathes ceiling repair

Below: Fixing lathes using headed stainless steel ringshank nails

a steel across the top of all the joists in the roof space, leaving a small gap between them. The beam can normally be supported at either end in the main walls (or party walls). Each of the old ceiling joists is then supported by individual steel straps hung down from the beam, looping

However, over time the plaster can lose its key, often as a result of water leaks, or sometimes due to pronounced vibration, perhaps from wild parties upstairs. Water seeping from defective pipes and showers etc will eventually weaken the 'nobbly bits' that hold the plaster into the laths; damp can also cause the nails holding the laths to rust and fail. One of the most

PATCH REPAIR TO LATH

1 Cut away loose plaster around the damaged patch until it feels solid.

2 Any defective timber laths must be repaired or removed and replaced.

3 Carefully cut around the surrounding edge of the adjoining plaster with a sharp knife. Leave it cut at an angle.

4 Loose patches of plasterwork can be secured by screwing a small washer plate through to the studwork frame.

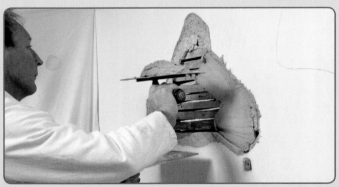

5 After dampening the adjoining plaster edges and the laths to kill suction, firmly press in fresh plaster to the patch so it 'keys' through the lath. Special gauged plaster can be applied to the full thickness in one coat, and also sets quicker.

6 The surface is 'screeded' with a board so it's flat with the surrounding wall.

7 Finally trowel on a fine finishing coat. Here a thin creamy mix comprises NHL2 in a 1:1 ratio with medium plastering sand, gauged with fine casting plaster. It is applied no more than 3mm thick so can appear virtually transparent.

All images courtesy
Studio Scotland Ltd
from
The Master Stroke
DVD Tutorial series.
To view DVD trailers go to
www.themasterstroke.com

Plastering to new traditional lath ceiling

Internal wall from landing in medieval timber frame house

common causes of damage to old ceilings is actually due to holes being cut to install concealed lighting.

Having resolved any structural issues, you need to consider whether the laths are firmly stuck to the joists, or have come loose or rotted so that they're no longer able to support the plaster. If you know the joists and laths are sound, then a deflecting ceiling must simply be due to some areas of plaster having lost their key and pulled away from their backing. Gently prodding the plaster should reveal whether it's still well adhered or is moving independently of the laths. It's often surprising just how secure old ceilings are, despite evidence of cracking and bulging.

It's not unusual to come across localised ceiling damage where small clumps of plaster have fallen away, exposing the naked laths behind. This type of small 'bald patch' can normally be repaired quite easily, as long as the laths are secure.

Where the laths have come loose, any sound ones can be re-fixed to the joists using long stainless steel screws with wide washers (nailing causes vibration). Additional support for loose laths can be provided by fixing new battens between the joists, working from above.

Where laths need replacing, first cut a rectangular-shaped hole to expose the joists on each side. Defective laths can be carefully cut out and removed and replaced with new ones (available from specialist suppliers), which are screwed to the undersides of the joists. The plasterwork can then be built up in two or three coats, depending on the required thickness.

Where an old ceiling is very badly damaged the part in poor condition can be taken down and reconstructed, reusing some of the sound existing laths. The new lime plasterwork can also incorporate some of the old lime plaster, ground-up and added to the mix – another example of how old buildings are incredibly sustainable.

Decoration

Internal surfaces were traditionally painted with soft distemper or limewash. Compared to modern emulsions (which began to replace them in the 1960s), these natural materials reflect light in a more subtle and pleasing way. They're still available today and are enjoying a resurgence in popularity. See Chapter 14 for full information on decorating old properties.

Internal walls

Internal walls were traditionally built from the same materials as the main external walls. However, in Georgian and Victorian houses with solid brick or stone main walls it's not unusual for some of the internal walls to be made of timber studwork, some with a brick noggin infill.

It's a popular misconception that if you tap a wall and it sounds hollow, it's not structural. Although some

Above: Thin stud wall to bedroom in 17th century cottage

Below: New traditional riven and sawn laths

Riven Oak

Riven Chestnut

Thick Sawn Oak

Sawn Oak

Sawn Larch

Right: Reed matting – a natural modern alternative to lath for wall lining

Below: Very old wattle and daub, covered with Victorian lath and lime plaster

Mikewye.co.uk

Heritage-house.org

Stud wall framework – where possible try to resist stripping lath & plaster

stud walls are simply partitions, many are likely to be load-bearing, supporting floors, roofs or walls above, so despite their relative thinness they should be treated as structural, especially any that incorporate the weight of brick infill.

Timber stud walls comprise a series of vertical posts spanning from the floor up to the ceiling, strengthened with horizontal timber strips in between, a time-honoured method still used today. The framework would then be clad with lath and plaster in a similar fashion to ceilings. Laths were traditionally made from hand-riven (split along the grain) chestnut or oak, although water reed was widely used as an alternative base for plaster in reed-growing areas. In the Victorian period cheaper, sawn softwood laths emerged as the predominant material.

Dry lining and studwork

Lining the internal faces of the main external walls is standard practice in new construction today, to help meet ambitious thermal insulation standards. But the builders of many old properties employed similar techniques. Instead of directly plastering the walls, in some more expensive houses they'd sometimes be clad with wood panelling or timber boarding. Alternatively, in some Georgian and Victorian properties, to help protect against damp a slim air gap was provided behind plastered laths fixed to the wall with vertical timber battens.

Lath and plaster surfaces are commonly found on internal timber stud walls, so it's important to be aware of their limitations should you need to fix something to the wall. It's best to avoid hammering nails into the lath as the wall will bounce, with a risk of fracturing the plaster nibs. Instead, pre-drill a couple of fine pilot holes in sound strips of timber lath – it may take more than one attempt to avoid the gaps between them. Then insert screws in the pre-drilled holes. Note that this technique is only suitable for supporting lighter objects, such as small picture frames. Any

weighty fixings need to pass right through the lath and plaster into the sturdy timber studwork posts or noggins behind. When it comes to supporting things like heavy shelves, to avoid damaging fragile plasterwork the traditional method was to first fix a stout horizontal batten across the main studwork frame and then secure the shelves to the batten. This is the same principle used for picture rails run along the upper walls.

Right: Timber embedded in wall ready to support new cistern

Below: New lath and matching studwork adjoining original oak

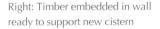

Mikewye.co.uk

Right: The natural charm of lime – with distinctive round edges to reveals

Mikewye.co.uk

Plasterwork

It's widely believed that the first job when renovating an old building is to start frantically hacking off all the plaster from the interior. But it's rarely necessary to remove old lime plaster – any cracks or gaps can normally be filled, and visual flaws are easily concealed with a coat of traditional limewash or distemper.

The appearance and texture of historic plasters and renders lends old properties character and beauty, as well as offering practical benefits. Traditional lime plaster allows walls to breathe, and because it absorbs excess humidity and is warmer to the touch (compared to plasterboard) it helps reduce condensation problems. It's also pretty straightforward stuff to repair. But most important of all, it just looks right.

Unfortunately a lot of old houses have been re-plastered in recent years with sterile modern gypsum plaster or hard cement

Hard modern gypsum plasters tend to crack as old buildings move and appear flat and uniform

render, in a misguided attempt to solve damp problems. And, as we saw earlier, many historic ceilings have been unnecessarily torn down and replaced with plasterboard. So if you're lucky enough to still have original plasterwork in your home, it's well worth conserving. Traditional plaster walls that aren't perfectly straight or regular are very much part of an old building's character, so don't be tempted to smooth them over when redecorating. Another interesting feature can sometimes be seen on internal corners of old walls. Whereas modern plasterers use concealed metal 'angle beads' to achieve a neat corner finish, in old buildings traditional rounded timber battens known as 'corner staffs' were often left visible.

Materials and mixes

In many older properties it's likely that at least some parts of the walls will have been re-plastered in recent years, most commonly the lower main walls. Modern gypsum plasters normally have a pinkish-brown colour (or occasionally light grey) and a harder and flatter finish than lime. But being highly rigid and inflexible, they have a tendency to develop cracks as the old walls continue to naturally flex. Worse, where damp-proofing works have been carried out there's usually a hard base coat of cement render beneath the surface plaster at lower levels. Although this is undesirable, hacking it off can sometimes cause even more damage, so in some cases conservationists may reluctantly advise that it's left undisturbed.

Modern gypsum plasters are generally incompatible with use on old solid walls that need to breathe. Whereas lime can happily tolerate dampness passing through it in small doses, gypsum plasters become saturated very quickly, drawing moisture out of walls and absorbing it from humid air. Gypsum plasters also tend

Fresh lime plaster mix

to retain damp, which eventually causes them to dissolve. So wherever possible traditional lime plaster should be used.

Traditional plasters were based on lime or clay (sometimes both) mixed with sand or, more rarely, chalk. Lime plasters, renders and mortars are basically the same mix (if anything plaster should be slightly richer in lime, say 1 part lime to 2½ or 3 parts sharp sand). Although a small amount of soft, fine sand is sometimes added to the mix to make it smoother, don't be tempted to only use soft sand as you'll just end up with lot of cracks. The main difference compared to lime mortar is the added ingredient of chopped animal hair as a binder to the undercoats, although sometimes hay was used. This is critical (especially for lath) as it dramatically reduces shrinkage and cracking as well as making the plaster stronger.

A plaster mix made from lime putty (ie non-hydraulic lime) is normally the best bet. This should provide excellent flexibility, which is important in old buildings prone to seasonal movement, whilst also offering maximum breathability. It can be purchased ready mixed, and even delivered to site by the tonne. The lime putty should ideally be at least three months old to ensure it's thoroughly slaked.

Where a tougher mix is needed, such as for plastering walls below ground in cellars, a moderately hydraulic lime such as NHL 3.5 could be suitable. However, stronger mixes have reduced breathability, so a weaker NHL 2 mix may be a good compromise.

Modern renovating plasters such as 'Limelite' are more robust than conventional gypsum plasters, and are claimed to allow walls to gradually dry out whilst limiting the absorption of salts. They also have a relatively porous face to help discourage condensation. But being cement-based they offer only limited breathability, so are never as suitable as the real deal, at least for main walls which need to breathe.

Gauging plaster

Lime plasters are sometimes gauged with gypsum to achieve a faster initial set and a more workable mix (although it still needs 3 days to cure). Once the raw lime 'coarse stuff' has been made up (e.g. 1 part lime to 3 parts sharp sand, plus hair) it is laid out on a board, and a small amount of gypsum powder mixed in. However this also has the effect of making the mix less breathable and more susceptible to salts. So it should only be used on walls or ceilings of lath construction (i.e. with an air gap behind). Gypsum must NOT be added to plaster for use on the inside faces of main walls.

Lime plaster coats

Plaster was traditionally applied directly on to brick or stonework walls, or alternatively on to a backing of timber laths. Depending on the quality of the building, it would comprise double or triple coats. The mix differed only slightly between each coat, the weakest being the topcoat which used finer sand for a smoother finish. To control suction (and prevent rapid drying out and cracking) surfaces would be dampened prior to plastering.

The first coat was known as a 'rendering coat' when applied to masonry, but when applied to a background of timber lath was called the 'pricking-up' coat – referring to the way the plaster 'pricks' through gaps between the laths (or so we're told). Alternatively both are sometimes referred to as 'scratch coats', because their surface is scratched in a diamond pattern to create a key for the next coat. This coat of 'hairy plaster' would need to be thick enough to even out irregularities in the wall (typically about 8mm thick on lath, and a shade thicker on masonry).

For better quality work, where achieving a very flat finished surface was important, an intermediate 'floating coat' or 'straightening coat' was applied to a similar thickness as the first coat. This would be carefully worked to get it dead flat. To even out bumps and hollows, particularly to ceilings, a length of straight timber known as a 'floating rule' would be passed across the surface ('screeded'). This intermediate coat was then 'scratched' to provide a key for the final coat, using a float with nails pricked through it known as a 'devil float', applied with a light circular motion. The final 'setting coat' or 'skimming coat', just a couple of millimetres thick, was a mix of lime putty and fine sand designed to create a smooth surface. Traditionally this work was often so smooth that it was sometimes mistaken for painted ashlar stonework. Alternatively, it could be given a slightly open, textured finish.

Damaged plaster

If you tap the surface of a masonry wall and it sounds hollow, it isn't necessarily cause for concern. Lime plaster is very resilient because the hair reinforcement binds it strongly together. This makes it act as a large sheet, even if a few smaller areas have parted company from the wall. That said, plaster at low levels can sometimes break up if it gets very damp (for example as a result of high ground levels).

Where a house has a history of damp, the internal plaster on the main external walls will have absorbed salts carried in solution.

As the moisture evaporates these crystallise on the surface of the plaster in the form of white salts. In small quantities these can simply be brushed off, but as we saw in Chapter 2, where larger amounts of salts have crystallised this can lead to a strange phenomenon occurring. Being hygroscopic they can absorb fresh moisture from the atmosphere of the room, giving the appearance of fresh damp. Although usually only superficial, any heavily salt-laden plaster is best replaced with two coats

Wall patch repaired in lime plaster, scratched for next coat

of new lime plaster (which is naturally breathable). But before re-plastering the source of the damp must first be resolved, and the wall allowed sufficient time to dry out. Any traces of salts must be brushed or vacuumed off, but not washed otherwise the water will dissolve the salts which will then leach back into the wall. A similar problem sometimes occurs on chimney breasts where salt-laden soot stains have leached through the plaster from moisture in unlined flues.

In more severe cases, one possible solution is to conceal salt contaminated walls and stained surfaces behind a new layer of dry lining. However, this is likely to involve considerable disruption to radiators, window reveals, skirting and architraves, and only suits walls without ceiling cornices and decorative features.

Traditional dry lining techniques can be applied by fixing a layer of timber laths to battens secured to the masonry. However, reed mat is now widely used as a less expensive natural substitute for traditional laths – see 'New plasterwork' below. Alternatively, dry lining with conventional plasterboard can be another option, since it allows a degree of breathability and the works are reversible. However, lime plaster doesn't adhere well to plasterboard.

If you plan to carry out dry lining works it may be worth going the whole hog and insulating the walls. See Chapter 16.

To deal with fine cracks a standard flexible filler can be used, such as decorators' caulk applied with an applicator gun. For small patch repairs lime plaster can be applied direct to masonry, or over traditional timber laths or sections of reed matting. Both are preferable to modern expanded metal lath (EML), which is unauthentic and can be prone to corrosion.

Mikewye.co.uk

Above and below: Cracks filled and ready for decoration

Mikewye.co.uk

Plastering to lath

1 Scooping out the prepared lime putty mortar with added horse hair.

2 Showing the consistency required.

3 Firmly working the lime mortar into the gaps in the lath.

4 Achieve a rough level and create an open texture before scratching.

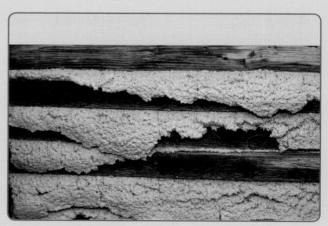

5 This shows the type of key required behind the lath to help prevent failure.

Decorative plasterwork

Freehand strapwork in the Jacobean style using a straight mix of course sand and fat lime.

A limewash finish is applied for aged look. Design copied from an early wood carving.

New plasterwork

Lime plaster adheres particularly well to surfaces that offer a degree of suction, such as old brickwork. It also adheres to some more absorbent types of modern concrete blockwork. Where surfaces are smooth or have poor suction a flexible resin can be added to the first coat, although this inhibits breathability.

If a completely new stud wall or ceiling needs to be constructed you can buy new traditional timber laths from specialist suppliers, although for larger areas this can work out quite expensive, as well as being very labour-intensive. Reed matting is an excellent alternative as a natural base both for internal and external work, and is much cheaper than lath. It's similar to the reed fence screening that you can buy in garden centres and is sold in rolls. The matting is quick and relatively easy to fix in place, secured with strips of lath screwed to the timber studwork or ceiling joists (or it can be applied using a nail gun). The 'pricking up' base coat can then be applied, with its finished surface 'devilled' and left to dry for at least a week or two before the setting coat is applied. For a dead flat surface, an intermediate floating coat may be necessary. Compared to modern materials lime plasters set relatively slowly by absorbing CO_2 from the air. During the drying process they tend to shrink, so any drying cracks will need to be periodically trowelled closed.

For rooms with a relatively humid atmosphere, such as kitchens and bathrooms, the plaster can be given a slightly coarser open-textured surface using a wooden float. This makes the walls more vapour-permeable, and a limewash finish should help absorb excess moisture.

Choosing a plasterer

To achieve a nice, stable, crack-free finish in lime plaster takes skill and experience, so it's better to wait to get the right person rather than risk employing a conventional plasterer who'll be learning on the job. There are three questions you can ask to help sort the true craftsmen from the boys:

1 'What mix do you intend to use?'
   Tip: Even a small amount of cement isn't acceptable.
2 'How many coats should be applied?'
   Tip: It should be at least two.
3 'How much time do you need to leave between coats?'
   Tip: It should be at least a week.

Standard plaster mix: lime putty

Used internally for ceilings and internal walls above ground. Used externally as render for softer backgrounds, eg lath, mud, soft brick and stone.

	1 Scratch coat or pricking-up coat on ceilings, and rendering coat on masonry	2 Floating coat or straightening coat	3 Setting coat or skim coat
Sand	3 parts sharp well-graded sand	As per scratch coat	1 or 2 parts silver sand (kiln-dried and sieved)
LIME	1 part mature lime putty (thick)	As per scratch coat	1 part mature lime putty (thick)
HAIR	Horse hair, goat hair or hay (2kg per tonne of plaster)	None, or sometimes a finer goat hair (2kg per tonne of plaster)	None

Special plaster mix: hydraulic lime

Used internally for below ground plastering, eg to basements. Used externally as render for harder masonry backgrounds.

	1 Scratch coat or rendering coat on masonry	2 Floating coat or straightening coat
SAND	2.5 parts sharp, well-graded sand	As per scratch coat
LIME	1 part NHL 2 or NHL 3.5	As per Scratch coat
HAIR	Horse hair or goat hair (2kg per tonne of plaster)	None

Internal joinery

It's surprising how much of the history and status of a property can be revealed from its internal joinery – the visible finished woodwork. If you take the trouble to look closely, old marks and imperfections can hold fascinating clues to the story of your house and its previous occupants. These are records from the past that grow in interest and character with the passing years, so shouldn't be automatically sanded smooth.

Features like original doors, shutters, picture rails, skirting boards and staircases all have a tale to tell, as well as being a source of considerable period charm that significantly adds to the value and character of an old house. Despite this, such irreplaceable features are often needlessly removed.

The quality of joinery can reveal a great deal about the property's status, and can be very useful for dating a building. According to ancient folklore old beams and panelling from demolished abbeys or grand houses were frequently re-deployed, so if you notice curiously shaped markings it could be indicative of unorthodox origins.

Historic joinery should be regarded similarly to antique furniture and cared for with the same zeal. Where damage is evident it should normally be possible to repair – after all, you wouldn't chuck out an 18th-century Hepplewhite dressing table just because one of the legs was damaged. Repair is normally the least

Old burn marks made by candles

expensive option as well as the most sustainable. Another good reason for retaining as much old joinery as possible is that the timber used in years gone by was far more durable than today's kiln-dried variety.

Where some of the original features have been misguidedly stripped out in the past, with a little detective work it's sometimes possible to track down suitable replacements. However, obtaining an exact match for original skirting boards and architraves can often be impossible today because of the infinite number of local variations in the past. If replacement or repair isn't possible it may be worth having matching items crafted using materials of a similar quality.

Doors

Traditional medieval 'ledge and brace' internal doors made from vertical timber planks were gradually superseded from the Georgian era by the more sophisticated panelled variety. If you're lucky enough to still have any of the original doors in an old house, a closer inspection may reveal mysterious marks and holes, evidence perhaps that they were made from ancient salvage, dating back centuries. Sometimes it transpires that an original door has been moved and altered for reuse in another location.

In properties with recent loft conversions the original internal doors may have been replaced to comply with fire regulations. If so they may have been stashed away in an outbuilding or basement. Sometimes such sacrifices are made unnecessarily, because it's

Baz Mogridge / E2BN

normally possible to upgrade the fire resistance of original doors using special paint or boarding and fitting intumescent seals to door linings.

Old door furniture can be a source of much delight. Ancient handles and hinges are often works of art in their own right, as well as revealing information about a house's history. Where hinges have become worn or damaged, rather than simply replacing them it's often a better option to leave them in place and supplement them with additional new matching ones. Similarly, it should be possible to repair and retain pleasingly stout old door locks, for which new keys can be made.

On Georgian and Victorian panel doors, fingerplates were sometimes fitted above doorknobs to keep dirty finger marks at bay. These later became unfashionable and are often missing. However, a closer inspection may reveal old screw holes or impressions in paintwork where such items of original door furniture have since been removed, providing sufficient clues to enable matching replicas to be sourced.

Panelling

Hardwood wainscotting

The origin of the timber skirting boards that run along the foot of our walls today was as a minimal form of panelling, harking back to the grander houses of the 16th and 17th centuries, where full-height carved oak panelling was a highly desirable feature. Early oak panelling tended to have quite small square panels, and would either be left plain or given a waxed or oiled finish. Intriguingly, in some properties – particularly those dating from the Tudor and Stuart periods – it's not uncommon to find false panels concealing sliding doors leading to long forgotten passages or 'priest holes'.

From the mid-Georgian era full-height room panelling began to go out of fashion, as it had the effect of making rooms feel rather gloomy, and was gradually superseded by wainscoting. This was a sort of halfway house, where only the lower wall was lined with

Painted Georgian full height wall panelling

timber panelling and the upper walls were plastered, with a painted frieze applied towards the ceiling.

Matchboarding

Georgian wainscoting typically comprises a horizontal moulded rail known as a 'chair rail' about a metre above floor level, designed to protect the wall from being knocked by chair backs, with continuous wooden panelling inserted between this and the skirting. Later, in Victorian times, the moulded rail was set higher and known as a 'dado rail'. Wainscoting was used to provide a partially panelled wall finish to many halls and staircases in more expensive houses. It was commonly made from softwood and painted or given a faux wood-grain appearance in imitation of dearer hardwood timber.

However traditional wood panelling was too expensive for most mainstream housing, so cheaper 'matchboarding' was applied to the lower walls of many Victorian hallways and sculleries. This comprised vertical planed, tongued and grooved softwood boards, similar to those used for flooring, topped with a horizontal run of moulded dado beading.

PANEL CONSTRUCTION

Timber panelling was made from a framework of uprights and cross members carefully jointed together with wooden pegs, glue and nails. This was infilled with timber panels slotted into grooves cut into the framing rather than being fixed in place, to allow for contraction and expansion independently of the framework. But appearances can be deceptive. Whilst some panels are made of sheet timber, others are formed from large planks laid vertically or horizontally, skilfully disguised by being filled and painted. At its simplest, this arrangement is essentially the same as that used to make panelled doors but on a larger scale. However, because of the complexity of construction it can prove extremely difficult to take wall panelling apart without causing damage, as it often employed 'secret fixing' to background timbers.

Where panelling has been in contact with damp walls or floors for long periods it may have suffered localised rot. To avoid unnecessary damage from dismantling, it may be possible to repair individual rotten sections without disturbing the rest. Where repairs are made it's important to source replacement timber of comparable quality to the original.

Shutters

The Georgian fashion for internal window shutters persisted to varying degrees through to the Edwardian era. Shutters were generally made from high quality imported softwoods, although in more expensive houses oak or mahogany would be the material of choice. The standard format comprised panelled leaves hinged to the window jambs designed to neatly fold into timber boxes at the sides of windows. Some shutters were divided horizontally into hinged pairs, allowing the householder to close the bottom section whilst leaving the top part open, thus letting in light whilst maintaining privacy. An alternative system, popular in the Victorian era, comprised

Storm windows

vertically sliding wooden sash boards. These were concealed within panelling beneath the windows and could be partially raised to provide security whilst admitting a certain amount of light.

Being remarkably unobtrusive these may appear to be an integral part of the wall panelling, particularly when disguised by numerous layers of paint, hence many householders today are unaware that their house even has shutters. If you're lucky enough to still retain the originals, they're well worth reinstating to their former glory, as they're very effective at keeping in the heat as well as deterring burglars.

Any small cracks can be filled with wood filler. Wider cracks can be filled with slivers of timber and sanded. Should the original shutters no longer exist, consider having replacements custom made.

Staircases

The medieval open hall house had no real need for stairs. Those that existed might comprise little more than ladders propped up at the end of the hall to access adjoining storage areas. In contrast, grander buildings such as castles and churches would contain stone spirals built into end walls or projecting turrets.

It was only with the advent of fireplaces and upper floors that stairs needed to be incorporated into residential dwellings. Many houses were modernised with simple timber winder stairs installed next to the new brick chimney breast. The space below these stairs sometimes housed a bread oven to the side of the fireplace. To avoid draughts it was common practice for stairs to be shut off by doors top and bottom. Many such early examples were subsequently replaced with easier to negotiate straight flights; the empty recesses, where the original ones stood, often survive as cupboards.

Larger houses would often have two or more staircases – a main one for the family and a discreet back one for servants, plus additional stairs serving basements and attic rooms.

Today even in the plainest houses an original staircase can be an absolute delight, with beautifully crafted newel posts,

banisters and balusters (spindles). But that doesn't mean they're always easy to live with. Many old stairs will be considerably steeper than today's maximum permitted 42°, with an alarming lack of headroom, and stair treads that bear little resemblance to the dimensions of modern feet. But even where they're in poor repair, that's no reason to replace them. Installing a new staircase requires Building Regulations approval, and it's rarely possible to fit new stairs into an old building without making major alterations.

Staircases were generally well built from good quality timber, or from hardwearing stone in the case of servants' stairs. Most problems today simply relate to normal wear and tear. Fortunately it should be a fairly straightforward job to replace a damaged or badly worn tread, although repair work will obviously be easier where access can also be gained from below, for example via a handy understairs cupboard. Where the underside is plastered, it's not usually advisable to risk damage by breaking it open.

The occasional broken spindle is a common maintenance issue, and it's normally possible to effect a neat repair by gluing

and temporarily clamping the two parts together. For additional strength a split spindle can be reinforced before gluing with a dowel drilled into the broken end of each piece.

The most serious defects with staircases are generally found where rot or beetle has taken hold, typically where there's a damp adjoining wall or floor. Repair or partial replacement usually requires some compromise, with a balance struck between conservation and safety.

Stripping and painting

Before setting out to restore joinery, consider whether the various marks and bumps would be better left on display as an interesting part of the building's life story. How best to prepare and decorate is covered in detail in Chapter 14.

12 FLOORS

Entrance porch featuring original with c.19th geometric and encaustic tiles

Above: Salvaged woodblock flooring

Left: Cast iron air grilles – original features that perform a key role

Below: Imperfections add character and are part of an old building's story

Many period cottages that sell today for eye-wateringly high prices started life as relatively humble dwellings with ground floors of bare earth. Even in better quality medieval houses, the floors were generally just strewn with rushes. The 'ground' floor was aptly named. Compacted earth remained the norm in crofters' cottages and much of rural Britain until as late as the 19th century, although for those who could afford them, flagstones might be adopted, or a layer of bricks or clay tiles placed directly on top.

By the Georgian era timber ground floors mimicking those upstairs were becoming established in townhouses, as a way of accommodating large basement rooms. But suspended timber ground floors were also starting to make an appearance in houses without basements. This was achieved by building small hidden 'sleeper walls' or brick piers to support the joists and raise them off the damp earth. To keep timber floors dry, small air grilles in the lower walls provided ventilation. This method of construction became virtually universal in Victorian houses for reception rooms, as well as for many entrance halls.

Timber floors

A really old floor can be a bit of a jigsaw puzzle, comprising various hand-sawn planks of different widths and thicknesses, smoothed by centuries of wear. Such floors are rarely uniform, and often contain a few boards that have obviously been cut and relaid at some point in the distant past. But such imperfections are part of the story and character of the house.

As a rule, the wider the floorboards the more ancient they are. Hardwood boards found in older properties, usually of native oak or elm, tend to be broader than later softwood ones, and are less likely to warp. Over time the introduction of machine sawing and imported softwood resulted in boards becoming more standardised, with a gradual reduction in sizes. So whereas a typical Georgian board might be about 200mm (8in) wide, later Victorian boards were generally narrower, at about 150mm (6in). Later tongued and grooved interlocking designs were manufactured to still thinner and narrower dimensions.

Lifting floorboards can sometimes throw a bit of light on the lifestyles of former occupants of your house. Amongst the

Below: A spot of light localised rubbing down may be all an old floor needs

Floor timbers had to be kept clear of hot hearths

Remnants of original floorboards in medieval building could be incorporated when repairs are undertaken

accumulated coal dust and cobwebs in the void above the ceilings you sometimes come across old artefacts such as cigarette packets, lost coins and beads, or even remnants of workmen's lunches, such as oyster shells. Voids to upper floors, especially those between the main bedrooms and servants' quarters in attics, were sometimes filled or 'pugged' with straw, grass, sand or wood shavings, in a bid to deaden sound transmission.

Most rooms had fireplaces, which needed a projecting hearthstone in front, incorporated within the floor (raised hearths are a modern practice). So that the timber joists didn't terminate under the hot hearth they were cut short and connected to a trimmer beam run parallel to the front of the hearth (ie at right angles to the joists). To form the hearth itself, deafening boards were fitted and packed with cinders or clinker and the hearthstone laid on top. The floorboards were then laid flush with the hearthstone.

Floor finishes

When you lift modern fitted carpets to expose an old timber floor you may notice something a bit puzzling – a pale oblong area

towards the centre surrounded by darker outer edges. This is because it was common practice before the days of wall-to-wall carpeting to place a large central rug in the middle of the room, with the area beyond stained black. One of the cheapest and most popular types of floor covering in Georgian and Victorian homes was oilcloth – a large rug comprising canvas sheet sealed with linseed oil perhaps decorated with a painted tiled pattern.

Georgian timber floors were sometimes left bare, or sprinkled with a little sand to 'self-clean' as people walked over them (sand adjacent to chamber pots also came in useful for absorbing gentlemen's nocturnal sprinklings). Today the preferable finish for treating old timber floors is to simply apply a natural breathable wax or a light natural oil that wears away gracefully and can be easily reapplied.

Repairing timber floors

Old floors are very much part of the charm of period houses and should be retained whenever possible, especially if you're lucky enough to have original hardwood boards. Fortunately most defects in timber floors are relatively straightforward to fix.

FLOORBOARD REPAIRS

Even floors that are perfectly sound structurally are likely to harbour the occasional loose or damaged board. However, removing old floorboards without causing collateral damage isn't always easy. The task is made harder because boards were traditionally laid using special large flat nails called 'brads' that

An old floor can be a bit of a jigsaw puzzle

A new batten screwed to adjoining boards

Most floors will show signs of past repairs

firmly grip them, preventing squeaks. Generations of plumbers and electricians carelessly prising up boards and cutting joists is a major cause of harm to old floors. Most obviously at risk are medieval houses where the floorboards are plastered on their underside to form a ceiling below.

To facilitate lifting, it can sometimes be necessary to cut across a board. For a neat result it's generally easier to cut it along the side of the joist, rather than at its centre, but this means a new batten will need to be screwed to the side of the joist, to support the cut end of the board when it's reinstated. For re-fixing boards it's best to use brass screws rather than nails. This allows for possible future lifting, and also protects delicate plaster ceilings below from hammer vibration.

As we saw in Chapter 8, most old houses will show signs of past wood beetle activity, something that's very common and normally superficial. So it's important not to overreact to old bore holes in floorboards. Only in extreme cases would the odd length of board be sufficiently worm-ridden to need replacing.

Where a length of old floorboard is genuinely damaged beyond repair, unfortunately you can't just slap in a bit of modern off-the-shelf softwood, as it will normally be too thin and narrow, as well as looking pretty obvious. Reclaimed boards are widely available, or it should be possible to have a matching one made from seasoned timber.

Fortunately, most problems can be remedied with a few straightforward repairs that make the most of the original materials, helping to retain the character of an old building. Weakened boards can be reinforced and strengthened by 'secretly' doubling them up with a length of new board fixed underneath, spanning between the joists. Alternatively, additional support can be provided by fitting new battens underneath, screwed to the adjacent boards on either side as long as they're in sound condition. Split boards can be glued and cramped back together. Where you've got localised damage to corners this can normally be repaired by splicing in small strips of new timber.

Gaps between boards can be useful to allow an old house to flex and stretch as well as providing ventilation, so it's best not to seal them up entirely. However, where draughts are a problem gaps can be filled with thin slivers of matching timber, or cosmetic repairs can be made by gluing papier mâché or strips of cork in

Edwardian woodblock flooring

place, which still allow slight movement. The alternative method of lifting all the boards and re-laying them butted tightly together isn't advisable because, inevitably, some of the boards will get damaged, and the process can weaken old floor structures.

Woodblock flooring was popular in more expensive houses in the Edwardian era. After a long period of time individual blocks sometimes come loose, and although it's relatively simple to have them reset any associated damp must first be resolved.

These floors are sometimes restored by sanding and varnishing, although conservationists generally prefer less harsh methods. For example, built-up layers of old polish can be removed using a suitable solvent, and the floor given a light manual sanding before applying a traditional finish of natural oil or wax polish. This method allows for occasional re-waxing or oiling, and is easier than re-varnishing when the surface becomes scratched.

Upper floors

The earliest upstairs floors comprised wooden planks laid across simple timber joists, although limeash plaster laid over wattle laths or reeds was sometimes used as a cheaper alternative to floorboards. As we saw earlier, plaster ceilings were originally applied directly to

Gaps between boards can allow an old house to stretch

Baz Mogridge / E2BN

Original oak floor boards in attic

the underside of the floor. Today exposed ceiling beams are one of the most appealing features in surviving medieval houses, but of course, these weren't put there simply to be admired.

Until the Great Fire of London, terraced houses were commonly built with the floor joists running from side to side, resting in the party walls between the houses. But this essentially created a linear run of timber along entire streets, heightening the risk of fire spreading from house to house. Subsequent legislation dictated that from the Georgian period onwards joists were instead run from front to rear, thereby allowing partition walls to act as firebreaks. But because floor joists could typically only span about 3m or 4m, in most terraced housing this necessitated the provision of internal supporting walls, which dictated room depths and layouts. However, such limitations could sometimes be overcome and hence larger room sizes created by supporting the joists on thick beams run underneath, instead of internal walls. If the span was too great, beams could be given a little extra support from a stout wooden post within the room.

Earlier oak or elm joists were often squarer and bulkier than later softwood Georgian and Victorian ones, which were typically sized about 8in x 2in (200mm x 50mm) and spaced fairly close together (about every 400mm). From a structural perspective, as well as holding up floors and ceilings, joists also provide crucial

Medieval jettied floor – from inside daylight is visible at base of wall

lateral restraint. Being built into the main walls, they help tie-in and strengthen the walls at each end of the house.

Inevitably builders were sometimes tempted to economise on materials, particularly in areas hidden from view, so cheaper houses were sometimes built with relatively thin joists spaced a little further apart than necessary. As a result some upper floors can feel a little springy. Many old floors have subsequently been further weakened by having notches and holes cut in them by plumbers and electricians. This is likely to result in floors deflecting, with consequential cracking to the ceilings below. Where floors suffer from being overly springy and weak they can normally be stiffened by wedging thick blocks of wood between the joists every 1.5m or so in order to brace them. It may be necessary to strengthen the floor by installing additional joists run between or alongside the existing ones. Where there are weak points in floor joists they can be stiffened by attaching straps or plates alongside, as described below.

In many earlier properties, where the upper floors are supported from beneath by chunky ceiling beams, it's not unusual for the beams to have sagged, and hence the floors to have dipped – sometimes quite alarmingly. But such movement is normally of an historic nature and may even have helped tighten the floor structure. Often all you need to do is adjust the legs on beds and wardrobes to accommodate a sloping floor. However, where a timber beam shows recent signs of stress and has cracked across the grain, it's usually because some additional loadings have been applied – perhaps a heavy cast iron bath has been installed upstairs. In such cases a structural engineer will need to advise on how best to beef up support without sacrificing historic fabric.

Structural repairs

Where an old timber beam has significantly weakened it's often as a result of fungal decay, sometimes aided and abetted by beetle attack. Floor beams in damp cellars are particularly vulnerable. Often closer inspection

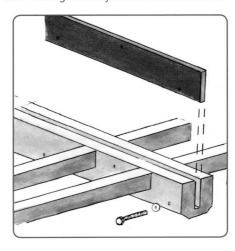

Flitch plate

will reveal that the damage is superficial, or limited to beam ends (see below). Where widespread weakening has occurred the obvious solution would be to simply replace it with a suitable steel. However, although this would provide a structurally appropriate solution it would destroy the original character of the floor. Alternatively a new oak beam could be installed, but this can be very costly and similarly would involve a loss of original fabric.

Fortunately there are ways that historic beams can be strengthened with the minimum of disturbance. Joists can be beefed up by bolting thick strips of plywood in place either side. But this takes up space as well as being visually obvious. A similar repair can be made using pre-drilled steel plates nailed in place, taking up much less space.

Where appearance is important, for example with exposed ceiling beams, steel reinforcements can be 'invisibly' sandwiched inside the beam. There are two main ways that such 'secret' repairs are carried out, in both cases working from above by lifting the floorboards to expose the top of the beam. One is to make a 'rod and resin' repair (as shown in Chapter 7). A deep slot is cut centrally along the full length of the beam, stopping short of the bottom (ie not so deep that it's cut in half). Into this channel, steel reinforcement rods are inserted. A resin mix is then poured on top to securely bed the rods and fill up the channel. Once set the beam should be as good as new, if not stronger. Where engineers specify epoxy resin in structural repairs it should be slow-setting, to allow it to soak into the timber.

Flitch plate repairs use a similar principle but are usually applied where a beam requires localised strengthening over a shorter span. Here a central slot is similarly cut into the beam, spanning the weakened section. Then a custom-made steel plate is inserted into the channel and securely bolted from either side. Both these repairs have the advantage of retaining an old building's irreplaceable original fabric while being virtually invisible.

ROTTEN BEAM ENDS

Traditionally joists were built into pockets in the main walls. But in properties where the external walls were particularly exposed to the elements, or poor maintenance allowed damp to penetrate, the embedded joist ends could eventually start to rot. One solution where floors are vulnerable from exposure to saturated masonry is to fit new galvanised steel joist hangers to keep the timber away from the wall.

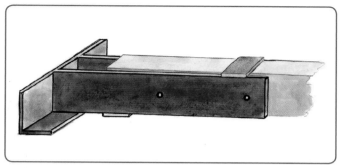

Steel joist extender

In extreme cases, lifting the floorboards adjacent to such walls may reveal that joist ends have been completely eaten away. Consequently there may now be a gap between the wall and the remaining body of the joist. A similar problem is sometimes found where walls have bowed or where the roof has pushed the upper walls out, so that they've parted company with the joist ends. A useful solution in both cases is to fit steel 'shoe' joist extenders that re-establish connection between the joists and the wall (see also Chapter 8). To carry out these works, the floorboards directly above the joist ends need to be lifted, as well as a small strip of the ceiling below. Once the joists have been extended and reconnected to the wall the boards are refixed in place, so you don't have to worry about such repairs looking pretty. However, where a weakened joist or beam end is visually important there are two main methods of achieving an 'invisible' repair. The traditional approach is to make a 'scarf' repair, replacing the defective section with matching oak or treated softwood, as described in Chapter 8. Alternatively, joists can be tied back in by inserting a steel bar through the wall from outside. This involves first drilling a suitable hole through the wall and into the joist. A special threaded stainless steel rod (known as a 'helical bar') with a fabric sleeve is then inserted, and the sleeve filled with resin to form a tight connection between the bar and the timber and masonry.

Ground floors

Timber ground floors are potentially more at risk of decay affecting the joist or beam ends embedded in damp walls. Before carrying

Scarf joint neatly blends new timber with remaining original joist

Sub floor void with brick pier supporting timber floor plate

Sub floor void with brick sleeper walls

Original limestone flags

out repairs, the causes of failure must first be remedied. The usual suspects are:

- High external ground levels, causing lower walls to become damp, hence joist ends resting in the walls can start to rot.
- Very wet ground, causing damp to rise via the masonry sleeper walls upon which the timber floor plates sit (perhaps where surface water from the garden has flooded in through airbricks). Hidden leaks from water supply pipes under suspended timber floors can remain undiscovered for surprisingly long periods, risking 'rising damp' to internal walls or, worse, settlement to the foundations. So it's worth lifting the occasional floorboard to check that the sub-floor void is dry and well ventilated.
- Blocked air grilles restricting the ventilation that helps keep timbers dry.
- A build-up of debris in the sub-floor void, forming a bridge between damp ground and floor timbers.

The good news is that damage is usually very localised. At worst it may be necessary to replace a few joists or timber floor plates. When reinstating timbers it's worth protecting them by inserting a strip of plastic DPC around joist ends sitting in walls, and under timber wall plates lying on top of sleeper walls.

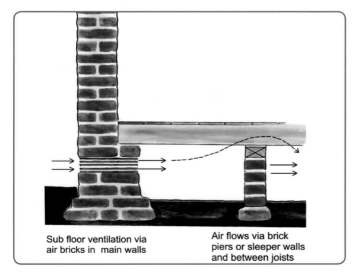

Sub floor ventilation via air bricks in main walls

Air flows via brick piers or sleeper walls and between joists

Solid floors

Until the mid-19th century it was common for flagstones or floor bricks to be laid directly on to the earth, perhaps over a sprinkling of sand for levelling. Alternatively a layer of limeash might be applied as a solid screed, a major improvement on the bare trodden earth floors traditionally found in many poorer dwellings. Slate was especially suitable as a flooring material, being impervious to water, making it ideal for use in cellars. In eastern counties, clay 'pamment' floor tiles were widely used and produced in a variety of different colours. But it was the Victorians who developed floor tiling into an art form, with universally available square quarry tiles or more exotic geometric and encaustic tiles echoing medieval monastic designs.

Grander mansions might have boasted elegant decorative marble floors. But what appears to be expensive marble may actually be scagiola – a cheaper material introduced in the 18th century made from glued gypsum with a polished surface of coloured stone or marble dust, skilfully stained to imitate the real thing.

Smaller tiles were held in place on a bed of lime mortar, but it wasn't considered necessary to incorporate damp-proofing into solid floors until well into the 20th century, even though most houses had DPCs built into walls from the mid-1870s onwards. This was probably because flagstones and floor tiles were water resistant, and any moisture in the ground could freely evaporate through the joints between them. As long as the ground wasn't marshy, and the floor was raised up a few inches higher than external ground level, then floors would remain comfortably dry.

Unfortunately many old floors have since been dug up, thanks to our present-day squeamishness about damp. Trying to retrospectively impose modern building standards has resulted in many old floors being replaced with concrete slabs and bland artificial tiles. But if you want an authentic farmhouse kitchen, then historic stone or clay tiles with all their slight imperfections and wear and tear are part of the experience.

Why problems occur

Traditional solid floors don't react well to being smothered by modern vinyl flooring or rubber-backed carpets and underlays. Where impermeable coverings such as these are laid directly over

Excavation for new limecrete floor

Any ground moisture is free to evaporate via joints

old solid floors, they trap moisture and become sweaty underneath. Over time, this encourages the growth of unsightly black mould, with an unpleasant musty smell permeating the room.

As a reaction to such problems, many old floors that had worked perfectly well for centuries were excavated and replaced with new concrete slabs laid over a compacted layer of hardcore and a plastic damp-proof membrane (DPM). Sometimes the original clay tiles or stone flags would be re-laid on the new slab, but more often they were chucked into skips in favour of fashionable alternatives.

Apart from the unnecessary loss of historic fabric, installing a concrete slab isn't usually a good idea because it can exacerbate damp problems elsewhere. This new impermeable barrier means moisture from the ground can no longer evaporate harmlessly away, and is forced to go somewhere else. The most likely route is along the underside of the new DPM until it reaches the first point where it's free to escape, usually up the walls. Such problems can be made worse in properties where there's a concrete path adjoining the walls on the outside, particularly if it slopes inwards towards the house.

Another obvious worry when it comes to excavating floors in old buildings is the risk that you could easily undermine the base of the walls, with their minimal foundations. The danger of excavations causing structural problems is why breaking up a thick modern concrete floor to reinstate an original floor needs to be undertaken with great care. It's common practice to leave the first metre or so of the slab adjoining the walls intact, in order to reduce such risks.

Dealing with damp

During periods of heavy rain, take a very close look at an old floor and you may notice a slight darkening of the joints between the tiles or flags. This isn't normally a cause for concern, simply a sign that small amounts of moisture are able to evaporate almost imperceptibly, which is how old floors are meant to function.

When you remove a carpet or other covering to expose an old solid floor there may initially be a smell of trapped damp. To allow the floor to dry naturally, the first step is to thoroughly ventilate the room. Once exposed it can take several weeks for floors to fully dry out.

Like human beings, traditional solid floors need to breathe and perspire. This is something that natural fibres readily accommodate, so loose rugs of wool or cotton (without a rubber backing) are well suited. The ideal floor covering is a natural

matting of seagrass, jute, sisal or coir, with a border of exposed floor left around the perimeter of the room. Once the house is warm and well ventilated, any slight moisture from the floor will be free to naturally evaporate without trace.

With all old properties there are a number of practical measures you can take to minimise dampness in the ground under the house. Removing concrete paths and replacing them with gravel next to the walls will allow moisture to evaporate. Common sense dictates that the ground around the house should slope away from the walls, so some minor landscaping to provide a shallow outward fall should help disperse surface water away from the building. Where gardens slope down towards the house, drainage channels can be provided in the ground within a few metres of the walls to intercept surface water heading downhill. Most important of all, the external ground levels should be kept significantly below the internal floor surface (ideally at least 150mm lower), as described in Chapter 2.

Floors over cellars

Some grander Georgian and Victorian properties had solid ground floors constructed over brick cellars built like small railway arches, in the form of vaults or tunnels. As floor loadings are applied the bricks or stones in the arches are compressed, and, acting in unison, they transfer the loadings by pushing out sideways. This is why the cellar walls at either side sometimes need to be propped with buttresses. So before cutting or altering such floors and walls, it's important to check the implications with a structural engineer, as it all works interdependently.

Mild salt staining is harmless

Traditional pammet floor being re-laid

Specialist-brickwork.com

Stone and brick floors

If you're lucky enough to still have the original stone flags, floor bricks or tile pavers in place, then all that may be required is a little light cleaning, as described below. But what if all you can see is a stark expanse of concrete? Despite appearances, it's just possible that underneath the modern slab the historic floor has survived intact. But this is only likely to be the case if the concrete was laid over a plastic sheet DPM that was first placed over the old floor surface. Or, in cases where a thin screed was applied on the old floor surface using a fairly weak cement mix, it may be possible to expose any surviving original tiles underneath without damage. One indication that a concrete screed was simply poured on top of the old floor rather than excavating it first is where the current floor level is significantly higher than the original.

Salts

We last encountered salt efflorescence in the form of white staining in damp masonry walls. But it can also occur in old solid floors where excessive moisture has been present. Some salts are hygroscopic, attracting moisture from the air, which can sometimes make floors appear damp, but as with salt-laden plasterwork this is normally harmless, although it may look unsightly. Loose salts can be brushed off or vacuumed, but shouldn't be washed because the water simply re-dissolves the salts, sending them back into the floor. In severe cases special pastes can be applied to draw out the salts, but a specialist firm will need to carry out such treatments.

Re-laying

It's quite common for individual flagstones, tiles or bricks to have come loose, rocking disconcertingly under the pressure of foot traffic. In most cases these can normally be re-bedded fairly easily with a dab of hydraulic lime mortar, but in severe cases there may be no alternative but for the entire floor to be re-laid. So that the floor can be correctly reinstated, as each stone or brick is removed it should be numbered in chalk and its position marked on a plan. If possible try to avoid disturbing the base (substrate). If the base has to be replaced, the procedure is to build up a new layer of hardcore and then re-lay the floor on a new bed of weak sand lime mortar. With many solid floors the stones or bricks were butted close and weren't originally pointed. Where pointing is required, use lime mortar to allow evaporation of moisture.

Tiled floors

Floor tiles were traditionally made from local clays in plain single colours (typically reds, buffs or blacks), and produced with square

edges and unglazed. 'Quarry tiles' (carré is French for square) date back to medieval times, their popularity peaking in the Victorian era but continuing in mainstream housing until well into the 20th century. They're commonly found in kitchens and sculleries on account of their remarkable durability. Most are 6in x 6in or larger (eg the 9in square terracotta tiles at Hampton Court).

Victorian floors are also well known for geometric tiles and exotically patterned 'encaustic' tiles. Geometric tiling comprises lots of small straight-edged plain tiles laid in patterns of two or more colours with a very fine grout line between. Commonly found on front garden paths and in entrance halls, geometrics were made in shapes such as triangles and rectangles and in a range of natural clay colours, from off-white through to red and brown to blue-black.

Encaustic tiles (literally meaning 'burnt-in') revived medieval techniques of inlaying clays of different colours to create patterns within each single tile. Decoration was achieved by stamping a design into the body of a plain clay tile before firing, and filling it with liquid clays of contrasting colours. Being relatively expensive, encaustics were often combined with quarry and geometric tiles to cover large areas at less cost.

As with stone and brick floors, once old tiles are released from years of enclosure behind suffocating layers of vinyl or carpet they'll need time to slowly dry out. There's often a grey bloom on the tiles but this can simply be brushed off.

The most common problem is where individual tiles have come loose or have broken. Usually they can be prised out carefully with a knife and re-laid. More extensive damage has usually resulted from movement in the base in which they're bedded. However, unless tiles are already loose or damaged, it's best to avoid trying to lift them, as they tend to be fairly brittle and prone to breakage. Where

Left: Marble is easily chipped and damaged

Below: Classic quarry tiling

Above: Geometric tiles

Right: Encaustic tiles

Floorer.co.uk

the tiles have been laid in a modern cement base (rather than soft lime), taking up and relaying them isn't practical, as many will suffer damage either in the lifting process or when cleaning off the mortar residue. If repairs can't be made without wholesale removal of tiles, there may be no choice but to replace the floor with a replica.

Maintaining solid floors

Most tiled or flagstone floors require very little maintenance, just occasional light scrubbing with a stiff brush and hot water with a dash of washing-up liquid. To prevent flooding the floor with excess water and to avoid soaking, mop and rinse as you go. Georgian and Victorian floor tiles were generally unglazed, and over time tend to develop their own natural sheen through the polishing action of wear from shoes. Even so, tiles may in some cases have become stained. Specialist tile cleaning products can be used sparingly to remove stubborn surface dirt, but must be rinsed off. Avoid detergents, caustic soda and acids. Never use abrasive cleaning methods such as rubbing with scouring powder.

Salvaged quarry tiles

Mikewye.co.uk

To bring out the colour of old stone flags or clay tiles, applying a smear of beeswax can be highly effective – but not too much, as it can make the floor slippery. Also take care to keep the joints clear of wax, so as not to block evaporation.

Do not use modern sealants,

as they trap moisture. Even exterior tiling (common to Victorian entrance porches and front garden paths) shouldn't be sealed, as it reduces its resistance to frost.

When it comes to maintaining marble floors, gentle cleaning and polishing is required because, despite its hard image, marble is easily chipped and damaged.

Limeash and plaster floors

Dating back to medieval times, limeash floors continued to be used as a cheap type of flooring, right up to the early 20th century. At its simplest, limeash comprised a mix of lime mortar and wood ash to produce a fairly hardwearing yet breathable solid floor that was commonly used for utility areas such as sculleries and kitchens. Similar 'plaster' mixes with added ingredients such as clay, burnt gypsum and aggregates were also used as a cheap method of 'boarding' upper floors. The construction process involved laying laths, boards or reeds over the floor joists and then trowelling the wet plaster mix on top. Once dry it formed a rigid slab with a similar appearance to concrete. Such floors can be repaired or re-laid from scratch, but this is fairly specialist work. To make patch repairs you can buy a ready-made dry product that just needs to be mixed with water.

Limecrete floors

Limecrete is a modern harder-wearing version of traditional limeash, retaining the latter's natural breathability. Where a new solid floor is required, limecrete is ideal. A mix of hydraulic lime, sand and insulating material, it can resist rising moisture without the need for a damp-proof membrane. It can even meet current Building Regulations by incorporating insulation and is compatible with underfloor heating.

In properties with limited headroom where it's necessary to dig down in order to accommodate the floor slab, it's advisable to consult a structural engineer, as the excavation work could disturb footings. Once a limecrete floor has been laid it can be walked on within hours, although you need to allow about four weeks for it to fully dry out before laying a final finishing coat.

LIMECRETE

Above and below: Limecrete layers

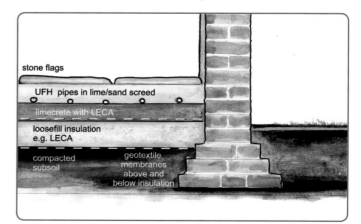

stone flags

UFH pipes in lime/sand screed

limecrete with LECA

loosefill insulation e.g. LECA

compacted subsoil

geotextile membranes above and below insulation

LAYING A LIMECRETE FLOOR

In this featured project the existing tiles were laid directly onto the soil. It was decided to replace the floor with a new limecrete slab finished with traditional flagstones (and to re-use the old tiles elsewhere).

Images courtesy Mike Wye & Associates Ltd and Matthew Clements'
houseintheenchantedforest.blogspot.co.uk

1 The first task is to check the height of the room – you need to allow a depth of about 350mm below the finished floor surface to accommodate the new limecrete slab and insulation material. Ideally the new floor surface should be at least 150mm above the outdoor ground level. The hard work can now commence – digging down to the required depth. Where excavation could disrupt the footings first consult a structural engineer.

2 It is essential not to disturb shallow foundations. Here the soil was dug out at a 45 degree angle, sloping inwards from the main walls leaving 150mm of cover above the foundations.

3 Here a total of 10 tonnes of soil was removed by hand .

4 The rough excavated ground must be levelled and compacted. To mark the levels for each layer of the new floor, a few wooden pegs can be hammered into the ground with marks on them, or timber shuttering boards positioned around the floor.

5 With the ground prepared the first sheet of geotextile membrane can be laid. This separates the next layer of loosefill insulation from the earth below. Where the excavated surface is still quite rough, a blinding layer of sand should first be laid to avoid damaging the fabric. Geotextile membranes are used rather than an ordinary plastic Damp Proof Membrane (DPM) to permit breathability. The membrane should be laid across the floor, overlapping at any joints, and folded up against the wall to contain the next layers.

6 Loosefill insulation material is laid to a depth of around 250mm*, ideally in the form of 'LECA' (Lightweight Expanded Clay Aggregate). These comprise baked clay beads (sized 10 – 20mm) with a honeycombed texture – a bit like small Maltesers (and are easily crushed). The thicker this layer is, the better insulated the floor will be. Specify coated LECA to resist capillary action and inhibit suction of moisture.

[Footnote: * Although to comply with Part L of the Building Regulations may require a greater depth of insulation, exemptions can apply for period buildings – this can be checked with Local Authority Building Control]

7 The loosefill is spread out and the depth checked. After levelling it should be lightly compacted by tamping – this is to prevent it sinking when the limecrete slab is laid on top. A second geotextile breather membrane is then laid above the insulation, which also helps protect it against the weight of the slab. It's important to avoid damage to the insulation beads when laying the membrane, so use temporary boards to walk on.

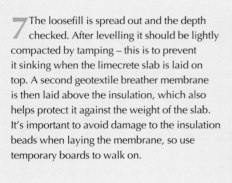

8 The limecrete can be prepared using a cement mixer (wear mask and goggles!). A simple mix might comprise 1 part lime (NHL 5) to 3 parts LECA insulation balls (uncoated and 0–20mm thick). Another common mix is 1 part lime (NHL 3.5) to 1 part sharp sand to 2 parts insulation material. Using LECA as the aggregate in the slab makes it lighter and further improves insulation (especially important where underfloor heating is being installed). Limecrete needs to be mixed to a thick porridge consistency and left quite dry – with just enough water so that it holds together when squeezed.

The insulation and the limecrete slab can be laid in stages. This also helps avoid any risk of crushing of the loosefill from excessive weights being moved across the surface.

9 Lay large temporary sheets of plywood to spread the load, then barrow in the mix. Trowel on the limecrete to form a slab at least 100mm thick. Once level it should be gently tamped – it will reduce in volume by about 10% when compacted. Using a straight edge ensure the floor surface is level.

The initial drying time of the slab will vary depending on humidity and temperature, but NHL can normally be walked on using boards after 24 to 48 hours (but not screeded just yet). In warmer conditions you may need to lightly mist the slab so it doesn't dry out too quickly.

10 The completed slab can be quite rough because of the insulation in the mix, so a surface screed is normally applied. Where Under Floor Heating (UFH) is to be provided, the pipes or cables can be laid over the limecrete – and tested before screeding.

11 Once the slab has been left to cure for approximately 2–3 weeks, the screed can be laid. This is the final layer and is mixed at ratio of 2 parts sharp sand to 1 part NHL5. The standard thickness is 50mm, unless you are installing UFH in which case it should be 75mm thick. However where the screed will be a bedding layer for floor tiles, it need only be 25mm thick. Curing times are as per the slab.

12 Floor tiles or flagstones are bedded onto a fairly weak hydraulic lime mix. Here limestone flags are laid onto a 25mm mortar bed (a thinner bed might use a stronger 2:1 NHL5 mix). However it's important to avoid any finish that could inhibit breathability, such as acrylic based tile adhesives. For the same reason, avoid applying modern sealants to the floor surface – a natural linseed oil finish is ideal.

Hybrid floors

Where excavating close to the walls might risk undermining shallow foundations, hybrid floors are sometimes used as an alternative to pure limecrete. The hybrid route is not for everyone but is better than a modern concrete floor.

1 Here only the middle of the floor is dug out, and to a lesser depth, hence there is less risk of disruption to the foundations.

2 UFH pipes can be installed to this central zone after the insulation has been laid. Some manufacturers of insulation recommended that a standard plastic sheet DPM is laid on top of the insulation below the UFH pipework.

3 Adjacent to the walls, a strip of about half a metre is carefully excavated to a shallow depth, and filled with limecrete laid over a geothermal membrane.

4 The limecrete around the edges is permeable and helps to dissipate any moisture vapour from the floor before it reaches the walls.

13 WINDOWS, DOORS AND EXTERNAL JOINERY

Keeping it real

Conservationists favour retaining as much original fabric as possible, but there's enormous pressure today to replace 'thermally inefficient' old windows with modern double-glazed units. However, fitting plastic windows and doors to a period house is one of the quickest ways to trash its visual appeal.

Nonetheless, it's important to take measures to ensure your house isn't leaking heat whilst ensuring its valuable historic authenticity is retained. The conservationist approach is to opt for 'reversible solutions', where in future the new fittings could if necessary be removed without trace. We know that traditional timber windows can last hundreds of years when correctly maintained, so the best option often tends to be overhauling and upgrading the originals, or if all else fails replacing them with authentic replicas.

Windows and doors define the personality of old buildings. Although after so many years many will have adopted a distinctly skewed, if not overtly lopsided stance, as one of the most important architectural features they should be retained and cherished. Fortunately even those in poor condition are normally repairable and can be sympathetically restored. It's very rare for complete replacement to be genuinely necessary. Retaining the originals also makes a lot of sense when you consider the quality of the materials used to produce them. Traditional hardwoods and naturally seasoned softwoods can last hundreds of years, in stark contrast to modern doors and windows, many of which have had to be replaced within a mere 20 years.

We sometimes forget what a gruelling environment doors and windows have to endure – not least when freezing winter conditions outdoors are pitched against a tropical, centrally heated indoor climate. So the occasional sticking door or window can be forgiven as part of the old house lifestyle. In fact, traditional wooden doors and windows have the enormous advantage that they can adapt to seasonal movement, being easily trimmed and adjusted with simple hand tools.

Discreet and very effective secondary glazing

Replacing doors and windows

Nothing causes more heartache with old buildings than the installation of inappropriate new windows and doors made from cheap short-life materials. There may sometimes be circumstances where repair is genuinely not possible, or the desire for double glazing is so pressing that the option of replacement needs to be considered. But what type to choose?

The first thing to say is 'don't believe the hype'. It's a popular misconception that UPVC lasts forever and is 'maintenance free'. In fact replacement typically becomes necessary after about 25 to 30 years, and maintenance issues commonly arise much sooner with defective handles, sealed unit cavities misting up, and white plastic fading and yellowing. Aluminium suffers from similar drawbacks. They're also unsuited for use in old buildings because they can't tolerate slight seasonal movement, and tend to distort.

Timber replacements would therefore seem to be the better option. But there are potential dangers with this route too. Standard-sized, off-the-shelf windows and doors rarely fit old openings, but the determination to make them do so at all costs has sometimes resulted in the most appalling botches. Rather than pay a bit more for custom-made units that are designed to fit properly, sometimes the house has been adjusted to fit the window, and the existing openings enlarged or made smaller.

Rectifying past wrongs

There is one increasingly common scenario where replacement can actually be welcome, and that's in houses where inappropriate replacements have already been installed. However, in the rush to rectify past mistakes it's sometimes not appreciated that with Listed buildings you need to obtain consent, even if you plan to

Good work – replacing 1970s aluminium horrors with new replica timber sashes

Original openings widened to accept charmless double glazed units

rip out gruesome 1970s horrors and install appropriate handmade replicas.

Undoing disfiguration caused by the past installation of inappropriate replacements, and reinstating authentic replica period sashes or casements, can have tremendous visual benefits.

Such improvements are more of a challenge in properties that have suffered from botched alterations in an attempt to fit wrongly-sized windows. Where the size of a window opening has been reduced it should be relatively simple to remove the infill material and reinstate the original. Enlarged openings are even more important to address, as they tend to stick out like a sore thumb, looking totally out of character in an old house. Reducing an outsized opening imperceptibly is likely to be easier for rendered walls. Otherwise the main challenge is to track down matching bricks or stone with which to reinstate the missing slice of wall. The condition of lintels should always be checked during such works – where an opening has been widened the original lintel will probably have been replaced, and if any structural repair work is required you'll need to notify Building Control first.

Timber lintels

Timber was the traditional material for lintels spanning openings above doors and windows. Even where the outer face of the wall has a brick arch or stone lintel there's often a secondary beam sitting behind it made of wood. Internally, timber lintels provided a useful surface for fixing laths for plasterwork, and therefore tended to be plastered over rather than being left exposed.

Thanks to the quality of the timber used in many old buildings, wooden lintels have generally performed extremely well. Oak is especially durable, but those of elm or softwood can equally endure for centuries as long as walls aren't subject to excessive damp.

Where problems do develop over time they tend to manifest themselves in the form of cracking to the external render or to internal plasterwork. But even where a lintel has started to rot, it may not automatically need replacing. The important thing is to expose it and allow it to dry out. This often requires the removal of cement renders or impervious modern paints that are trapping damp.

Where it's necessary to replace a lintel it's important to specify a matching new timber one, otherwise before you know it the builders will have instinctively whacked in a bog-standard steel or concrete beam. The best option is to use semi-dry oak, but

Left: Lintel to medieval cottage window is supporting additional loadings from ceiling beam

Right: Stripping away plaster reveals timber lintel nestling behind facing brick – common in Georgian & Victorian houses

it's probably worth first consulting a structural engineer with a good knowledge of timber. Builders are mostly used to buying prefabricated lintels off-the-shelf, but these can cause problems in thin walls with 'cold bridging' around windows and doors. This leads to condensation and mould staining, and can also cause problems getting lime plaster and render to adhere to steel or concrete when making good around the window or door opening later.

Replacing a rotten lintel

1 Timber lintel shows signs of decay and is sagging. It can no longer safely support loadings from masonry above and from ceiling beam.

2 Strongboy props inserted in wall to support loadings and ceiling beam cut away and propped.

3 After hacking off plaster, old lintel can be carefully eased out.

4 New lintels are installed with end bearings resting on padstones to reduce crushing.

5 Substantial new oak lintels in place and new ceiling beam installed resting in main wall, not above window.

6 Why it had to go: old lintel has suffered from fungal decay and beetle infestation.

Windows

Early windows comprised small openings or 'wind eyes' without any form of glazing, glass being a highly prized material reserved for use in churches and manor houses. By Shakespeare's time glazed windows were starting to become established for domestic use but remained something of a status symbol to the extent that homeowners would sometimes pack them up to accompany them when they moved house.

The appeal of glazing was dealt a severe blow in 1696 with the introduction of a levy on the number of window openings in a house in the form of the Window Tax. This inevitably inspired evasive measures, most famously bricked-up window openings, which were sometimes later painted to look like windows. This was sorely resented as 'a tax on air and light' and meant that many servants and others of constrained means were condemned to live in airless rooms. This long running tax was eventually reduced in 1825 and finally repealed in 1851.

Despite the punitive tax regime, Georgian sash windows were central to the elegance of 18th- and early 19th-century architecture. To achieve the desired classical proportions in larger houses, a rule of thumb was applied so that the height of a window would be between 1.25 and 1.75 times its width. Window heights reflected the importance of particular floor levels, so the principal first-floor rooms often boasted taller, more elegant windows than ground floors. Later fashions for exaggeratedly tall windows, sometimes running from floor to ceiling, are found in many houses of the period providing access to gardens or balconies. The fashion for elegant sash windows continued throughout most of the Victorian era until the revival of traditional casements around the turn of the 20th century.

Today we seem to have a less respectful attitude to the surviving eyes and souls of period buildings. As a nation we seem to be inextricably wedded to the idea that replacement windows

Wind eye

are a good thing. But the fact is, keeping your originals intact and fitting custom-made secondary glazing is often a superior solution, as well as being considerably less expensive. Alternatively it may be possible to install special super-thin double glazing into existing windows. Where there's no other option but to install new windows, an authentic appearance can sometimes be created using a single larger sheet of double glazing with fake glazing bars applied over each side. This may be worth considering for new extensions as a way of satisfying the Planners whilst complying with energy efficiency standards in the Building Regulations.

Ye Olde tax avoidance. Window on right is deceptive - a painted 'trompe l'oeil'

Custom made replica Georgian sash windows incorporating high performance super-slim double glazing

The vast majority of original windows in period houses are of wood, although cast or wrought iron isn't uncommon. There are two basic opening types – hinged casements and sliding sashes. Those that don't open are known as fixed lights.

The most common points for failure are found anywhere that water can penetrate or collect and 'pond'. Sills and lower joints tend to be the most vulnerable areas, and flaking paint may conceal early signs of decay, particularly to bottom rails and lower sashes.

Timber repairs

It's nearly always possible to repair timber windows, although most simply require occasional adjustment and smartening up. Many originals have lasted more than 200 years and are capable of performing good service for at least another century. As always, regular maintenance is key to a long and healthy life. A day or two spent rubbing down and painting every four or five years can work wonders. Above all, any surface cracks in putty or gaps that have opened up against the glass should be filled and painted before the frost gets a chance to blow it loose or decay sets in.

In situ window repairs are often possible

Woodlouseconservation.co.uk

Workshop repairs may be necessary for more substantial repairs

Sashconsultancy.co.uk

As good as new: localised decay cut out and new timber strip expertly spliced in .

Georgian sashes removed for overhaul and fitting of high performance slim double glazing units

Sashconsultancy.co.uk / Slenderglaze Ltd

Small areas of rot can be cut out and filled with putty or filler. Fillers have become more versatile in recent years and have the advantage of minimising the loss of original timber. Often filler can be applied without the removal of window frames, which helps reduce the risk of damage to historic glass.

Loose joints are a common problem. The simplest form of repair is to strengthen the corner of a window with an angle bracket made from non-corroding brass or stainless steel. Once any decay has been cut out and filled the bracket can be secured in place and concealed.

Alternatively, loose joints can simply be re-glued. This normally requires taking the windows out and cramping the glued frames in a workbench. But in old properties the frames may not be perfectly square, having evolved in shape over time in tune with the walls. So once glued they can instead be placed back in the opening, using small wooden wedges to keep joints tight until the adhesive is fully set.

Where larger areas of timber are defective they can be cut and replaced with matching timber. New sections to frames, rails, stiles and glazing bars can be scarfed in, and a good joiner should be able to minimise the loss of original material. Another thing to bear in mind when restoring old windows is that historic glass is easily scratched. So before sanding the frames it's a good idea to protect the glass with masking tape or plastic safety film. Old glazing also tends to be very fragile and doesn't take kindly to being disturbed, so great care must be taken when removing defective old putty.

Sills

Sills are a notorious weak point, and can often be repaired by cutting the rotten face back to sound wood and then planting in a new piece, using glue and non-ferrous screws. This should be a relatively easy job for a joiner, but it's important to specify good quality seasoned timber.

Period sash windows normally have small timber 'sub-sills' at the base of the window, which in turn sit upon a large projecting stone sill. But with most other types of window the timber sills themselves project out from the wall, and it's important to ensure there's a clear drip groove on the underside (usually set back a few millimetres from the outer edge). These help disperse rainwater safely away from the wall below, but can sometimes become damaged or blocked (eg with paint) with the result that water soaks through the wall below.

Sash windows

One of the defining features of Georgian and Victorian urban architecture was the sash window. Unlike the original Dutch

versions on which they were based, these normally comprised two sashes of equal proportions – an upper and lower sash designed to slide vertically. Each sash is suspended on cords (or sometimes chains) connected via small pulleys to pairs of counterbalance weights of cast iron or lead concealed in a box frame either side.

However there was a simpler, older version known as the 'Yorkshire sash'. Developed from medieval sideways-sliding shutter boards, these have horizontally sliding sashes that operate without the need for weights.

Sash windows were far more expensive to install than traditional hinged wooden or iron casements, and hence were often inserted only in the front facade, with casements to the rear and sides or anywhere that small windows were required, such as dormers. But by the mid-18th century many old timber-frame houses were having their old leaded casements replaced with fashionable sashes.

Early Georgian sashes were quite cumbersome, with large wooden sections and often with only the lower sash moveable. In lieu of counterbalance weights, windows were kept open at a particular height by pegs inserted in notches cut into the grooves, or were held in place with metal hooks.

Sash Repairs Ltd

Horizontal sliding sash windows.

Joints to sash window frames commonly suffer localised decay but can normally be repaired. Here the lower sash has been removed for thorough overhaul

Fortis & Hooke / sash-windowrenovation.co.uk

Sash Repairs Ltd

Rotten timber sills can be cut out and replaced

Early solid wood glazing bars were relatively flat and heavy, but by the mid-18th century they'd become much thinner, often no more than an eighth of an inch (3.2mm) thick, in timber or metal.

Sash window maintenance

Sash windows are fairly straightforward to overhaul and can nearly always be repaired. To do this properly it's best to remove the sashes from their frames, which can be done from inside. This involves levering off the nailed beading that retains them, which needs to be undertaken with care to avoid splitting the beading. In Scotland the lower sashes were sensibly designed to open into the room for cleaning and ease of maintenance.

One common problem is where sliding sashes occasionally stick or become jammed, usually due to a build-up of paint or a lack of lubrication. To ensure smooth running the channels in the frame on either side in which they slide should be lubricated with linseed oil or wax. Also the pulley wheels over which the cords loop on the upper sides require a periodic drop of oil – and while you're at it, check that they haven't seized.

Sash cords occasionally break due to wear, but new cords can be fitted fairly easily. This requires partial dismantling of side sash boxes. New sash cords made from natural fibres are widely available; these are supplied ready-waxed and pre-stretched and are preferable to nylon cords, which are prone to stretching. Where new thicker replacement glass is installed in an old sash frame, the sash weights may need to be adjusted to balance the increased weight.

Although neglected sash windows are sometimes prone to being a bit breezy, fortunately it's a fairly easy job to draught proof them, as described below.

Reducing noise and heat loss

Part of the price of owning an old house is that sometimes you're confronted with dilemmas that simply wouldn't arise if, for example, you'd bought a new Barratt home. Top of the list is how to benefit from 21st-century levels of insulation and yet still retain all that charming historic fabric.

Estate agents consistently advise that unspoilt period properties with original features tend to command higher prices, with strong demand even during market downturns. So although it may be tempting to replace entire windows with new double-glazed versions, the negatives of doing this can easily outweigh the potential benefits. Loss of genuine antique components that give a house its history, combined with an often detrimental aesthetic impact, can result in unsympathetically 'modernised' properties

Looks worse than it is; good quality original timber is surprisingly durable

Secondary glazing can be highly effective …

… and very discreet

New replica originals with 'high-E' glazing

suffering a permanent reduction in value. However where the original windows no longer exist or are genuinely beyond repair, installing new custom-made replicas that faithfully reproduce windows from the correct period may be the best option . Otherwise you might be better off selecting one of the following less expensive low-impact choices.

SECONDARY GLAZING

The best solution is often to retain the existing windows and fit custom-made secondary glazing tailored to the individual opening. This way you can get the best of both worlds – improved thermal insulation whilst retaining the special 'sparkle' of original period windows. Modern secondary glazing is far less visually intrusive than some less refined earlier types. Individual units can be designed to discreetly match the original frames, making them virtually invisible from outside, especially where you specify a powder-coated finish to match your paintwork. Thanks to the deeper air gap between the main windows and the inner secondary glazing, sound insulation performance is actually superior to that of double glazing. You can choose from a range

Best of both worlds – 'invisible' secondary glazed units allow retention of originals with improved thermal efficiency

of designs with neatly hinged openings, sliding units or lift-out magnetic panels that can be removed in summer.

CUSTOM SEALED UNITS

The obvious compromise is to retain the original sashes or casements and simply replace old window glass with new thermally efficient sealed units. The problem here is that the rebates in which the glass sits often aren't deep enough to accommodate thicker glazing. However, specially developed thin double-glazed units have been developed precisely with old buildings in mind, and are well worth exploring. However, Conservation Officers might resist the loss of original glass.

OVERHAUL

Rattling or sticking windows can be overhauled so that they run smoothly and silently. Sash windows often have a central fastener with a cam which, when closed, draws the upper and lower sashes together. However, where layers of paint have built up these may have become inoperable, requiring localised stripping and oiling. Where missing, replica cam closers are readily available in DIY stores.

DRAUGHTPROOFING

Self-adhesive draught strips are cheap and easy to apply. Sash windows can be draughtproofed with inconspicuous brush strips that can be fitted by specialist firms. This is done by removing both sashes so that grooves can be routed into their edges (the top edge, the meeting rails and the parting beads), and brush strips fitted into the grooves and virtually hidden. This also helps improve sound insulation.

RETRO LIFESTYLE

The traditional method of reducing draughts and keeping in heat at night was to close window shutters and fit heavy curtains. This can be surprisingly effective and is well worth reinstating.

However, before enthusiastically setting about sealing up every nook and cranny, bear in mind that old houses need a certain amount of background ventilation to help carry away moisture and avoid the build-up of condensation and damp. There's little point sealing up every tiny gap around windows if it means you then need to add some new form of ventilation, such as trickle vents – which are required even on new triple-glazed windows. In other words, there needs to be a balance between comfort and ventilation. Fortunately the need to retain the special character of historic buildings when improving thermal efficiency is recognised in Part L of the Building Regulations, which permits a number of exemptions for old houses.

Metal windows

Many period houses have historic metal casement windows. Early examples were made from wrought iron produced in a local blacksmith's forge and glazed with leaded lights. From the mid-18th century handmade wrought iron was increasingly supplanted by cheaper manufactured cast iron. These were produced in standardised designs that were often quite elaborate, and are commonly found in Georgian and Victorian cottages. Cast iron

was made by pouring or 'casting' molten iron into moulds formed by creating impressions in fine sand using a timber 'pattern'. Today it's possible to create new replica components in the same way, as long as you can find an identical component elsewhere from which to make the template.

Steel windows later replaced cast iron, becoming popular from the interwar period. Earlier ones can be very prone to corrosion, whereas later steel windows were far hardier thanks to hot-dipped galvanising techniques, employed from around the mid-1950s.

Maintenance

The most serious problem that can afflict all types of metal windows is rust. As the metal corrodes it expands, causing

distortion which can eventually cause the glass to crack. Another problem that's easier to remedy is excessive build-up of paint. Failed hinges and fittings can also be an issue, but even windows that appear to be beyond repair can normally be successfully overhauled and given a new lease of life.

SURFACE RUST

Where rust only affects the surface it can simply be cleaned off with a wire brush. Note that red lead was a commonly used primer historically, but is highly toxic, so precautions must be taken before starting work. Iron casements are most susceptible to rust anywhere the paint is chipped, but usually there's sound metal underneath once the rust is removed.

CORROSION

Any corroded sections of wrought iron windows can be cut out and new replacement sections welded in. Local blacksmiths can often repair wrought iron, although there's a risk that use of intense heat can crack the glass or loosen old handmade metal joints. Repairs to cast iron are more difficult as it's almost impossible to weld, and may require a 'cold-metal stitching' process.

TREATMENT

Once all rust is removed, apply a good quality metal primer before painting. Flame-sprayed zinc primer is an excellent pre-paint treatment for ferrous metals.

DRAUGHTPROOFING

Silicone sealant can be injected into the gaps between the closed window and the frame, after first coating the surface of each opening casement with a release agent. Once dry it should neatly fill these gaps.

Leaded lights

Because early glass could only be made in small panes, leaded lights provided a way of knitting individual pieces together to create larger glazed panels for windows. This was achieved by using thin H-shaped strips of lead or 'cames' to hold the small panes of clear or coloured glass, known as 'quarries', which were often diamond-shaped. The cames were packed with special cement to securely grip the individual panes, and where cames overlapped the joints were soldered. The whole matrix was then sealed with special thin black putty to form a surprisingly durable piece of glazing.

Glass-making technology eventually made medieval leaded lights redundant, and in the Georgian period many leaded casements were replaced with fashionable sashes. However, the tradition was revived in late Victorian and Edwardian houses, some featuring small panes of coloured glass. Where original stained glass windows have survived they should be regarded as valuable antique works of art, with their repair and restoration entrusted to experts.

Leaded lights are sometimes criticised for being fragile and draughty, but that's no reason to condemn these classic windows. Something as simple as fitting secondary glazing can often provide an effective solution.

evident where cracked panes were traditionally mended *in situ* many years ago by sealing along the crack with new strips of lead.

Where it's not possible to save cracked panes, they can usually be repaired on site by 'stopping in' a new piece of glass to match. Glass is cut to size and the lead carefully bent back to allow the new piece to be inserted. It's then sealed with special stiff cement. However, opening and re-sealing lead cames isn't as easy as it sounds, so repair tends to be specialist work.

Many old leaded lights have 'saddle bars' or 'stanchion bars' running across their width. Made of iron, steel or wood, these aren't for security but to help the panel withstand wind loadings. Where they're held on with copper ties the mix of dissimilar metals can eventually cause corrosion. Metal bars can also rust

LEADED LIGHT REPAIR

It's very rare that leaded panels get blown out or fall out, but if they rattle in the wind or let draughts through then it's likely that the cement used to seal them has disintegrated. Deterioration of the leadwork over many years can allow water to seep through, or may eventually cause general weakening, with whole panels buckling or bulging. With luck some panels may only need flattening and localised soldering. In fact, old lights can sometimes be very obviously bowed and still be perfectly serviceable – the distortion may have existed for centuries and is often simply due to an original tight fit, the glass having expanded slightly when warmed by the sun. Traditional diagonal patterns are generally more resistant to buckling, although square grids often concealed metal rods used to strengthen the cames (known as 'ferramenta').

In more severe cases, or where there are major areas of breakage, a complete rebuild might be necessary. Here the entire leaded light is removed and a new panel is made reusing the old glass, known as a 're-lead'. However, before dismantling them it's important to keep a record with photos and drawings, or by taking a rubbing.

Leaded lights are predominantly associated with iron casement windows. Where these have suffered from rust, the expansion of the corroded metal can sometimes cause cracking to individual panes. This is likely to require removal of the window for dismantling and rebuilding in a workshop. Once the cause of the problem has been remedied it should be possible to retain any cracked original glass panes by 'invisibly' gluing them back together using special adhesive, prior to the window being professionally re-leaded. Sometimes less subtle old repairs are

and expand, damaging stonework if set directly into it. The usual remedy is to replace them with replica stainless steel bars that are given a powder-coated black finish.

Glass

One of the most enchanting features of period houses is the quaint design of their windows. But we sometimes forget that these simply reflected the limitations of glass-making technology at the time – from medieval leaded lights with their tiny panes of thick glass, to classic Georgian sashes with their trademark 'six over six' pane design which later evolved into Victorian four-pane sashes. Larger heavier panes without glazing bars were made possible with the advent of plate glass in the late 19th century.

Depending on how old your house is, and whether or not

it's been modernised, you may find a variety of different ages and types of glazing. You can normally detect whether glass is of historic origin with a simple test: try moving your head slowly from side to side as you look through the window (at the risk of alarming the neighbours) – if there's no distortion evident then it's likely to be modern float glass.

Conservation Officers are normally keen to retain old glass wherever possible because it's part of a building's history and adds to its charm. Where you need to replace a broken pane, new handmade glass incorporating subtle imperfections can be sourced from specialist suppliers, and can even be specially produced in the form of safety glass.

Types of glass

The Romans first made window glass in Britain, and this was reintroduced in the Middle Ages. But as we saw earlier, window glass was a rarity in domestic buildings until well into the 1600s. Even in the largest houses, often it was only the most important rooms that were afforded the luxury of glazed windows, shutters being used elsewhere. Lower down the economic scale, windows remained glassless until costs eventually decreased with large-scale glass manufacturing from the early 19th century. This was boosted by the abolition of two long-standing taxes – in addition to the infamous Window Tax, glass itself had been subject to a punitive levy dating from as far back as 1746. Glass Duty was based on the weight of glass in windows – one reason why it was made thin and weak – and was abolished in 1845, six years before the final demise of the Window Tax.

As glass-making technology developed, the style of windows evolved, so today the type of glass is an important clue to the age of a property.

CYLINDER, MUFF OR BROAD GLASS
Made by collecting molten glass on to the end of a blowpipe (or 'pontil') and blowing it into a long sausage-shaped cylinder (with the skilled application of much twisting and turning). The ends were then cut off and the cylinder of glass split lengthways, before being opened, flattened out and allowed to cool. The resulting product is characterised by straight ripples and occasional tiny bubbles.

CROWN GLASS
Crown glass predominated in the Georgian period and was of much higher quality than the older cylinder type. However, it was relatively expensive, so many smaller houses continued to make do with the cheaper cylinder variety. The name relates to the slightly convex or crown shape of the glass. It was made by blowing molten glass into a balloon, which was spun to form a large circular sheet like a flat plate or disc about 1.5m (5ft) in diameter. The outer portion of the disc would be cut into small panes, but the central core where the blower's pontil had been attached famously comprised a distorted 'bull's eye'. Because that part of the glass was flawed it escaped glass duty, and was sold as a cheaper offcut,

developing a certain appeal amongst the frugal. Bull's-eye panes were particularly popular for less important windows at the backs of homes where quality wasn't an issue.

Panes of crown glass have a characteristically rippled surface (reflecting the rings of the disc) and a pale bluish tinge from impurities in silica sand. Although crown glass is no longer produced, a good alternative today is Cordele (pronounced 'cor-delay'). Also referred to as 'P1' glass, this can be ordered ready-cut to shape.

PLATE AND SHEET GLASS

The invention of plate glass (so called because the molten glass was spread across tables known as plates) allowed really large panes to be produced, but it was enormously expensive to make. In 1838 a cheap method of producing larger sheets was developed, known as sheet glass (or 'drawn sheet'). This had most of the virtues of plate glass but cooled much faster and

needed less polishing. Sheet glass became common in houses from the mid-Victorian period, changing window fashions as multi-paned glazing became obsolete. To support the increased weight of larger, heavier sheets of glass, thicker sash window frames were introduced with 'horns' on their lower edges for added strength.

MODERN GLASS

Machine-drawn glass was developed in the early 20th century, followed by flat-drawn sheet glass. In 1959 the invention by Pilkington of modern float glass revolutionised the manufacturing process, with a higher quality product manufactured at a cheaper cost.

Glazing repairs

Where a pane of glass has suffered localised minor damage, such as a crack across a corner, think twice before replacing it. If in doubt, it's always worth seeking the advice of a Conservation Officer. In the rare cases where a window frame is completely beyond repair,

Putty lamp

it's worth trying to at least salvage the old glass. However, it can be difficult to release the pane intact, so dismantling a decayed frame for restoration is best undertaken in a workshop rather than *in situ*.

A common problem is where cracked or loose putty is letting in water, or the odd bit has dropped off. The ideal solution is to remove cracked putty and replace it, but unfortunately this can be almost impossible to do without breaking the pane. Although heat guns can soften old putty, their use isn't advisable because the glass is similarly heated, which can cause it to crack. Fortunately, in most cases, it should be sufficient to periodically fill cracks in putty by warming up some new linseed oil putty and rubbing it in with your finger. Where sections of putty have come loose, gently remove them and simply re-putty the gaps.

'Low–E' super thin glazing

Special thin double-glazed units with cavities as thin as 3.9mm have been developed that are suitable for use in many period properties. The best examples can appear virtually indistinguishable from the originals, even replicating aesthetically pleasing historic crown or cylinder glass in the outer panes – with the option of patterned or etched glass. Inner panes made from 'low emissivity' glass reflect heat back into the room, and the use of inert gas-filled cavities means that U-values in the range of 1.9 to 1.3W/m2K can be achieved. The use of Polymer-rich glazing putty that remains flexible and watertight to resist any risk of units becoming 'misted' due to breakdown of seals.

Where complete removal is advisable, such as on windows that are very exposed to the elements, a specialist joiner can use a 'putty lamp' that applies focused infrared heat, softening the putty prior to removal. The infrared rays pass through the glass without heating it so the pane isn't damaged.

Re-glazing

Sometimes the need to re-glaze an old window is unavoidable. The best advice is to use replica replacement glass that's made using similar traditional methods to the original. Alternatively, where appropriate, you may wish to consider custom-made super-slim 'heritage' double-glazed units.

USEFUL RE-GLAZING TIPS

■ When measuring for new panes remember to deduct about 1.5mm from the frame size to allow sufficient clearance when fitting.

■ Always clean and prime the rebate before puttying in a new pane, to prevent oils in the putty from being adsorbed and drying out too quickly.

■ On larger panes, once the glass is bedded in place fixing pins known as 'sprigs' are gently hammered in to the front of the new pane. But before hammering, the adjacent glass should be protected with a thin protective sheet (*eg* of Perspex), leaving a small gap between the sprigs and the glass to prevent fracturing.

■ Apply fresh linseed oil putty using a putty knife, wetting the knife for a smooth surface – note that it requires plenty of patience to achieve a neat finish!

■ Leave the freshly applied putty for at least one week (assuming a warmish environment) before painting.

Safety

House surveys sometimes point out that glazing at lower levels should be made from safety glass or toughened glass, to comply with current Building Regulations. However, this only applies to new construction, with no requirement to sacrifice existing old glass. Where safety is an issue, for example where you have young children, plastic film can be fitted over it or, better still, secondary glazing installed. Reproduction period glass is available in toughened or laminated form, ideal for replacing broken glass in sensitive locations.

Doors

The front door of a period property is fundamental to its identity and character. Regrettably, as with old windows, some misguided owners have ripped out and replaced the originals in the belief that it will somehow improve their property and boost its value. But with old houses the exact opposite is usually the case – original features are much sought-after, and many potential buyers will be put off. The fact is, installing inappropriate replacements, no matter how thermally efficient, is usually the quickest way to trash the character and value of historic houses – even devaluing the entire street!

The good news is that replacement of old doors is rarely necessary. Even where decay has taken hold, they can usually be repaired, although any major works will need to be carried out on a bench. As with all external joinery, the timber most at risk is at any point where water is able to penetrate or accumulate; so decay to doors tends to occur at the joints towards the bottom, at the sills, and to the lower doorframe near the ground.

KEY POINTS TO CHECK WHEN MAINTAINING DOORS

- Deterioration due to damp is usually very localised. Often it's just the base of a doorframe that's rotten, or decay has set in along the very bottom edge of the door. Damaged wood can be cut out and patch-repaired by scarfing in new lengths of seasoned timber cut to size.
- Because doors comprise quite a large surface area they're prone to shrinking and swelling with seasonal changes in moisture and temperature. This can be up to several millimetres, enough to cause sticking in damper months. The extent of movement can be minimised by keeping the timber well decorated.
- To decorate a door thoroughly you need to temporarily remove it at the hinges so that all the edges can be fully primed and finished.

A skilled joiner can repair even the most ravaged historic doors. Weak points for decay are commonly found at joints and ledges at lower levels where water has become trapped

BMulfordHistoricCarpentry.co.uk

Early plank and batten door
.

Ledged and braced 'cottage' main door – note that the braces point downwards towards the hinges.

Framed and panelled front door with fanlight.

Door types

Main entrance doors have evolved over the centuries from simple arrangements comprising vertical boards into more elaborate solid frames with integral panels.

The earliest and simplest form is the 'plank and batten' door, in which vertical planks are nailed on to four or five horizontal timber battens or 'ledges', later augmented with diagonal braces. Some external doors were of double thickness, with timber fillets applied to cover the joints between planks. These were gradually superseded by lighter panel doors comprising a frame of rails and stiles with thin inset panels. Georgian and early Victorian front doors generally have six or sometimes eight panels, arranged in two columns. Classic Victorian four-panel front doors predominated in the mid-19th century, commonly incorporating large, glazed upper panels, and glass lights above the doorframe. From the 1870s front doors became more elaborate, some with their panels arranged in three columns or with coloured leaded fan lights, with six-panel designs regaining popularity from the end of the century.

Fanlights

Glazed fanlights began to appear in the 1720s as a way of providing natural light to hallways. Unlike some modern 'Georgian-style' doors, these were always separate from the doors themselves, which were unglazed. The highly intricate nature of fanlights, especially those with cast lead glazing bars, means that great care is needed when maintaining or repairing them.

Traditional method of draughtproofing – thick curtains can be surprisingly effective

Reducing heat loss

It was common practice in days gone by for thick curtains to be fitted on rails to the backs of entrance doors, automatically lifting as the door was opened. A close inspection may reveal clues to the former existence of such a device, which could be reinstated.

We tend to think of draughtproofing as being a relatively modern concept, but cover-plates for keyholes are nothing new. Unprotected keyholes in entrance doors can allow a surprising amount of cold air to come blasting through, so where none of the originals survive brass replicas of period cover-plates can be fitted.

Letter-flap plates can also be guilty of letting in cold air. If this is a problem, replacing old worn springs can sometimes help, or you could simply adopt the traditional custom of hanging a heavy piece of cloth against the inside or installing a wooden inner flap to insulate it. Fitting fabric draught excluders along the bottom of doors is also a good way to cut draughts.

Whilst on the subject of gaps, cutting holes to insert catflaps into historic doors, needless to say, isn't exactly welcomed by conservationists. The obvious solution where an old property has been extended is to insert it instead through a modern door or wall. If there's no other option, sometimes the original lower panel of an old door can be temporarily removed and substituted with a plywood panel accommodating the catflap.

Ironmongery

There's something fascinating about unearthing historic artefacts in period houses. Old items of ironmongery that have been

overlooked for many years may at first glance resemble an amorphous mass, having been painted over countless times, but a spot of careful cleaning can reveal delicately moulded mini-masterpieces of brass, bronze or cast iron, with intricate detailing. As well as adding considerable charm to an old house, they may also reveal something of the property's history.

Early ironmongery was hand-forged in wrought iron by local blacksmiths. Later Georgian and Victorian door furniture was mass-produced in cast iron, with polished brass reserved for the better off. Designs for doorknobs, knockers, locks and hinges echoed classical themes, such as shields, lions' heads, Medusas, dolphins and urns. Today, depending on how many layers of paint have accumulated over the centuries, a close inspection may reveal the beaten quality of older wrought iron, compared to the much smoother finish of manufactured cast iron.

Latches

Forged wrought iron thumb latches (aka Norfolk or Suffolk latches)

were widely used throughout Britain between the 17th and 18th centuries. Known in Northern England as 'snecks', some latches had locking pins for privacy.

Letter flaps

One of the most visible details on a front door, these were originally of brass or iron. However, these are only as old as the postal service itself, first appearing in 1840.

Hinges

If a hinge fails the door will drop, causing it to stick, with resulting problems with lock alignment. If replacement is necessary try to match like with like. For medieval doors, traditional large surface-mounted 'T' hinges may be appropriate. For Georgian and Victorian panel doors, try to match the original 'H' or 'HL' hinges.

Escutcheons

Pronounced scratching is often evident around keyholes as a result of multiple key-insertion attempts on the part of former residents. We sometimes forget that less than a century ago houses were engulfed in pervading darkness outside of daylight hours, relieved only by an occasional

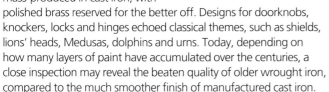

flickering flame, which may, as much as inebriation, explain such key-fumbling. Either way, to protect the woodwork from damage small brass or iron surrounds would be fitted around keyholes. Known as escutcheons, these often incorporated swing-down cover plates that acted as automatic draught excluders.

LOCKS

The oldest forms of door security comprised hefty metal bolts and thick wooden planks used as crossbars. Today there are two basic types of door lock – surface-mounted rim locks, and mortise locks embedded within the fabric of the door. Rim locks originally appeared in grander houses in the 18th century, fitted to the face (or rim) of internal doors, whereas mortises were in common use a little later in the century. Modern cylinder locks such as the Yale became more widely used in the Victorian period. Where original locks have survived they're an important part of the history of the house and are best retained, particularly where surface-mounted and visible. Old locks can usually be brought back to life by a little oiling and adjustment. New keys can be cut to replace long-mislaid originals.

Security

Today, we tend to regard the subject of security as a relatively modern concern, but many Georgian and Victorian houses were built with very effective defensive measures, such as internal wooden window shutters and stout bolts on sturdy main doors. Iron railings defended front gardens with rows of spear-like bars, deterring potential intruders by a combination of physical barrier and visual exposure (except, obviously, where rampant hedge growth has overwhelmed a garden).

Despite the desirability of preserving old locks, such antique security measures are unlikely to offer the level of security required by today's insurance companies, so they may need to be augmented with new security devices. A little diligent lock-hunting should track down suitably discreet locks and bolts. But such works need to be undertaken with care, because historic doors and windows can be damaged by trying to fit new security devices.

It makes sense to upgrade all door locks where possible, using new ones that won't damage the fabric – a five- or seven-lever mortise deadlock is recommended. However, bear in mind that any lock is only as good as the strength of its fixing.

Modern mortise locks can be fitted inside an opening cut through the edge of the door, so they're virtually hidden. The best solution is to buy locks that fit existing mortise openings without having to cut or drill new holes (but don't chuck away the originals once they've been replaced). When buying replacement mortise locks remember to check the 'backset' – the distance of the keyhole and handle from the side edge of the door.

For windows as well as doors, fitting robust internal bolts is a simple way to improve security. Specially designed locking bolts for sash windows are reasonably inconspicuous and easy to fit. Simple window restrictors can also be used to limit the extent of opening.

When it comes to installing intruder alarms, it can require a lot of damaging drilling and cutting of holes for detectors and contact points on doors and windows, which can weaken them. To limit the damage, wireless intruder alarms are a better option because all the individual detectors around the house communicate with the alarm base via wireless signals, which saves having to run lots of wires.

External joinery

On some older properties the windows and doors comprise the full extent of the external joinery, but from the Georgian era onwards it became increasingly common for houses to be embellished with carved or moulded timbers, to areas such as roof lines and porches. As a rule, the more expensive the property, the more decorative timberwork would be displayed.

Much of this joinery is found at high level, at the eaves and gable ends. Horizontal timber fascia boards at the base of the roof slopes provided a handy place to fix gutter brackets. Fascias were sometimes attached directly to the upper wall masonry but more commonly would be fixed to the rafter feet, forming 'box eaves', with a soffit 'ceiling' underneath made from lath and plaster or timber.

Similarly, decorative bargeboards were commonly fitted under the verges at gable walls (hence their original name 'vergeboards'). But many old houses were built without external joinery of any kind at roof level. Instead, verges often featured corbelled or decorative 'dogstooth' brickwork, and eaves were traditionally left open with rafter feet projecting, exposed to the elements – a feature that's recently been revived in much new housing.

Because external timberwork is permanently exposed to the ravages of the British weather, it can potentially be vulnerable to decay. However, thanks to the quality of the timber and the skill of the original joiners much of it has proved surprisingly durable. Where localised decay has set in there's usually a contributing factor, such as a leaking gutter. The solution is pretty much as described for dealing with decay to windows and doors. Localised small areas of rot can be cut out and the remaining timber treated and filled. More extensive decay will need replacement with good quality new timber cut and spliced in to match the original.

Paint

Keeping external joinery well protected from the weather is fundamental to preventing the onset of serious problems. It's interesting to note that the original paints used until the mid-19th century performed very differently from their modern counterparts. Traditional paints tend to powder or flake with age, allowing damp timber a chance to dry off, whereas modern gloss paints simply seal in damp. As we're about to see in the next chapter, there's a real art to getting decoration and wall finishes right on period buildings.

Above: New timber finial post being made identical to original

Right: Saved: skilled joinery repairs with sound original timber retained where possible.

Left: Antique original joinery should be retained - a stitch in time can save much later expense

BMulfordHistoricCarpentry.co.uk

14 DECORATIONS AND FINISHES

The natural feel and subtle shading of a limewashed wall

A surprising amount of damage has been caused to old houses by well-intentioned 'smartening up'. In some cases centuries of history have been unwittingly obliterated in the space of a few minutes. So before reaching for your paintbrush, it's worth taking time out to do a spot of detective work.

Traditional crafts revived

Concealed wall surfaces in cupboards or behind old fittings can often provide a fascinating insight into a property's history. Things as simple as the pattern of wear on old floors and curious markings on antique joinery are all part of a building's provenance. It's generally better to retain the visible clues to its past life, not just because it makes the property more interesting but also because history can enhance house values. In medieval houses wall paintings were commonly applied to the timber framework and to wattle and daub infill panels, and original artwork of this age predates most of the paintings displayed in the National Gallery.

Today, many houses suffer from being over-restored, and it's no exaggeration to say that buildings can be put at risk simply by being decorated with inappropriate modern materials. So the greatest benefit for many old buildings is likely to come from the removal of damaging modern masonry paints and replacing them with traditional finishes.

Help- I'm suffocating!

Cleaning masonry and paint removal

Vinyl emulsions, modern gloss and masonry paints have been in use for the last 50 years or more, so by now nearly all old properties will have been decorated with them. The reason this is an issue is because non-breathable modern paints have a similar effect on an old house as putting moist washing in a plastic bag – it never gets dry because the moisture can't escape. And as we saw in Chapter 2, traditional buildings need to breathe, so the main reason for stripping paint is to restore breathability.

But a build-up of paint might also be obscuring fine details of historic mouldings in plaster, stone or timber. So having decided to do the right thing and strip away modern layers of paint that are slowly suffocating an old building, the next question is how best to go about it. Mistakes have been made in the past with paint removal and cleaning techniques that were far too aggressive. Picking the wrong method can cause the destruction of layers of irreplaceable history in a few moments. Some processes can also be damaging to human health.

Before you start

From a health perspective, you need to take precautions when stripping or rubbing down old surfaces. Many old paints applied until as late as the 1970s contained lead, which can be dangerous if dust is breathed in. Also, some of the more aggressive stripping and cleaning methods need to be applied with due regard to personal safety. For example, some chemical strippers are highly caustic, and fumes from burning paint can be toxic as well as being an irritant.

Also before starting, you need to be aware that consent may be required for certain stripping and redecoration work – if you're in any doubt at all, check with your local Conservation Officer.

Transformed – wonderful 'polychromatic' brickwork released from behind a century of grime

Cleaning stone and brickwork

The first question should always be whether cleaning is really necessary. In the past there have been many disasters, where blasting with high-pressure sand or water have actually accelerated surface decay. Aggressive chemical treatments that successfully removed dirt from stonework sometimes also permanently discoloured it, and the resulting chemical stains may not now be removable. Botched attempts at cleaning have left behind roughened wall surfaces that attract lichen and facilitate moisture ingress, with fine carved stone detailing eaten away. The mistakes of the past mean that consent is now normally required for stone cleaning to Listed buildings and for some work in Conservation Areas.

It's now understood that as soot staining accumulated over many years from smoke pollution, it formed a hard crust on the exterior surface of stonework. Blasting, sanding, or high-pressure flushing and chemicals can easily strip away this 'protective skin', leaving the walls cleaner but more vulnerable. So where there's a build-up of soot and surface dirt on a masonry wall the best approach is to start with some small-scale testing.

It's important to first analyse what type of stone you're dealing with. Limestone and sandstone have very dissimilar chemistry and therefore need different cleaning methods. Where dirt has built up on limestone it's usually water soluble, and should respond to gentle washing techniques using a minimum amount of water. But with sandstone the use of chemical cleaning agents may be necessary, and these must be selected specifically for compatibility with the particular type of stone. This is where advice from your local Conservation Officer can be useful. Once chemical cleaning is complete it's critical to follow neutralising instructions, otherwise the chemicals can continue to eat into the face of the masonry for many weeks.

Brickwork on old buildings may similarly appear perfectly hard and resilient when in fact it's easily damaged. Bricks have an outer protective skin formed during the firing process which can be destroyed by sandblasting; once exposed the softer core will be highly porous and can allow water to penetrate through the brick. Fortunately, today there are some gentle yet effective ways to clean both brick and stonework.

RECOMMENDED TREATMENTS

Cleaning masonry needn't be a full-scale assault. The best approach is to carefully target the areas that need cleansing to avoid any weaker or sensitive parts of the building's fabric. Simply brushing with a scrubbing brush and water can often be surprisingly effective. Conservationists sometimes also favour specialist systems using steam or superheated hot water in controlled amounts. These are the big brothers of the humble home wallpaper stripper. Operated by specialist contractors, such systems are designed to be gentle, although success depends on the skill of the operator, as jets of hot water in the wrong hands are capable of burrowing into mortar. Their use should also be restricted to the warmer seasons to allow plenty of time for the fabric to dry out prior to winter, otherwise the walls could be at risk of frost damage. This is a different process from high-pressure water cleaning, which is best avoided, as blasting large amounts of water at old buildings risks damaging them and can introduce damp problems.

Laser-based cleaning systems are the latest technology, and these have the enormous advantage of being able to clean the face of the wall with absolutely no contact other than light.

Paint removal

Today, we have at our disposal an extensive armoury of proven and effective paint-removal methods. By adopting a targeted approach it's now possible to remove most types of modern impermeable paint from a variety of different surfaces without damaging the building's underlying original fabric.

Steam strippers of the type used for cleaning can also prove highly effective for paint removal, as can some environmentally friendly chemical strippers. The recently developed Vortex system uses a gently abrasive technique for paint removal. In the hands of a skilled operator it can even strip paint without damage from relatively soft materials such as pine. But as this can generate quite a lot of dust it's best suited to use in vacant buildings. The full range of options is described in the boxout overleaf.

PAINT REMOVAL FROM MASONRY WALLS

Conservationists sometimes point out that if you leave a painted wall long enough the paint will eventually peel off naturally, saving

High temperature water jet system (120° C) suitable for the hardness and texture of the brick.

the need for stripping. But this would mean putting up with an unsightly appearance for years on end whilst damp remained trapped behind the more resilient layers. So direct action is normally required.

Where paint is adhering poorly and flaking it should be fairly simple to remove it using a metal scraper. But you need to be careful not to damage the surface of old bricks and lime renders, which are comparatively soft and easily scored. Where masonry paint is more stubbornly attached to a wall it should respond to treatment with a wallpaper steamer, although there may be a few diehard patches that it simply isn't possible to shift. The most effective modern systems use superheated steam that can simply melt modern plastic paints. These are quite gentle and consume a minimum amount of water. The most challenging surfaces are roughcast or pebbledash renders which incorporate small pebbles, making total removal of paint difficult to achieve.

However, where walls are rendered with cement there's no point going to the trouble of stripping paint. Instead, the impermeable coating of cement will first need to be removed and replaced with lime render.

Left and below: Where paint is adhering poorly it should peel off fairly easily using a metal scraper

Above: Time travel: several layers reveal old lead paint and varnish

Right: Black beams are so 'last century'

PAINT REMOVAL FROM TIMBER

Although water-based strippers and flushing are preferable, solvent-based paint strippers are very effective for removing layers of modern paint. These can either be painted on or applied as a thick poultice. Older oil-based paints can be dissolved using alkaline-based removers. Caustic soda dissolved in water will often remove tar and linseed oil. Extra care is obviously required with joinery to windows because old glass is easily cracked and scratched, so flame guns and abrasive treatments are best avoided. It's quite common to send doors and other items of internal joinery to be stripped in chemical baths, but there are some potential risks (see boxout). Veneered timber should never be stripped, as it will delaminate.

Beams stripped using gentle low pressure (25psi) aluminium silicate scouring process

The JOS system is another recently developed process that can be used to remove black paint from beams and bring out the colour of the wood while retaining the charm of its natural imperfections and age. Although this is a wet abrasive system it uses relatively soft calcium carbonate and allows pressures to be controlled to a very fine degree.

In timber-frame buildings the exposed internal posts and beams may simply need scrubbing down to remove layers of ancient grime, and given a coating of boiled beeswax to bring out the natural colour. Beeswax polish was also the traditional finish for oak and elm floorboards, and can be a good option today for hardwood joinery, as can natural oil-based varnish. However, raw linseed oil isn't recommended for beams or floorboards because its finish is slightly sticky, which attracts dust.

PAINT REMOVAL FROM METALWORK

Built-up layers of paint often obscure fine detail on antique ironwork, so it can be well worth stripping. Chemical removers are usually most effective, but heat guns can be used, and wire brushes can be useful for removing surface rust.

Paint removal methods

	A	B	C	D	E	F	G	H
	Water-based eco strippers	Brush-on solvents	Alkaline strippers	Poultices	Dipping in caustic baths	Hot air guns	Steam wall-paper strippers	Abrasive methods
Brick and stone	✔	✔	✔	✔			✔	
Timber	✔	✔	✔	✔	✔	✔	✔	
Plaster	✔	✔	✔	✔				
Marble	✔	✔	✔	✔				
Metalwork	✔	✔	✔	✔	✔			✔

Notes

A – Water-based, solvent-free 'eco strippers' are non-toxic and can be painted on. These are preferable to chemical strippers for a wide variety of surfaces.

B – Solvent strippers are paint-like gels that are brushed on, causing paint to blister so that it can be scraped away and the process then repeated. Some manufacturers can mix specially formulated chemical strippers if you send them a sample of the paint to be stripped. But it's important that the chemical is washed off after use

Solvent stripper reveals beautiful oak

so that it doesn't continue to attack the new paint. Note, however, that some chemicals can permanently discolour timber.

C – Alkaline (caustic) strippers work by softening the paint so that it can be removed with a scraper.

D – Poultices with longer contact times can be used to draw out deep-seated contaminants.

E – Caustic chemical baths are used, hot or cold, for dipping whole items, such as doors that need to be taken down and sent off for treatment. Ironmongery and door furniture should first be removed. But there's sometimes a risk that timber can either become bleached or darkened. If the chemicals dissolve animal glue used in joints it might cause parts to work loose, or may lead to shrinkage and distortion.

F – Heat applied by hot-air guns softens paint so that it can be scraped off.

But great care is required to avoid scorching timber and leaving unsightly black marks, and also to avoid cracking adjacent glass in doors and windows. Many conservation organisations ban hot paint stripping, as it poses a potential fire risk, for example to hidden wood shavings in old sash boxes; hidden pockets of old straw or sawdust may smoulder undetected for some time before eventually catching alight. The release of toxic fumes is another concern. Naked flame blowtorches should never be used.

G – Steam wallpaper strippers are a simple and benign way of removing plastic paints, although they're not always successful

Black scorch marks on stripped door

at shifting stubborn patches. Care must be taken not to allow moisture to penetrate too deeply into old lath and plaster or it may weaken the surface.

H – Abrasive methods such as sanding with power tools and wire brushes should be restricted to metalwork, but even gentle sanding can release toxic dust into the air from old lead paint.

Other than for stripping some metal surfaces, sandblasting is now considered inappropriate as a paint removal technique on historic buildings. The ferocity of the abrasive blasting can damage the surfaces being stripped, for example turning an antique piece of timber into driftwood. When grit is fired at a painted wall it tends to bounce off hard surfaces but can penetrate gaps in the paint, attacking and scarring the softer old wall behind. It also generates unpleasant clouds of dust.

What old walls want
– limewashing

Blistering evident
behind coat of
modern gloss

Decoration

When you're doing up an old house, choosing the right materials is key. Not only does paint have to look right, it also has to serve the essential function of protecting the building. So as well as enhancing the overall period feel, applying a suitable paint will help improve the building's performance.

Conventional modern paint

Today's paints are mostly formulated from plastics – synthetic latex, vinyl or polyurethane and acrylic resin – hence the term 'plastic' paints. Modern emulsions, masonry paints and solvent-based oil paints work by forming a plastic skin on the surface of the wall. Polyurethane varnishes (which superseded traditional natural varnishes from the 1970s) similarly form a protective skin that resists breathing.

However, the appeal of modern paints hasn't arisen without good reason. They have fewer limitations in use compared to traditional natural paints such as limewash that can't be used throughout the winter months. They are also easier to apply and take less time to dry out, needing fewer coats. But crucially, modern paints aren't breathable – even water-based products aren't usually breathable to any useful extent.

There is, however, an even more damaging material that should never be used on period properties. Long-life wall treatments are aggressively promoted by 'Never Decorate Again!' firms promising to 'shield your walls'. Such finishes may be fine for modern cavity-wall houses, but not for traditional solid-walled properties. Claims that treated walls will be able to breathe are misleading, as any minimal amount of breathability will be nothing like enough to be of any practical benefit for old buildings.

Traditional paints

Paint is made up of three parts: a binder to make it stick to the surface; a solvent to make it spreadable and which evaporates, causing the paint to solidify; and pigment for colour.

However, there are some key differences in the way traditional paints perform compared to today's paints sold in DIY stores. Most importantly, old paints are breathable and can cope with damp. They're also relatively flexible and can accommodate small amounts of movement.

Modern paints work by totally repelling damp and are designed for use with modern non-porous building materials. In contrast, old houses were built with softer, more permeable materials. And because damp will inevitably find its way into the fabric of old buildings from a variety of routes – not just from rain – it's important that it's free to escape, so that the walls can dry out.

Because old houses are prone to slight seasonal movement, applying a brittle film of modern paint will, over time, result in cracking and blistering. The cracks admit water and the blisters act like small reservoirs, so the damp fabric behind has little

What old walls don't want – plastic masonry paint

Natural finishes exude warmth and charm

What's in lead paint?

Lead was the key ingredient in traditional oil-based paints until it was finally banned in Britain in 1992 (it was banned in the US in 1978). Lead paint normally comprised 'white lead' (lead carbonate) bound in linseed oil. It was also coloured with various pigments and dyes, sometimes including small amounts of toxins such as arsenic (greens and whites), cadmium (yellow), cyanide (blues) and cinnabar (the parent ore of mercury, used for reds).

Linseed oil (squeezed from the seeds of the flax plant) was an essential ingredient because it hardened into a tough film. Its one dramatic downside was that it's extremely combustible – a single pot of linseed oil could, in the presence of an open flame such as a candle, ignite spontaneously – and was the source of many devastating house fires.

Oil paints were originally pretty glutinous and difficult to use, a bit like spreading tar with a broom. Only the discovery of turpentine, a natural thinner distilled from the sap of pine trees, made the paint easier to apply, and painting became smoother. Adding turps (turpentine) also gave the paint a matt finish, which became a fashionable look in the Georgian era.

Painting was especially skilful because, until the first ready-mixed paints appeared in the mid to late Victorian period, painters had to create their own colours by grinding their own pigments. Paint had to be mixed in small portions and used at once, so the ability to make matching batches from day to day was a real skill. They also had to apply several coats, since even the best paints had little opacity.

Blues and yellows were two or three times more expensive than duller colours like off-white and stone, so they tended to be used only by the wealthier classes. Most expensive of all was bluish green verdigris, made by hanging copper strips over a vat of horse dung and vinegar and scraping off the oxidised copper. Rich colours generally denoted expense, since you needed a lot of pigment to make them.

However, there were two very basic colours that didn't exist until well into the 19th century. The brightest available white was a dull off-white, and it wasn't until titanium oxide began to be added to paints in the 1940s that really intense, long-lasting whites became available. Also missing was a strong black. Permanent black, distilled from tar and pitch, wasn't popularly available until the late Victorian period, so glossy black front doors, railings, gates, lampposts, gutters, downpipes, and other fittings that are such an element in many restored properties today are actually quite a recent phenomenon. In Dickens' time almost all ironwork was green, light blue or dull grey.

chance to dry out properly, being screened from sun and wind by waterproof paint.

In contrast, limewash has the magical ability to self-heal, sealing up minor cracks. And because traditional limewashed walls can breathe you don't have to worry about any rain getting into the odd hairline crack, since the wall shouldn't retain water for long. Painting old houses with limewash also makes them look much more authentic, thanks to its softly varied colour.

Lead paints

Painted joinery, both externally and internally, would normally have been finished in natural oil-based paints. These combined a base, usually of lead carbonate (to provide body and a white pigment), mixed with a binder of linseed oil (to make it stick), plus pigment for colour and thickening agents like wax or soap. Varnish was similarly produced, but with resins added to the linseed oil instead of pigment. The higher the lead content, the more durable and the more expensive the paint.

Despite their toxicity these paints remained popular into the 1960s. Today lead paint is banned almost everywhere except for a handful of specialist uses, notably on Listed buildings (Grades I and II* or Scottish Grade A). It is much missed by conservationists because it gave a depth of colour and a mellow air that modern paints really can't match. Although predominantly used for decorating joinery and metalwork, in some grander buildings it was also applied to plasterwork and stuccoed facades.

In most old houses layers of lead paint will be lurking under later coats of modern gloss. Lead paint testing kits can be used to check if necessary, but it's safest to assume that the material is present. However, there's only a potential health risk if lead compounds are ingested or inhaled, usually from sanding, so simple precautions should be taken against ingesting dust when rubbing down.

Old lead paint frequently has a creamy or soft colour. If it looks faded and has a slightly chalky surface, it's probably lead paint. Rather than splitting, blistering and peeling away from its background like today's paints, traditional paints tend to fade away more gracefully over time. It was actually the lead content that enabled it to weather into a powder. An old door, for example, will become matt and dusty rather than crack and peel. However, it can eventually shrink into large oblong pieces, with fine cracks at roughly 50mm (2in) intervals. The cracks only require filling with linseed oil putty before recoating. From a technical point of view the best new overcoat would be the same paint, but this isn't normally permitted. The next best option is to use modern natural oil paints where the lead content has been substituted by salts of other metals.

From medieval times limewash was commonly applied as a finish to timber surfaces

Limewash

Limewash is one of the oldest building materials, familiar to the ancient Greeks and Romans. Traditionally it was used to protect and decorate stonework, brickwork and plaster, mostly as an external coating. From medieval times it was also commonly applied as a finish to timber-frame buildings, covering both timber and render surfaces alike.

Limewash is made by diluting lime putty with water. Its natural complexion is a pleasing shade of soft white, but it can be coloured with earth or mineral pigments or with vegetable dyes. As a rule, the less additives the better, as they reduce breathability. So that it's not overloaded, the amount of pigment should be no more than about 10% of the mix. Traditional pastel colours, from yellow ochre to orange and terracotta, were based on natural earth pigments sourced from crushed earth or soft rock.

Additional ingredients were sometimes added to limewashes to modify their performance and durability, included linseed oil, tallow, salt and casein. Today some ready-made paints include a small quantity of added linseed oil to help reduce 'dusting' and improve external water shedding. However, adding modern PVA building adhesive makes limewash non-breathable and is best avoided, other than where you've got a few remaining 'islands' of cement render on a wall that it otherwise wouldn't stick to.

Painting the walls of an old house with limewash imparts a pleasingly authentic matt finish that mellows over the years in a different way from modern paints. In contrast to today's standard masonry paints with their uniform colour and sheen, limewash softens over time, its colour variations becoming more apparent. Because limewashes are porous the colours temporarily deepen in tone in rainy weather as moisture is absorbed until it naturally evaporates away.

The finish isn't perfectly uniform, but has subtle imperfections rather like antique parchment, adding character to a building. Because its chalky matt finish varies across the surface it helps to disguise lumps and cracks in old walls. In skilled hands the addition of a little fine sand can help disguise irregularities in the wall, and the gently varying surface can be textured by special brushing.

Modern eco paints

Limewash remains king of external paints, offering breathability and durability plus a natural aesthetic that's hard to match. However, a new generation of water-based silicate masonry paints can offer a useful alternative to limewash, and are easier to apply. So where access for repeated applications is difficult, such as at higher levels, these are sometimes used by conservationists as they're longer-lasting and more durable. Silicate paints are claimed to be highly breathable and are suitable for all permeable masonry surfaces including brick, stone, and lime plaster and render. They require one primer plus two coats, with a drying time of 4–12 hours.

But choosing modern alternatives to limewash can be a bit of a minefield. Some adverts for 'microporous' paints promise great things, but even if the small print on the tin says it's breathable, that doesn't automatically make it suitable. It probably won't say exactly how breathable, and that's important. The fact is, unless paint is usefully breathable it doesn't belong on the walls of an old house. The best advice is to first check with your local Conservation Officer.

Because limewash is porous the colours naturally deepen in tone as moisture evaporates

Authentic, natural, breathable finish

Mikewye.co.uk

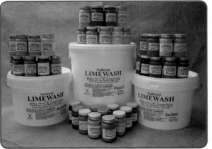

Mikewye.co.uk

External decoration

Most old houses have acquired numerous layers of different types of paint over many years, so before applying fresh paint a certain amount of stripping may first be required, as described earlier. As always, surface preparation is key to achieving good results.

Making your own limewash

Materials
- Lime putty
- A supply of water

Tools
- A clean plastic dustbin with lid
- Cordless drill with a whisk mixer attachment (as used by plasterers)
- A clean metal trowel
- Protective goggles and gloves

1 Pour fresh water into the dustbin.
2 Add lime putty to an approximate ratio of one part lime to three parts water.
3 Use the whisk to mix the lime and water. Wear goggles!
4 To check the consistency of the mix, dip in a trowel. The mix should be the thickness of semi-skimmed milk, coating the trowel but translucent enough that you can see the steel through it.
5 If the mix is too thick, add more water; if too thin add a bit more lime.
6 To add colour mix a *small* amount of pigment in powder form (available from lime suppliers).
7 Keep the dustbin covered with a lid to ensure a long shelf-life. It will settle after a few weeks and need remixing before use.

Limewashing masonry walls

Limewash is the perfect finish for most old walls. As well as being relatively cheap it works in harmony with traditional lime mortars and renders, sharing their flexibility of movement, and can even help heal damaged surfaces. To save time limewash can be purchased ready-mixed in plastic tubs, in a range of colours. But it can be very rewarding, as well as cheaper, to have a go at making it yourself from lime putty and water. Always use a good quality lime putty that doesn't first need to be sieved through a pair of old tights (which can be put to better use for wine making).

Preparing external wall surfaces

Thorough preparation of the wall surface is essential. For any work at height use a safe work platform set back slightly from the wall. Before commencing limewashing the surface should be prepared as follows:

- Repair any defects in the wall surface.
- Use a stiff-bristled brush to remove any loose particles and wash any dust and dirt from the surface.
- Mask doors, windows and joinery using polythene sheeting and tape.
- Any mould or lichen growing on the surface can be removed with a fungicide, such as a weak bleach solution, which should be rinsed off before limewashing.

Lime render is the ideal backing for limewash because it's naturally permeable and absorbent, but sometimes old limewashed or distempered surfaces have been coated with sealant in a past attempt to get modern paints to adhere to the surface; and where freshly applied limewash isn't able to soak into a reasonably porous background material it will instead sit on the surface, making it prone to flaking or premature weathering. Similarly, it will struggle to get a grip on cement-rendered walls, where in any case there's little benefit to using it since its prime quality – breathability – will be wasted.

A similar problem can arise where you have a 'mixed surface', where it hasn't been possible to entirely strip all the old masonry paint as a few stubborn patches have adhered too strongly; and where cement render has to be hacked off a wall and replaced

with lime it's not always possible to completely remove the odd part without risking damage. So a few small islands of hard cement can remain, typically around windows and to ancient wattle and daub panels. The challenge is therefore to find a suitable finish that lets the main part of the wall breathe, but that can also stick to these enduring areas of plastic paint or cement.

The traditional way of increasing the 'stickability' and durability of limewash was to add casein (from skimmed milk), common salt or tallow. The fact that additives tend to reduce breathability shouldn't matter when applied to impermeable surfaces. An alternative solution may be to use limewash made with feebly hydraulic NHL with an added earth pigment, to achieve a good cosmetic finish combined with breathability. Or try using modern silicate masonry paints.

Applying limewash

You'll need a large short-haired emulsion brush (or one that can hold a lot of liquid, such as a thick creosoting brush for fences). An additional smaller brush can come in useful for crevices and awkward bits. Limewash is caustic, and getting it in your eyes can be extremely painful, so be sure to protect them with goggles; plus it's not a bad idea to slip on a pair of surgical gloves to preserve your complexion.

The ideal weather for limewashing is mild and slightly drizzly. On sunny days try to work on walls in the shade, so do the east wall in the afternoon as direct sunlight can make it dry out too quickly. It should never be applied in temperatures below 5° or when there's a risk of frost.

The key to a good limewash finish is to apply several thin coats to a damp surface to slow down the drying-out process. So before brushing on your first coat it's important that dry surfaces are first dampened (this shouldn't be necessary with new lime render or plaster that's still moist). Using a hose with a spray gun set to 'mist', spray the area with water and allow it to soak in. Pre-wetting the surface should prevent the water being rapidly sucked out of the newly applied limewash.

A litre of limewash should cover 3–6m² for one coat, depending on the smoothness and porosity of the surface. Before you start

Working with limewash

Working with limewash is fairly straightforward, but for a good result you need to understand its qualities and limitations:

- Limewash is caustic, so it's essential to protect your eyes and to wear gloves.
- It likes traditional porous surfaces and will readily stick to soft brick, stone, lime plaster or roughcast.
- It isn't readily compatible with non-porous surfaces such as modern cement render, plastic masonry paints or hard modern bricks.
- Four or five thin coats will usually be sufficient for new plaster or bare brick/stone. As a rule of thumb, it lasts a year for every coat applied, plus a couple more in sheltered situations (where it should last around seven years).
- Three coats may be sufficient to freshen up previously limewashed surfaces.
- It doesn't tolerate frost until properly dry.

whisk the limewash thoroughly, to disperse any putty which has settled. Then proceed as follows:

- Working from the top down, re-wet roughly 1m² of wall and brush the limewash on to the dampened area.
- Work the limewash well into any cracks or joints, but don't let it build up too thickly as it can craze on drying out. Don't worry if it looks very thin – it will appear transparent on application but will dry opaque. Remember that several thin coats are better than one or two thick ones.
- The limewash becomes lighter and cloudier as it absorbs CO_2 from the atmosphere. Coloured limewashes dry to a much lighter shade than when first applied.
- Allow 24 hours between coats and repeat the operation. Four coats (five for white) are recommended on new external lime render, or three coats on new internal lime plaster. For each further coat, follow the same procedure of misting well in advance and allow the limewash to dry out slowly, with a little light spraying if required.
- Protect each external coat of limewash from the weather if necessary. A thin coat curing slowly in the presence of moisture will form a harder-wearing surface, as opposed to a chalky finish if a thick coat dries out too quickly.
- Limewash continues to strengthen for several weeks after application and it can take a few days for the true colour to become apparent. Remember that it's normal for limewashed walls to darken a little when they get wet.

Access for decorating at height must be safe

Left: Vapour permeable stains can be a good option. Below: Where timbers were originally limewashed, go with tradition

Painting timber

Historically, limewash was commonly applied to the exposed framework of timber-frame houses. Alternatively external oak would be preserved with a clear breathable coating of boiled linseed oil diluted with natural turpentine (the oak weathering to a silvery colour after a few years).

As we saw earlier, traditional oil-based paints were later developed containing lead as a key ingredient. Today, for most period properties, the best finish for external joinery is the modern equivalent – natural linseed oil paints. These are similar to the original but use substitutes such as zinc in place of lead, and can be applied over existing sound lead paint, or direct to bare sanded wood.

Bare wood was traditionally treated with a primer coat or two of raw linseed oil, warmed up to about 60°C to make the oil thinner so that it soaked in more easily. The same method can be used to good effect today. Any cracks can first be filled using a linseed oil-based putty. This can be painted over before it's dried with the first coat of linseed oil paint. Each subsequent coat should be allowed to dry and given a light sanding. Linseed oil paints take longer to dry than today's plastic paints and should not be applied in cold, damp weather.

These natural paints require greater skill to use compared to modern non-drip paints, as they're thinner (and thus drip more), becoming thicker as they dry. They need to be applied in several thin coats or they can wrinkle when dry. However, linseed oil paints have the major benefit of lasting considerably longer than conventional modern paints – often 15 years or more. Their remarkable longevity is because the oil soaks into the wood rather than just sitting on the surface ready to flake off, like modern solvent-based paints. Also the finished surface has a certain amount of elasticity so it isn't as physically hard and prone to cracking as modern paints. Above all, because they're breathable they don't trap damp behind a surface 'skin' of paint. Although more expensive to buy, using natural oil paints should work out significantly cheaper in the long run.

Alternatively, where ease of use is a key factor modern vapour permeable paints and stains can be a good option. Most are water-based, solvent and acrylic-free, with a flexible microporous finish that doesn't seal in moisture.

Iron

Unlike most surfaces in old buildings iron has no need to breathe, so the use of modern paints should hold no horrors. Cast iron components like gutters, downpipes, window frames and railings are tough enough to withstand the scraping and abrasion required to strip off past layers of paint. However, the use of heat guns should be avoided since cast iron is very brittle and can crack with heat. Bear in mind also that old layers of paint may contain lead.

Always make sure the surface to be painted is clean, dry and free of any rust. A zinc-based primer should be applied to chemically protect bare metal from rust. Normally two coats of primer are needed followed by a suitable surface coat. Special MIO (micaceous iron oxide) paint gives excellent protection from knocks, but being rather thick can obscure detail on decorative ironwork.

Natural linseed oil paints soak into the wood and last for many years

Chris Gare / Gare.co.uk

Internal decoration

Tempting though it can be to smarten things up, sometimes it can be a better option to leave old surfaces alone, displaying their patina of age and retaining their ingrained history. Sometimes doing nothing is the best option. Where redecoration really is necessary, the first decision is often whether to take a dedicated conservationist approach and only use traditional materials throughout the building, or to allow modern materials where appropriate. And as we have seen, breathability is a key factor for surfaces where moisture needs to escape. However, this isn't generally such an issue with ceilings, internal joinery and some internal partition walls. Although breathable internal surfaces can help absorb airborne vapour from condensation, it's worth remembering that even some original paints had quite limited performance in this respect (for example, those with additives to enhance their durability or colour).

A good compromise is to use modern acrylic-free, water-borne emulsions, clay paints and casein paints. These combine ease of use and a good range of colour with a useful amount of breathability.

When it comes to matching period wallpapers, specialist suppliers keep old designs or can even reproduce new ones from an old sample. The original glues used for wallpapering were animal- or vegetable-based, and much more breathable than today's impermeable pastes. So if re-wallpapering, try to use a similar natural adhesive when pasting walls (sizing).

Glazed wall tiles were another Victorian favourite. As well as adding considerable aesthetic charm tiles served a practical purpose, solving the problem of clothing getting marked from brushing against whitewashed surfaces. Tiles were even manufactured in the form of glazed dado rails. But because old buildings tend to move slightly, rigid tiles sometimes develop hairline cracks. Fortunately there are many good reproductions of old patterned tiles now available.

Soft distemper

Distempers were a popular type of whitewash used for internal decoration until eventually superseded in the 1960s by vinyl and acrylic emulsions. Soft distemper was made from powdered chalk or lime, bound with glue or casein (a resin with good adhesive qualities derived from solidified milk – hence the traditional name 'milk paints'). A typical recipe might consist of chalk dust ('whiting') mixed with hot water to a creamy consistency, which was combined with 'size' (a sticky gel made from rabbit-skin glue dissolved in hot water). This produced a thin, inexpensive paint that gave a gentle white finish known for retaining its brightness on dry surfaces. It was sometimes tinted in pastel colours.

Soft distemper was widely used for ceilings and decorative plasterwork. Ceilings required regular redecoration because of the extensive amount of smoke from sooty candles and open fires, plus of course nicotine staining from pipes, cigars and cigarettes. But instead of just slapping a new coat of paint on top of the existing layers the old dirty coat first had to be washed off.

INTERIOR LIMEWASHING

Limewash is very forgiving and will happily accommodate changes in your choice of colour. But bear in mind that when first applied the tone will be significantly deeper than when fully dried out. In this example, after the first coat in beige it was decided to opt for a warmer peach colour.

1 Wall surfaces filled and repaired using lime putty plaster

2 First application of beige limewash with brush

3 Repairs clearly visible as first coat is being applied

4 First coat of beige limewash drying out

5 Beige limewash a couple of hours later still looking relatively dark and blotchey

6 After the beige colour, a coat of peach limewash goes on

7 First coat of peach limewash drying out up to 4 hours

8 First coat of peach after 14 hours of drying

9 Second coat of peach being applied

10 Decoration complete but not quite dry as the repairs still hold a little moisture

11 Drying out

Images courtesy Mike Wye & Associates Limited

This had the benefit of preventing a build-up of thick paint over many years obscuring the detail on intricate mouldings.

Soft distemper has an opaque, chalky appearance. Although relatively breathable it's not recommended for any areas prone to damp, or for external use. One less desirable characteristic was that it tended to rub off as a chalky powder on clothes if people casually brushed against it. Attempts were made to address this problem on walls by sometimes applying harder-wearing, oil-bound distempers. Linseed oil distempers also had the advantage of being able to support darker colours, although this made them less breathable.

Today the use of modern distempers can add an authentic period feel, and can also visually heal minor cracks in old walls or ceilings. Specialist firms can mix distemper to order, but it has a limited shelf life.

Old coats of distemper should wash off when brushed with warm water containing a small amount of added wallpaper stripper to give it a boost.

Limewash

Traditionally limewash was used less widely for internal decoration than distemper. Its relatively thin, milky consistency made it more time-consuming and messy to apply to ceilings However, limewash was traditionally recognised for its antiseptic qualities, and was sometimes used in sculleries to help 'keep the flies away'. It was also suited to use on any damp areas of internal walls, being able to cope with high levels of moisture evaporation. Today it's ideal for use on lime plaster on a damp wall that's still drying out. Tubs of ready-mixed coloured limewash prepared for use on internal surfaces can be purchased, and impart a lovely traditional finish to old plastered walls. But it can take a little getting used to, appearing transparent and darker as it's being applied, starting to dry to an opaque finish after a few hours. For a colour finish, the undercoats can be left white if required, with just the final two coats coloured with added pigment.

Interior eco-paints and trade emulsions

Today a new generation of eco-paints is available, categorised into water, mineral or plant based. When choosing a compatible breathable paint, check its resistance to water vapour permeability – the lower the better. Clay-based emulsions are especially effective and can be used to unify a patchwork wall where the surface comprises a mix of older and newer materials. Modern casein paints are claimed to be 'the most natural paint available',

being constituted primarily from lime and milk protein with added chalk, clay and earth pigments.

Conventional modern wall-primer undercoat emulsions are another possible alternative, and are widely available from DIY stores. These are used by trade decorators to apply a first coat on new gypsum plasterwork while the walls are drying out. Because they don't contain vinyl they permit a useful degree of breathing. They dry to a matt finish with no sheen.

Preparation of internal surfaces

Time spent on preparation is key to achieving a decent finish. Any loose and flaking paint should first be gently removed using a stripping knife. And as we saw earlier, where a surface has a coating of old distemper it will need to be washed off before redecorating. In areas where breathability is important, such as the

Use a steamer to strip modern wallpaper

Small cracks and holes can be filled with a standard flexible filler

Time spent on preparation will be repaid with a successful finish

main walls, layers of modern vinyl emulsion should be removed. It should peel away quite easily where it was applied over an original layer of distemper or limewash.

However, as we saw earlier, there are usually a few patches of paint that are virtually impossible to remove, particularly where applied to modern gypsum plaster. All you can do then is to give it a through rubbing down to provide a key. Often you're left with a wall or ceiling that's a patchwork of old lime plaster interlaced with some gypsum plaster repairs, plus various hairline cracks and a few firmly adhered patches of paint. Small cracks and holes can be filled with standard powder-based filler mixed with water. Any large areas can be filled with lime plaster and sanded down when dry.

This is where old houses require a different mindset – surfaces don't have to be perfectly smooth and even. A certain amount of unevenness is a characteristic of old lath and plaster, and is part of the building's period charm that you want to preserve. Bear in mind also the danger that overly vigorous stripping of old wallpaper can remove layers of history with it, so a careful approach can reap rewards.

Internal wall surfaces

The simple act of emulsioning an old wall has sometimes drawn attention to the presence of some low-level damp. Where moisture is naturally evaporating from within a wall (normally the main walls), applying a coat of emulsion effectively forms a vinyl skin over the surface and traps it. This can lead to a rash of unsightly bubbles forming under the surface film of emulsion.

To make matters worse, this would often then be misdiagnosed as rising damp, setting in motion the needless and harmful process of injecting an ineffective chemical DPC. Even more damaging, the lower wall would then be re-plastered in hard cement render and given a finish coat of pink-coloured gypsum plaster. So in many properties the lower part of the main walls may no longer comprise the original lime plaster.

Where you have a mixed surface – part lime plaster and part modern gypsum plaster – traditional distemper won't adhere to the more recent plaster. The best option is to use a breathable clay paint that can adhere to both kinds of background. But where walls are damp they should be allowed to dry out as much as possible before redecorating. See also 'Hygroscopic salts' in Chapter 2.

Gypsum plaster isn't necessarily a problem when applied to internal partition walls, but on the main walls hard gypsum surfaces can harbour damp, especially in winter as warm moist air from the room condenses. This can result in emulsion peeling off and black mould forming.

Where the original lime plaster has survived, stripping off coats of modern emulsion and replacing them with a traditional paint will allow the wall to breathe once again. This is especially important for the main walls exposed to the full force of the elements externally. But, as with ceilings, breathability tends to be less of an issue with internal partition walls. Although the lower portion of a ground floor internal wall might have absorbed damp (for example from leaking pipes or moist ground), most partition wall surfaces normally harbour no significant moisture content. They're also far less prone to condensation, which is more of a concern on colder main walls, particularly those in steamy bathrooms and kitchens. So simply decorating over existing emulsion can often be technically acceptable, although they'll lack the authentic 'feel good' factor conferred by lime.

Ceilings

Stripping emulsion from ceilings may not be necessary or even advisable. Unlike main walls, ceilings have no urgent need to breathe, and in any case the upper surface of the lath and plaster concealed within the floor void remains 'naked' and breathable. Another reason to be wary of disturbing old lath and plaster ceilings is that many were lined with thick wallpaper. Although a steam wallpaper stripper can be very effective at removing emulsion, it will also weaken any lining paper that's helping to unify and retain old plaster.

In many houses some of the original ceilings will at some point in the past have been replaced with plasterboard, evident from its smooth, uniform surface, often with hairline cracks visible along rectangular board joints. A good compromise can be to decorate over existing sound emulsion with modern clay paints, which are claimed to give a more authentic look than new emulsion.

If stripping is essential (for example to remove textured paints, described below) a simple hand scraper is usually sufficient to get the surface layers to part company from underlying original distemper, but take care not to gouge the plaster. Emulsion can be much harder to remove where the original chalky distempered surfaces were primed with a sealer to stabilise them and enable over-painting.

Where a few stubborn islands of emulsion might remain, the slightly proud edges can be smoothed using a small amount of filler. After cleaning with sugar soap and rubbing down to provide a key, ceilings can be decorated with a modern clay or casein paint.

Artex

The fashion for textured ceilings is today, thankfully, a thing of the past, but many houses still have Artex-type ceiling coverings which were popular from the 1970s, and which may contain very small amounts of asbestos fibre. This means that stripping must be carried out with care. Use of power tools and sanders should be avoided, as inhalation of the fibres is a health risk. Stripping can normally be carried out successfully using a wallpaper steamer accompanied by the energetic use of a scraper.

Cornices and ceiling roses

One of the great joys of restoring a classic property is the opportunity to bring back to life old decorative features that

have long been obliterated under multiple layers of paint. But you need to plan your stripping campaign very carefully. Successful removal depends on picking the right method that's compatible with the material the antique ornamentation is made from. Decorative plaster can be quite fragile and is easily softened by steam strippers. Most delicate of all are mouldings made from papier-mâché or gesso (a traditional compound resembling hardened putty). Fortunately, where layers of modern emulsion have been applied over existing distempered surfaces it should come off quite easily, and using a flexible plastic spreader blade it may be possible to gently peel back the overlying coats of paint. In more stubborn cases good results can sometimes be obtained using chemical poultices, but always do a pilot test on a discreetly located section first. If it looks like it could damage the material, the best option is to leave well alone.

Internal joinery

Conservationists aren't overly keen on the word 'restoration'. This may seem a bit precious, but many homes have been 'restored' to an imaginary past that never actually existed. For example, the late 20th century fad for stripped pine interiors would horrify any self-respecting Georgian or Victorian. Softwood joinery was traditionally regarded as a cheap and inferior material, despite

being of far higher quality than most equivalent timber available today. Pine (red or yellow deal) would be disguised by being painted, or was sometimes camouflaged with skilled fake graining to resemble more expensive woods. Better quality hardwood, in stark contrast, would either be left unfinished in all its naked glory, or given a simple waxed or oil finish to enhance its natural beauty for all to admire.

However, because the quality of old joinery was generally very high, stripping it can be a good way to show off the original workmanship. Stripping away coatings of modern paint and exposing original hardwood can bring back to life beautiful features that have been hidden for generations. But avoid stripping where historically inappropriate – for example, wainscoting was normally painted in the Georgian period.

When it comes to painting internal joinery, conservationists generally prefer linseed oil-based paints, which are similar to ones traditionally used since the 1700s. These can be applied over old lead paint if it's sound, or direct to bare wood.

Natural linseed oil paints should be applied in very thin layers, otherwise they form a skin on the surface, remaining soft underneath. Each layer should be allowed to dry thoroughly and lightly sanded between coats. Three thin coats will usually suffice. The drying time is longer than with today's plastic paints (one to three days), but they last considerably longer.

15 SERVICES

When most period houses were built the services that we today take for granted were unknown. Only by the later Victorian period were significant numbers of homes supplied with piped water and connected to a public sewer. Although gas was becoming increasingly popular from the 1890s for lighting, electricity remained an elusive concept for all but the wealthiest households until well after the First World War.

Over the years most old buildings have been repeatedly adapted to accommodate new services. Intriguing remnants of what are now long-defunct fittings, pipes and cables are quite often encountered today when carrying out work. Curious items such as cast iron gas pipes embedded in fireplace walls, or dark brown Bakelite light switches, can offer a fascinating glimpse into lifestyles from bygone eras. Lifting floorboards sometimes reveals networks of old wires that were once connected to servants' bells, even in homes of comparatively humble status.

Minimising damage

As new technologies evolve, the challenge remains of trying to incorporate them without the destruction of historic fabric or spoiling the character of old properties. Careful planning of new cable and pipe runs is key to minimising damage. The following top tips should help prevent disaster:

SURFACE-RUN SUPPLIES
New pipework and cabling can often be run along wall surfaces (above the skirting or in corners) instead of through floors. Boxing them in with timber casings or plastic conduit painted to match the wall can make new surface-run supplies very discreet and yet retain excellent accessibility for maintenance.

DON'T CUT HISTORIC FABRIC
Try to avoid knocking holes in walls or chasing plaster for cable or pipe runs. Where unavoidable, ensure making-good is done in appropriate materials. It's especially important to avoid cutting through fragile old wattle and daub wall panels, or through lath and plaster ceilings and walls, as even small cuts can cause collapse. Also avoid cutting historic features.

REUSE EXISTING CONDUITS
Most houses will have redundant conduits that can be reused to run new pipes or cabling, saving disruption. Old buildings often contain voids, such as disused chimneys, that can sometimes be used to accommodate new services.

JOIST CUTTING
Try to avoid cutting notches in joists, as it will inevitably weaken the floor structure. Pipes can often be run parallel to joists. Where cutting is unavoidable notches should not exceed one eighth of the depth of the timber, because structurally the depth of a joist provides greater stiffness than its width. Cutting should always be made from the top, and not within the first 300mm of either end. Fitting a metal plate over the open notch to cover the top of the pipes helps reduce the weakening effect, and also protects pipes from any subsequent clumsy nailing in floorboards.

FLOORBOARD CARE
Lifting old floorboards without causing damage isn't as easy as it looks – a joiner is the best person for the job. When it comes to re-fixing lifted floorboards it's advisable to use screws rather than nails. This way they can easily be re-lifted in future. It also prevents the risk of vibration from hammering causing damage to delicate plaster ceilings.

Even correctly cut notches weaken joists

Common causes of damage

Electrical wiring

Much damage has been caused by deep chases cut into historic plasterwork and holes cut through walls for new cable runs. To reduce their impact, cables should where possible be surface-run and contained in a plastic conduit. If there's no other option, holes through floor joists should be drilled approximately halfway down, and located no closer together than three times the diameter of the hole. To minimise damage to the fabric, new sockets and light fittings can be surface-mounted instead of being recessed. Alarms can use remote wireless technology with no need for cabling.

High level supply cables add stresses to old structures (and are a potential danger with building works)

Central heating pipework

With careful planning it should be possible to route pipework so that any cutting is minimised. It helps to use modern flexible plastic pipes or narrower 8mm microbore copper pipes, which only need small holes. Best of all, have new pipework surface-run.

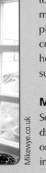

Mikewye.co.uk

Meter boxes and external services

Some properties have been horribly disfigured with big ugly meter boxes stuck on to historic walls – or even physically inserted into them. Installing low-level meter boxes in the ground is usually a better option. Ideally fit internal smart-meters that are read remotely, tucked away somewhere discreetly. When running external fittings try to screw the clips into mortar joints to save damaging old masonry.

Satellite dishes and solar panels

Special care is needed when walking on fragile old roof coverings. Ensure installers use appropriate access equipment to spread loads.

Left: Rare period vent pipe – worth preserving

Below: Rainwater and grey water shouldn't be mixed

Drainage

Drains have enormous potential to wreak havoc. Hidden away underground, persistent pipe leaks often go unnoticed for years on end – until disaster strikes. Defective drains are one of the main causes of subsiding foundations. Yet this is a subject we rarely give much thought to until accosted by foul stenches or overflowing toilets. So it's worth taking an interest to prevent such disasters arising in the first place.

Drainage is normally divided into two separate systems, foul waste and surface water. The relatively clean rainwater that collects as 'surface water' from roofs and hard surfaces is usually channelled to soakaways or into nearby watercourses. A separate foul waste system delivers 'grey water' from bathrooms and kitchens etc to mains sewers, or in more rural areas sometimes to private drainage systems. Problems arise where the two systems get mixed up. Foul waste misconnections are illegal, as well as a source of pollution. A simple example might be where a dishwasher is connected into a handy nearby rainwater downpipe, causing the soakaway under the lawn to bubble with detergent. The same scenario with a WC macerator would have more disturbing consequences. Conversely, surface water is sometimes

Separate systems, but top of soil pipe is missing – heavy cast iron toppling can present serious dangers

misconnected to foul waste systems. This may not sound too serious but it can be a recipe for disaster in storm conditions, as sewage works become deluged with tsunamis and the contents overspill. Either way the consequences are likely to be unpleasantly wet and sticky.

Drain history

In many older houses the drainage system will be a relatively recent addition. In most towns and cities the drains usually date from Victorian times, whereas in rural areas many mains systems were installed in the post-war period, or they may rely on private systems such as septic tanks.

Until the mid to late 20th century most underground pipework connecting the house to the main sewer comprised salt-glazed clayware pipes with spigot joints, typically of 100m (4in) or sometimes 150mm (6in) diameter. Inspection chambers were built of brick, often rendered internally, and with pipes bedded in weak cement mortar benching.

Above-ground foul waste

In older properties the waste pipes serving WCs, bathrooms, kitchens and sculleries were originally made of lead or cast iron, but many have subsequently been replaced or supplemented with

new pipework. Because of their relatively large diameter (typically 30–50mm diameter, and 100mm for WCs) waste pipes should not be run within timber floors – cutting huge chunks out of floor structures to accommodate them obviously isn't a good idea. Even where it's possible to run waste pipes parallel to joists it isn't normally advisable because hidden leaks can develop, resulting in outbreaks of rot.

Waste pipes in older properties normally feed out through the wall as branch pipes connected to a larger bore soil and vent pipe (SVP) running vertically up the side or rear of the house. The job of the SVP is to channel foul waste safely down into the underground drainage system. These were traditionally manufactured from cast iron, although some examples made from bespoke leadwork with decorative brackets still survive. Despite their utilitarian function, these can be miniature works of art that add to the character of old houses, and should be preserved. Try not to modify or replace interesting old pipework with bland modern plastic components. Any new additions to the system are best made from authentic cast iron components (which

shouldn't be hard to source). Alternatively, suitable salvaged items may be obtainable.

Like funnels, the tops of SVPs are always open in order to ventilate the drainage system and alleviate pressure. This means foul odours can be emitted, so the top needs to project well above the level of upstairs windows. Normally terminating above eaves level is sufficient to disperse any malodorous wafts (unless there are roof windows at higher level). Problems can occur where SVPs become blocked, for example if birds are nesting in their open tops. One solution is to fit small protective 'wire balloon' cages over them.

Inside the house foul sewer smells are kept safely at bay thanks to the U-shaped traps under sinks and baths etc. These retain (or 'trap') sufficient water at the base to act as a seal. If it wasn't for the ventilation provided by the SVP, every time you pulled out the plug the waste water rushing down the pipe would create a

vacuum in its wake, sucking out the water sitting in the traps and allowing foul sewer gases to rise up and pervade the house. This curious phenomenon, known as 'siphonage', can also be caused by branch pipes that are too long or set to incorrect falls.

Ye Olde foul waste systems discreetly painted to blend in

Spaghetti school of plumbing: Old SVP sprouting numerous modern additions

The distinctive waft of sewers – soil pipe close to bedroom window

All clear: traditional brick inspection chamber

Underground systems

Clay pipes were traditionally used for underground drainage systems, together with brick-built inspection chambers to provide access for maintenance. The last chamber in line before the main sewer should have an interceptor trap as a barrier to smells and rats, with a cleaning eye or stopper above the trap where drain rods could be inserted to clear blockages. At least, that's the theory. In reality many old properties may have no inspection chambers at all, or just a solitary specimen.

Often the first challenge is to actually locate old drains. They may be hard to trace, disappearing under buildings or weaving

Low level sewer vents helped relieve pressure – common in some older systems

around obstacles in a way that modern regulations wouldn't permit. Many old drain runs are surprisingly shallow and can be fractured by ground movement. Damage is sometimes also caused by heavy vehicles parked on top, or by excavation work in close proximity.

Over time ground movement sometimes affects the fall of underground pipe runs, which traditionally were laid to a very slight incline (1 in 40 for a 100mm pipe). And where waste water can't flow easily, blockages are likely to occur. The most common weak points are at pipe joints, which are sometimes infiltrated by roots of trees and shrubs aggressively seeking moisture.

To check whether drains are flowing freely, the simplest test is to lift inspection chamber covers and then run the taps and flush WCs. Adding coloured dye can help identify the path of waste water from different locations.

Testing for leaks and blockages between two inspection chambers can be done by plugging the outlet entering the lower chamber (ie the one furthest from the house) and filling the upper chamber nearest the house with water. Then wait to see if the water is retained or leaks away through the pipe linking the two chambers. Of course, not every house has the luxury of two inspection chambers, in which case the best way to spot problems like fractures and infiltration of roots in underground drainage systems is to instruct a professional drainage survey where a CCTV camera is passed through the drains.

Where an old system is defective, replacement with new pipework is normally advisable. Modern plastic pipes and ready-made inspection units are easier to install than in the past. Even where an old system appears to be operating satisfactorily, if access is poor it's a good idea to add new inspection chambers at major bends in pipe runs. But as always with old houses, deep trenches mustn't be dug too close to shallow foundations because of the risk of destabilising the wall. Note also that changes to drainage systems normally require Building Regulations consent.

Private drainage

Many homes in rural areas don't have the luxury of mains drainage and instead rely on a private system comprising a cesspool or septic tank. A cesspool (aka cesspit) is simply a large storage vessel buried in the ground. It acts as a temporary repository for foul waste until it can be emptied and carted away on a fairly frequent basis (sometimes as often as once a month). Hence the importance of ensuring adequate access for tanker lorries.

Septic tanks are more like miniature sewage works, comprising a series of buried chambers where natural bacteria break down the waste into relatively harmless run-off. The solids are retained as a crust or sludge whilst the effluent is discharged into the ground via a network of pipes or land drains, or into a nearby stream or to surface water drains. Because septic tanks only retain the solid waste, they can be smaller than a cesspool. Accumulated sludge needs to be pumped out by a tanker lorry once or twice a year. Both types of tank were traditionally built of brick, and tend to be prone to leakage; modern manufactured plastic chambers are more efficient. Septic tanks and cesspools should be located at least 12m away from the house, with sufficient access for emptying. If you plan to install a new system it's worth considering more sophisticated solutions such as Mini Treatment Plants (MTPs), which can process waste more efficiently.

When buying a property with private drainage, bear in mind that it's an offence to make a sewage effluent discharge to surface waters without an environmental permit. Systems that discharge effluent must be registered with the Environment Agency (cesspools are unaffected) or have an exemption permit in place, otherwise they may need to be upgraded at some cost.

Old cesspits and septic tanks are often hidden by foliage

Left: Surviving original water pump and trough

Right: Original feature - lead supply pipe

Below: Old house and modern suite living in harmony

Plumbing

Internal pipework supplying hot and cold water was traditionally made from cast iron or lead. Although lead is no longer considered suitable for drinking water supplies, in hard water areas the insides of such pipes will have long ago developed a protective coating with natural deposits of limescale. In soft water areas lead water pipes should be replaced. Lead was also a constituent in solder for some types of copper pipework until finally banned in 1987. Today new cold supplies are run in plastic or copper pipe, usually with push-fit or press-fit joints.

It's surprisingly common for old buildings to have suffered from small leaks that have persisted unnoticed over a long period of time, from hidden pipes or sanitaryware. The chief offenders, however, are acrylic shower trays and plastic baths, which commonly develop leaks at the seals around the edges, allowing water to quietly seep into the fabric of the building. Power showers are notorious for injecting water under pressure through even the tiniest of cracks. The resulting timber decay to floors and stud walls may only become evident as a result of a pervasive damp smell.

When installing new hot or cold pipework in old buildings, modern materials offer some significant advantages. Flexible plastic pipes in particular are easier to thread through awkward

Incoming cold supply with trademark bulbous joint where connected to copper pipe

New plastic cold supply replacing defective old cast iron pipe

Sanitary fittings

Original bathroom fittings are a valuable part of a property's history. Surviving cast iron baths can normally be overhauled and re-enamelled. However, most period properties were built with little, if anything, in the way of plumbing, traditionally relying on water pumped by hand from a nearby well.

Until the later Victorian period a large tin bathtub placed by the fireside would normally suffice for bathing, supplied in wealthier homes by hot water ferried in cans carried by servants. Day to day, most households washed themselves from small washstand basins or jugs and bowls in the corner of the bedroom – later to become a room of its own.

Although many late 19th century houses had a water supply to the kitchen and perhaps to a downstairs WC, most lacked a proper bathroom because there wasn't enough pressure in the pipes to get water upstairs. Existing houses had to later be adapted with baths fitted in wherever space permitted, usually taking the place of a bedroom, or jemmied into alcoves or other odd corners. Ironically, some of the last properties to have plumbing installed were those of the super-rich, who had little need for piped water supplies as servants continued to perform this function well into the 20th century.

Toilet facilities were traditionally limited to commodes or chamber pots kept in bedroom cupboards. Some Georgian dining rooms also famously harboured pots stored in sideboards or hidden behind curtains 'for the relief of gentlemen when drinking after dinner once the ladies had retired into the drawing room' (history does not record how the ladies coped with similar calls of nature).

Most Georgian houses had an outside privy, or an ash or earth closet with a wooden seat over a cesspit (cesspool) in the backyard or garden. In wealthier households privies were sometimes installed indoors with a cesspit dug below the ground floor that had to be emptied periodically by 'nightsoil men'. However, many such vessels were badly built and leaked into nearby domestic wells or into rivers providing drinking water. Many fatal illnesses of the period such as cholera and typhoid were the result of such practices. Today, where long-forgotten sealed-up cesspits are unearthed in old houses, there can be a potential risk from any trapped, highly explosive methane gas.

The 1848 Public Health Act was a turning point, requiring every new house to have a 'WC, privy, or ash-pit', usually located in the backyard. Despite such progress, many people soldiered on with the familiar comforts afforded by chamber pots, which were emptied the next day into an outdoor toilet. Such reluctance to abandon tradition may have had something to do with the fact that early water closets often didn't work well. Until the development of the U-bend (and S-bend), with its integral water-sealed trap at the bottom, every toilet bowl acted as a conduit for smells of cesspit and sewer. The backwaft of odours, especially in hot weather, could be unbearable, hence the custom of locating privies outdoors. Worse, some primitive early WCs could backfire, filling the room with what the horrified user had hoped to dispose of. Even successfully flushed waste might only travel as far as an overflowing cesspool in the backyard, or perhaps via a short brick drain pouring waste into the nearest stream or river. The breakthrough came with the construction of urban sewer systems from the mid-1860s onwards. Legislation followed soon after requiring all new houses to have running water and internal drainage. Modern ceramic flushing 'wash-down' WCs with pedestal bases and enclosed traps became popular from the 1880s. However, poorer households had to make do with a shared communal toilet in the yard and a single tap supplying water for several families.

Above: Original mahogany and marble bath circa 1880s

Left: Privy waste was collected from back alleys via small doors by 'nightsoil men'

Below: Traditional privies used ash or earth in 'lieu' of water

Right: Early low level cistern flushing WC with mahogany seat

Below: Twyfords – well known toilet pioneers

spaces, reducing the need for cutting; and thanks to push-fit joints plumbers needn't use blowtorches on solder joints, minimising the risk of fire. However, before work starts it's important to confirm where the pipes are to be run and how they're to be boxed in – otherwise plumbers will route them the easiest way, regardless of the damage to the building.

Isolation valves should be fitted to hot and cold pipes serving baths, basins and WCs etc. This will allow future maintenance work to be carried out to individual taps and fittings without having to turn off the supply to the entire house. Bear in mind also that it's important to provide access for maintenance to concealed pipes, cisterns and traps etc.

When installing heavy new fittings such as baths or water tanks it's essential to carefully consider how the weight will be supported. A Victorian cast iron bath, for example, can weigh up to 200kg, and hold at least 150 litres of water, with a combined load (when in use) equivalent to five or more adults. With all the loadings transmitted via tiny claw feet, the pressure per square centimetre can be more than a Challenger tank. Additional support and strengthening is likely to be required to floors.

Electrical installations

When you buy a house there's every chance that the electrics will be flagged up by the surveyor as being in some way inadequate, if not downright dangerous. Even where the switches and sockets appear perfectly modern, they may be connected to ancient rubber- or fabric-clad cables run in metal pipe conduits.

This is an area where old isn't necessarily best. As we saw earlier, electricity supplies didn't exist when period houses were built (except for the occasional Edwardian mansion). Nonetheless, this can still pose something of a dilemma for conservationists, as redundant old fittings are part of a property's history. So although ancient fuse boxes, switches and fittings won't comply with current safety standards, once disconnected they should if possible be left on display as interesting features.

When having new electrical work carried out it's important to decide in advance where you want new sockets and switches located – and to mark the exact position in pencil on the wall in advance, or they'll inevitably end up in the wrong position.

In thatched properties, try to avoid running cables in lofts, because it's not unknown for mice to chew through cables with a consequent fire risk. PVC cables run within thick layers of loft insulation can potentially overheat, so as a precaution they should either be laid on the surface or higher capacity cabling should be used. New cabling can be made vermin-proof by running it in conduits. Alternatively specify mineral insulated MICC cable (aka 'pyro' cable), which is a thin, flexible copper tube that's fire resistant.

Above: Newly installed traditional basin

Below: All mod cons – original indoor water pump and stone sink, plus zinc bath tub and 'copper' and washboard for laundry

Above: Edwardian light switches

Below: Gas lights in kitchen later converted to electric

Lighting

Seductive lighting can really bring period properties to life, highlighting charming features and creating a warm, homely atmosphere. But illuminating an old property can also present challenges, and there are some key points worth bearing in mind:

Recessed downlighters should not be installed in lath and plaster ceilings, as cutting even small holes will weaken them, as well as breaching the building's fire resistance. Downlighters are ideally suited to modern plasterboard ceilings (such as in kitchen extensions). If all else fails it might be possible to construct a suitable suspended ceiling below the original, where there's sufficient headroom.

Transformers for low-voltage lighting give off heat and can potentially present a fire hazard in confined spaces where there may be accumulated dust or old, dry timber. LED lights are preferable as they consume less energy and run at lower temperatures.

Old cottages often have low ceilings that restrict the use of conventional pendant lights. One alternative solution is to have table lamps or standard lamps wired so that they can be operated from the main light switch. This type of lighting can look very atmospheric, and is preferable to fitting wall lights that necessitate cutting into plasterwork.

Fire alarm systems

Modern alarm systems can be lifesavers, alerting slumbering residents to the risks of fire and the dangers of deadly carbon monoxide. Smoke detectors and heat alarms must be mains-powered, with battery backup. They must be linked to one another on the same circuit or via radio interlink, so that if one detects a fire they all go off. Such measures are vital in historic properties, and in thatched houses an additional alarm should be fitted in the loft (somewhere reasonably accessible).

To work effectively smoke alarms must be positioned correctly, sited away from corners of rooms (which smoke tends to avoid). The Building Regs require at least one smoke detector fitted on each storey, no more than 3m away from bedroom doors. In halls and landings they should be fitted within 7.5m of the door to each habitable room. It's also advisable to locate them away from cooking areas, heaters and bathrooms, since steam and fumes can accidentally set them off. Also avoid fitting them in kitchens or garages.

Security alarm companies can provide phone-linked monitoring services that automatically alert the fire service in an emergency. If your house was unoccupied this could prevent the disaster of losing everything in a blaze. As with all services, alarm systems need to be installed with sensitivity to respect the building's fabric.

Sprinkler in medieval timber frame house

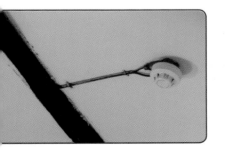

TV aerials and satellite dishes

Installers usually want to locate aerials and satellite dishes wherever it's most convenient for them, regardless of whether it blots out centuries of history. To avoid ruining the appearance of your property, avoid installation on main elevations. Bear in mind also that cable runs clumsily dangling across the walls or nailed into old masonry can deface and damage the facade. It's best to site them within lofts or in the garden well away from the house – satellite dishes can work just as well on the ground and still get good reception. Perfectly good TV reception is often possible from aerials located in lofts, without the need for amplifiers or signal boosters.

Gas

Original Victorian mains gas supply pipes were of cast iron, but in recent years suppliers have undertaken a major programme of replacement with yellow polyethylene underground pipes.

Such was the fear of explosion that gas didn't become established in homes for cooking or heating until well into the 20th century. Yet as early as the 1860s some fashionable townhouses had a central gaslight hanging from the ceiling in each of the main reception rooms, with a ventilation grille concealed in the decorative ceiling rose above. The largest pendant fittings had several burners and were known as 'gasoliers'. Gas wall brackets were commonly fitted to chimney breasts, and even some staircases were lit by lights attached to newel posts. It goes without saying that where such curiosities survive they should be retained. It can even be worth exploring the possibility of making them safe and reusing them.

Gas supply run under floor in void

Heating

Traditionally the only heat in the home was provided by open fires or kitchen ranges. With just the living room or kitchen heated, keeping warm in other rooms was simply a matter of 'putting a jumper on'. Today we demand much greater levels of warmth (and hence energy consumption) than in the past, preferring to heat all the rooms in the house and wear fewer clothes.

Central heating is a relatively recent addition to British homes, only becoming a standard feature in new properties from the 1960s. However, pioneering central heating systems had been installed in some larger houses as far back as the late Victorian period, with varying degrees of success. These comprised large-bore cast iron pipes fed by gravity and the natural circulating force of hot water. Surviving pipes of this vintage can often be adapted for use with modern pumped systems. Old cast iron radiators are very much back in fashion and are a visual asset well worth preserving. New replica period radiators or salvaged originals can look just right in a period house. However, the charms of antique boilers are as a rule best avoided. Labour-intensive solid fuel stoves

or bad-tempered furnaces have thankfully been consigned to history (although worth preserving as a curiosity if still in existence).

Boilers and flues have considerably reduced in size in recent years, but installations of new energy-efficient systems still need to be very carefully planned. One of the most important considerations is the position of the flue, as without due care this can easily damage the fabric of an old building and scar the exterior. If a conventional wall flue is inappropriate, vertical steel flues can be an option, venting via a (less visible) roof slope or utilising a redundant chimney.

Internally, the flow and return pipework to radiators should ideally be surface-run to minimise cutting of the building's fabric, as noted earlier. Also bear in mind the potentially damaging drying effects of central heating on old joinery; so, for example, radiators should be positioned away from timber panelling. A newly installed heating system should be initially run at low output to allow the building to gently acclimatise.

Any rooms with gas appliances that take their combustion air from within the room, such as living flame fires, are likely to require additional room ventilation to comply with Building Regulations. This usually necessitates cutting air vents into the main walls, so such works must be carefully planned in advance to prevent damage.

Oil-fired appliances

Many owners of period properties in more rural locations rely on oil for heating and cooking. Oil-fired cookers (such as Aga, Rayburn, Redfyre etc) operate by drawing oil from a storage tank by gravity, often without the need for a mechanical pump. The oil passes via a control unit into the burner, where it vaporises and burns. However, in recent years some owners have experienced problems caused by hard deposits forming in the burner base and oil feed pipes. This coincided with a 50% reduction in sulphur to oil supplies brought about by an EU directive in January 2008. Cookers are very sensitive to fuel quality changes and a number of vaporising issues resulted from the introduction of low-sulphur fuel. The use of additives may be required to compensate.

Underfloor heating (UFH)

Old buildings are well suited to the gentle, constant, background heat provided by UFH systems, compared to the sudden bursts of heat generated from conventional radiators. UFH is also excellent for heating large rooms with high ceilings, and the lack of radiators frees up wall space, with less damage to historic fabric from pipe runs and fixings.

The predominant type of UFH system consists of loops of plastic pipes embedded in the floor through which warm water circulates. Alternatively 'dry' systems use electric cabling in the form of thin mats, which are better suited to retrofitting, and useful for smaller areas such as bathrooms. Both types suit solid floor construction and are ideal for floors surfaces such as stone or tile. They can also be fitted to timber floors.

The downside is that taking up an old solid floor can damage the character and history of an old house. However, UFH may be worth considering where the original floor no longer survives, or in modern extensions. New solid floors made from natural limecrete are compatible with UFH and can be installed as described in Chapter 12.

Solar PV panels – contentious to old properties when visible to front

Renewables

Before spending money on generating renewable energy it's important to ensure the house is as well insulated as possible so that it can hang on to all that expensive heat, rather than allowing it to simply leak away. How best to insulate different types of period property raises some important issues (see next chapter). Some traditional buildings are better suited than others to retaining energy. Buildings with thick masonry walls have the advantage of 'high thermal mass' that makes them very efficient at storing natural warmth.

In the rush to generate green energy, it's important to minimise the impact of new installations on the structure, fabric and aesthetics of old houses – not least, all the associated cabling and pipework will need to be sensitively routed around the building.

Of the array of renewable options, wind turbines are rarely compatible with old houses. Those fixed to buildings generate relatively low amounts of power, and there can be issues of structural damage from loadings and vibration, not to mention disfigurement. Freestanding turbines can cause noise as well as aesthetic concerns. The following are likely to be the most suitable options.

Wood stoves and biomass

Traditional open fires are notorious for losing 75% or more of their heat straight up the chimney. In comparison, the most efficient wood-burning stoves operate at efficiencies of over 80%. Some new-generation stoves are made with 'soapstone', which holds and emits heat long after the fire has gone out. However,

Charnwood stoves

if you prefer the appearance of a beautiful traditional fireplace modern cassette fires can be worth considering. These have the appearance of traditional open fires but operate at above 50% efficiency thanks to a double-skin that superheats cool air between metal plates before venting it back into the room.

A key factor when burning logs is to be sure the wood is well seasoned, with a moisture content below 20% (wood needs to be stored in a well ventilated space for at least six months before use). Biomass stoves are also well suited to older properties. Although their usual fuel is wood chips and pellets they can consume a wide variety of renewable fuels, producing large quantities of heat very rapidly, and can even be fully automated. However, installation costs are relatively expensive. All such installations must be undertaken by a HETAS-approved heating engineer or inspected by Building Control prior to use.

Solar PV and solar water-heating

Both solar photovoltaics (PV) electricity and solar water-heating (SWH) are popular options. However, historic houses are vulnerable to disfigurement by solar roof panels, hence their use is restricted in Conservation Areas and isn't permitted on Listed buildings. Hidden roof valleys may be suitable if they face SE to SW without overshadowing. Mounting solar systems on old roofs can also have structural implications, and requires building regulations consent. Alternatively solar PV panels can be set away from the house at ground level, where they can work perfectly well provided they're not obscured. Garden-sited panels can even be adjusted for greater efficiency to face the full sun more of the time. SWH is less expensive to install than PV, as well as requiring significantly less roof space, and is ideally suited to underfloor heating systems.

Installation of virtually invisible 'solar slate' PV panels

Solar Slate Ltd

Heat pumps

Ground-source heat pumps work by using a series of long, continuous loops of pipe buried underground to collect the heat. The pipes are laid in long trenches about 1.5m deep and hence they only suit larger plots. Because the water produced is at a relatively low temperature, these systems work best combined with UFH systems, but can also be compatible with old heavy iron radiators. One downside with heat pumps is the electricity consumption required to pump large volumes of water through circulating pipes. Using similar technology, air-source heat pumps absorb heat from the outside, even in sub-zero weather, and are cheaper to install.

Lightning protection

From time to time a dramatic news story breaks featuring buildings hit by 'freak' lightning strikes. The risk of a lightning strike relates primarily to a property's degree of exposure, hence structures that reach higher into the sky, such as church spires, are especially vulnerable (though large trees, hills or buildings etc nearby can provide some protection). Old houses with prominent high-level features such as tall chimneys or lofty projecting finials can also be at risk, and hence would benefit from a lightning conductor. These comprise a metal strip or rod, usually of copper or aluminium, connected at the bottom to an electrode driven into the ground, the purpose of which is to direct a lightning strike to earth safely, without harm to the building or its occupants. Larger properties may need more than one, and they should be positioned unobtrusively.

16 LIVING FOR TODAY

Boosting energy efficiency and making more space

Oakwrights.co.uk

Period properties are a scarce and increasingly valuable resource, becoming ever more desirable over the years. The trouble is, much of their appeal and value can be lost simply by making a few clumsy 'improvements'. This is especially apparent where charming old buildings are permanently disfigured as a result of poorly planned extensions. But where new space is added with sensitivity and flair it can actually enhance the character of an old property and add real value.

However, the biggest challenge facing many owners of historic buildings today is how best to upgrade their energy performance. In the rush to boost thermal efficiency ratings in old houses there's a real danger that, in the process, the historic qualities that make them so desirable will be destroyed.

Green living

Today we hear a lot about 'sustainable' building, but to discover what this actually means you need to go back in time. It is a fact that old houses are generally far more eco-friendly than modern homes – they were sustainably built and are long-lasting and easily repaired. The one area where they sometimes fall short is in 'hanging on to their heat'. Fortunately, most properties are capable of being sensitively upgraded. But first let's remind ourselves why old buildings are inherently so green:

- **Localism** – Period properties were built from locally-sourced natural materials that have often lasted for centuries. Trees from nearby woodlands were cut for timber, and cornfields provided a source of thatch. The clay for bricks and tiles was often dug close to the site. Mortars, glass and iron were traditionally produced by local cottage industries.
- **Environmental impact** – Windows, doors and joinery were made from high-quality timber that can be adjusted and repaired over time, rather than needing periodic replacement with energy-intensive manufactured new units.
- **Carbon footprint** – Lime mortars, plasters and renders absorb large amounts of CO_2 when setting.
- **Recycling** – Whole buildings can be recycled. Old bricks or stones set in lime mortar can be dusted off and reused (something modern cement makes impossible), lime mortar and plasters can be ground down and remixed with new. In fact just about everything in them is recyclable.

Building conservation is about maintaining this traditional, sustainable approach. Conservationists can sometimes come across as being a bit po-faced and 'stuck in the past', but the philosophy of consuming less and conserving more is very much in tune with 21st-century thinking. This translates into minimum replacement of the existing fabric and getting maximum life from the old, while favouring traditional materials and repairs instead of unnecessary replacement with newly manufactured ones.

Despite our stock of old houses being some of the greenest and most sustainable buildings on the planet, they're routinely 'marked down' by Energy Assessors simply because the levels of insulation are less than in new houses. The danger is that owners can be panicked into carrying out damaging 'improvements' in the rush to boost thermal efficiency. So what's worth doing and what isn't?

Energy efficiency

Old houses were constructed with far lower levels of insulation than is required for new homes today, although those built with thick stone or earth walls are naturally well insulated, benefiting from high thermal mass that helps store heat. But other traditional forms of construction can be relatively cold and draughty by modern standards. In times past insulation was applied to the human body, which was actually a far more efficient use of energy than the modern practice of keeping every cubic metre of a house permanently heated so that summer clothes can be worn all year round. When it comes to the subject of energy efficiency, a key part of the equation is usually disregarded – the lifestyle of the occupants. The fact is, if lights are left on in empty rooms or heating turned up to maximum with windows left open, it's hugely wasteful, no matter how super-efficient the building.

Embodied energy

There are two forms of energy use – the consumption of 'new energy', and the stored 'old energy' that was originally expended in building the house, referred to as 'embodied energy'. The longer

Embodied energy – with potential

the house lasts the more efficient it is in terms of embodied energy use, spreading the original environmental impact over many years.

Modern buildings are designed to be energy efficient in use, but they consume enormous amounts of resources and energy in the process of construction. So conserving existing old buildings is always a far greener option than demolishing and replacing them. This makes government commitments to 'sustainable development' questionable, given the fact that new houses are zero-rated for VAT but repairs are charged at the full rate – even for conserving Listed buildings.

Repair is always a more sustainable option than replacement, yet current energy policy is designed to steer homeowners towards wastefully replacing sound old windows with expensive new manufactured short-life products on the grounds that they take less energy to run. This, of course, completely ignores the energy and resources used to manufacture the new products, as well as the embodied energy in the old ones that are thrown away. The fact is, the amount of energy consumed in the manufacture, transportation and installation of a new double-glazed unit is likely to far exceed the amount it saves during its entire thermally efficient lifespan.

Energy ratings

All residential properties being sold or rented must by law have an Energy Performance Certificate (EPC). These measure the energy efficiency of buildings, based on a few key facts keyed in to a laptop by an Energy Assessor. But the standardised recommendations churned out by a computer program can be inaccurate for older or more quirky buildings. For example, no allowance is made for the insulation afforded by thatched roofs. More worryingly, it has recently come to light that the software used to calculate SAP ratings significantly underestimates the thermal efficiency of most solid-wall houses. Consequently lots of older buildings are wrongly assessed and homeowners provided with flawed reports. And if inappropriate advice is unthinkingly acted upon, it can cause real damage.

Sealing up homes with double glazing or insulating walls and blocking ventilation can reduce the ability of moisture in the fabric of the house to evaporate, leading to future problems with damp and decay. Many perfectly sound historic windows have been ripped out and replaced with cheap modern double-glazed units on the assumption that this will achieve significant improvements. But alternative solutions such as secondary glazing can be just as effective and consume far less energy.

Draughtproofing is one of the most cost-effective and least intrusive ways of improving comfort and reducing heat loss in (often over-ventilated) period houses – provided that sufficient ventilation is retained for the health of the building and its occupants (especially for the safe functioning of open fires and cookers). So checking things like letterboxes, keyholes, cat flaps and loft hatches can pay dividends.

No one disputes the fact that creating a better insulated building 'envelope' can improve energy efficiency. The important thing is to specify worthwhile improvements that can sensibly be carried out to old properties.

Insulation

Improving insulation to reduce energy consumption needs to be undertaken with great care. Products intended for the insulation of modern houses can sometimes damage old ones, particularly if they prevent walls from breathing or block ventilation.

Fortunately the Building Regulations recognise that applying newbuild standards to traditional properties can be counter-productive, with the danger that you could end up with a warmer but damp interior. Whereas new homes are required to be airtight, imposing similar requirements on old buildings could compromise their need to breathe. Indeed, a certain amount of ventilation is critical to the way they function.

One associated problem is 'interstitial condensation'. This can occur where warm, moist air inside the house can't disperse harmlessly away and instead seeps into the fabric of the building. When it reaches a cold part of the structure, such as the roof space or cavities in walls, it condenses back into water. This is rather like exhaling warm breath through a scarf in winter – the scarf becomes wet as your breath condenses. Crucially, once insulation becomes wet, its effectiveness is massively reduced. And any timber in contact with damp insulation will be more at risk of decay. So good ventilation is essential to help disperse moist air and thus reduce the risk of condensation causing the 'damp scarf' effect.

	Fibreglass insulation	Sheep's wool insulation
What's good	* Cost * Available in DIY stores	* Breathable * Retains thermal performance even when damp * No health risk * Production uses minimal energy and resources
What's not so good	* An irritant – not user-friendly * Poor performance when damp * Contains toxins * Can retain moisture * Produced using larger amounts of energy and resources	* More expensive * Greater thickness needed to achieve equivalent U-values

Natural insulation materials

Breathable natural materials are ideal for old buildings. There are a number of alternatives:

Cellulose fibre

Recycled newspaper processed back to its raw fibrous state is well suited for loft insulation. The product is available either as loose lay or in compressed bales or 'batts'. It's pre-treated with inorganic salts for fire resistance and to protect against fungal and rodent attack (in contrast to toxic fire retardants and pesticides found in many conventional insulation products). UK-manufactured Warmcel 100 is supplied in bags that can simply be emptied into the loft space. As loose fill it's effective at reaching gaps around pipes etc. Other types can be mechanically blown into position by specialist contractors.

Sheep's wool

A natural fibre from a renewable resource, wool has the ability to absorb and release water vapour rapidly, which increases its effectiveness as an insulant. It's simple to install and doesn't irritate the eyes, skin and lungs like conventional mineral products, so can be installed without the need for protective clothing. Normally supplied in rolls or as batts in various widths and thicknesses with sufficient rigidity to adapt to the shape of rafters and joists etc. It can be placed over ceilings, as loft insulation, built into walls, or used to insulate suspended timber floors. Wool is pre-treated with inorganic salts (such as borax) to improve fire-resistance and to make it insect-proof. Brands like Thermafleece are very effective at both thermal and acoustic insulation and can be installed as a 'sandwich' between two sheets of lath.

Hemp

Hemp fibres combined with recycled cotton fibres produce a highly efficient insulation material that's flexible and robust. It's easy to handle and install, plus it doesn't irritate the skin. Like wool it can absorb and release water vapour. Being cellulose-based makes it less attractive to rodents or insects, but it's treated with inorganic salts for pest and fire resistance. It's claimed to smell like newly cut hay (in contrast to the chemical aroma of polyurethane boards). Although famously sourced from the same crop as its distant cousin cannabis, hemp has no mind-altering qualities (it might be worth mentioning this to the builders, in case handfuls start disappearing in sandwich bags!).

Reed

Natural reed formed into boards is sold as a base for plastering internal walls and ceilings. It's an ideal way of adding a layer of wall or ceiling insulation, particularly for timber-frame or earth buildings. Reedboard can simply be screwed into place using stainless steel screws and special plastic washers to prevent thermal bridging.

Other natural stuff

There are some other imported insulation materials that are both natural and non-toxic, such as strawboard, flax, cork, and Pavadentro interlocking wood-fibre boards made from waste softwood.

Insulating the building envelope

The percentage heat loss attributed to different parts of a typical property's envelope are widely quoted as:

- Roof 25%
- Walls 35%
- Floor 15%
- Doors and draughts 15%
- Windows 10%

Some of these areas are easier and more cost-effective to insulate than others, so let's take a look at each in turn.

ROOFS

The roof space is probably the least contentious area to insulate. As everyone knows, heat rises, so the loft is one of the most effective places to insulate a house, as well as usually the easiest. Loft insulation can be laid in rolls or as loose lay. A depth of 300mm is generally considered sufficient. However, there are some key issues to consider:-

- It can be tempting to seal up draughty eaves but these ventilation paths at the edge of the roof are important for keeping roof timbers aired and dry. Sealing ventilation can promote timber decay. Traditionally tiles and slates were laid without any roofing felt underneath, which allowed plenty of air to enter via lots of very small gaps, making roof spaces nice and airy. But many old roofs have subsequently been lined with underfelt, hence any remaining ventilation paths at the eaves etc are all the more important. So in order to maintain a clear ventilation gap between the underfelt and the top of the insulation quilt, purpose-made ventilation trays can be inserted between the rafters at the eaves.
- If electric cables are buried deep within insulation they can potentially be prone to overheating. Instead, PVC cables can be run on the surface or within conduits. Alternatively, specify higher capacity cable.
- Avoid sprayed plastic foam treatments that are aggressively advertised with misleading claims. Spraying the undersides of old roofs with a patchy layer of polyurethane provides virtually zero thermal insulation. It can also block essential ventilation and seal in moisture to roof timbers, making them susceptible to decay.
- To protect against frost, cold-water tanks should be well insulated, and pipes run through lofts should be lagged. This should prevent pipes bursting due to water freezing in winter and will also reduce the potential for condensation forming on cold surfaces and dripping down to cause damp problems. Although rarely encountered, old asbestos-based insulation materials are sometimes found on pipes and tanks, requiring specialist removal. However, asbestos cement water tanks aren't considered to pose a health risk and can be left *in situ*.

Fibreglass quilt and rolls of mineral wool (made from volcanic rock) have long been the most widely used materials for loft insulation. They also have the additional beneficial quality of providing fire resistance and good sound insulation. However, both materials

Strengthened ceiling with loft insulation

Baz Mogridge / E2BN

are irritants to the skin and respiratory system, so some are now produced in pre-wrapped form. New 'eco' loft quilts made from recycled plastic bottles are also available and claimed to be free from floating fibres. However, to maintain breathability natural insulation materials such as Warmcel or sheep's wool quilts are generally a better option for older buildings.

Instead of laying loft insulation above bedroom ceilings, roof spaces can also be insulated higher up at rafter level – although this normally only makes sense where you want to use your loft space to justify the cost of keeping it heated. To achieve sufficient thermal performance, you might need to install approximately 50mm depth of rigid insulation between the rafters, with another 70mm or so lining the undersides of the rafters. Natural wood-fibre boards are a popular material for this purpose.

To comply with Building Regs, an air gap of at least 50mm must normally be left beneath the roof tiles for ventilation, although this may not be necessary where the roof tiles aren't underfelted. Alternatively, modern multifoils can be used to provide under-rafter insulation by being stapled in place to the rafters and secured from inside the loft with horizontal timber battens. These sheets of silver-foil insulation comprise several thin layers of reflective and insulating material. They're heat-reflecting, and although only 30mm or so thick claim performance equal to much thicker insulation quilts. However, to achieve optimum efficiency an adjoining air space of about 20mm needs to be maintained. Multifoils can be useful for insulating awkward narrow spaces in old houses.

If you need to strip the roof anyway, or you want to insulate smaller subsidiary roofs, it may be possible to re-lay the tiles over new insulation placed on top of the rafters, such as sheets of woodfibre sarking board, although this will raise the height of the roof, which may have planning implications.

WALLS

When it comes to insulating walls, period houses fall into the 'hard to treat' category. Solid-wall construction obviously rules out the option of pumping in cavity insulation that's so effective for insulating more modern homes.

Old walls can be difficult to insulate because of the need to maintain breathability. The danger with adding layers of insulation is that it can potentially act as a barrier to the natural breathing

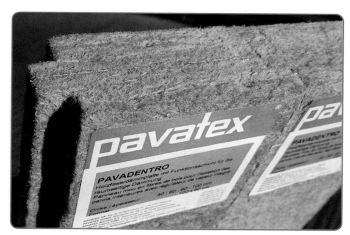
Woodfibre boards – natural and breathable

process, trapping moisture and causing condensation within the building's fabric.

The other main concern with period houses is that their aesthetics and history are precious and easily damaged, so the worry is that in the rush to cut energy bills such works can cause damage to fragile fabric. Nonetheless, with careful planning it should be possible to make significant energy efficiency improvements. In theory walls can be lined externally or internally – at the risk of altering their appearance and concealing old features.

External insulation

Cladding the walls externally with thick insulation boards can give excellent thermal performance. However, it raises a number of practical problems, such as how to integrate it with roof overhangs, window sills and adjoining walls next door, plus the headache of trying to reroute downpipes and flues etc. Visually, external cladding often makes more sense on less visible side or rear walls (particularly in Conservation Areas) and is likely to be more appropriate in houses with rendered walls.

However, sealing up old solid-wall buildings by sticking giant slabs of polyurethane to their outsides can be a recipe for disaster. Fortunately there are other more appropriate ways of insulating externally. The obvious one is to apply traditional breathable external claddings such as tiling or timber boarding, although this is only likely to be appropriate where it matches the local vernacular. Alternatively wood fibreboards with a coating of hemp/lime plaster can provide a new breathable surface. These tongue-and-groove or butt-jointed boards can be screwed on to the external wall before being rendered and colour-washed.

Traditional timber-frame buildings can be more challenging to insulate. One possible solution where cement-rendered panels need completely replacing is to insert lightweight insulation batts in the voids between the timber frame (for example sheep's wool, woodwool board or hempcrete). These naturally breathable panels can then be lime-rendered externally to a wattle base.

A similar approach can prove very effective with weatherboarded timber-frame houses, with resulting improvements in comfort levels and reduced draughts. Once the voids have been insulated an external cladding of woodfibre boards can be fixed over the exposed outer side before replacing the weatherboarding.

Internal insulation

Lining the main walls internally is generally less effective in terms of performance than cladding the outsides. It also tends to involve considerable disruption to heating systems and electrical sockets and switches, plus there's the added risk that temporarily removing old joinery such as skirtings and architraves could damage them. In addition, things like staircases and historic features such as cornices are hard to integrate into thick, new wall linings. Despite this, for homes where the amount of disturbance needs to be minimal, lining the walls internally is often the least bad option. Mid-terraced houses, for example, have fewer main wall surfaces that will need upgrading. But the increased thickness of the insulated walls will inevitably mean some loss of room space.

New stud framework wall lining

The main worry when insulating the inside of solid walls is the risk that warm, moist air from indoors could penetrate through the new lining and condense on the cold main wall surface; and where such interstitial condensation forms unseen within a wall it can lead to a hidden build-up of moisture, causing rot problems – something that's especially of concern in timber-frame buildings.

One solution is to leave a space between the new insulation layer and the main wall. For example, a new 100mm timber studwork insulated inner leaf can be constructed leaving a 25mm air gap between the studwork and the main wall. This should prevent the risk of the studwork potentially masking condensation problems. If possible *any* moisture in this cavity should be able to escape via a void above. The studwork can be filled with natural sheep's wool, cellulose or hempwood batts and lined on the room side with 20mm woodfibre board for a traditional lime plaster finish.

A similar ventilated cavity can be formed by applying lime plaster to a traditional lath background set on battens some 30 or 40mm off the face of the wall. Lime plaster itself is a

Thermafleece infill to studwork

Natural wall insulation

INSULATING WITH REED BOARD

Wall being prepared for insulation

The board is marked and cut to size (reeds are bound with zinc coated wire)

Reed board can be cut with a saw (hand or powered) and wire cutters or secateurs used to cut wire

Boards can be held in place with dabs of plaster, then carefully trimmed and the wire adjusted. Minimum 20mm must be left at edges of cut boards to avoid wire slipping

Drilling for special fixings

Reed bedded to wall in lime mortar helps prevent voids

Reed partially fixed to wall

All images courtesy Mike Wye & Associates Limited

Reed insulation fitted around oak window and slate sill. Ready for lime plastering

INSULATING WITH WOODFIBRE BOARD

Woodfibre boards provide thicker breathable insulation ideal for bathroom and kitchen walls:-

Woodfibre insulation board fixed in place to inner face of an external wall

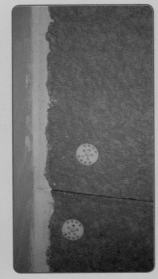
The board is secured in place with easy-to-use insulated fixings

Lime plastered wall ready to decorate

Fully redecorated in vapour permeable paints. Ceiling left as original as possible to show history

relatively good thermal insulator, especially with aggregates like hemp added to the mix, and the air cavity provides an additional insulating layer. A natural paint finish will maintain the breathability of the walls.

An alternative solution may be to fit a natural wall insulation material such as hemp mats between timber battens directly against solid walls (eg Thermo Hemp, available in 100mm-thick mat form). An 'intelligent' breather membrane (eg Intello Plus) is then taped in place on the room side. The aim of this is to provide a vapour check that stops water vapour from the internal environment entering the wall, yet allows any trapped moisture in the structure to escape. The insulation is then lined with a breathable wallboard, such as woodfibre, which is given a lime plaster finish. Regular gypsum plasterboard is reasonably breathable as long as it's not foil-backed, but is unsuited to lime plaster.

Hemp plasters or reed boards can be fixed directly on to the walls, following the contours, and retaining a certain amount of character compared to flat boards fixed to studwork. Some woodfibre boards have a built-in vapour check to reduce the amount of vapour that can pass from the room to the cold inner wall surface.

There's some debate about whether it's appropriate to fit standard non-breathing insulation boards to the inside of the main walls. In some properties, as long as the walls aren't damp and are free to breathe on the outside, this may be an option. It also helps if the works are carried out in late summer when the walls should normally be at their driest. But the problem with making walls impervious on the inside is that it hinders the drying-out of masonry after prolonged exposure to rain. So it's normally best to allow walls to breathe on both faces.

The latest generation of interior insulation systems use high-performance polyurethane foam panels which incorporate a series of holes. These are pre-filled with a special mineral that has a high capillary action and hence readily absorbs moisture. The panels are bonded to the walls with a mineral glue, and coated with a highly porous, lightweight plaster to about a centimetre thick. This enables the old walls to still breathe while providing excellent thermal insulation with relatively thin construction. It can also absorb moisture from the indoor atmosphere, helping to regulate the room climate.

HOLLOW WALLS

Although cavity walls and period properties generally belong to different eras, a small number of early cavity brick-wall houses were built in the late Victorian and Edwardian periods. These have relatively thin cavities with simple cast iron wall ties, and the ventilation through cavities helps disperse moisture. Although injecting such walls with cavity wall insulation may be feasible, there's a potential risk that some early wall ties can rust quicker if surrounded by insulation should it become damp.

Other more ancient types of 'cavity walls' include Tudor timber-frame houses that were re-clad with new brick or stone facades, leaving thin gaps in between that allow a degree of ventilation. Also, many traditional thick stone walls actually comprise two separate skins of stonework with the gap between filled with rubble. Modern injected foam insulants are inappropriate for such buildings because they insert a barrier that seals the wall internally, restricting its ability to breathe.

WINDOWS

Many older houses were built with very small windows that consequently don't waste as much heat as the larger openings in some more modern properties. Nonetheless, the march of the double-glazing salesmen is relentless and it is widely believed that fitting replacement sealed units can only ever be a 'good thing'. However, it's not always correct to assume that new windows will deliver significant improvements. The official statistics show that it can take as long as 90 years to recover the cost of fitting new double glazing, in terms of the likely 'payback period' calculated from resulting savings in fuel bills. Yet the lifespan of UPVC windows that are popularly believed to 'last for ever' is typically only 30 years or less. As we saw earlier, UPVC is vulnerable to UV degradation and cannot be adapted and repaired like timber, plus sealed units commonly fail and become 'misted'. The fact that DIY stores now sell special paint for plastic windows and doors only confirms the fact that they're not maintenance-free products. In some countries such as Sweden, Germany and Austria they're either banned altogether or there are restrictions on the use of PVC on environmental grounds.

There are often more appropriate solutions such as overhaul and draughtproofing. Fitting secondary glazing can provide an excellent solution, with superior performance to many double glazed windows. A number of different designs are available, including some that operate very discreetly like shutters, and

Ideal combination: discreet new secondary glazing with original shutters

Stormwindows.co.uk

others where the frames are held in place with magnets, facilitating easy removal in summer.

The big risk with replacing windows is that it could seriously damage the historic nature of the property, if carried out insensitively. As we saw in Chapter 13, rather than replacing entire widows it may be worth re-glazing existing frames with special slim double-glazed units designed for heritage buildings, especially where the original glass no longer exists.

However, it isn't always possible to simply slot replacement panes into old frames. A new double-glazed pane will inevitably be far thicker than the original, and may not fit existing rebates. Even where replacement is feasible, Conservation Officers will generally want to resist the loss of original glass

It's also worth bearing in mind that double glazing generally has something of a chequered history. In the not too distant past some sealed units have failed prematurely. In some cases the use of oil-based putty in rebates is thought to have reacted with the butyl edge sealant, letting in moisture. Problems have also been caused by new sealed units being jammed into rebates too tightly. To accommodate the expansion and contraction of wooden frames, a 3mm gap should normally be left between the sealed unit and the rebate.

At the end of the day, the most cost-effective way to cut energy use might simply be to follow in the footsteps of previous generations. Donning a thick woolly jumper, drawing heavily lined curtains to windows and external doors, and closing shutters at night can be surprisingly effective. Such simple remedies were traditionally used to retain heat and keep cold and draughts at bay, and in combination can actually achieve insulation values approaching those of double glazing.

FLOORS

Suspended timber ground floors are almost ubiquitous in Victorian and Edwardian properties. Georgian townhouses also featured timber upper ground floors, usually with a basement storey down below.

With this type of floor, a through-flow of air to the underfloor void is essential to keeping the timber structure free from damp, and hence rot and beetle. Ventilation is provided by small airbricks in the lower walls. However, this can sometimes result in draughts through the odd gap between floorboards. Draughtproofing is fairly easily achieved by plugging any such gaps (see Chapter 12).

Above: Snug fleecy sheepswool floor

Right: Gaps between boards can be sealed with slivers of wood

To insulate timber floors, rigid insulation boards can be wedged between joists. Alternatively loft quilt or sheep's wool can be laid in nets fixed over or under the joists. However, it's not advisable to take up an entire floor simply to insulate it because inevitably some of the old timber boards will be damaged in the process.

Netting over joists holds mineral wool

Cutting heat loss

Studies by English Heritage into the thermal performance of traditional sash windows show that even the most basic repair and improvement works can produce impressive results.

- ■ Air infiltration through a sash window in good condition can be reduced by as much as 86% by draughtproofing.
- ■ Closing thick curtains was found to reduce heat loss by 41%, and closing plain roller blinds reduced heat loss by 38%.
- ■ Installing good quality, low-emissivity secondary glazing can reduce heat loss by 58%, achieving U-values as low as 1.7, which more than meets current Building Regulations targets.
- ■ Shutters can reduce heat loss through a window by up to 50%, whilst also helping to reduce noise.

Outlet for new extractor minimises disruption to masonry and can be hidden behind new terracotta grille

The ideal situation is where there's a cellar or basement below permitting easy access to the exposed floor structure. But in most cases ordinary suspended floors have a generous amount of 'crawl space' to the void below, so it should be possible to gain access simply by lifting a small number of boards. Insulation can then be wedged between joists from below.

While you've got access it's a good idea to check the condition of joist ends and sleeper walls, and to check that the oversite ground is dry. It may also be worth taking the opportunity to run any new pipework or cabling, and to lag any naked pipes in the floor void to protect them from frost.

Upstairs floors generally have no need for insulation unless they're located above cold passageways. However, where improved acoustic insulation would be beneficial mineral wool quilt laid between joists can be very effective at sound-deadening.

Solid ground floors can be more of a challenge when it comes to boosting insulation. Excavating historic floors is obviously not an option from a conservation perspective. However, rigid insulation boards can sometimes be laid on top, preserving the original floor. But in practice the associated disruption to internal joinery, fittings, plumbing etc can be immense (as well as potentially damaging). Modern polyurethane foam boards provide the most thermally efficient floor insulation, but sealing old floors can push extra moisture towards the lower walls, with potential damp issues. So it's better to use breathable floor insulation slabs, such as hempcrete blocks laid with a breather membrane on top of an old floor, as a reversible improvement.

Where an old floor has already been substituted by modern concrete you might want to consider excavating it (this should be done very carefully near the walls and in case the old floor remains buried underneath). Concrete floors can be replaced with lime concrete (limecrete) mixed with ceramic bead insulation, even incorporating UFH (see step-by-step feature in Chapter 12).

The importance of ventilation

Old houses need to be kept well ventilated to prevent damaging levels of damp building up from airborne moisture. Any excess humidity from washing, cooking and other human activities was traditionally dispersed through open flues and via draughts, or absorbed by breathable lime-plastered surfaces (fireplaces provided a very useful source of what's now called 'passive stack' ventilation). Today condensation forming on cold walls, floors and windows, particularly in steamy kitchens and bathrooms, can significantly add to the amount of water vapour in the atmosphere of the house, hence the importance of effective ventilation. As we've seen, a good cross-flow of ventilation is also important in lofts and under suspended ground floors to keep timbers healthy and free from decay.

As a rule of thumb, old buildings require twice the level of ventilation of a modern home. But this doesn't mean you have to put up with howling gales blowing through the house (although if your constitution is robust enough, allowing the odd draught to circulate can be beneficial). The aim is to have controlled ventilation, for example with the use of mechanical extractor fans or simply by getting into the habit of opening a window for 15 minutes after showering. But if you fit new extractors it's important to carefully consider whereabouts they'll be located on the external walls, so as not to unwittingly spoil the character of the house.

Photo: Bluebeard

Alterations and extensions

Over the centuries old houses have had to adapt to changing lifestyles. Some have been radically enlarged with extensions, or drastically altered with fashionable makeovers or the addition of entire new facades. Others may have had windows blocked up in a bid to avoid taxes. All have at some point been adapted to accommodate the sort of creature comforts that today we take for granted, such as central heating and modern bathrooms.

As a result we have inherited buildings with many 'layers' pertaining to different eras, something that enriches the history of old houses, making them fascinating to unravel and explore. However, this does beg the question as to how we should today go about altering and extending these residential heirlooms with future generations in mind. Is it possible to both conserve a building and to alter it?

Classic 'Victorian' extension

Extensions

A good extension should enhance the existing architecture. This normally means a sensitive design built to an appropriate scale with pleasing proportions both internally and externally. With Listed buildings and those in Conservation Areas, clearly the planners are going to raise the bar that much higher, but the fundamental rule with all new extensions is that they should respect the original historic building and not interfere visually with the main views of the property.

Builders steeped in traditional skills should be able to produce an authentic new 'period' extension that echoes the character and appearance of the original. But unless you're confident in the ability of your designer and builders to replicate the original architectural style, there's a danger of ending up with a clumsy pastiche. However, there are some types of extension that always seem to blend well with period houses. A well-crafted 'Victorian' addition will often complement properties dating from earlier periods, giving an old house the appearance of having evolved organically over the years. Traditional green oak frame extensions also seem to enhance all manner of old homes and are generally popular with the planners.

With the focus of today's Building Regulations set firmly on thermal efficiency, it's highly unlikely that you'd be allowed to build an extension in traditional solid-wall construction. However, the Planners may insist on a design that faithfully replicates the original. To resolve this apparent conflict, the challenge is to disguise modern insulated cavity construction so that, viewed externally, it authentically resembles a traditional solid wall – for example by using imperial-sized handmade bricks set in lime mortar in a faux solid Flemish bond pattern (with 'split headers').

However, extending your home doesn't mean you have to be a slave to history. After all, the Georgians didn't fiddle about trying to replicate Tudor architecture – they displayed supreme confidence in developing new building techniques and materials (although styles were classically influenced).

Good new design can sometimes work extremely well alongside period buildings. So why not go for a contemporary look? Strange as it may sound, even ultra-modern pure glass 'boxes' juxtaposed against an old house can often be acceptable to Conservation Officers. There's a strong argument that the integrity of the original house is preserved because you can still see the old building through the glass. Neutral and anonymous, the transparent nature of pure glass extensions makes them almost invisible.

Conservationists like any major new work on period properties to be as reversible as possible. New additions should therefore be designed so that they could, if necessary, be removed in future

Perhaps a traditional timber frame extension…

… Or maybe high performance glass?

Cutting to old structures can be minimised by adapting existing openings

Oakwrights.co.uk

without leaving scars. So the main problem is how to attach them to the walls of an old house without causing damage.

To minimise destruction of original fabric, new doorways can be formed from existing window openings rather than knocking holes for completely new ones. You may even be able to transplant the removed old window so that it's re-employed in the new extension.

One key technical point to bear in mind when designing extensions to old buildings is the risk of differential movement. When an extension with deep foundations is built next to an old house with shallow foundations, the old structure will still want to move slightly in accordance with changes to ground conditions, whilst the new one remains rock solid. This inevitably leads to cracking at or near the point where the two structures meet. So it's important to design a flexible junction that allows them to move independently.

Another peculiarity sometimes encountered when excavating foundation trenches in close proximity to period houses is the presence of old wells. This may necessitate expensive remedial work to stabilise the ground.

Conservatories

Conservatories were a Victorian development and aren't necessarily appropriate, on a purely historical basis, for some older houses. Even then, a Victorian or Edwardian rectory might have had one, but not a crofter's cottage. In terms of materials, timber is obviously more suitable than UPVC or aluminium, and glass is always preferable to cheap polycarbonate sheeting. Where consent is required, a smaller, well-designed conservatory made of timber is more likely to be approved.

Loft conversions

It's often possible to convert your loft space with minimal visual impact externally. A couple of conservation skylights to the rear, or a discreet window to a side gable, may be the only noticeable change, making this an attractive proposition for properties in Conservation Areas. However, loft conversions add enormous loadings to existing

structures – and of course, old buildings have relatively shallow foundations and often fairly weak lintels. Old walls that lean or bow may be perfectly stable – until massive new loadings are added.

Converting a loft will also have a

Permitted development

It's not always realised that a significant amount of extending is normally allowed to properties without the need for planning consent. The Permitted Development Rules provide the following 'free allowance' for most properties:

Front
Small porches are normally permitted (except in Conservation Areas or for Listed buildings).

Side
Single-storey extensions up to 4m height, with a maximum width up to half the width of the house (except in Conservation Areas or for Listed buildings).

Rear
Single-storey extensions up to 4m deep for detached houses, or 3m for terraces and semis. Two-storey or higher extensions up to 3m deep (including the ground floor) and no higher than the main house. No balconies. Only a single storey is permitted in Conservation Areas. (Nothing is permitted on Listed buildings.)

Materials and roof pitches should match the existing house and extensions within 2m of a boundary must have a maximum eaves height of 3m. Loft conversions are normally permitted even for a large box with dormers, as long as they don't face a highway.

A fuller account of the rules can be seen on the website **www.period-house.com**

major impact on the interior of the existing house. Deciding where to install the new stairs can mean sacrificing a bedroom, effectively cancelling out the benefit of new space gained in the loft. Also, complying with fire regulations can mean having to replace all the internal doors to habitable rooms en route down to the main entrance with new fire doors. However, in some circumstances it may be possible to upgrade existing historic doors. The fire regulations become more draconian when adding new loft rooms to houses more than two storeys high, or where the new loft floor is 7.5m or more above ground level. This may, for example, require the fitting of sprinkler systems, an external fire escape, or enclosing the stairs with a fire door at the top or bottom.

The necessary structural work normally involves introducing steel beams to take loadings diverted from the roof and to support new loft floors. But as always with old houses, it's essential to design the additional structural elements so that there's minimal loss of fabric, taking particular care to protect fragile historic plasterwork to ceilings below.

Specialist firms may be good at carrying out standard loft conversions in modern houses, but they may not know much about old buildings. The best advice is to consult a structural engineer experienced in conservation to produce the necessary calculations and drawings. Above all, never cut any joists, rafters or other roof timbers until alternative support has been provided.

One final challenge is how best to retro-insulate the roof (see page 222). Bear in mind that Building Control may require additional air vents to eaves and ridges to ensure a free flow of air around roof timbers. A vapour barrier lining should be installed to

Above and right: Original doors can often be retained with upgraded fire resistance

Lining rafters with insulated plasterboard

prevent moisture from the room condensing under the roof slopes, before the new loft room is clad internally with plasterboard secured with dry-wall screws. Where your house has an original attic room, the main challenge will be how best to upgrade insulation whilst minimising the loss of original fabric.

Cellars and basements

A cellar is an underground room used for storage, which is often windowless. Although not a very congenial space it at least has the compensating virtue of providing access to the lower structure of the house. A basement, on the other hand, is a habitable room commonly taking the form of a 'semi-basement' with part of it extending above ground level. If your house boasts a basement it was probably once the 'downstairs' occupied (along with attic rooms) by servants, and in many Georgian houses was the location of the kitchen and scullery.

In terms of potential for conversion to liveable space there's not usually a lot you can do with cellars, on account of their low headroom and lack of windows. The nuclear option – excavating and rebuilding at enormous cost – is rarely advisable. Better to content yourself with the thought that cellars can make a great wine store or can come in handy as a space to accommodate fridge-freezers, storage safes or boilers – or even tanks for rainwater harvesting systems.

However, one thing cellars and basements have in common is the tendency to suffer from damp – although this needn't be an issue where they're simply used for storage. Where damp is more severe, such as where standing water has accumulated, it can normally be dispersed with a pump. However, if it turns out that the water table is higher than the level of the cellar floor there's a good chance that it will simply be replaced by the ingress of new groundwater. This requires specialist advice, as it may be necessary to install an external land drain. Although old wells are sometimes found in cellars or under ancient floors, such long-established 'water features' are rarely a problem.

Converting an existing basement into habitable space can be a realistic proposition. However, there are still likely to be significant limitations, not least the cost. Issues such as damp-proofing, light and ventilation, access, headroom and the potential risk of flooding all need to be carefully weighed up. All works should comply with BS8102.

If structural work is required, this can be damaging to old foundations. Old structures don't take kindly to being violently disturbed. Even when such works are done competently they can have a similar effect to part of the building being underpinned, resulting in differential movement.

There are two main methods for making basements damp proof:

1 Ventilated cavity systems

Ventilated dry lining systems work by isolating the original wall surfaces behind a new inner lining, leaving a ventilated air gap in between. This is achieved by installing a special dimpled plastic sheet between the basement walls and a new interior layer of dry-lined studwork, creating a ventilated air gap. To the floor, a screed is laid over a damp proof membrane. This method has the advantage of not taking up much space and also allows walls to breathe, but good ventilation is vital. Provision should be made for any water that may penetrate into the cavity to be collected and drained or pumped away.

In basements where damp is likely to be more prevalent, a more robust solution can be to build a new 'room within a room'. This is achieved by constructing a new floor and blockwork walls that are

Above and above right: Ventilated cavity systems

Right: Pump installed to discharge any water collecting within cavity

Tanking to basement brickwork

isolated from the main structure by DPMs and a drained cavity. The main disadvantage is that the blockwork takes up more room space.

2 Tanking

Probably the best-known method, tanking uses waterproof material to totally seal the walls and floor, forming a 'tank'. The work can be carried out either inside or outside the building. However, it's generally considered to be the most invasive and least effective system. For some older properties it can lead to longer-term problems, such as where tanked walls cause damp to be driven up the masonry walls to affect the structure above.

Adding a new bathroom

Installing a new bathroom or cloakroom needs to be planned carefully. While pumps and macerators can make it theoretically possible to locate such new facilities virtually anywhere in the house, in practice the associated pipework often needs very long runs and can be ugly and intrusive. If all your existing drain runs and soil pipes are over in the 'east wing' but you insist on siting your gleaming new bathroom in the 'west wing', it's obviously going to necessitate a lot of additional cutting and unnecessary damage to historic fabric. So it makes sense to locate such new facilities where they can be linked in with the existing infrastructure.

When it comes to installing new sanitary fittings there's another practical problem that's sometimes encountered in old houses:

upstairs floors are rarely perfectly level, which can play havoc with conventional floor-standing basins and WCs. One solution is to fit wall-mounted units, which have the added advantage of leaving the old floor surface exposed, allowing easy access for cleaning.

Bathrooms, of course, generate enormous amounts of steamy air that, unless expelled, can seep into the fabric of the building and condense, causing damp. Hence the importance of fitting effective extractor fans.

Adding a new kitchen

Incorporating a new kitchen sympathetically in an old house can be something of a challenge. As always, the priority should be to avoid disturbing the original building more than necessary, but physically installing standard kitchen units in properties with uneven walls, floors and ceilings can be a nightmare. So rather than opting for a conventional fitted kitchen it's often preferable to select free-standing kitchen furniture. A traditional dresser can provide a generous amount of storage space whilst imparting a suitably authentic period feel. It may even prove less expensive than installing fitted units. A free-standing range cooker can similarly make life easier, as well as looking the part.

As with bathrooms, pipework for the hot and cold water and waste plumbing needs to be carefully thought through, along with the location of electric supplies, gas or oil pipes and the position of sinks and appliances.

Cooking is a major contributor to the amount of indoor water vapour, so a cooker hood with a powerful extractor fan should be installed to extract steam and dispatch stale cooking smells to the outdoors. This is an essential part of your armoury in the war against damaging condensation, but the amount of hole-cutting in walls and ceilings for vents should be kept to the minimum.

Last but not least, there's the question of whether to pick a traditional or modern design. In fact both styles can work well in old houses; if anything, modern designs are better suited to being located in relatively new extensions.

Right: Sparse original 19th century kitchen

Below: New period style timber framed kitchen/diner

Oakwrights.co.uk

17 OUTDOORS AND MAINTENANCE SUMMARY

It's surprising how many period features frequently survive within the surroundings of old houses. Fascinating clues to the building's history

can often be found lurking in gardens or grounds. Old tiled paths, ancient outbuildings and original boundary walls or railings all have a story to tell. Sometimes drinking wells or water pumps that date back centuries are unearthed. But the surroundings of a building are also important for another reason: many of the defects discussed in the preceding chapters originate from neglect to the adjoining land. This all-important comfort zone can have a direct bearing on the well-being of the house.

Paths and drives

The setting in which a period property stands is central to the way it's perceived. A medieval cottage, for example, is unlikely to look right set within a landscape of tarmac or concrete with all the charm of a supermarket car park. That doesn't mean you need to lavish a fortune on luscious landscaping, but a little attention to paving and driveways can reap big dividends. The natural materials traditionally used for paving were pleasingly irregular, so to recreate such an attractive environment, replica handmade

tiles can be obtained. Alternatively new stone paving can look very appealing when divided into smaller areas or set within gravel, which is relatively inexpensive.

The presence of hard, impervious materials such as concrete next to old walls can be a concern for more practical reasons. The simple fact is that rain splashing on hard surfaces can soak adjoining walls, becoming a source of damaging internal damp. This is particularly problematic where ground levels are high or gutters are leaking. It will also have the damaging effect of preventing moisture evaporating, trapping damp against the walls.

Patio slabs often have the undesirable effect of raising the ground level next to walls – a common contributing factor to damp problems. Just to complete the happy picture, raised paving is often implicated in blocking essential ventilation via airbricks to timber ground floors.

Clearly where an old property is at risk from such low-quality landscaping, prompt action needs to be taken. Where you have concrete paths abutting the main walls, the section closest to the house should be cut out to at least 300mm width and removed. As we saw in Chapter 2, with a small amount of excavation a simple French drain can be formed comprising a shallow gravel-filled ditch. The gravel should drain freely and allow the walls to breathe again.

To judge whether a property is at risk of flooding from surface water, the obvious starting point is to observe the lie of the land. Where the surrounding ground slopes down towards the house, surface water could surge towards the property in storm conditions, sometimes entering airbricks and soaking the floor under the house. Provision may therefore need to be made to divert it safely away to a nearby watercourse, soakaway or surface water drain via new drainage channels and gullies. Surface water can also cause problems anywhere that rain can accumulate without being able to disperse, such as driveways with hard surfaces. Hence the SUDS planning requirements (sustainable urban drainage systems). These stipulate that planning permission is required for all new or replacement driveways larger than 5m² where the surface is to be covered with an impermeable material – but not where permeable paving such as gravel is used.

Outbuildings

Substantial old outbuildings often survive in the gardens of many period houses, forming an important part of the property's setting and history. Many such structures were remarkably well designed, and were generally constructed using traditional building techniques. Despite their evident quality, many are left languishing in dire condition often overgrown and in need of rescuing from profuse ivy growth.

Old maps can often reveal clues to where long-demolished original outbuildings once stood. For example, old privies may have been removed or abandoned once superseded by indoor WCs. Cart sheds and stables were often converted into garages or workshops.

Many surviving such buildings, however, are generously sized and can often be given a new lease of life as useful workspace. However, where alterations are proposed to old outbuildings (*ie*

The proverbial brick privy

pre-dating 1 July 1948) it's important to first check their planning status. Those that lie within the original curtilage of a Listed building are usually protected, as are features such as garden walls and railings.

Garden walls

Even where money has been lavished on the upkeep of an old house, the surrounding boundary walls and structures are often sadly neglected. The original front garden fences, hedges or walls may have been knocked down or uprooted to make way for car spaces. This can pose a potential risk when buying a Listed property or a house located in a Conservation Area, should the planners require you as the new owner to reinstate an illegally demolished wall. The cost of rebuilding it in matching stonework and lime mortar could easily total two or three times the price of an equivalent wall built using modern materials.

Original garden walls come in all shapes and sizes, depending on the type of materials available locally at the time of construction. Often they comprise materials left over from building the main house, or stones collected from surrounding fields. Dry stone walls are common in many rural areas, particularly to the north and west. But one thing you won't see in old garden walls,

Will your insurance cover it?

Old garden walls can cost serious money to maintain – not least the thatched variety

no matter how far they extend, is expansion joints. Whereas modern walls built with brittle cement mortar need frequent vertical joints to prevent cracking, traditional lime can naturally accommodate movement in long expanses.

In terms of maintenance, garden walls are pretty much like main house walls, with a possible need for occasional re-pointing in lime mortar. However, the lifespan of any freestanding wall will be enhanced if the coping stones on top are properly maintained so that rain is effectively shed away from the masonry below. A common cause of damage to boundary walls is from roots of saplings growing nearby that eventually disturb the structure, often resulting in serious instability.

Metal gates and railings

Original railings and gates are part of the architecture of a period property, so if you need to source replacements it's important they match and complement the house. Often some will have survived to other buildings in the local area, or if all else fails you can check out old photos.

Georgian and early Victorian railings were mostly made in wrought iron, later superseded by cast iron. Wrought iron is a malleable iron heated up and hammered into shape, capable of fine detailing. Cast iron is moulded into individual components that could be bolted together on site. Today, most off-the-shelf

metal railings and gates are made from mild steel, often replicating standard original patterns. However, where authenticity is important it should be possible to have replicas made to order that match period pieces.

Metal railings were commonly embedded in a masonry wall plinth, although some were of a stand-alone type. Sometimes you come across small square stumps of metal set into the rendered top of low-level garden walls – the remnants of the original railings cut off as part of the war effort in 1940.

Trees and gardens

Like the Lost Gardens of Heligan, an overgrown garden may contain fascinating clues to a distant past of horticultural splendour. As with the archaeological remains of old greenhouses

And finally...

Owning a period house is to belong to an exclusive club. Old houses have a special kind of value, as unique pieces of 'living history' handed down across the generations. Hopefully the advice in this Haynes Manual will prove useful in making the most of this responsibility – if only to show that doing nothing is sometimes the best policy!

In essence, caring for old buildings can be boiled down to a few simple rules:

- Work in harmony with the building, aiming wherever possible to repair and maintain, rather than to replace.
- Respect the fact that old houses need to breathe, and it will go a long way to preventing problems with damp and rot.
- Use natural materials and traditional methods; and always avoid modern 'miracle solutions'.
- Be cautious when it comes to accepting advice. Many surveyors, architects and builders have little experience or understanding of old buildings. If in doubt, check with your local Conservation Officer.
- Old houses are some of the most sustainable buildings on the planet. Be wary of Energy Assessors armed with computer printouts who suggest otherwise.
- Enjoy all aspects of your home's history – even the tiniest marks and blemishes can provide unique clues to past lives.

Above all, the key to good health in old houses lies in spotting potential problems and tackling them before they get out of hand. By nipping any deterioration in the bud you can prevent the onset of far more damaging problems that would otherwise arise later, requiring far more expensive repairs. So how better to finish than with a checklist of things to keep a watchful eye on? – a simple way of ensuring that your valuable antique property enjoys the best of health into the future.

and privies, it may be possible to trace the outlines of former paths or flower and vegetable beds.

However, some garden life can be surprisingly pernicious and aggressive. One shrub to be especially wary of is fast-growing Japanese knotweed. So seriously is this highly invasive weed regarded that mortgages can be declined where infestation is evident. It has become fairly widespread in recent years and left untreated can become strong enough to damage foundations, concrete, and tarmac. Complete eradication is difficult because the roots can penetrate to depths of 3m, requiring a mix of weeding and pesticide. Knotweed-contaminated soil is classed as controlled waste that has to be removed by a licensed operator to a designated landfill site. Control and eradication is an expensive, specialist job.

As we saw back at the start of the book, you may not necessarily be at liberty to cut down trees even in the privacy of your own garden. Sometimes they're legally protected by a Tree Preservation Order – although this normally applies to more substantial specimens. Similarly, those in Conservation Areas enjoy automatic legal protection. It's an offence to fell or prune such a specimen without permission. An application for work to such a protected tree needs to be submitted to the arboricultural officer at your Local Authority, and can take six to eight weeks to process.

This means that where you plan to carry out building works in the vicinity of a protected tree, the trunk, root zone and canopy must be protected from damage – usually by installing fencing around the edge of the tree canopy.

Left: Unwelcome in any garden – the dreaded Japanese knotweed

Maintenance checklist

Old houses generally command a market premium, and in many ways are more akin to valuable antiques than somewhere to live. Yet despite their enormous value both financially and culturally, probably the greatest threat to our surviving stock of heritage buildings is neglect.

As with human health, prevention is better than cure, so keeping a watchful eye on things can reap dividends. Intelligent ownership means being alert to danger signs and ensuring regular maintenance is carried out.

The following list shows some key areas to check – each is covered in more detail in the relevant chapters.

INTERIOR

Infestation and rot
- Damp is one of the main causes of internal problems, often due to water leaks. If you spot a defect, always deal with the underlying cause rather than relying on dodgy quick-fix solutions such as instant 'spray-on damp cures'.
- Air movement is vital to reduce moisture in old houses, so don't be too fanatical about sealing up draughts.
- Annually check for signs of rot and beetle attack to timbers, particularly to any areas of damp on walls, under the stairs, in cellars and in cupboards.

Heating and pipes
- Check radiators and pipework for leaks, and have boilers serviced annually.
- Check oil tanks for leaks.
- Ensure that both hot and cold water pipes in unheated areas are lagged (lofts, larders, cellars, outbuildings etc) and water tanks are fully insulated.
- Check seals at the edges of baths and showers for cracks and leaks.
- Check connections of WC soil pipes at junctions with pans.
- Turn off stopcocks to check they work.

Loft
- From the underside of the roof tiles (assuming they're visible, *ie* not lined) check for leaks and any large gaps where tiles have slipped.
- Check the chimney in the loft for leaks, for example at mortar joints, using a smoke pellet burning in each fireplace.
- Check levels of insulation (300mm depth is recommended).

Fire
- Be alert for potential fire risks – get into the habit of closing doors to habitable rooms at night.
- Clean and test smoke alarms annually and replace batteries.
- Arrange for the electrics to be professionally tested every ten years or upon moving house.
- Check escape routes that you would use in the event of fire.

EXTERIOR

Roofs
- Give the roof a quick look over with a pair of binoculars every six months or so, as well as after any storms or gales. Strong gusts of wind may dislodge tiles or lift leadwork, so check for any debris on the ground from broken tiles.
- Replace any slipped or missing tiles promptly.
- Check flashings and mortar fillets at junctions to stacks and parapets for cracks and leaks.
- With thatched roofs, look for signs of decay, especially to the ridge.

Rainwater fittings
- Neglected guttering and downpipes are a very common cause of damp penetration and timber decay. Softening of the ground adjacent to the foundations can cause structural movement.
- Check for leaks at gutters, often due to defective joints, blockages or poor alignment.
- Check the backs of any cracked or rusted downpipes to see if water can seep out.
- Clear any open gulleys at the base of downpipes.

Drains and plumbing
- Check for blockages to foul drains by lifting inspection chamber covers.
- Arrange a drains test if blockages regularly occur or leakage is suspected.
- Check outside taps and overflow pipes for dripping and leaks.

Main walls
- Ensure earth is not mounded up at the base of walls. Ground levels around the building should ideally be around 200mm below the internal floor level, and should not be sloping towards the house.
- Clear airbricks using a stick.
- Re-point any badly eroded mortar joints and repair damaged render.
- Reapply limewash regularly.
- Note any cracking and monitor it.
- Clear away climbing plants and any large shrubs at the base of walls. Ivy roots are especially invasive and can force open lime mortar joints and penetrate roofs.
- Keep any trees or large shrubs in close proximity to the house well pruned to restrict their water consumption.

Joinery
- Check windows, doors, fascias and bargeboards for timber decay, and ensure that painted joinery isn't flaking.
- Ensure that rainwater cannot accumulate in 'ponds' on sills and ledges etc where it could rot the timber.
- Look for small cracks in paintwork around timber windows and especially on sills. Rubbing linseed oil glazing putty into small cracks in painted woodwork can help until the weather is right for redecoration.

Chimneys
- Ensure that flues in use are swept regularly. Disused flues should be caped and vented.
- Check flashings for cracks and leaks.
- Where spark arrestors are fitted to pots on thatched roofs, ensure they do not clog up.

BIBLIOGRAPHY

Title	Author	Publisher
Survey and Repair of Traditional Buildings	Richard Oxley	Donhead
The SPAB Old House Handbook	Roger Hunt & Marianne Suhr	Frances Lincoln
At Home: A short history of private life	Bill Bryson	Black Swan
Structural Surveys of Dwelling Houses	Ian Melville & Ian Gordon	Estates Gazette
The Georgian House	Richard Reid	Bishopsgate Press
Old House Care & Repair	Janet Collings	Donhead
Maintaining and Repairing Old Houses	Bevis Claxton	Crowood
The Victorian House Manual	Ian Rock	Haynes

INDEX